跨文化双边对话
文化的语境：地域·人类·历史

—— 第三届中美文化论坛文集

A Binational Conversation on Bridging Cultures
The Context: Place·People·History

THE THIRD CHINA-U.S. CULTURAL FORUM
COLLECTION OF THE THESES

贾磊磊 主编

Editor in Chief
Jia Leilei

文化艺术出版社
Culture and Art Publishing House

第三届中美文化论坛(北京)
The Third China-US Cultural Forum (Beijing)

第三届中美文化论坛（南京）
The Third China-US Cultural Forum (Nanjing)

目录

序言

1　共同搭建中美文化交流的跨世纪桥梁
　　王文章　中国艺术研究院院长，中国非物质文化遗产保护中心主任

开幕致辞

7　赵少华　中华人民共和国文化部副部长

15　[美] 詹姆斯·利奇　美国国家人文基金会主席

第一单元　文化与人类

29　"将无同"——文化融合是人类未来的大趋势
　　刘梦溪　中国艺术研究院中国文化研究所所长

39　文化与人类：非物质文化遗产的传播、翻译与转化
　　[美] 玛格丽特·巴尔杰　美国国会图书馆"美国国家民俗中心"名誉主任

51　超越黑白两分
　　黄平　中国社会科学院美国研究所所长

62　建立档案与美国印第安研究间的桥梁
　　[美] 斯科特·曼宁·史蒂文斯　美国纽伯瑞图书馆"美洲印第安人和原住民研究"达西·麦克尼克尔中心主任

73　中国当代艺术：在全球与本土之间
　　范迪安　中国美术馆馆长

88　文化与教育交流
　　[美] 阿瑟·泰　"美中学术交流委员会"北京办事处主任

104 利玛窦的发现
余秋雨 著名文化学者

121 中国非物质文化遗产保护的创造性实践
李新风 中国艺术研究院·中国非物质文化遗产保护中心常务副主任

第二单元 文化与历史

139 保护文化遗产，践行国际公约
刘魁立 中国社会科学院荣誉学部委员，民族文学研究所研究员

151 纪念一种新的美国史和美国文化
[美]克莱门特·普莱斯 "杰出贡献教授理事会"成员，历史学教授，罗格斯大学纽华克分校"种族、文化与现代经验"学院院长

163 论中国社会发展背景下的陶瓷艺术创作
朱乐耕 中国艺术研究院艺术创作研究中心及陶瓷艺术研究中心主任

176 文化权利是国家主权和国家利益的组成部分
摩罗 中国艺术研究院中国文化研究所研究员

182 我们怎样阅读与写作：社会网络与文学社群
[美]凯思琳·菲茨帕特里克 美国现代语言学会学术传播部主任，美国波莫纳学院媒介研究教授

195 中国电影表述的文化价值观
贾磊磊 中国艺术研究院院长助理，文化发展战略研究中心主任

第三单元 文化与地域

223　中国城市社会的来临与挑战 —— 城市多元化及其融合
　　　宋林飞　江苏省人民政府参事室主任

231　窥视，沉醉，理解：论空间与文学
　　　[美] 克里斯托弗·梅瑞尔　美国爱荷华大学国际写作计划主任

247　地域文化的价值倾向
　　　毕飞宇　江苏省作家协会副主席

254　思维定势与世界观：对空间如何决定思想的反思
　　　[美] 詹森·帕滕特　南京大学–约翰斯·霍普金斯大学中美文化研究中心美方合作主任

267　美国文学教学与研究在南京
　　　王守仁　南京大学外国语学院教授，当代外国文学与文化研究中心主任

277　江苏及南京地域文化简述
　　　徐耀新　江苏省文化厅厅长

292　美国/墨西哥边境地区的文化与空间
　　　[美] 拉蒙·萨尔迪瓦　美国斯坦福大学英语与比较文学系教授，"人文与科学学院"霍格兰德家庭教授

305　全球化冲击下的文化融合与文化差异
　　　蔡佳禾　南京大学–约翰斯·霍普金斯大学中美文化研究中心副主任

闭幕致辞

325 詹姆斯·利奇　美国国家人文基金会主席
331 李鸿　中华人民共和国文化部对外文化联络局 副局长

339 与会学者论点撷英

新闻综述

389 沟通·融合·将无同
　　　任慧 中国艺术研究院文化发展战略研究中心副研究员
405 构筑文化交流与认知的世纪平台
　　　肖庆 中国艺术研究院文化发展战略研究中心助理研究员

Contents

PREFACE

1   Jointly Build a Cross-Century Bridge for China-U.S. Cultural Exchanges
Wang Wenzhang , President of the Chinese National Academy of Arts, Director of China Intangible Cultural Heritage Protection Center

Address at the Opening Ceremony

11   Zhao Shaohua, Vice Minister of Ministry of Culture, People's Republic of China

18   James Leach, Chairman of US National Endowment for the Humanities

Unit One: Culture and People

34   Jiang Wu Tong— Cultural Integration is the General Trend of the Future of Humanity
Liu Mengxi, Director of Institute of Chinese Culture, Chinese National Academy of Arts

45   Culture and People: Transmitting, Translating and Transforming Intangible Cultural Heritage
Margaret Bulger, Director Emerita of the American Folklife Center at the Library of Congress

57   Beyond Black and White
Huang Ping, Director of United States Institute of the Chinese Academy of Social Sciences

68   Bridging the Divide between the Archive and American Indians
Scott Manning Stevens, Director of D'Arcy McNickle Center for American Indian and Indigenous Studies , Newberry Library

81	Contemporary Chinese Art: Between Globalization and Localization Fan Di'an, Director of National Art Museum of China
96	Cultural and Educational Exchanges Arthur Tai, Director of the Beijing Office of the US Committee on Scholarly Communication with China
113	Matteo Ricci's Discovery Yu Qiuyu, Famous Cultural Scholar
126	Creative Practice of China's Intangible Cultural Heritage Protection Li Xinfeng, Executive Deputy Director of China Intangible Cultural Heritage Protection Center, Chinese National Academy of Arts

Unit Two: Culture and History

145	Safeguarding Cultural Heritage and Implementing International Conventions Liu Kuili, Honorary Academician of Chinese Academy of Social Sciences, Research Fellow of the Institute of Ethnic Literature
157	Commemorating a New American History and Culture Clement Alexander Price, Board of Governors Distinguished Service Professor of History and Director, The Rutgers Institute on Ethnicity, Culture, and the Modern Experience, Rutgers University
170	Artistic Creation of Ceramics in the Context of Social Development in China Zhu Legeng, Director of Art Creation Center and Ceramic Art Center, Chinese National Academy of Arts
179	Cultural Right is an Integral Part of National Sovereignty and National Interests Mo Luo, Research Fellow of Institute of Chinese Culture, Chinese National Academy of Arts

189　How We Read and Write: Social Networks and Literary Communities
　　Kathleen Fitzpatrick, Director of Scholarly Communication, Modern Language Association; Professor of Media Studies, Pomona College
206　Cultural Values Presented in Chinese Movies
　　Jia Leilei, President Assistant of Chinese National Academy of Arts, Director of Cultural Development Strategy Research Center, Chinese National Academy of Arts

Unit Three: Culture and Place

227　Arrival and Challenges of the Urban Society of China—Urban Diversification and Melting
　　Song Linfei, Director of Counsellors' Office of Jiangsu Provincial People's Government
240　Peering, Absorbing, Translating: A Note on Geography and Culture
　　Christopher Merrell, Director of International Writing Program, University of Iowa
251　Value Orientation of Regional Culture
　　Bi Feiyu, Vice President of the Writers' Association of Jiangsu Province
261　Mindset and Worldview: Reflections on How Place Shapes the Mind
　　Jason D. Patent, American Co-director of The Johns Hopkins University-Nanjing University Center for Chinese and American Studies
272　Teaching and Study of American Literature in Nanjing
　　Wang Shouren, Professor of the Foreign Language College of Nanjing University, Head of the Center for the Studies of Contemporary Foreign Literature and Culture
284　On Regional Culture of Jiangsu Province and Nanjing
　　Xu Yaoxin, Director of Jiangsu Provincial Department of Culture

299   Culture and Place on the US/Mexico Border
Ramón Saldívar, Professor of English and Comparative Literature and the Hoagland Family Professor of Humanities and Sciences at Stanford University

312   Cultural Integration and Cultural Differences under the Impact of Globalization
Cai Jiahe, Deputy Director of The Johns Hopkins University - Nanjing University Center for Chinese and American Studies

Address at the Closing Ceremony

328   James Leach, Chairman of US National Endowment for the Humanities
334   Li Hong, Vice Director-General of the Bureau for External Cultural Relations, Ministry of Culture, People's Republic of China

363   **Collection of Scholars' Viewpoints**

News Roundup

397   Communication, Integration and Jiang Wu Tong
Ren Hui, Associate Research Fellow of Cultural Development Strategy Research Center, Chinese National Academy of Arts

411   Build a Century Platform for Cross-cultural Communication and Understanding
Xiao Qing, Assistant Research Fellow of Cultural Development Strategy Research Center, Chinese National Academy of Arts

序 言
共同搭建中美文化交流的跨世纪桥梁

王文章
中国艺术研究院院长，中国非物质文化遗产保护中心主任

由中华人民共和国文化部和美国国家人文基金会共同主办、中国艺术研究院和江苏省文化厅共同承办的"跨文化双边对话：第三届中美文化论坛"圆满闭幕了。根据双方的约定，我们将参加论坛的五十余名中美专家、学者和艺术家发表的学术论文和精彩的发言记录以中英文编辑出版，这对于我们中美双方来说都是一件具有意义的事情，它不只是一份跨文化研究的历史文献，同时也是中美两国学者之间思想交流与文化对话的珍贵记录。

中国是目前世界上最大的发展中国家，美国是最大的发达国家，中美是两个在政治、经济等方面存在着不少差异的大国，能否进行建设性的合作与对话，在某种意义上，取决于双方能否理解彼此的文化，能否尊重彼此的文化价值观。"中美文化论坛"正是立足于这样一个文化交流的长远目标，为促进中美两国人民之间的思想沟通，为促进相互理解和信任，共同搭建起一座跨文化交流的世纪桥梁。我们相信，这对于推动两国关系的健康发展乃至世界文化的繁荣都具有重要意义。

中美两国地处地球上的两大洲，不同的历史传统和地理环境孕育出了不同的文化。浩瀚深邃的太平洋并没有阻隔两国人民相互了解和交流的脚步，中美很早就开始了文化艺术领域的交流与对话。尤其是1979年中美正式建交，联合签署了《中美文化交流协定》，从此开创了中美文化交流的新纪元。现在，中美两国互派留学生和访问学者的人数逐年递增，2012年中国赴美国的留学生人数达到近二十万人，两国高等院校与文化机构之间的合作也越来越多、越来越深入。美国的电影、流行音乐在中国几乎家喻户晓。美国动画中的米老鼠、唐老鸭更是受到中国少年儿童的喜爱。中国的京剧、昆曲、功夫、茶叶等等也受到美国人民的欢迎，许多美国学校开设了有关中国文化的课程。

根据中华人民共和国文化部和美国国家人文基金会的共同约定，2008年12月8日至9日，第一届"中美文化论坛"在北京隆重召开。中美双方的专家、艺术家围绕"数字化时代的文化遗产保护和展现"这一主题，针对数字技术在文化遗产保护中的作用、数字技术与当代文化发展等论题进行了广泛、深入的对话与研讨。作为此次会议中方主办单位的代表，我在开幕式致辞中指出，数字技术的广泛应用不仅有利于传统文化艺术的保护和发展，同时也冲破了各种文化类型相对封闭的自然状态，为不同文化之间的交流与发展提供了现实的空间，为它们创造了进行深入了解和借鉴的机遇。不论是文字、音乐，还是图画、影像，各种文化内容都借助于数字化媒介在互通、互融过程中逐渐形成了全球共享的文化资源，进而扩大了人类文化成果在全球的广泛传播。但是，我们也应该看到，技术不可能直接转变为人类的智慧，数字技术最终也不可能代替人的精神。因此，如何充分利用数字技术保护、开发、利用传统文化资源，充分借鉴和认真汲取前人的智慧与经验，促进人类的和平发展与和谐进步，以及更好地保持人类文化的多样性，必将是世界各国共同面临的重大发展课题。

2009年11月，中国国家主席胡锦涛和美国总统奥巴马在北京签署《中美联合声明》，其中专门写到两国要合作办好"中美文化论坛"。2010年5月，中国国务院国务委员刘延东和美国国务卿希拉里·克林顿在北京联合主持了"中美人文交流高层磋商机制成立仪式暨第一次会议"，再次强调了办好"中美文化论坛"的共同意愿。这显示了两国领导人对"中美文化论坛"以及中美文化交流的高度重视。

2010年10月15日至16日，我带队出席了在美国加利福尼亚大学伯克利分校举行的第二届"中美文化论坛"。加州大学伯克利分校是全美第一个成立中国文化研究中心的高等院校，在这里举办"中美文化论坛"具有特殊的意义。五十余名来自中美两国的专家、学者和艺术家、作家汇集一堂，以"跨文化双边对话"为主题，从文化艺术领域回顾了中美交流的历史，探讨了两国文化交流的现实路径，以期推动中美人文社会科学和文化艺术的发展、交流与合作。会议期间，我与美国国家人文基金会主席詹姆斯·利奇进行了友好的会见，交换了对中美文化交流的意见，并聆听了专家的发言。我在论坛开幕致辞时强调,"万物并育而不相害,道并行而不相悖",不同文化的交流会使我们更加了解对方而尊重对方,会使我们在学习与借鉴对方文化发展经验的同时,提升我们各自在文化艺术领域建设发展的创造性。中美两国文化机构和专家学者、艺术家们不断加强交流与合作,符合两国人民的根本利益,有助于增进两国人民的了解与友谊,它必将造福于两国和两国人民,同时也有利于促进东西方文明的相互沟通与和谐发展,成为推动人类文明不断进步的重要动力。作为会议的成果之一,美国国家人文基金会和中华人民共和国文化部签署了《谅解备忘录》,决定将论坛持续举办下去。

2012年9月6日至8日,第三届"中美文化论坛"如期在北京和南京隆重举办。来自中美两国的专家、学者和艺术家围绕"文化的语境:地域、人类、历史"的议题,探讨中美两国由于不同的地理环境、民族渊源、历史发展等原因形成的文化特质,从而寻求相互认知、理解与认同的基础,以推动中美两国文化的深入交流,促进两国人民之间的友谊。

我了解到两国学者对于促进中美文化交流与发展的精辟见解。如美国国会图书馆"美国国家民俗中心"名誉主任玛格丽特·巴尔杰认为,美国公民的祖先来自于世界各地,"美国文化"的独特性正是源于世界文化的融合和/或共存;中国艺术研究院文化研究所所长、终身研究员刘梦溪指出,世界上不同的文化、不同的"文明体国家",并不是会必然发展为冲突,而是需要通过交流与对话达成文化的互补与融合;"美中学术交流委员会"北京办事处主任阿瑟·泰全面回顾了过去三十多年中美文化与教育交流复兴概况,并展望了前景。通过阅读这些充满睿智和哲理的论文,我亲身感受到,"中美文化论坛"正在达到它预想的目标。连续三届"中美文化论坛"的成功举办,已证明中美双方在文化艺术领域建立了一个具有公共性、开放性、互动性的国际交流平台。这对于推动中美文化交流得到长久、持续、深入的发展,建立相互尊重、合作共赢的新型大国关系具有重要意义。

21世纪是经济全球化的世纪,也是文化多样性的世纪。中华民族历来以友好、开放、兼容并包的态度对待其他民族的文化,崇尚"和而不同"、"有容乃大"的文化理念。尽管不同文化之间存在着种种差异,但它们并没有高低优劣之分。不同国家、民族的文化只有相互尊重、相互交流、相互借鉴,才能健康发展。正是多元文化的辉映、碰撞和交融才成就了世界历史波澜壮阔的巨流。中国人民正在努力建设自己的文化强国,强调在弘扬中华优秀传统文化、推进当代文化创新的同时，也要积极吸收借鉴国外优秀文化成果，建设中华民族共有精神家园。"中美文化论坛"的成功举办，标志着中美文化交流正在向着制度化、高端化的境界迈进。我们希望进一步总结经验、加强合作，使论坛取得更加丰硕的成果，为增进中美两国人民的友谊和情感、推动人类文明进步作出更大贡献。

PREFACE
Jointly Build a Cross-Century Bridge for China-U.S. Cultural Exchanges

Wang Wenzhang
President of the Chinese National Academy of Arts
Director of China Intangible Cultural Heritage Protection Center

"The Third China-U.S. Cultural Forum: A Binational Conversation on Bridging Cultures", co-sponsored by the Ministry of Culture of the People's Republic of China and the US National Endowment for the Humanities, and jointly organized by the Chinese National Academy of Arts and the Jiangsu Provincial Department of Culture, has successfully closed. According to the agreement between China and the United States, we now collect and publish in both Chinese and English the academic papers submitted to the conference by over 50 experts, scholars, and artists from the two countries and the texts of their fantastic speeches, which is a matter of significance to both sides. It not only contributes to the literature of transcultural studies, but also serves as an important document attesting to cultural dialogue and communication between the Chinese and American scholars.

China is the largest developing country, while the United States is the largest developed country in the world. They have significant differences in politics and economy. Whether they can carry out constructive cooperation and dialogue in some sense depends on whether one can understand and respect the values of the other culture. As a bridge between cultures, the China-U.S. Cultural Forum works hard towards the long-term goal of promoting cultural exchanges and fostering communication, mutual understanding and trust between the two peoples. We believe that it is of great significance to the healthy development of China-U.S. relations and to the prosperity of world cultures.

China and the United States are located on two continents, and different historical traditions and geographical environment have brought about different cultures. The vast Pacific Ocean that separates the two countries has never prevented the efforts of the two peoples to understand and communicate with each other. China and the United States have begun exchanges and dialogue in the fields of culture and art long before. Especially in 1979, the establishment of the diplomatic relations and the signing of a cultural accord between China and the United States marked a new milestone in China-U.S. cultural exchanges. In recent years, the number of students and visiting scholars studying in each other's country has witnessed continued increase. In 2012, nearly 200,000 Chinese were studying in the United States, and the cooperation between the institutions of higher learning and cultural institutions of both countries has increased in depth and breath. American movies and pop music go down well in China. The images of Mickey Mouse and Donald Duck are very popular among Chinese children. In the same vein, the Peking Opera, Kunqu Opera, Chinese Kungfu and Tea are very popular among American people. Many American schools have introduced courses on Chinese culture.

As agreed between the Ministry of Culture of the People's Republic of China and the US National Endowment for the Humanities, on December 8-9, 2008, the first China-U.S. Cultural Forum was held ceremoniously in Beijing. Revolving around the theme of "Preservation and Presentation of Cultural Heritage in Digital Age", the experts and artists from both countries held wide-ranging and in-depth discussions on the role of digital technology in the preservation and development of cultural heritage, and in the development of contemporary culture. When I addressed the opening ceremony of the forum on behalf of the Chinese sponsor, I spoke of the extensive application of the digital technology, which has not only contributed to the preservation and development of traditional culture and art, but also has broken the barriers that had previously distanced different types of cultures. It has thus provided a valuable opportunity for the exchanges between different cultures and their development, and an opportunity for them to better understand and learn from each other. Whether in the form of words, music, pictures, or images, various cultural contents have become globally shared cultural resources in the process of cultural exchanges and fusion with the aid of digital media. This has doubtlessly facilitated world-wide dissemination of the cultural achievements of mankind. However, we must also be alert to the fact that technology can not be directly translated into human wisdom, and that digital technology will never take the place of the spirit of humankind. Therefore, how to preserve, develop, and utilize traditional cultural resources through digital technology so as to fully and earnestly draw on the wisdom and experience of our forefathers, to promote peaceful development and harmonious progress of mankind, and to better maintain cultural diversity of humankind, will surely become an important challenge for all countries in the world.

In November 2009, Chinese President Hu Jintao and American President Obama signed in Beijing the China-U.S. Joint Statement, which stressed the importance of the China-U.S. Cultural Forum. In May 2010, Chinese State Councilor Liu Yandong and U.S. Secretary of State Hillary Clinton co-chaired in Beijing the "Launch Ceremony cum the First Meeting of the High-Level Consultation Mechanism for People-to-people Exchanges", and emphasized again the common wish to jointly organize the China-U.S. Cultural Forum. This indicates that the leaders of both countries have attached great importance to the China-U.S. Cultural Forum and cultural exchanges between the two countries.

On October 15-16 2010, I led a delegation to attend the Second China-U.S. Cultural Forum held at the University of California, Berkeley. The Center for Chinese Studies of the University of California, Berkeley is the earliest of such centers at American colleges and universities, and the convening of the China-U.S. Cultural Forum here is of special significance. Centering on the theme of "Binational Conversation on Bridging Cultures", more than 50 experts, scholars, artists and writers reviewed the history of China-U.S. exchanges in culture and art, and discussed the realistic approaches of China-U.S. cultural exchanges, with a view to promoting the development, communication and cooperation in the fields of humanities, social sciences, culture, and art. During the conference, I had a friendly meeting with Jim Leach, Chairman of the US National Endowment for the Humanities. We exchanged our opinions on China-U.S. cultural exchanges, and listened to the presentations of the experts. In my speech at the opening ceremony of the forum, I emphasized that "All living creatures grow together without harming one another; ways run parallel without interfering with one another". Exchanges between different cultures promote our mutual understanding and mutual respect, and enhance our creativity in our respective cultural and artistic fields through learning the experience of each other. The continued strengthening of communication and cooperation between the cultural institutions, the experts, scholars, and artists of China and the United States conforms to the fundamental interests of the people of both countries, and may foster understanding and goodwill between them. It will surely benefit both countries and both peoples. Meanwhile, it will also help promote mutual communication and harmonious development of western and oriental civilizations, and will effectively drive forward the constant progress of human civilizations. As one of the achievements of the conference, the US National Endowment for the Humanities and the Ministry of Culture of the People's Republic of China signed a Memorandum of Understanding to make the forum a long-standing mechanism.

On September 6-8, 2012, the Third China-U.S. Cultural Forum was held as scheduled in Beijing and Nanjing. Experts, scholars and artists from both China and the United States discussed the theme of "the Context: Place, People, History", and explored the cultural traits of China and the US resulting from different geographical environments, ethnic origins, and historical development, with a view to establishing a foundation for mutual understanding and acceptance, and to deepening China-U.S. cultural exchanges and friendship between the two peoples.

I have known about the insightful opinions of the scholars from both countries on facilitating the cultural exchanges and cultural development of China and the United States. For example, as Margaret Bulger, Director Emerita of the American Folklife Center at the Library of Congress, pointed out, American citizens have ancestors and forebears from literally every corner of the World, and the unique traits of "American culture", come from the fusion and/or co-existence of world cultures. Liu Mengxi, Lifelong Research Fellow and Director of Chinese Studies Institute of Chinese National Academy of Arts, believes that the differences in cultures and civilizations of the world will not necessarily escalate into conflicts, and that cultural fusion and mutual complementation can be achieved through exchange and dialogue. Arthur D. Tai, Director of the Beijing Office of the US Committee on Scholarly Communication with China, reviewed the revival of China-U.S. cultural and educational exchanges in the past three decades and analyzed their prospects. Through reading these papers that are permeated with philosophical wisdom and insights, I feel that the China-U.S. Cultural Forum has achieved its pre-defined goals. The successful holding of the three consecutive China-U.S. Cultural Forums proves that a public, open and interactive international exchange platform has been established in the fields of culture and art of the two countries. It has played a very significant role in fostering the long-term, persistent and in-depth development of China-U.S. cultural exchanges, and in establishing a new-style, mutually respectful, cooperative, win-win relationship between the two important countries.

The 21st century is a century of economic globalization, and of cultural diversity. Chinese people have been treating the other cultures with a friendly, open, and embracing attitude, and it has been enshrining the cultural philosophy of "harmony without sameness" and "tolerance and accommodation". Despite the differences between cultures, there are no such differentiations as the superior or inferior, and the good or bad. The cultures of different countries and ethnic groups can only develop healthily on the basis of mutual respect, mutual exchanges, and mutual learning. It is the co-existence, clashes and fusion of distinct cultures that has shaped the fascinatingly diversified cultural landscape of the world in history. In the process of enhancing its cultural competence and building the cultural haven for its people, China not only emphasizes the promotion of its own excellent cultural tradition and contemporary cultural innovation, but also draws strength from the excellent foreign cultural achievements. The success of the China-U.S. Cultural Forum marks great progress in the high-level mechanism of China-U.S. cultural exchanges. We hope to further sum up the experience and strengthen cooperation so that the forum can achieve more fruitful results and make greater contribution to enhancing the goodwill and friendship between the Chinese and US people and to promoting the progress in human civilizations.

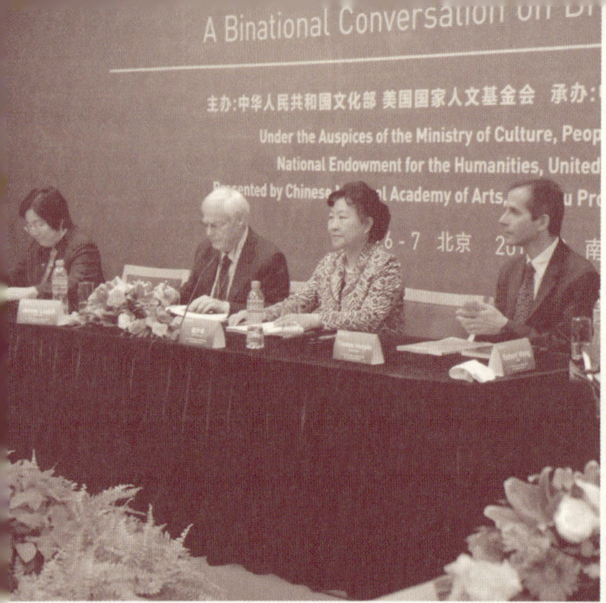
A Binational Conversation on
主办:中华人民共和国文化部 美国国家人文基金会 承办:
Under the Auspices of the Ministry of Culture,
National Endowment for the Humanities,
6 - 7 北京

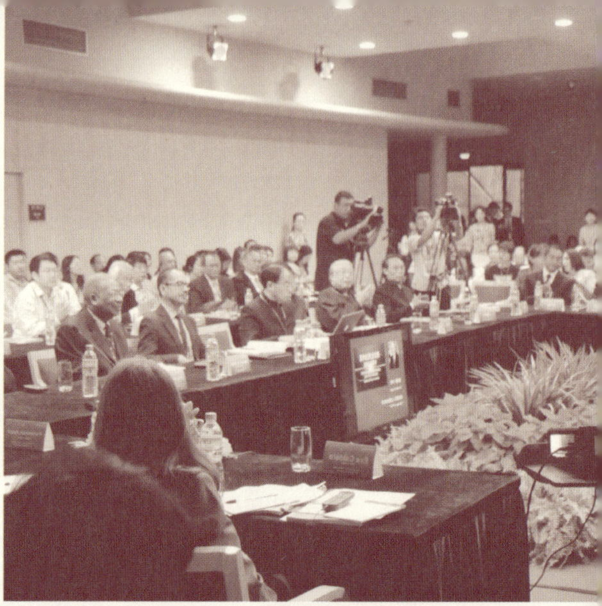

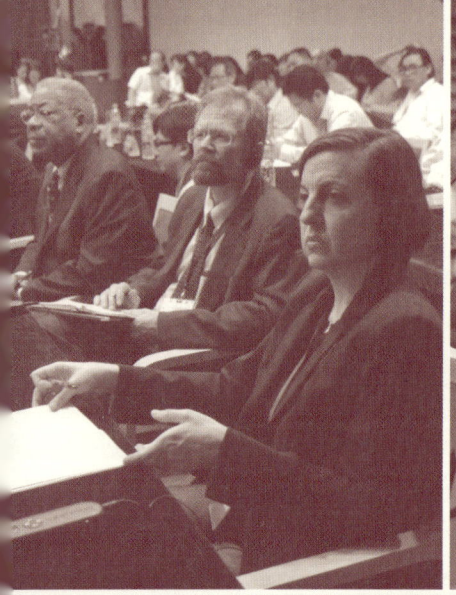

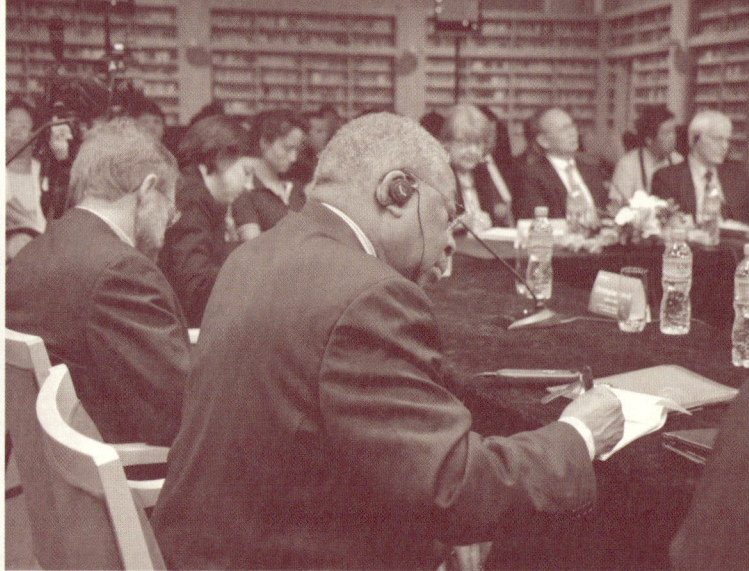

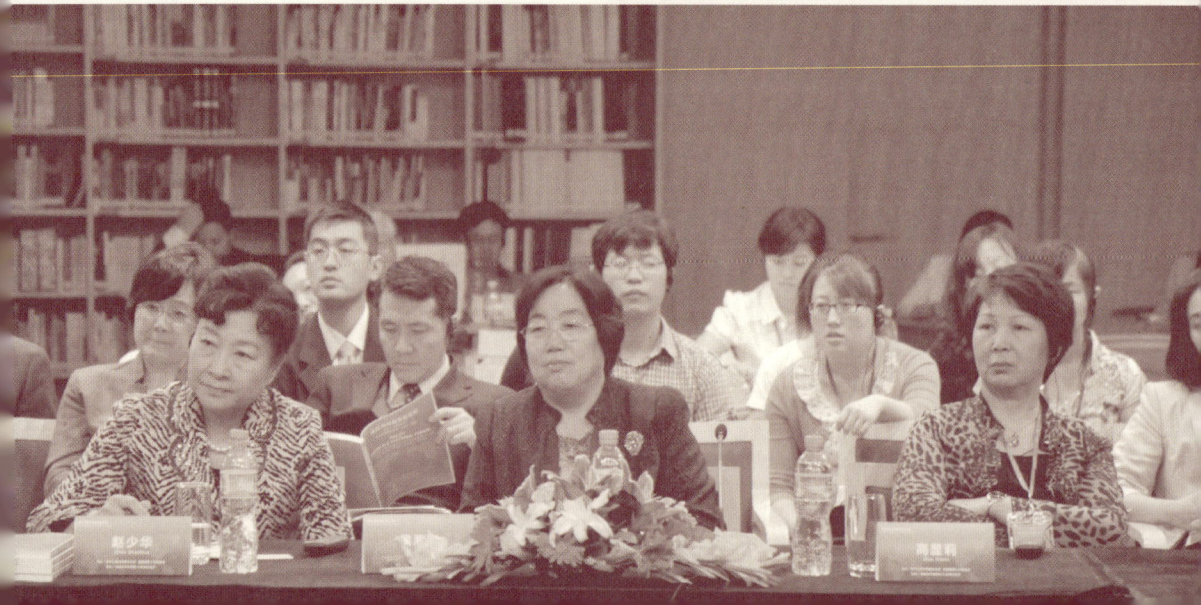

Opening Address

开幕致辞

中华人民共和国文化部副部长赵少华开幕致辞
Address at the Opening Ceremony by Zhao Shaohua,
Vice Minister of Ministry of Culture, People's Republic of China

美国国家人文基金会主席詹姆斯·利奇开幕致辞
Address at the Opening Ceremony by James Leach,
Chairman of US National Endowment for the Humanities

赵少华

★

中华人民共和国文化部副部长

尊敬的利奇先生、王晓珉公使，
女士们、先生们、朋友们：

大家上午好！

第三届"中美文化论坛"今天在中国北京如期开幕，在此，我谨代表中国文化部、代表蔡武部长对论坛的召开表示热烈的祝贺，向远道而来的美国国家人文基金会利奇主席以及代表团全体成员表示热烈的欢迎；同时，也向来自中国文化界、学术界的专家学者和新闻媒体的朋友们表示热烈的欢迎。同时，向给予本届论坛大力支持的中国艺术研究院、国家大剧院和江苏省文化厅表示衷心的感谢。

在中国文化部与美国国家人文基金会的共同努力下，"中美文化论坛"已经成功举办了两届。2008年12月的首届论坛，以"数字化时代的文化遗产保护和展现"为主题，在北京举行。两国学者围绕数字技术在保护历史文化遗产、传承传统文化艺术、推动文化教育等方面的作用进行了深入地交流和对话；并在文化遗产保护和图书馆、博物馆合作等领域达成了诸多合作意向。

2010年10月，在美国加利福尼亚大学伯克利分校举行了第二届论坛，主题是"跨文化双边对话"。两国学者就"中美文化关系的历史回顾"、"文学遗产与创造性"、"视觉艺术的传统与创新"、"表演艺术比较观"以及"中美文化关系的未来展望"等多个论题展开讨论，系统回顾了中美两国在各艺术领域的交流与合作，并对中美文化关系的发展前景进行了积极地展望。

今天，经过双方的精心筹备，第三届"中美文化论坛"将分别在中国的北京和南京举行。论坛将以"文化的语境：文化与地域，文化与人类，文化与历史"为主题，从宏观层面探讨中美两国由于不同的地理环境、民族渊源、历史发展等原因所形成的文化特质，从而寻求相互认知、理解与认同的基础。

从地域、历史与人类发展的角度，对比中美文化，将给予我们更为宏大、高远的视角来看待两国文化与两国关系。首先，从地域或空间的角度看，位于太平洋两岸的中国与美国都是幅员辽阔的大国，领土面积分列世界第三、第四位。两国彼此广博壮丽的土地、山川、河流孕育着杰出的人民和灿烂的文化。美国诗人惠特曼的《草叶集》中有这样的诗句："哪里有土、哪里有水，哪里就长着青草"；中国同样有类似的名言："一方水土养一方人"，一方人孕育着一方文化，这一方文化又滋养着这一方人，并赋予他们特有的民族性格和精神气质。

其次，从历史或时间的角度简单勾勒，具有五千年文明史的中国，历经两千多年的封建王朝更替，于20世纪初摆脱了封建统治的枷锁，掀开了百年民族自强不息奋斗的序幕，启动新文化运动，1949年成立了新中国，历经曲折，迎来了近三十年的黄金建设期。当下中国正倡导推行具有中国特色的社会主义和谐文化建设，传承创新、博大包容。而位于地球另一端"新大陆"的美国，在短短二百多年间，融合、转化西方文明，创造了现代文明，构建了多元、包容、开放的文化体系，彰显出强盛的生命力。

从人类发展和文明特性的角度看，中华文明能够生生不息、薪火相传，取决于其独特的文明特质。中华文化长期以人伦关系为基准，重视修身，关注家庭，热爱国家，心忧天下，并且推己及人、由近及远，表现出宽广的博爱精神和慈悲情怀，并不断印证着其博采众长、开放包容、追求和谐、平衡的理念。而具有二百多年历史的美国，历经了多种族移民的艰苦奋斗和文化融合，在广泛吸纳西方文明成果的基础上，逐渐凝聚形成独特的美国精神和价值观。其强烈的个人自由观，鲜明的劳动致富观，民主平等的理念，为美国的进步、发展提供了深厚的精神土壤，使这块土地上的人们得以保持旺盛的进取和奋斗精神。自古至今，由近及远，由己及人，中美两国不同的地域、历史和价值观为我们了解彼此的文化提供了最佳的视角。

纵观中美两国的交往，1784年美国商船"中国皇后号"抵达广州，揭开了两国近二百余年的交往历史。新中国成立后，40年前的1972年，尼克松总统成为第一位踏上中华人民共和国土地的美国总统,标志着中美关系正常化的开始。经过40年的发展,今天,两国已经互为对方的第二大贸易伙伴,中美关系已成为当今世界上最为重要的双边关系。当前,中美间从政府、机构、组织到个人,从政治、经贸、文化乃至军事,正进行着全方位、多层次的交往与合作。

诚然,中美两国在文化传统、社会制度和发展阶段等方面存在着较大差异和不同。问题的关键是如何对待差异和不同。基辛格博士在他的新书《论中国》中通过比较中国围棋和西方象棋的不同,得出中西战略文化思维的不同。西方的象棋是逻辑,是一种绝对游戏或者零和的游戏概念,即国家间的游戏更多是一场"你死我活"的游戏。中国所秉持的则是一种"围棋"逻辑,这是一种相对的游戏,或者是非零和的游戏。在这里,作为中国的文化部长,我真诚地希望,两国的有识之士今后能够更多思考如何减少由于中美两国之间存在的差异和不同所造成的误读、误解乃至误判,努力在增进文化间的互相了解上下工夫。作为全球最大的发展中国家和最大的发达国家,中美双方加强交流、增进互信、促进合作无疑对于两国、乃至全世界来讲都是最大的福音,也是我们共同的意愿。

今年5月,中国国务委员刘延东在第三轮中美人文交流高层磋商期间指出,"面对共同的挑战与责任,唯有增信释疑、求同存异才是正确选择,唯有包容理解、平等合作才能互利共赢。"克林顿国务卿目前正在中国访问,她也曾表示,"我不会宣称我们的人文交流努力能消除我们两种制度以及我们文化和历史进程之间存在的差异。但我确实认为,它将加强并增进理解、共鸣和信任。"

文化在中国被看作是"至柔至善的水","润物无声的春雨"。文化能化育心灵、沐浴社会、滋养世界。历史的经验告诉我们,文化交流在推进人类历史和平发展方面可以起到积极作用。冲突能够在文化交流中缓解,矛盾可以在相互认同中消弭。近年来,我们两国在文化领域开展了卓有成效的交流与合作,为增进两国人民的相互了解、拉近两国人民的情感距离发挥了桥梁作用。

朋友们,"中美文化论坛"是中美人文交流高层磋商机制框架下文化领域的重要项目,论坛举办以来吸引了两国众多的文化机构和有识之士,双方本着真诚友好、平等互鉴和开放包容的精神,从不同视角进行了深入探讨与交流。本届论坛从地域、历史和人类发展的角度出发,或许将帮助我们回归本源，在比较中重新审视两国文化发展的根基、厘清发展的文脉。我们也期待在两国日益密切的文化交流中，能够涌现更多闪光的思想火花，为帮助我们更好地认清未来提供文化的智慧与力量。

最后，再次感谢大家。衷心预祝第三届"中美文化论坛"取得圆满成功！

Zhao Shaohua

───────────── ★ ─────────────

Vice Minister of Ministry of Culture,
People's Republic of China

Honorable Chairman Leach and
Deputy Chief of Mission Dr. Robert Wong,
Ladies and gentlemen, dear friends,

Good morning.

The Third China-US Cultural Forum has opened as scheduled today in Beijing. I hereby offer the warmest congratulations on the opening of the forum on behalf of the Chinese Ministry of Culture and Minister of Culture Cai Wu, and extend a warm welcome to Dr. Leach, chairman of National Endowment for the Humanities (NEH), and all the members of the delegation. I also extend a warm welcome to experts and scholars from China's cultural and academic circles and our friends from the news media. Moreover, I express my sincere gratitude to Chinese National Academy of Arts, National Center for the Performing Arts, and Jiangsu Provincial Department of Culture for their strong support for this forum.

Thanks to the joint efforts of the Chinese Ministry of Culture and NEH, the China-US Cultural Forum has been successfully held twice. The first forum was held in Beijing in December 2008 with the theme 'Preservation and Presentation of Cultural Heritage in Digital Age'. Scholars from both countries had in-depth exchanges and dialogues on the application of digital technology to protecting historical and cultural heritage, passing down traditional art and culture, and promoting cultural education. Intent of cooperation was reached in areas like cultural heritage protection and cooperation in libraries and museums.

In October 2010, the second forum was held at UC Berkeley with the theme 'A Binational Conversation on Bridging Cultures'. Scholars from both countries discussed topics like 'A Retrospect of China-US Cultural Relations', 'Literary Legacy and Creativity', 'Visual Arts: Tradition and Innovation', 'A Comparative View on Performing Arts', and 'the Prospect of China-US Cultural Relations'. They made a systematic retrospect of communication and cooperation between China and the US in various areas of art and aired positive opinions on the prospect of China-US cultural relations.

Today, after careful preparations, the Third China-US Cultural Forum will be held in Beijing and Nanjing. With the theme 'The Context: Place, People, History', it will explore on a macroscopic level the cultural traits of China and the US formed by different geographical environments, ethnic origins, and historical development in order to seek a foundation for mutual understanding and acceptance.

A comparison between Chinese culture and American culture in terms of place, history and humankind's development will enable us to view their cultures and the relations between them from a more lofty and macroscopic perspective. First of all, in terms of place, China and America, which are respectively situated on the east and west shores of the Pacific, are both great powers with a vast territory, ranking the third and the fourth in size in the world. Their magnificent land, mountains and rivers have nurtured outstanding peoples and splendid cultures. In Leaves of Grass, the American poet Walt Whitman wrote, 'This is the grass that grows wherever the land is and the water is.' China has a similar saying, which goes, 'A particular place nurtures a particular group of people.' A particular group of people creates a particular culture, which in turn nourishes these people and gives them the unique national character and ethos.

Secondly, a brief summary can be made of the histories of China and the US: China, which has a 5,000-year-old civilization, was ruled by one dynasty after another for more than 2,000 years until the early 20th century, when it was freed from the yoke of feudalism. That marked the beginning of the New Culture Movement and a century of national self-strengthening efforts. In 1949, the People's Republic of China was founded. After some twists and turns, it entered a golden age of development that has lasted nearly three decades. Now China is advocating the socialist culture of harmony with Chinese characteristics, which is characterized by a broad-minded and eclectic combination of tradition and innovation. As the New World on the other side of the earth, the US has assimilated and transformed civilizations of the West and created a modern civilization in less than three centuries. It has built a cultural system marked by diversity, inclusiveness and openness, which is exhibiting strong vitality.

In terms of humankind's development and characters of civilizations, the amazing longevity of the Chinese civilization depends on its unique character. Chinese culture has always been based on human relations, with emphasis on self-cultivation, family, love of the country, and concern for the nation's destiny. Moreover, it advocates the spirit of treating others as one would like to be treated and extending one's love of his or her neighbors to other people as well, showing broad-minded fraternity and compassion, and constantly practicing the concept of learning widely from others' strengths, being open and inclusive, and pursuing harmony and balance. In comparison, the US, which has a history of over 200 years, has witnessed multi-ethnic immigrants' arduous struggle and cultural fusion, and has developed a unique American spirit and unique values based on a wide incorporation of the achievements of Western civilization. The strong sense of individual liberty, the clear preference for getting rich by hard work, and the concepts of democracy and equality have provided a profound cultural foundation for US progress and development, enabling its people to maintain a lively spirit of enterprise and struggle. The differences between China and the US in geographic environment, history and values provide us with the best perspective to understand each other's culture.

Here is a brief retrospect of the history of China-US relations: in 1784, the US merchant vessel 'Empress of China' arrived in Guangzhou, which marked the beginning of over 200 years of dealings between the two countries. After the founding of the People's Republic of China in 1972, or exactly 40 years ago, President Nixon became the first US president to step on the soil of New China, which marked the beginning of the normalization of China-US relations. Over the past four decades, the two countries have become each other's second largest trade partner, and China-US relations have become the most important bilateral relations in today's world. Now, China and the US are having all-round, multi-level exchange and cooperation between the governments, institutions, organizations and individuals on political, trade and economic, cultural and military levels.

It is true that there exist considerable differences between China and the US in cultural tradition, social system, and stage of development, but the crux of the problem is how to deal with such differences. In his new book On China, Dr. Henry Kissinger has found out the difference between the strategic cultures of China and the West by comparing Chinese go with Western chess. The latter is an absolute or zero-sum game based on logic; likewise, games between countries tend to be of the life-and-death kind. In contrast, China follows the logic of go, which is a relative or non-zero-sum game. Here, as the Chinese Vice Minister of Culture, I sincerely hope that insightful people from both countries could think more about how to reduce misinterpretation, misunderstanding and misjudgment between China and the US that arise from their differences and work hard at enhancing mutual understanding between them. It will be the best blessing for the world and our common wish for the two countries to improve communication, enhance mutual trust, and promote cooperation as the world's largest developing country and largest developed country.

In May this year, during the Third Meeting of the China-US High-Level Consultation on People-to-People Exchange, State Councilor Liu Yandong remarked, 'Faced with common challenges and responsibilities, the right thing to do is to enhance trust, dispel misgiving, seek common ground and reserve differences. Only inclusiveness, understanding, equality and cooperation will lead to win-win progress.' Secretary of State Hillary Clinton, currently on a visit to China, also said, 'I do not claim that our people-to-people efforts will eliminate the differences between our two systems, our cultural and historical experiences. But I do believe it will increase and enhance understanding, empathy, and trust.'

In China, culture is compared to 'the ultimate softness and goodness of water' and 'spring rain that silently moistens everything'. Culture can edify minds, harmonize society, and nourish the world. History tells us that cultural exchange can play a useful role in the peaceful development of mankind. Conflicts can be relieved in cultural exchange, and disputes can be dissolved in mutual understanding. In recent years, China and the US have conducted successful exchange and cooperation in culture, which has helped to enhance mutual understanding between the peoples and bridge their emotional gap.

Dear friends, China-US Cultural Forum is an important cultural project within the framework of the China-US High-Level Consultation on People-to-

People Exchange. Since its initiation, it has attracted a large number of cultural institutions and people of insight from both countries. In the spirit of sincerity, friendship, equality, mutual complementation, openness and inclusiveness, they have had in-depth discussions from various perspectives. With the theme of place, people and history, this year's forum may help us to return to the origin and re-examine the foundations of both countries' cultural development and chart the course of such development through comparison. We also hope that more brilliant ideas will emerge from the ever-increasingly close cultural exchange between the two countries, which could provide cultural wisdom and strength for a better vision of the future.

Finally, let me thank you all again and express my sincere wish for the great success of the Third China-US Cultural Forum.

詹姆斯·利奇

美国国家人文基金会主席

蔡武部长、赵少华女士，尊敬的各位与会嘉宾：

本次会议重点关注一系列文化问题，在会议开始之际我想首先对会议主办方表示敬意。

纵观人类文明史，中国在创新方面长久以来发挥着独一无二的作用。中国的发明推进了商业和农业的发展。中国学者使哲学思想得到进一步丰富。诗歌激发了中国艺术家和工匠灵魂深处的创作灵感，使其在纸张、丝绸和各色瓷器上描绘出了壮美河山。

是中国人率先发明了纸张、印刷机、指南针和火药。是中国人率先用锄头和犁耕地促进作物生长。中国的锻造技术在欧洲工业革命发生前几个世纪就已经相当成熟，用铜制作出了精良的炊具。中国早于亨利·福特几千年就开始应用组装技术，中国人懂得如何高效组装，比如如何在西安兵马俑的躯干上安装手臂和腿。中国的各种哲学思潮，从儒家思想到道家学说，从孙子的治国之道到邓小平的经济发展理论，百花齐放，蜚声海外。

我的国家美国则是一个年轻的国家（至少在后殖民地意义上如此），但是拥有蓬勃发展的历史。我们很幸运地拥有一个社会能够获得的最慷慨的援助——源于圣地的道德价值观：摩西和基督的教义；佛陀、穆罕默德以及古希腊时期和欧洲启蒙时期的哲学家们的思想：柏拉图、亚里士多德、马基雅维里、孟德斯鸠、洛克、休谟、黑格尔和斯宾诺莎。

来自全球各地的移民使美国拥有丰富多样的技术、力量、文化和传统。基于对信仰的承诺、独立的思考方式和人类力量，我们的先辈共同造就了美国第一届政府，并对其不断加以完善。美国人认为他们生来拥有不可剥夺的权利。美国的首届政府由民选产生，具有自下而上建立的合法性。

虽然美国的历史并不悠久，但是我们面临的挑战却十分严峻。这些挑战有的来自内部，有的来自外部，20世纪中期我们来到亚洲与中国人民并肩作战抗击法西斯的侵略便是挑战之一。

我们为美国所取得的科学和技术成就而骄傲，从爱迪生到爱因斯坦，从数字计算机到芯片，以及现在的 IPhone 和 IPad。我们也为美国多元化的艺术而自豪，从格兰特·伍德具有地方特色的画作，杰克逊·波洛克的抽象表现主义，到马克·吐温的幽默写作风格，再到斯坦贝克、海明威、福克纳笔下描述的或重或轻的忧伤，他们亦如参加第二届中美文化论坛的中国代表莫言一样，通过虚构城市和人物捕捉生命的悲怆。

中美两国的文化虽有差异，但这并不意味着我们不能尊重彼此的创造、社会成就以及更重要的人类环境，即使公众的分歧变得十分明显时亦是如此。毕竟，政府政策具有短暂性和可逆性。另一方面，文化的内涵比政府的概念更深远、更持久。政府是文化的组成部分，反之则不然。文化是海洋、是环境，而国家则像船只，航行在文化的滔滔巨浪之中。

民族国家之间的差异及其人民和既得利益的不同有时难免会深化。但是，如果人们尊重彼此的文化，认识到不同背景下人们面临的共同挑战，就可以大大降低因差异导致矛盾的可能性。

这就是为什么人文领域——历史、文学、哲学及相关学科，包括语言艺术和比较宗教——的会议和研究如此重要的原因，人际交往也是如此。

在当今时代，国与国之间的关系完全是政府政策的职能，而外交仅仅是政府间开展的对话。其实，与政府官员相比，能够更准确界定国家之间关系基调的往往是商人、企业家和未当权的善良民众，无论他们是艺术家、科学家、运动员、学生，还是人文学者。

政府代表关注权力和安全问题，这一点可以理解，尤其是当我们处于一个四分五裂的世界中时。相反，文化交往更多涉及核心价值观和人文精神的广度。而且更重要的是，在商业世界中，文化交往与寻求共同利益、促进互利共赢息息相关。

人们若要实现相互尊重，就必须具有人文层面的共同价值观。没有人性——表示理解的握手，信任、团结和国家安全便无从实现。

人生和国家命运是一个不断寻求平衡的过程，就如同行走在钢索上的马戏团演员。当今世界瞬息万变，平衡困境不断增加，后果愈发严重。为了说明问题，我想列举当今时代三种特别敏感的困境：

1. 贸易中的竞争与合作之间的平衡。若要维持建设性的关系，国家和公司之间必须实现互利。

2. 地方化和全球化之间的平衡。美国20世纪杰出议员之一、众议院议长蒂普·奥尼尔的名言是：所有政治都是地方政治。一个不断被强化的结论值得关注：所有的地方政治都受到全球性事件的影响。当政治（包括由贸易问题引发的关注）变得愈发全球化时，外交政策便愈发本地化，不再是统治精英的专属特权。政府在决策时必须以某种方式兼顾城市和农村民众的情绪。

3. 国家自由与内、外部秩序的平衡。在世界许多地方，这种平衡变得越来越不稳定。没有任何一个国家能够避免做出抉择，或规避与他者判断的分歧。

态度愈发强硬、宗教和历史的差异日趋深化是当今地缘政治的特点。人文因素，例如人性弱点和利益冲突，在政府决策中永远不会受到低估。但是，不管领导人如何用心良苦，也难免会犯下错误，引发严重后果，特别是对于缺乏应对挑战经验的领导人。

在这一发人深省的背景下，中美双边关系需要不断关注政策层面。如果中美关系处理不当，发生冲突和经济危机的可能性就会增大。另一方面，如果谨慎处理中美关系，经济繁荣和世界和平所带来的利益也将同样巨大。

因此，除了一些重要的例外情况，在国际交往中保持谨言慎行是当今世界的不二法则。很少会出现只由某个人或某个国家单独决定某一合理方式的情况。

不甚完美的判断是人类环境的特点之一。无论一个人知道的或多或少，都必须注意不要轻下断言。也许，无所不知比知之甚少更为可取，但最优秀和最聪明的人也难免会犯下重大错误。这也解释了为何谦卑是一个非常重要的品质，以及为什么在文明世界中共同学习和共享经验是如此重要。

谢谢！

James Leach

— ★ —

Chairman of US National Endowment for the Humanities

Minister Cai Wu, Madam Zhao Shaohua, distinguished conferees and guests:

In this conference addressing broad questions of culture, I would like to begin by paying deep respect to our hosts.

In the development of civilization, China has through the ages played a uniquely innovative role. Chinese inventions have advanced commercial and agricultural enterprise. Chinese scholars have embellished philosophical thought. Chinese artists and artisans have stimulated the creative instincts of the soul with poetry, landscapes on paper and silk scrolls, and ceramics of various kinds and dimensions.

It is here in China that paper was first processed and the printing press first used. It is in China that the compass, the rotating gimbal, and gunpowder were first developed. It is in China that the hoe and the plow first knifed through the soil to spur growth of seeds into plants. It is in China that forging capacities were advanced centuries before the industrial revolution in Europe to produce sophisticated brass cooking pots. It is in China that assembly-line techniques were used, millennia before Henry Ford used the approach to building cars, to craft efficiently and attach, among other things, arms and legs to the torsos of the terra cotta warriors in Xi'an. And it is in China where philosophical movements from Confucianism to Daoism, from theories of statecraft of Sun Tzu to theories of economic development of Deng Xiaoping, have flourished and influenced millions beyond its borders.

As for my country, America has a young (at least in a post-colonial sense) but vibrant history. We have been blessed with the most generous foreign aid ever given a society – moral values springing from the Holy Land and points East: the creeds of Moses and Christ, Buddha and Mohammed, mixed with the philosophical ideas and ideals emanating from ancient Greece and the Enlightenment in Europe: Plato and Aristotle, Machiavelli and Montesquieu, Locke and Hume, Hegel and Spinoza.

America has also been munificently gifted with the skills, energy, and cultural traditions of immigrants from all corners of the earth. This mixture of faith-based commitment, independent thinking, and human energy has made possible the forging and subsequent refinement of the first government whose revolutionary legitimacy springs from the bottom-up, from individuals self-evidently born with inalienable rights.

Through our short history we have faced a series of challenges, internal and external, one of which in the middle of the 20th Century brought us to Asia in alliance with the Chinese people to fight together fascist aggression.

We are proud of our achievements in science and technology, from Edison to Einstein, from the digital computer to smart phones. We are proud of the diversity of our arts, the regional paintings of Grant Wood and the abstract expressionism of Jackson Pollock, the humor-laced writings of Mark Twain, and the traumas, large and small, depicted by Steinbeck, Hemingway and Faulkner, who like Mo Yan, one of China's representatives to the Second China-U.S. Cultural Forum, captured the pathos of life by placing fictional characters in an invented city.

China and America have different cultures but that doesn't mean we cannot respect each other's creativity and social achievements and, more importantly, human condition even if public differences become stark. Governmental policies, after all, are fleeting and reversible. Culture, on the other hand, is vastly larger and more sustaining than government. Governance is a component of culture, not vice-versa. Culture is the ocean – the circumstances – and nations are like ships attempting to navigate culture's tumultuous waves.

Differences between nation-states, their peoples and vested interests, inevitably heighten from time to time. But if people have respect for each other's culture and for the mutual challenges individuals of all backgrounds face in the sea of life, the chances that differences will cause conflict vastly diminish.

This is why conferences and studies in the humanities – history, literature, philosophy, and related disciplines, including the language arts and comparative religion – are critically important. So are people-to-people exchanges.

A myth of our times is that relations between countries are exclusively a function of government policy and that diplomacy is simply a government-to-government dialogue. Actually, it is businessmen and businesswomen, unelected people of good will – be they artists or scientists, athletes, students, or scholars in the humanities – who are often more integral to defining the tone of relations between states than public officials.

Representatives of governments understandably dwell on power and security issues, especially in a fractured world. Cultural engagement, by contrast, is more about the centrality of values and the breadth of the human spirit. And, importantly, in the business world it is about probing common interests and promoting mutual advantage.

If people are to develop mutual respect, values must be brought to bear on a human scale. Without humanization – handshakes of understanding – there can be no more than minimal trust, minimal security for family or nation.

Like a circus performer walking on a suspended tight rope, the life of peoples and countries in the 21st Century is a balancing act. In a world of escalating change, balancing quandaries grow rapidly in number and consequence. To illustrate, I would like to reference three particularly sensitive quandaries of our times:

1) The balance between competition and cooperation in trade. For constructive relations to be sustainable, mutual advantage must accrue to countries as well as companies.

2) The balance between localism and globalism. One of the preeminent American legislators of the 20th Century, Speaker of the House Tip O'Neill, was fond of asserting that all politics is local. A fast strengthening corollary deserves attention: all local politics is affected by global events. When politics, including trade-driven concerns, becomes globalized, foreign policy comes to be a localized consideration, rather than the near exclusive province of governing elites. In one way or another, public sentiment in cities and rural hamlets must be factored into policy considerations.

3) The balance between freedom and order externally as well as internally in the affairs of the state. In many parts of the world this balance is increasingly precarious. No country escapes the necessity of choice-making and the ramifications of the judgment calls of others.

Geo-politics at the moment is characterized by a hardening of attitudes and a sharpening of religious and historical differences. The human factor – foibles and conflicts of interest, for instance – can never be underestimated in governmental decision-making. But leaders, no matter how well-intentioned, can make mistakes that carry monumental consequences, especially when challenges lack precedent.

It is in this sobering context that the bilateral relationship between China and the United States demands the constant attention of policy stewards. If this relationship is ill-managed, the likelihood of conflict and economic trauma will be great. On the other hand, if the relationship is managed prudently, the benefits in terms of economic prosperity and world peace will be commensurate.

Accordingly, with important exceptions, the case for restrained rhetoric and caution in statecraft fits best the world in which we now live. Seldom is there only one proper path determinable by one individual or one country.

Imperfect judgment characterizes the human condition. Whether a person knows a great deal or very little, care should be taken about being certain of very much. To know a lot may be a preferable condition to knowing little, but the best and the brightest are not immune from great mistakes. That is why humility is such a valued character trait, and why shared learning and shared experiences are so important in a civilized world.

Thank you!

UNIT ONE: CULTURE AND PEOPLE

第一单元 文化与人类

中国艺术研究院中国文化研究所所长刘梦溪做主题发言
《"将无同"——文化融合是人类未来的大趋势》
Liu Mengxi, Director of Institute of Chinese Culture, Chinese National Academy of Arts
"Jiang Wu Tong——Cultural Integration is the General Trend of the Future of Humanity"

美国国会图书馆"美国国家民俗中心"名誉主任玛格丽特·巴尔杰做主题发言
《文化与人类：非物质文化遗产的传播、翻译与转化》
Margaret Bulger, Director Emerita of the American Folklife Center at the Library of Congress
"Culture and People: Transmitting, Translating and Transforming Intangible Cultural Heritage"

中国社会科学院美国研究所所长黄平做主题发言
《超越黑白两分》
Huang Ping, Director of United States Institute of the Chinese Academy of Social Sciences
"Beyond Black and White"

美国纽伯瑞图书馆"美洲印第安人和原住民研究"达西·麦克尼克尔中心主任斯科特·曼宁·史蒂文斯做主题发言
《建立档案与美国印第安研究间的桥梁》
Scott Manning Stevens, Director of D'Arcy McNickle Center for American Indian and Indigenous Studies, Newberry Library
"Bridging the Divide between the Archive and American Indians"

中国美术馆馆长范迪安做主题发言
《中国当代艺术：在全球与本土之间》
Fan Di'an, Director of National Art Museum of China
"Contemporary Chinese Art: Between Globalization and Localization"

"美中学术交流委员会"北京办事处主任阿瑟·泰做主题发言
《文化与教育交流》
Arthur Tai, Director of the Beijing Office of the US Committee on Scholarly Communication with China
"Cultural and Educational Exchanges"

著名文化学者余秋雨做主题发言
《利玛窦的发现》
Yu Qiuyu, Famous Cultural Scholar
"Matteo Ricci's Discovery"

中国艺术研究院·中国非物质文化遗产保护中心常务副主任李新风做主题发言
《中国非物质文化遗产保护的创造性实践》
Li Xinfeng, Executive Deputy Director of China Intangible Cultural Heritage Protection Center, Chinese National Academy of Arts
"Creative Practice of China's Intangible Cultural Heritage Protection"

刘梦溪

中国艺术研究院中国文化研究所所长

"将无同"
——文化融合是人类未来的大趋势

内容提要： 世界上不同的文化、不同的"文明体国家"，不必然发展为冲突，而是需要通过交流与对话达成文化的互补与融合。冲突是人类文明的"反动"，是礼仪文化的"弃物"。所以孔子说："礼之用，和为贵。""和"才能成礼，冲突是愚蠢的失礼行为，为人类文明所不取。人类如果因文化的差异与"不同"而出现偶然的对立，彼此当事方应该采取"和而解"的态度，而不是走向"仇而亡"。这是中国古老文化的智慧，也是人类本性和人类理性所应该指向的目标。

一、"三语掾"

"将无同"这三个字，出现在中国历史上学术思想最活跃的魏晋时期，约为公元220—420年。当时流行的学术思潮是玄学。学者们围绕"名教"和"自然"的主题，展开激烈的辩论。看法虽然不同，双方的风度很好。他们不轻视对手，只论理，而不在意对手地位的尊卑。

"竹林七贤"是当时一个有名的知识分子群体，诗人阮籍和音乐家嵇康是"七贤"的领袖。他们的立场倾向于与"名教"对立的"自然"方面，狂简任达和思想自由，是他们追寻的目标。王戎是"七贤"最小的成员，比他大20岁的阮籍，本来与王戎的父亲王浑友善，后来接触到王戎，相见大乐，此后便只愿意和这个年仅15岁的"阿戎谈"，置王浑于一旁而不顾。

清谈者的姿容仪态也很讲究，最尊崇有范儿的是王戎的从弟王衍，据说他清谈的时候，"神情明秀，风姿详雅"，手里拿的麈尾以玉为柄，因皮肤白皙，手和麈尾的玉柄浑然无有分别。另一位清谈名家乐广，以渊默简要著称。王衍和乐广，极尽当时名士风流之盛，成为魏正始时期的清谈领袖。

清谈在哲学层面发生的争论，是关于宇宙世界的"有"和"无"的问题。中国古代两位天才的思想家王弼与何晏，就活跃于此一历史时刻。关于"有"和"无"的争论，参与的人比较少，"名教"与"自然"的争论牵连面广，参与的人多，持续的时间相当之长。"名教"关乎政治伦理秩序，"自然"关乎个体生命的自由。王弼的观点主要见于他的《老子注》一书，何晏则注《论语》，两人都从儒家和道家的最高经典追溯自己思想的源头。哲学论争和"名教"与"自然"的争论互为表里，包括高人、雅士、名流在内的魏晋知识分子群体，鲜有置身于这一时代主题之外者。

但到了下一代，情况发生了改变。《晋书》记载，阮籍的从侄孙阮瞻，一次拜见当时已经位至"三公"的王戎。王戎问这位年轻人："圣人贵名教，老庄明自然，其旨同异？"王戎回答说："将无同。"当时圈内人士称阮瞻的回答为"三语掾"。"将无"是不含实义的语助词，"将无同"就是没有什么不同，也就是"同"。前辈们争论不休的"名教"与"自然"问题，到下一代人那里，已超越对立，摆脱执著，变成无须争论不必争论的问题了。

《世说新语》的类似记载，是王衍和阮籍的侄儿阮修的互相对问。诚如大史学家陈寅恪先生所说："答者之为阮瞻或阮修皆不关重要，其重要者只是老庄自然与周孔名教相同之说一点，盖此为当时清谈主旨所在。"①《晋书》记载，王戎听了阮瞻的回答，不禁"咨嗟良久"，最后表示认同。当年持论甚坚的清谈领袖，在时代前行的年轻人面前低下了高贵的头颅。

二、破除"迷执"

事实上，人类历史上的许多惊心动魄或者惊天动地的争执和论争，到后来都因趋同而化解或由于折中而和合。人类的思维之路之所以无限

---

① 《陶渊明之思想与清谈之关系》，陈著：《金明馆丛稿初编》，第203页。

曲折，是由于人们有"执"："执于"一"，而不知有"二"；执于此，而不及于彼；执其始，而不知所终，未能做到孔子说的"扣其两端"。《华严经》上说："一切众生具有如来智慧德相，但以妄想执著而不证得。"这是说，人类本身并非不具备拥有"智慧德相"的条件，只是由于自身的"妄想"和"迷执"，不能够实现"证得"。"证得"就是"证悟"，亦即思想的"觉悟"。不能"证得"，就是不得"觉悟"。

三、文化自觉

我国已故的老一辈文化社会学家费孝通先生，晚年提出"各美其美，美人之美，美美与共，世界大同"的文化论说，即主张世界上各种不同的文化，都有其优长之处，我们既要看到自己的长处，也要看到他者的长处。所以需要"各美其美"，也要"美人之美"。也就是尊重差别，尊重文化的多样性。"美美与共"，指人类的文化最终会走向融合。这是费先生的关于"文化自觉"的理论，对陷入"迷执"的今天的人们而言，无疑是"润物细无声"的春日喜雨。

我国另一位百科全书式的大学者钱锺书先生，他在早年的著作《谈艺录》中，也说过："东海西海，心理攸同；南学北学，道术未裂。"钱先生的意思，东方和西方，各个国家民族的不同人群，彼此的心理结构和心理指向，常常是相同的。已故的哈佛大学中国学学者史华慈教授，提倡"跨文化沟通"，甚至提出语言对于思维并不具有人们想象的那样大的作用。所以有时尽管语言不通，也不是完全不能交流，甚至还可以发生爱情。人类的"同"其实远远多于"不同"。

强调人类的"不同"，是因为"有执"，包括"我执"和"法执"。还由于"理障"。各种预设的不正确的"论理体系"，有时会成为隔断人类正常交往与交流的围墙。过多地强调人类的"不同"，是文化的陷阱。

四、"与人同者，物必归焉"

中国最古老的文化经典《易经》，其"系辞"写道："天下何思何虑？天下同归而殊途，一致而百虑。"这个意思是说，人类的不同在于方法和途径，也就是"化迹"的不同，最终的结点总是要走在一起。《易经》"睽"

卦的"象辞"也说:"君子以同而异。"所以不同,是因为有同。与其标立彼此之"异",不如首先认同求同。这一道理,《易经》的"序"卦,有更为直接的论证:"与人同者,物必归焉。"亦即要达至众望所归,得到他人的认同,自己必须首先"与人同"。大家熟知的孔子的名言"君子和而不同",讲的也是这个道理。

不同也可以共处在一个统一体中,不同也可以达成"和"的泰局。

五、"仇必和而解"

对这个问题阐释得最深刻的是中国宋代的思想家张载。他在自己的代表著作《正蒙》中,用四句话表达了他对整个宇宙世界的看法。这四句话是——

> 有象斯有对,
> 对必反其为,
> 有反斯有仇,
> 仇必和而解。

我把这四句话,称作张载的"哲学四句教"。因为他还有另外的"四句教",即"为天地立心,为生民立命,为往圣继绝学,为万世开太平",表达的是宋儒的群体政治理想。

张载的"哲学四句教"意在说明:宇宙万物,山川河流,微尘草芥,个体生命,这一个个有形的物体,都可叫作"象"。"象"不重复,人有人象,物有物象。同为人,象也不同。所谓"佳人不同体,美人不同面"。而"有对",就是指"象"的不同和不同的"象",它们各自所处的位置。西哲说,"世界上没有相同的两个体",也是此义。"象"不是静止的,它运行流动,无往不在,无处不在。不同的"象",流动的方向不完全相同,因此象与象之间"反其为"的情形时时会出现。第三句"有反斯有仇",不必理解为仇敌的仇。这个字的古写,作"雠",校雠的雠,两只短尾巴鸟,叽叽喳喳地争短论长。不是一个吃掉另一个,而是互相校正,你校正我,我校正你,存异求同,和合共生。

关键是最后一句："仇必和而解。"简单地说，宇宙间万事万物，不过是对待、流行、校正、和解而已。对待与流行的结果，不是吃掉、消灭，而是通过校正，达至和解、共生。"度尽劫波兄弟在，相逢一笑泯恩仇"，这是中国大作家鲁迅一首诗里的话，最能得张载义理的真传。

六、结语

张载哲学启示我们，世界各文明之间，虽然存在差异，却不必然发展为冲突。人类的未来，世界历史的大趋势，是走向文明的融合而不是相反。因此我个人无法赞同前些年哈佛大学亨廷顿教授提出的"文明冲突论"。他把西方文明跟伊斯兰文明及儒教文明，视为不可调和的"冲突体"。这个理论是站不住脚的。他只看到了不同文化不同文明之间的差异和纠结，没有看到不同文化之间的对话、沟通和"化解"；只看到了"文明的冲突"，没有看到文明的融合。

世界上不同的文化、不同的"文明体国家"，不必然发展为冲突，而是需要通过交流与对话达成文化的互补与融合。冲突是人类文明的"反动"，是礼仪文化的"弃物"。所以孔子说："礼之用，和为贵。""和"才能成礼，冲突是愚蠢的失礼行为，为人类文明所不取。人类如果因文化的差异与"不同"而出现偶然的对立，彼此当事方应该采取"和而解"的态度，而不是走向"仇而亡"。这是中国古老文化的智慧，也是人类本性和人类理性所应该指向的目标。

Jiang Wu Tong

— Cultural Integration is the General Trend of the Future of Humanity

Liu Mengxi
Director of Institute of Chinese Chlture, Chinese National Academy of Arts

Abstract: Conflict is not inevitable between different cultures and civilizations in the world. Instead, it is necessary to achieve cultural fusion and mutual complementation through exchange and dialogue. Conflict is 'reactionary' to human civilization and something 'eschewed' by ritual culture. That is why Confucius said, 'In the application of the rites, harmony is to be prized.' Only harmony can lead to propriety, whereas conflict is a foolish breach of propriety to be avoided in human civilization. In the case of occasional confrontation arising from cultural differences, the parties involved should try to become reconciled instead of hating and trying to beat the other. Such is the wisdom in the ancient Chinese culture and also an objective that human nature and reason inclines one to.

I. The 'Monumental Three-character Reply'

The three-word epigram 'just the same' (jiang wu tong) dates back to the Wei and Jin Dynasties (c. 220-420 AD), a period which saw the liveliest academic thoughts in Chinese history. The prevailing trend of thought was metaphysics, and scholars had heated debates over subjects like the Confucian ethnical code and naturalness. Despite their different opinions, they always maintained gentle manners. They focused on theoretical discussion, never looking down upon their opponents or minding their status.

The Seven Sages of the Bamboo Grove was a well-known group of intellectuals led by the poet Ruan Ji and the musician Ji Kang. They were inclined toward naturalness as opposed to the Confucian ethical code, preferring a simple, unrestrained and unconventional way of life and pursuing freedom of thinking. Wang Rong was the youngest of the seven. Ruan Ji, who was twenty years his senior, had been good friends with his father Wang Hun. When he met Wang Rong, however, he was so delighted that, from then on, he would only talk with the fifteen-year-old A Rong and ignore the boy's father.

Those who engaged in 'pure talk' (qingtan) were quite particular about their appearance and bearing. One of the most stylish figures was Wang Yan, who was Wang Rong's cousin. It was said that, when he was having a 'pure talk', he had a bright and charming look and a poised and elegant bearing. He held an ornamental duster with a handle made of jade, and his skin was so fair that it was hard to tell his hand from the jade handle. Another famous 'pure talker', named Yue Guang, was known for his profound and laconic style. Both representing the acme of refinement for literary celebrities, Wang Yan and Yue Guang became leaders of 'pure talk' during the Zhengshi period of the Wei Dynasty.

The philosophical debate in 'pure talk' concerned the existence or non-existence of the universe and the world. It was during this period that Wang Bi and He Yan were active as two of the most gifted thinkers of ancient China. The debate on existence versus non-existence involved fewer people than the argument about the Confucian ethical code versus naturalness, which touched upon a wider range of subjects and lasted a considerable period of time. The former had to do with political and ethical order, while the latter concerned individual freedom. Wang Bi expressed his views mainly in his Commentary on Lao Tzu, while He Yan wrote a commentary on The Analects. They traced their thought back to the highest classics of Confucianism and Taoism respectively. The philosophical debate and the argument about the Confucian ethical code versus naturalness, which were inter-dependent, formed the theme of the times, which influenced almost all of the Wei and Jin intellectuals, including eminent thinkers, men of letters, and distinguished personages.

However, the situation changed in the next generation. According to Book of Jin, Ruan Zhan, a great grandson of Ruan Ji's cousin, once paid a visit to Wang Rong, who had become one of the three highest-ranking officials in the imperial court. Wang Rong asked the young man, 'The sages preached the Confucian ethical code, but Lao Tzu and Chuang Tse advocated naturalness. Are their main ideas the same or different?' Ruan Zhan answered, 'Jiang wu tong (just the same).' This was known among the literati as the 'Monumental Three-character Reply'. Jiang-wu is an auxiliary word with no specific meaning, so jiang wu tong means simply tong, or 'just the same'. Earlier scholars had had incessant dispute over 'ethical code' and 'naturalness'; the younger generation of scholars, however, overcame doggedness, and debate over the issue was rendered irrelevant.

There is a similar account of this anecdote in Shi Shuo Xin Yu, except that the two persons concerned are Wang Yan and Ruan Ji's nephew Ruan Xiu. As the great historian Chen Yinque remarked, 'It doesn't matter who answered the question, Ruan Zhan or Ruan Xiu. What matters is the opinion that Lao Tzu and Chuang Tse's concept of naturalness is the same as the Confucian ethical code attributed to the Duke of Zhou and Confucius, which was a major theme of "pure talk" at the time.'[1] According to Book of Jin, Wang Rong marveled at Ruan Zhan's answer for a long while before finally saying that he agreed with the latter.

---

[1] 'On the Relationship between Tao Yuanming's Thought and Pure Talk', in Chen Yinque: Initial Edition of the Golden Bright Study Manuscripts, p. 203

Thus a leader of pure talk who used to hold steadfastly to his opinion bowed his head in front of a young man who stood in the forefront of the times.

II. Getting rid of doggedness

In fact, many fierce or earthshaking debates and arguments in history were eventually resolved by a tendency toward common ground or reconciled through compromise. The reason why the human intellectual history is laden with twists and turns is people's 'doggedness'--they cling to 'one idea' doggedly but turn a blind eye to' another'; they preoccupy themselves doggedly with 'this' but forget about 'that'; they are obsessed with the 'origin' but lose track of where it will lead to. In a sense, they have failed to do as Confucius instructed--'to thrash a matter out with pros and cons'. Avatamsaka Sutra says, 'All creatures are endowed with the wisdom and virtue of Buddha, which they fail to realize because of their wrong thinking and obsession.' To realize such wisdom and virtue would be to attain enlightenment; failure to do so would preclude one from enlightenment.

III. Cultural consciousness

As one of the first cultural sociologists in China, the late Professor Fei Xiaotong posited in his twilight years the notion that 'the world will be a harmonious place if people appreciate their own beauty and that of others, and work together to create beauty in the world.' There exist diverse cultures in the world, and each has its own strengths. We should be aware of the strengths of others as well as those of ourselves. Therefore we need to respect differences and diversity. Eventually all cultures of humankind will become unified. Such is Professor Fei's theory on 'cultural consciousness', which may nourish the minds of today's obsessed people like a spring rain that 'moistens everything gently and silently'.

A similar remark was made by Qian Zhongshu, another great encyclopedic Chinese scholar, in one of his earlier books On Arts, 'From the east or west, people think in the same way; in the south and north, the Tao is nothing dissimilar.' This means that people's psychological structure and preference tend to be the same in various countries of the East and the West. The late Professor Benjamin Schwartz of Harvard, a scholar of Chinese studies, advocated 'cross-cultural communication' and even said that language does not have such a significant influence on thinking as we imagine. Sometimes, language barrier does not totally prevent communication; in fact, it may even help to engender love. We are actually far more 'the same' than 'different'.

To stress difference among people is because of obsession, which includes egocentrism and dharma-graha, and 'theoretical barriers'. Presupposed incorrect 'theoretical systems' sometimes become walls that cut off normal dealings and exchange among people. To place too much emphasis on difference is a cultural pitfall.

IV. 'If you identify with others, you'll find everything in the world in your favor.'

The Great Treatise on Book of Changes, one of China's oldest classics, says, 'Why is there so much dissension in the world? All different paths lead to the same goal. Despite the same goal, different ideas arise.' That is to say, difference among people lies in methods and approaches which eventually lead to the same end. One of the classic commentaries on the hexagram of kui (polarizing) goes, 'The gentleman finds sameness in difference.' Therefore it would be wiser to recognize such commonality than to demarcate differences. A more direct argument for this is given in the hexagram of xu: 'If you identify with others, you'll find everything in the world in your favor.' That is, you have to think from others' angles to win their favor. The same idea is expressed in the well-known adage by Confucius: 'A gentleman seeks harmony rather than ostensible agreement.'

Differences can also coexist in a unified entity and result in peace and harmony.

V. Antagonism must be resolved through compromise

This issue has been most profoundly discussed by Zhang Zai, a Chinese thinker of the Song Dynasty. In his magnum opus Zheng Meng, he expresses his view of the whole universe in four lines:

Each phenomenon has its opposite;
Two opposite things must be in conflict.
From conflict arises antagonism;
Antagonism must be resolved through compromise.

I refer to these words as Zhang Zai's 'four-line philosophical teaching'. He has another four-line teaching--'to establish the soul between heaven and earth, to define the meaning of life for people, to carry on the learning of sages of the past, and to usher in everlasting peace', which expresses the collective political ideal of Song Confucians.

By his 'four-line philosophical teaching' Zhang Zhai means the following: Everything in the world--a mountain, a river, a particle of dust, a blade of grass, or an individual--in other words, every visible object, can be called a 'phenomenon'. Human phenomena differ from non-human ones, and each person is a unique phenomenon (as the saying goes, 'Each beauty has a unique body and unique face.'). Each phenomenon has something opposite to it. The same meaning is expressed in Western philosophy as 'there are no two identical things in the world'. Phenomena are not static, but dynamic, flowing, and omnipresent. Different phenomena may not flow in the same direction, so 'opposition' arises between phenomena from time to time. 'Confrontation' (chou) in the third line can be interpreted as 'correction', as in the word jiao-chou (collation), rather than 'hostility', as in chou-di (enemy). The ancient character chou in jiao-chou represents two birds engaging in a chattering argument, which does not end with one eating another, but rather involves mutual correction, an effort to seek common ground while reserving differences, and harmonious coexistence.

The most important is the last line--'Which always ends in reconciliation'. To put it simply, relationships between all things in the universe can be classified into opposition, prevalence, correction, and reconciliation. Opposition and prevalence do not lead to annihilation, but to reconciliation and coexistence by means of correction. 'For all the disasters the brotherhood has remained; a smile at meeting and enmity is banished'--this line from a poem by the great writer Lu Xun best illustrates Zhang Zai's doctrine.

VI. Conclusion

Zhang Zai's philosophy tells us that differences between civilizations of the world do not necessarily give rise to conflicts, and that the future of humankind and the general trend of world history is the integration of civilizations, not the opposite. So personally I cannot agree with the theory on the clash of civilizations proposed by Professor Huntington of Harvard University, who says that there exists irreconcilable conflict among Western, Islamic and Confucian civilizations. This theory is untenable because he only sees differences and contradiction between civilizations but fails to see dialogue, communication and 'reconciliation' between cultures; he only sees the 'conflict of civilizations', not their integration.

Conflict is not inevitable between different cultures and civilizations in the world. Instead, it is necessary to achieve cultural fusion and mutual complementation through exchange and dialogue. Conflict is 'reactionary' to human civilization and something 'eschewed' by ritual culture. That is why Confucius said, 'In the application of the rites, harmony is to be prized.' Only harmony can lead to propriety, whereas conflict is a foolish breach of propriety to be avoided in human civilization. In the event of occasional confrontation arising from cultural differences, the parties involved should try to become reconciled instead of hating and trying to destroy each other. Such is the wisdom in the ancient Chinese culture and also an objective that human nature and reason inclines one to.

文化与人类：
非物质文化遗产的传播、翻译与转化

玛格丽特·巴尔杰

美国国会图书馆"美国国家民俗中心"名誉主任

内容提要：文化往往被视为地球上某个特定地区的财产和遗产。但事实上，文化是由个体的人创造和传播的，而人是流动的，并不是根植在某一个位置的。美国公民的祖先可以说来自世界各地。只有那些美国土著部落的文化表述才能被视为是完全意义上的"本土"文化表述。而对于所谓的"美国文化"的其他组成部分来说，它的独特性正是源于世界文化的融合和/或共存。我认为，这种多样性对于维护21世纪可持续发展的文化社群至关重要，这不仅仅限于美国范围内，也同样适用于整个世界。我们致力于在全世界范围内保护和支持全球所有非物质文化遗产，同时我们必须认识并尊重由于人口流动和不可避免的文化元素共享所形成的整体文化表述。有一个事实是无法否定的：即文化是瞬息万变的，它的演化过程与人们的文化学习、文化保护和文化传承活动是相伴相随的。基于我作为美国公共民俗学者的四十多年经验，我建议倡导一种策略，即在保护传统文化表述的同时，应当对这个流动化、全球化、依赖于新技术并维护知识产权的现代世界中可能出现的文化变化持支持态度。

与会的美国发言者都是文化领域的专家和著名的人文学者。但由于其来自不同的学科，每个人都有其独特视角。我是一位民俗学者，因此，我的报告反映了我在该领域的培训和工作情况。民俗学的观点与历史学、人类学、社会学、文学、民族研究以及艺术史的观点既有交叉，又有不同。

什么是民俗

我要说明为什么民俗学是将构成人文学的各学科紧密相融的关键因素。经常有人问我："什么是民俗学？"简而言之，民俗学就是是一切通过口述、风俗和实践留传下来的知识。我在中国的民俗学同仁都知道，民俗和民众生活中蕴含着重要的文化元素，如民间艺术、手工艺和乡土建筑等，以及各种口述传统，如口述历史、史诗、传说、神话、笑话、谚语、民间诗歌和个人叙事等。它还包括农村地区的织网、农耕、打鱼和打铁等传统职业技能，以及驾驶出租车、当警察、经营餐馆等现代城市技能——实际上，任何职业或事业都有与其相关的民俗知识体，通过老一代从业者传承给年轻一代。

总之，我们所知和所传承的大约90%都是民俗。我们认为这些知识非常重要，应当亲自教给子孙后代，而不是留给学校和教授们去灌输。传承民俗文化的重要因素之一是人与人之间亲密而持续地交流。有人邀请我谈一下"文化与民族"，这十分切题，因为民俗不是一件"事物"，它是一个过程，是人类文化薪火相传的过程。在美国乃至全世界，人们对所谓的"民俗"存在着诸多误解和成见。不是只有生活在农村地区的贫穷的、少数族群的或者未受过教育的人才能拥有民俗——我们都会把自身传统的文化表述传给下一代人。这种知识往往成为我们自身的一部分，以至于我们甚至没有意识到它是一种文化表述——我们只当它是生活。在今天的国际对话和谈判中，"民俗"一词已被两个新词所代替——"非物质文化遗产"和"传统文化表述"。世界各地的人们也都认识到了这种材料的巨大价值。

文化与民族

进入21世纪，我们经常能在国际会议中看到文化商品大放异彩。文化往往被视为地球上某个特定地区的财产和遗产。但事实上，文化是由个体的人创造和传播的，而人是流动的，并不是植根在某一个位置的。美国公民的祖先可以说来自世界各地，只有那些美国土著部落的文化表述才能被视为是完全意义上的"本土"文化表述。而对于所谓的"美国文化"的其他组成部分来说，它的独特性正是源于世界文化的融合和/或共存。我认为，这种多样性对于维护21世纪可持续发展的文化社群至关重要，这不仅仅限于美国范围内，也同样适用于整个世界。我们致力于在全世界范围内保护和支持全球所有非物质文化遗产，同时我们必须承认并尊重由于人口流动和不可避免的文化元素共享所形成的整体文化表述。

有一个事实是无法否定的：即文化是瞬息万变的，它的演化过程与人们对传统的学习、保护和向下一代的传承活动是相伴相随的。

美国文化

世人眼中真正的传统美国文化实际上是世界文化的混合体。有时，这些文化元素在与外来文化接触后相融，进而调和形成新的文化表述；有时候，文化元素被原样地接受和信奉，如从中国、希腊或埃塞俄比亚输入美洲新大陆的传统。在北美新世界文化中随处可见欧洲、非洲、拉丁美洲以及其他各地的传统文化表述。

例如，让我们看一下美国标志性的传统音乐——兰草音乐。这种独特的音乐流派产生于文化融合，进而形成一种新的文化表述。所有兰草音乐乐队都包括吉他、班卓琴、小提琴和曼陀铃。班卓琴来自非洲，小提琴和吉他来自欧洲，而曼陀铃则源自中东的乌得琴。当几种乐器同时演奏，并配以明快的节奏以及和谐的音乐时，你就会欣赏到兰草音乐。如果没有移民输入的音乐传统，就不会有美国的兰草音乐。

佛罗里达

作为民俗学家，我的职业生涯开始于美国最南部的佛罗里达州。我成为该州第一位"州级民俗学家"，我的工作是对佛罗里达州的民间艺术和文化进行实地调查。1975年发生了很多事，我也在这一年有了很多重大发现——我开着我的1969年产福特皮卡跋涉5000多英里（约8000多公里），走遍了佛罗里达州的每一个角落。众所周知，佛罗里达州以其宜人的气候和美丽的海滩吸引了大批退休人员。我的一个发现就是，退休后的美国人似乎还是愿意与和自己相近的人待在一起。我在此次旅行中造访了塔彭斯普林斯。这里居住着超过12000名希腊裔美国人，他们中的许多人都是希腊海绵渔民的后裔。这些海绵渔民于19世纪80年代来到塔彭斯普林斯，靠从墨西哥湾捞取天然海绵为生。此外，还有许多是从纽约、芝加哥、波士顿以及其他大城市退休的希腊裔美国人。今天，如果你来到塔彭斯普林斯，肯定会感到已经离开了美国，身处多德卡尼斯群岛。城镇广场上随处可见希腊东正教教堂，美国区的大主教也居住在这个小镇上。这里有希腊饭店，还有只招待男性的咖啡屋，里面煮着希腊诸岛传统的浓香咖啡。在这儿，人们读希腊报纸，街道上飘荡着 tsasbouna 和 bouzouki 音乐。建筑全都采用白灰泥。希腊国旗到处飘扬。塔彭斯普林斯也因其独特的希腊遗风成为著名的旅游景点。

与此类似，贝尔维尔的居民全是来自美国各大城市的波兰裔退休人员。他们认同并继续维持其东欧传统（包括针线活、饮食习惯和复活节仪式传统）。贝尔维尔的波兰人甚至从华沙请来一位东正教神父，用其本土语言向大众传教。沿着贝尔维尔德道路走下去，就是马萨里克镇。这个镇以捷克斯洛伐克独立领导人的姓名命名，居住着以养鸡为生的捷克裔美国人。再向南就到了大西洋沿岸的莱克沃思镇，这里居住着25000名芬兰裔美国人。他们仍然保留着一个红色芬兰厅和一个白色芬兰厅。莱克沃思镇的芬兰人仍然演奏和欣赏卡累利阿人的音乐，每个人都有一间桑拿浴室——即便走出门你就能享受到佛罗里达的天然桑拿。佛罗里达州北部的捷克逊维尔市是一个大型的黎巴嫩裔美国人社区。这个城市标志性的三明治被称为"骆驼骑士"——皮塔饼加火腿和奶酪。大多数人都知道，迈阿密拥有除古巴外最大和最具活力的古巴社区，社区的中心是"Calle Ocho"。但你可能不知道，距离这里仅一英里（约1.6公里）远的椰树林镇是一个巨大的巴哈马人社区。而在另一个方向的一英里（约1.6公里）外，聚集着大批海地裔美国人，那里被贴切地称为"小海地"。这样的例子不胜枚举，但我想你已经明白了我的意思。美国的生活和文化是丰富多样且永远处于变化中的，这是好事。我们需要了解文化如何在现实世界中发挥作用。它是流动性的、灵活的和可变的。

美国国家艺术基金会的"民俗与传统艺术项目"中有一个项目专为表彰国家遗产的传承者——他们是美国活着的文化瑰宝。这是授予我国民间艺术从业者的最高荣誉，以下杰出人士都曾获此殊荣，他们反映了美国文化的异质性：

莫莉·帕克，美国土著人，她是巴萨马瓜迪族的编筐艺人，居住在缅因州。她的艺术属于美国的本土文化。

其他获此殊荣的人还有：

卡马拉·纳拉雅楠——Bharantanatyan 印第安舞蹈大师。她在印度长大，现定居纽约。

弗拉科·希门尼斯——Tex-Mex 音乐演奏家，来自墨西哥，现定居得克萨斯。

卡林霍斯·奥罗 —— 狂欢节打击乐大师。来自巴西里约热内卢，现定居加州。

还有：

王玉坤和徐正丽（音译）—— 中国撑杆偶（又称"杖头偶"）表演艺术家。生于北京，现居俄勒冈州奥罗拉市。

齐淑芳（音译）—— 京剧名家，现居纽约州伍德黑文。

所有这些传统艺术都来到了美国，并传授给青年一代。这些传统艺术丰富着我们的文化社区，改变着人们对美国文化的观念。

传统文化表述的保护

联合国教科文组织以及世界知识产权组织关心"传统文化表述"以及"非物质文化遗产"的保存与保护，然而，文化的保存和发扬光大无法单纯依靠法律和条约实现。文化只能由那些实践、珍视并认为它极为重要而应传给下一代的人来保护 —— 无论他们身在何处。我们无法通过立法规定延续文化元素，但能够真实记录今天存在的文化表述，并利用新媒体将其音频与视频材料保存到未来。通过记录下这个特定时间与空间的文化，学者和研究者（以及下一代）即可了解民间文化表达的起源和历史。我们也借此研究创造了我们当代文化元素的那些变化。

总之，我们必须应对这样一个事实：文化不会一成不变 —— 功能性是文化保留的主要驱动力。而功能会发生变化，以满足现实世界人们的需求。21世纪的文化表述是在逝去时代的民俗基础上发展而来，但它们同样拥有对于当今世界至关重要的独特元素。

语言的保存

我们知道，语言与文化难解难分，失去语言无异于损失一个生物物种。然而，我们应该更现实地看待为保存世界语言所作的努力。语言肩负着人与人之间传递信息的功能，并从中获得发展。如果没有一定数量的使用者，语言就丧失了其主要功能，进而濒临灭绝。如果一种语言仅拥有少数使用者，它就很难在需要国际交流和即时翻译的世界上拥有一席之地。因此，捕捉那些濒危语言的声音、词汇和语法十分重要。目前，美国土著语言正在以惊人的速度消失，因此，国家人文基金会正在开展一项极为重要的工作，即协助在全国范围记录这些语言。中国正在拥有的语言有100多种，我猜想这种情况在中国同样存在。随着现代技术的发展和人员的流动，许多语言正在丧失其主要功能。因此，我们必须开始记录下这些文化和语言。据我所知，中国正在全力记录和保护非物质文化遗产，我期待更深入地了解这方面的情况。

多元文化的中国

过去三个世纪以来，美国发生了翻天覆地的变化，大批移民来到这里寻求新的商机与社会发展。中国也一样，随着人们不断寻求经济机会，新的文化表述汹涌而至。中国幅员辽阔，拥有56个民族，他们的祖先世代居住在这里。经济发展与现代化交融，使得民族之间的文化共享和社会接触成为必然。新的文化表述将被创造出来，而旧的民俗和语言却可能丧失。但庆幸的是，眼下，中国政府正努力记录这个国家正在实践和讲述的传统文化表述——因为下一刻就有可能发生不可逆转的变化。

今天，看到大批民俗学家和人类学家正在中国各地努力开展研究和学习工作，作出重要贡献，我深感欣慰。只有举国上下齐心协力，传统文化才能得以保护。

总之，无论是美国人还是中国人，都拥有各自的宝贵文化。每当有长者逝去，我们就失去了一部分历史。中美两国都拥有丰富的民族传统和文化宝藏，也都在不断适应全球化和网络贸易发展以及人员流动日益活跃的现实。有鉴于此，我们今天相聚在这里讨论和规划如何记录并传承我们两国文化之事，实在是再合适不过了。

Margaret Bulger

Director Emerita of the American Folklife Center at the Library of Congress

Culture and People: Transmitting, Translating and Transforming Intangible Cultural Heritage

Abstract: Culture is often seen as being the property and heritage of a particular place on the Earth. But, the fact is, culture is created and carried within individual people and people are mobile, not rooted in one place. In the United States, our citizens have ancestors and forebears from literally every corner of the World. The only American cultural expressions that can be considered "indigenous" are those of the many Native American tribes. As for the rest of what is known as "American culture", the fusion and/or co-existence of world cultures is what makes it unique. I believe that this heterogeneity is essential to sustainable cultural communities in the 21st century, not only in the United States, but throughout the world. Our international attempts to safeguard and support the world's intangible cultural heritage must recognize and respect the full spectrum of cultural expression that results from human mobility and the inevitable sharing of cultural elements. One fact cannot be denied -- culture is ever-changing and will evolve within the people who are learning, cherishing and passing on traditions to new generations. Drawing on my 40-plus years of experience as a public folklorist in the United States, I will suggest a strategy for the safeguarding of traditional cultural expressions while embracing the cultural changes that will occur in a world that is mobile and global, relies on new technologies, and is concerned with intellectual property rights.

Each of the speakers here from the United States is an expert on culture and a noted humanities scholar. Yet, each speaker comes from a different discipline with a unique perspective. I am a folklorist, so my remarks reflect my training and career in that field. That perspective overlaps, but is distinct from, the perspectives of history, anthropology, sociology, literature, ethnic studies, and art history.

What is Folklore

I want to make clear why folkloristics is so vital to the mix of disciplines that comprise the humanities. The most common question that I am asked is "What is folklore?" Simply put, folklore is all of the knowledge that is passed down by word of mouth, custom and practice. As my esteemed Chinese folklorist colleagues know, folklore and folklife would encompass material culture such as folk arts, crafts, and vernacular architecture. It would also include oral traditions such as oral history, epics, legends, myths, jokes, proverbs, folk poetry and personal narratives. It would also include traditional occupational skills such as net-making, farming, fishing, and blacksmithing from rural areas, and contemporary urban occupations such as cab-driving, policing, running a restaurant – in fact, any occupation or career will have a body of folk knowledge that is associated with it and is passed on by older practitioners to young recruits.

In short, about 90% of what we know and pass on is folklore. This is the knowledge that we deem to be important enough to teach to our children and grandchildren ourselves – we don't leave this pedagogy to schools and professors. The one element that is essential to the transmission of folklore is intimate and sustained communication between individuals. I have been asked to speak on "Culture and People", and this is fitting because folklore is not a "thing", it is a process, the process of people transmitting their culture to the next generation. There are many misconceptions and stereotypes in the United States and around the world concerning the so-called "folk". One does not have to be poor, rural, ethnic or uneducated to possess folklore – we all pass on our traditional cultural expressions to the younger generations. Most often, this knowledge is so ingrained that we don't even recognize it as an expression of culture – it's just life. In today's international discussions and negotiations, the term "folklore" has been replaced by two new phrases – "intangible cultural heritage" and "traditional cultural expressions" and a new awareness of the immense value of this body of material has taken hold throughout the world.

Culture and People

In the 21st century, we have seen the commodification of culture taking a major role in international meetings. Culture is often seen as being the property and heritage of a particular place on the Earth. But, the fact is, culture is created and carried within individual people and people are mobile, not rooted in one place. In the United States, our citizens have ancestors and forebears from literally every corner of the World. The only American cultural expressions that can be considered "indigenous" are those of the many Native American tribes. As for the rest of what is known as "American culture", the fusion and/or co-existence of world cultures is what makes it unique. I believe that this heterogeneity is essential to sustainable cultural communities in the 21st century, not only in the United States, but throughout the world. Our international attempts to safeguard and support the world's intangible cultural heritage must recognize and respect the full spectrum of cultural expression that results from human mobility and the inevitable sharing of cultural elements. One fact cannot be denied -- culture is ever-changing and will evolve within the people who are learning, cherishing and passing on traditions to new generations.

American Culture

What the world considers to be authentic and traditional American culture is actually an amalgam of world cultures. At times, these cultural elements have fused and adapted upon contact to create new cultural expressions, and at other times, cultural elements are accepted and embraced just as they are, remaining (for instance) as imported Chinese, Greek, or Ethiopian traditions in the New World. The New World culture of North America is firmly grounded in the traditional cultural expressions of Europe, Africa, Asia, Latin America and every other point on the Globe.

As an example, let's look at an iconic American musical tradition – Bluegrass. This unique musical genre arose from a cultural fusion and has resulted in a new cultural expression. All bluegrass bands must have these musical instruments – guitar, banjo, fiddle, and mandolin. The banjo is from Africa, the fiddle and guitar are from Europe, the mandolin is descended from the ouds of the Middle East. When you put them together with a hard-driving rhythm and close harmony, you have Bluegrass. Without the imported musical traditions of immigrants, there would be no American Bluegrass.

Florida

When I first began my career as a folklorist, I came to the state of Florida in the deep South of the United States. I was the first "State Folklorist" and my job was to conduct a field survey of the folk arts and culture of Florida. I was amazed at what I found in that eventful year of 1975 – traveling to every corner of the state in my 1969 Ford pick-up truck. I logged over 5000 miles in that journey of discovery. Most people know that Florida is a destination for new retirees, who are attracted to the warm climate and beaches. However, when Americans retire, it appears that they still seek the company of their peers. In my travels I visited Tarpon Springs, which is home to over 12,000 Greek-Americans, many are the grandchildren and great-grandchildren of Greek sponge-fishermen who came to Tarpon Springs to harvest natural sponges in the Gulf of Mexico in the 1880s. They have been joined by Greek-Americans who have retired from jobs in New York, Chicago, Boston and other large cities. If you visit Tarpon Springs today, you would swear that you just left the United States and you are in the Dodecanese Islands. The Greek Orthodox Church dominates the town square and the Archbishop for the USA is based in this tiny town. There are Greek restaurants, men-only coffee houses brewing the muddy thick coffee of the Greek isles, people are reading Greek newspapers, tsasbouna and bouzouki music spills into the streets, the architecture is white-washed plaster, Greek flags are flying everywhere. Tarpon Springs is a tourist attraction due to the unique Greek heritage that has shaped this town of Americans.

Similarly, the town of Belleville has been settled entirely by Polish retirees from every major American city who identify with and continue to practice their Eastern European traditions (including needlework, foodways, and ritual Easter traditions) The Poles of Belleville even have brought a Catholic priest over from Warsaw to say the masses in their native tongue. Just down the road from Belleville, Mazaryktown is named for the founder of Czechoslovakian independence and is populated by Czech-American chicken farmers. Further South, on the Atlantic coast, Lake Worth is home to 25,000 Finnish-Americans who still maintain a Red Finn Hall and a White Finn Hall. The Finns of Lake Worth still play and enjoy Karelian music and everyone has a sauna – even though you can walk outside and Florida provides a natural sauna. In North Florida, Jacksonville has a large community of Lebanese-Americans and the signature sandwich for the whole city is known as the "Camel Rider" – ham & cheese on pita bread. Most people know that Miami has the largest and most vibrant Cuban community outside of Cuba, centered around "Calle Ocho", but you may not know that just a mile away, in Coconut Grove, you have a huge Bahamian community, and one mile in the other direction, the city is home to so many Haitian-Americans that the neighborhood is now known as "Little Haiti". I could go on and on with this, but you get the point. American life and culture is heterogenous and ever-evolving. This is a good thing. We need to recognize how culture functions in the real world, and it is fluid, flexible and adaptable.

The Folk and Traditional Arts Program of the National Endowment for the Arts in the United States has a program to honor and celebrate the National Heritage Fellows – they are the United States' Living Cultural Treasures. This is the highest honor given to practitioners of folk art in our nation and the recipients reflect our cultural heterogeneity. Included in these exhalted ranks are:

Molly Neptune Parker who is Native to America, she is a Passamaquoddy basketmaker living in Maine. Her art is indigenous to the United States, but other fellows are . . .

Kamala Narayanan – a master of Bharantanatyan Indian Dance who makes her home now in New York, but was raised in India.

Flaco Jimenez – Tex-Mex conjunto virtuoso, originally from Mexico and now in Texas.

Carlinhos Pandeiro de Ouro – Carnival Percussion master from Rio de Janeiro, Brazil who makes California his home.

And also . . .

Yuquin Wang & Zhengli Xu – Chinese rod puppeteers, born in Beijing and now living in Aurora, Oregon, and

Qi Shu Fang – Star of Beijing Opera and a resident of Woodhaven, NY. All of these traditional arts have come to the United States, they are being taught to younger generations, and they are enriching our cultural communities and changing the notion of what is American culture.

Safeguarding Traditional Cultural Expressions

UNESCO and the World Intellectual Property Organization are concerned with preserving and safeguarding "traditional cultural expressions" and "intangible cultural heritage", however, ensuring the preservation and proliferation of culture cannot be accomplished through laws and treaties alone. Culture can only be safeguarded by the people who practice it, cherish it, and deem it essential enough to pass on to the next generation – no matter where they reside. One cannot legislate that cultural elements must be continued, however, we CAN ensure the documentation of the expressions of culture as they exist today, and provide for the preservation of that resulting audio and visual material into the future, as new media is developed. By documenting culture as it exists at this particular time and place, we provide scholars and researchers (as well as future generations) with an understanding of the provenance and history of folk cultural expressions and we allow a way to study the changes that have created our contemporary cultural elements.

In sum, we must come to grips with the fact that culture will not remain the same over time – functionality is the primary driver of cultural retention, and function evolves to meet the needs of people in the real world. The cultural expressions of the 21st century are based upon the folklore of past generations, but they have unique features that are relevant and essential for the world as it exists today.

Language Preservation

We know that language and culture are inextricably entwined and the loss of a language is akin to the loss of a biological species. However, we need to be realistic about our efforts to preserve the languages of the world. Languages develop with a function -- to communicate information from one person to another. Without a critical number of speakers, languages lose their primary function and they are in danger of being silenced forever. If a language is limited to a few speakers, it is extremely difficult to create a place for that tongue in a world that requires international communication and demands instantaneous translation. It is essential to capture the sounds, vocabulary and grammar of our endangered languages. In the United States, the National Endowment for the Humanities is doing a critically important job of supporting documentation efforts across the nation, since we are losing Native American languages at an alarming rate. I would surmise that the same situation exists here in China, where the number of languages spoken are over 100, and with modern technology and personal mobility, many of these languages are losing their primary function. The time to document culture and language is now. I know that China is doing much to document and safeguard intangible cultural heritage and I look forward to learning more about these efforts.

Multi-cultural China

Just as the United States has gone through enormous change in the past three centuries, with huge numbers of immigrants arriving for new economic and social opportunities, China is experiencing an enormous influx of new cultural expressions as people arrive seeking economic opportunity. And the vast land area that is the People's Republic of China is home to over 56 ethnic minorities who have centuries of ancestry here. Economic growth and modernity will combine to make inter-ethnic cultural sharing and social contact inevitable. New cultural expressions will be created, while some of the older folklore and language may be lost. It is fortunate that at this point in China's history there are important efforts to document the nation's traditional cultural expressions as they are practiced and spoken today – for tomorrow may bring irreversible change.

I am pleased to recognize the important work by folklorists and anthropologists who are researching and studying throughout China today. Only with this sort of concerted national effort will there be preservation of traditional cultural heritage.

In short, culture lives in the many individuals who reside both in the United States and the Peoples' Republic of China. With the passing of each elder, we lose a part of our history. It is fitting that we are all here today to discuss and plan for the documentation and support of culture in two nations that are replete with ethnic traditions and treasures and that are adapting to the realities of globalization, internet commerce and expanded human mobility.

超越黑白两分

黄平
中国社会科学院美国研究
所所长

内容提要： 我们都把自己视为当然的启蒙之传人和弟子。而且，"启蒙"今天对于非西方世界的意义甚至大于对于西方的意义，这个原因，在很大程度上，是因为走向现代性的过程或"进步历程"在西方如果还没有完成的话，在非西方就更是远远没有完成。非西方世界走向现代性的历程也常常被看作是"西化"的过程。这是因为，相信进步的人们以为，所有的国家，或迟或早，都要发展成为所谓现代的、民主的、自由的或开放的社会。问题的关键，不在于一个社会究竟是现代的还是传统的，民主的还是威权的，自由的还是封闭的，而在于面对现代性问题的二元对立思维：未来与过去，现代与传统，西方与非西方，民主与专制，落后与进步，文明与野蛮等。这样的二元的、非此即彼的思维模式阻碍了我们去认识在黑白两极之间无数的可能性，使我们更看不到在这两极之外的无限可能性。超越此种二元对立的思维套路，可以追溯到中国古代的哲学，尤其是《易经》所包含的思想，其关键是阴阳之间的完美结合，其中，阴与阳构成了彼此存在的必要条件，所以，问题就不在究竟是要在黑白之间二选一，而在于找到中庸之道，并因此寻求和谐的多种可能。

谢谢文化部和美国人文基金会的邀请，就我所知，这已经是第三届中美的文化论坛了。中美之间现在论坛很多，安全、外交、经济、环境、能源、气候等，好几十个对话，可以说，论坛不是太少而是太多了，可是，这个文化论坛我自己是非常非常喜欢的。我也参加中欧的和中国与周边的（比如日本和印度的）文化对话。其中我今天这个题目，第一次讲是15年前在日本东京的时候，题目叫作"超越边界"。现在这个题目实际上是就在一年以前我们在这隔壁做了一整年的中德之间的"启蒙的对话"，而这个对话也是很高层次和很有文化品位的，也是由文化部亲自来引领。我对"启蒙对话"

的最大疑问是：如果启蒙当初本来是为了解放（Enlightening）我们的思想，那么，它所提供的思想武器、思维方式，有没有反而又束缚了我们的思想？

在这样一个文化对话的时代，我感到这个问题好像比十五年前与日本同行对话的时候更加突出了！所谓"中西对话"，我们已经有一个西方和东方、过去和现在的预设，这就是启蒙运动给我们带来的二元论的、二分的、非此即彼的"选择"：先进还是落后、文明还是野蛮、东方还是西方、发达还是不发达等。

这个预设，恰恰是启蒙带给我们的。

所以，我今天这个话题虽然在中美文化论坛是第一次讲，但实际上这二十多年来，我在英学习、在美教书，现在在与美国沟通中，一直在我头脑里的问题，也是我越来越感觉到需要我们人文学者——包括艺术家、思想家、建筑学家、文化学者、历史学家，大家来沟通、讨论这样的思想问题、文化问题，这比我们直接讨论汇率、进出口的不平衡之类，也许更有意义。至少，我们可以不可以先把那些属于正常的经贸摩擦放在一边，而来讨论一下多年来一直困绕着我的这个问题：不是哪个野蛮、哪个落后、哪个还有待启蒙，而是这个背后的思维路径，这样一个启蒙以来给我们自以为理所当然的二元论，把西方与非西方简单地用文明与野蛮、黑与白、善与恶来区分，应该不应该超越？有没有可能超越？怎样超越？

刚才刘梦溪先生专门讲到《易经》，我觉得其实中国古代的哲学——其中《易经》是最典型的，当然也不只是《易经》——很深刻地揭示了古希腊叫作辩证法的道理。前苏格拉底的哲学跟中国古代的哲学是很相通的，古代印度也一样，那个时候我们处理世界的问题的时候，并不是这样一种截然两分，而其中最有代表性的就是《易经》，它里面最基本的概念就是阴和阳，而不是善与恶，不是非此即彼，要么阴要么阳，相反，每一块，或者叫每一极，正好是另一块另一极的前提，而不是这两个之中必须也只能选一个。如果没有阴就没有阳，没有阳就没有阴，所以，问题就不是哪一个是好的，哪一个是坏的。而正因为阴和阳的同时存在，构成了彼此得以存在的条件。两个都存在就是我们说的和，其实这个和包括和平、和善、和谐，也包括合作、妥协、共存，我们讲的和平共存、和平共处、和而不同，其实这个理念背后最重要的东西，我认为有两个，第一个就是：在两极之间，中间还有很多可能性。

我刚刚从科罗拉多的阿斯彭回来，在那里参加了一个中美欧论坛。我在那儿拍了一张黑白的桦树林照片，我想学亚当斯，他是拍黑白照片最有名的，七十多年前他那幅最有名的桦树林也是在那儿拍的。其实黑白照片的真正的艺术价值不在于要把黑和白分开，而恰恰是黑白和中间的无限的灰色，这样来构成一个意境，就是看能不能在黑白之间利用无限的灰色构成一个艺术品。

我说这个的意思是，超越黑白第一个最重要的就是能不能发现在两极之间还有无限的可能性。我们以前讲的中庸之道，优点类似西方艺术中讲的黄金分割线。这个既是艺术，其实也是政治，就是能否找到那个最佳的结合点，而不是在两极之间非此即彼来回折腾。我们要在这个黑白两极之间看到无限的可能，无限的灰色或者中间地带，这是第一个超越。

第二个超越也许更难，那就是：在两极之外，还有更大的空间。比如说，如果说曾经我们假设西方是一极，东方是另一极，至少在东西之外还有大量的社会地带和文化空间，它们是两极之外的。我自己学社会学出身，那个时候最喜欢读的书是老师推荐的一个小册子，叫《社会学的想象》，是一位美国社会学家写的。其实我们今天需要更大的想象，这就是：在现存世界找到两极之间的无限可能性，更在东西之外去找到更新的事情。这个不仅是书生气，或者说不仅是一个文字游戏。

我现在提两个概念，大家看有没有可能是有意义的。

第一是城乡一体化（Rubanization）。过去社会学、人类学的研究，不只是在中国，也包括在印度，甚至是在墨西哥、泰国，在西欧和北美，一说城乡关系，就是先进、落后、发达、不发达，基本上是用两元对立、彼此矛盾的眼光来看待，城市最后要取代农村，因为农村落后。我们今天在提倡城乡一体化，在这个概念之前，比如说英语里我第一次听说有这个概念是在印度，在那里的克拉拉邦。那里就像我们的贵州，地域很偏远，人均收入很低，但是那个地方发展出一种模式，当地人叫rubanization，城乡一体，彼此结合在一块儿，是共存、共生、共荣、共赢。

第二是本土全球化（Glocalization）。我们自己有那么一个地方，就是云南的香格里拉。我和一些同事在那里做过多年的研究，了解当地的社会、经济、文化和历史。刚才刘梦溪先生介绍的费老提倡的"文化自觉"，香格里拉的人是自己在那儿实实在在地做，身体力行文化自觉，虽然并没有什么学术的论述，但是实际做出来了。我们去了解，发现不是随着全球化我们地方的文化就要消失，因此我们只好去保护它们，把它们弄到博物馆来，然后人类唯一结局就是走向那个一维的全球化。在香格里拉，我们可以看到一个活生生的藏族地方文化怎么既是地方的又是最全球化的，比如说传统和我们所说的现代的自然而完美的结合，而不是一个吃掉另外一个。我把这个现象叫作本土全球化。

刚才刘梦溪先生讲的那个文化自觉，费老生前我也听他讲过很多很多次，15年前我在日本讲超越边界的时候也是引用他这个"各美其美，美人之美，美美与共，天下大同"，并把它写到大黑板上，让日本的听众能够看得明白。

按照费老的逻辑，我们应该：首先，尊重自己，为自己的文化和历史而骄傲，看到我们自身文化的那些特色与优势，这在全世界高速现代化过程中有些甚至是容易被遗忘的，因为都在拼命往前走、往前赶；其次，不论我们自己的文化有多么优美多么美好，也应该学会欣赏别人的文化，叫美人之美，而且这个所谓"别人的"也不只是西方的，包括我们说的第三世界，也包括今天常常被污名的阿拉伯世界、伊斯兰世界；最后，在这个基础上，还要美美与共，共享美德、美术、美丽，最后形成这么一个天下大同的世界，包括孔子说的和而不同的境界。

回到最原本的东西，生物多样性和文化多样性，这两个东西应该是我们所有的人得以生存和发展的基础、前提。然后我们在中美之间进行比较，一方面是中国自认为有很悠久的历史，三千年、五千年，甚至更长；另一方面是美国自认为有很优越的文化，"山巅之城"，无比例外。一边是悠久的，一边是优越的。但是有没有这种可能：不论我的历史多么悠久，也不论你的文化多么优越，我们放下各自的架子，以最平常的心来探讨，跨越我们现有的文化的屏障、束缚、边界？

这样又涉及现在中国知识界、文化界、学界也包括媒体争论得很多的问题，怎么样的文化是普世性的问题。我觉得有没有可能与大家分享这么一个类似科学表述的命题，我自己以前说过，后来也在中文刊物上发表了，这个命题就是：任何一种东西，比如说是文化，如果它跨越的时间越长，它覆盖的空间越广，它涉及的个体越多，那么很可能，它所包含的普遍性就越强。

这里，我故意用了一个"很可能"，就是说不要把话说得那么死，特别是中国人自己，因为很容易说我们中国文化很长，时间很漫长，空间也很广大，个体更是多得吓人，那么我们的文化里是不是包含有很强的普遍性呢？难道它仅仅是个个案、是个局部现象、是个另类？但是我说"很可能"，就是自己不要太武断，有没有、有多少普遍性，让别人去说，让后人去说，让历史去说，但是如果一定要说只有西方的文化才有普遍性，似乎不那么能满足科学的一般性原理和常识。

但是，不论普遍性有多强，或者跨越时间有多长，覆盖的空间有多大，涉及的个体有多么多，有没有可能跨越它、超越它？最重要的是，这个东西本身有没有多样性，包括文化的多样性，以及背后生态的多样性？我想与大家分享的第二个命题是：任何东西，越是多样的，就越具有包容性和开放性，因为他自身越多样，他的生存能力就越强，而它的生命力越强，其影响力也很可能——我仍然用了"很可能"，因为这并非是自然的——就越强。

实事求是地说，这个问题是非常难处理的，包括我们最近多年开展的中美战略与经济对话，也时时涉及到这个问题，但是很不容易做到费老讲的那三个境界，各美其美比较容易，美人之美就很难，美美与共就实在太难太难。美人之美不仅需要换位思考，更需要己所不欲勿施于人（而不是己所欲施于人！）的精神，否则各种各样的美就很容易被遮蔽掉。

现在，我们所谓的全球化，实际上是一个跨越国家边界的过程（Transnational），而不只是国家之间（International）的现象，不仅是你有一个东西，我有一个东西，各自边界很清楚，然后我们俩来发生关系。其实这个和国际关系的研究碰到的问题也是类似的，国际关系有一个大的问题就是始终在国家间的关系里面搅，越搅越搅不清楚，但是实际上全球化是这么一个过程，它不断跨越国家之间的界限，也是一个跨越国家边界的过程(Transnational)。

如果我们把全球化不只是看成一个经济的、贸易的过程，而且也是信息、商品，乃至于还有人本身不断跨越各种边界的过程，那么，就不难发现，其实在美国和中国之间，是有一个很大的共同点的。刚才说我们中国认为自己的历史很悠久，美国认为自己的文化很优越，似乎差距很大，谈不到一块儿，但是有一点是共同的，那就是我们都是包含着多样性的大陆型文化、大陆型经济，我们在这方面非常相似：第一是大陆型的，而不是地区型，更不是城市型的；第二是都包含着多样性，文化、经济，都是多种形式并存，而不是单一的。

那么，如果我们这样来探讨跨文化交流的作用和意义，就不只是所谓文化搭台、经济唱戏，也不只是一个边缘化的，可有可无的。其实，它很可能更重要，比如说经济有点像天气，它一会儿好一会儿坏，它是一会儿快一会儿慢，或者说有点像我们的身体，今天精神一点儿，明天又疲劳一点儿。但是，文化的脉络是，有人把它形容为盐溶于水，或者雪融于水，你好像看不见，但是其实每天都在摄入，我们每一个人都生活在文化里。即使偏远山区里的没有受过正规教育的老百姓，他们身上的文化底蕴和文化修养也是非常丰富和深邃的。我们还有很多专家今明两天要讲文化的保护和文化遗产的弘扬，甚至通过法律来保护。但是其实这个文化是每一天在每一个人的身上和心里，甚至是在骨子里和血液里，这样的文化生命力和影响力，我觉得才是我们要真正探讨的。

这样我们生活的意义就出来了，有了这个东西再来讨论文化和文化交流，从文化间对话（Intercultural dialogue）到跨文化共享（Transcultural sharing），我们就不会只是不停地批判、不断地挑毛病，还没完没了地怨天尤人。

Beyond Black and White

Huang Ping

Director of United States Institute of the Chinese Academy of Social Sciences

---

Abstract: We all regard ourselves as the natural inheritor and disciple of the Enlightenment. Enlightenment today means more to the non-Western world, as the modernization process is further from completion in the non-Western world than in the Western world, and the modernization of non-Western world is often regarded as a process of westernization. Adherents of progress think that all countries will develop, soon or later, into the so-called modern, democratic, free or open society. However, what holds the key to these issues is not whether the society is modern or traditional, democratic or dictatorial, free or isolated, but a polarized, dualistic approach to modernization: future vs. past, modern vs. traditional, Western vs. non-Western, democratic vs. dictatorial, backward vs. advanced, and civilized vs. barbarian, etc. Such a dualistic, either-or mentality prevents people from recognizing a wide spectrum of possibilities between black and white, without mentioning the infinite possibilities beyond the two opposite ends. Endeavors to transcend this way of thinking may be found in ancient Chinese philosophy, especially in the Book of Changes, which advocates the perfect combination of Yin and Yang. As Yin and Yang are the preconditions for each other's existence, the question is not to make a choice between black and white, but to take a middle course to seek possibilities of harmony.

I am glad and grateful to be invited by the Ministry of Culture and US National Endowment for the Humanities. This is already the third edition of the China-US Cultural Forum. There are dozens of forums or dialogues between China and US --- far too many perhaps. They address a wide range of issues including security, diplomacy, economy, environment, energy and climate. This cultural forum, however, remains one of my favorites. I have attended a number of cultural dialogues between China and Europe and between China and neighboring countries (such as Japan and India). I have touched this topic in my speech called "Cross the Boundary" in Tokyo 15 years ago, and my speech today is based on our one-year-long work on China-Germany "Enlightenment in Dialogue" Series right beside the venue last year, another high-end and culturally important event also under the leadership of the Ministry of Culture. The biggest question, as I have raised in the dialogue, is whether the ideology and way of thinking brought by the Enlightenment, which was expected to enlighten and to inspire in the first place, turns out to be a straitjacket for us.

In such an era of cultural dialogue, I am bothered even more by this question than 15 years ago when we engaged in a dialogue with our Japanese colleagues. An important presumption for China-West dialogues is the division between the West and the East, the past and the present. That is the dualistic or dichotomic approach of the Enlightenment — advanced or backward, civilized or barbarian, Eastern or Western, developed or underdeveloped, etc.— a presumption brought by the Enlightenment movement itself.

Therefore, although I addressed this topic for the first time in this forum, it has always been on my mind in the past two decades when I studied in Britain, taught in US and communicate now with US scholars, and I feel an even more pressing need for us humanities scholars including artists, ideologists, architects, cultural scholars and historians to communicate for and discuss such ideological and cultural problems, which is perhaps more meaningful than discussion on the foreign exchange rate and imbalance between import and export. At least, we can perhaps put aside normal economic and trade frictions, and discuss the question reoccurring on my mind for years: the question is not to distinguish what is barbarian, civilized or to be enlightened, but whether we should transcend the underlying way of thinking, i.e., the dualism that we have taken for granted ever since the Enlightenment and that draws a clear dividing line between Western and non-Western, civilized and barbarian, black and white, good and evil? And is it possible to do so and how?

Mr. Liu Mengxi just mentioned the Book of Changes. I think ancient Chinese philosophical classics, of which the Book of Changes is only one most representative example, reveal principles which were called dialectics by ancient Greeks. Greek philosophy before Socrates shares much in common with that of ancient China as well as ancient India. The ancients viewed the world in a different way from dichotomy, and they did not divide things into sharply contrasting opposites. The Book of Changes best represents this way of thinking. The basic concepts in the Book of Changes are Yin and Yang, rather than good and evil. Yin and Yang are not complete opposites but preconditions to each other. They are by no means two mutually exclusive options. Without Yin, Yang does not exist at all, and vice versa. Therefore, people do not have to define which one is good or bad. Yin and Yang are conditions for the existence of each other. Together, they make up "harmony", a broad concept implying peace, good will, cohesiveness as well as cooperation, compromise and co-existence. I think one important implication of concepts like peaceful coexistence and harmony without sameness is the vast possibilities between two opposites.

I have just come back from a China-US-Europe forum held in Aspen, Colorado where I took a black-and-white photo of the birch wood. The most prestigious black-and-white photographer Adams created his famous work on birch trees there over 70 years ago. The real artistic value of the black-and-white photo is not the sharp contrast between black and white but the infinite continuum of grey tones which hold a particular artistic appeal and are often ingeniously used to produce a real work of art.

I mean the first and foremost to transcend the black-white dichotomy is whether we can find the infinite possibility between two poles. The Doctrine of Mean we have talked before is similar with the golden section in Western art. It is about art and also politics. We should seek the best combination between the two, rather than make an either-or choice. We should see infinite possibility, infinite area of grey between black and white. This is the first transcendence I am talking about.

The other transcendence may be more difficult, i.e., the much broader space beyond the two poles. For example, we once supposed the west and the east as two poles, but there are broader space of society and culture beyond the two poles. When I was a sociology student, I once read a book recommended by my teacher. It is called Sociological Imagination written by an American sociologist. As a matter of fact, we should give more free rein to our imagination to find the infinite possibility between two poles and new things beyond the Eastern-Western division. That is not bookish; it is not a word play, either.

I would like to propose two concepts for discussion.

The first is rubanization. When dealing with the urban-rural relationship, the sociological and anthropological studies in China, India and even in Mexico, Thailand, Western Europe and North America used to deem urban and rural areas two contradictory opposites and describe them as advanced or backward, and developed or underdeveloped, and backward rural areas were expected to be finally replaced by cities. I knew for the first time the English word of rubanization in Kerala, a remote place in India, somewhat like Guizhou in China. Despite low per capita income, the local people have developed a pattern called rubanization which means rural-urban integration, or more specifically, coexistence, mutual prosperity and mutually beneficial development of rural and urban areas.

The second is called glocalization. Shangri-La in Yunnan province, China is an example. My colleagues and I have conducted research there for years to know about local society, economy, culture and history. Mr. Liu Mengxi introduced the idea of "cultural consciousness" advocated by Mr. Fei Xiaotong. People in Shangri-La have practiced this idea, although they haven't produced any academic writings. We found that local cultures do not vanish along with the globalization, so we had to protect them and preserve them in museums, only leading to the one-dimensional globalization for the whole of mankind. In Shangri-La, we see how the authentic Tibetan culture becomes global while remaining local. For example, the traditional and the modern can perfectly and naturally blend rather than replace each other. I would like to call this glocalization.

I have heard the concept of "cultural consciousness" many times from Mr. Fei Xiaotong when he was alive. In my speech addressed in Japan 15 years ago, I wrote on the blackboard before Japanese audience (in order for them to better understand) Mr. Fei's idea of "cherish one's own value and appreciate others' and realize harmony through sharing".

According to Mr. Fei, we should first of all respect ourselves, be proud of our own culture and history, and know clearly about its distinctiveness and advantages which tend to be easily forgotten in an era of rapid modernization across the globe. Second, no matter how brilliant our own culture is, we should learn to appreciate other cultures not only including Western culture, but also cultures of the third world and those of the Arab world and Islamic world. Finally, on this basis, we should share the beauty of culture, moral values and art and finally realize harmony across the world, including the harmony without sameness advocated by Confucius.

Let's come back to the most essential question regarding the biological and cultural diversity, the foundation and precondition for survival and development of humanity. Take China and US for example. China is proud of its long history that spans 3,000 to 5,000 years or even longer, while US also boasts advanced culture. However, is it possible for us all to cross the cultural barrier, confinement and boundary for an unbiased discussion, no matter how long our history is or how advanced our culture is?

That leads to the cultural universality which has caused numerous disputes in China's intellectual, cultural and academic communities as well as in the media. I want to share with you here something like a scientific preposition, on which I once wrote an article for a Chinese journal. The preposition is: it is of great possibility that great time span and spatial coverage of anything, for example culture, and the high number of individuals involved in it correlate positively with its universality.

I say "great possibility" to leave more room for exceptions. Chinese people always say the Chinese culture has long history and involves vast geographic space and great number of individuals. Does it have great universality? Or does it only refer to particular cases, specific phenomenon or just exceptions? By "great possibility", I try to avoid arbitrary conclusions, and let others, later generations and the history make proper judgment. However, the argument that only the Western culture is universal seems not to abide by general scientific principle and common sense.

Is it possible to transcend it despite its universality, history, coverage and number of individuals involved? More importantly, is it diverse in culture and biology? The other proposal is greater diversity implies better inclusiveness and openness, as it indicates better vitality and perhaps greater influence. By "perhaps", I mean it is not necessarily so in all cases.

In fact, it is a difficult problem to deal with. China-US strategic and economic dialogue in recent years often touched this question, but can hardly achieve what Mr. Fei has envisaged. It is comparatively easy to cherish one's own value, but hard to appreciate others' beauty and ever harder to sharing one's best part with others. To appreciate others' beauty, we should think through the point of view of others, and do not do to others what you don't want to be done to you, otherwise, beauty or value in many other forms may well be ignored.

The so-called globalization is actually a transnational process, rather than a simple international phenomenon, and it is more than interactions between people who own different things within clear boundaries. That is quite similar with the issue of international relations which are harder and harder to deal with as we are confined in relations between countries. In fact, globalization is a transnational process, during which people keep breaking the confinement of boundaries.

If we see globalization as not only an economic and trade process, but also involving information and goods, and human endeavors to cross various boundaries, we will find China and US share a great common ground. There seems a great gap between China and US which take pride in their long history and advanced culture, respectively, but they both have diverse continental, rather than regional or urban, culture and economy which take diverse forms rather than being monotonously the same.

The discussion on the role and value of cross-cultural exchange is neither a cultural activity for economic purposes nor a marginalized event of little relevance. Rather, it is very likely to be more important than it is usually deemed. Economy is somewhat like the uncertain weather, or like our body, energetic today but tired on the other day. But culture is like salt in water or snow in water. You cannot see it but take it every day, as we all live in a certain culture. Even poorly-educated people living in remote areas have rich and profound cultural background and attainment. Many other scholars will share their ideas today and tomorrow on cultural protection and the preservation of cultural properties even through legal means. But what we really need to discuss, I think, is the cultural vitality and influence, as culture is in our mind, daily life, and even in our flesh and blood.

Then we will see clearly the meaning of our life, and stop criticizing and blaming others in the discussion on culture and cultural communication, if we turn from intercultural dialogue to transcultural sharing.

建立档案与美国印第安研究间的桥梁

斯科特·曼宁·史蒂文斯

美国纽伯瑞图书馆"美洲印第安人和原住民研究"达西·麦克尼克尔中心主任

内容提要: 我的论文涉及了几个问题,这几个问题是图书馆及其他致力于收藏美洲印第安人资料的文化机构所长期面临的。其中最主要的一个问题,就是如何建立研究机构(如纽伯瑞图书馆)和它所代表的美国印第安人社区之间的最佳联系。1911年,爱德华·E·亚逸向纽伯瑞图书馆(1841—1927)捐赠了17000多件与美国印第安人历史有关的藏品。由于亚逸的捐赠,该图书馆一跃成为全球领先的一家致力于美国印第安人历史和文化研究的博物馆。

作为一位美国印第安人研究领域的学者,以及美国印第安人研究中心的主任,我曾与各方面的专业选民和民族选民进行过交流。很快,我意识到需要解决图书馆所面临的几个问题。首个问题就是藏品的使用问题。在纽伯瑞,图书馆资源对于公众而言是自由的、开放的,这一点使我们备感自豪。但图书馆本身位于美国的一个主要城市,对于居住在遥远的保留区的许多美国印第安人而言有些遥不可及。通过建立一些创新项目吸收美国原住民学者到纽伯瑞工作,并尽力吸引居住在城市里的美国印第安人,我们可以打造一种使图书馆和美国印第安人双方互惠互利的关系。图书馆有义务使馆藏的文化材料尽量不脱离美国印第安人的生活,而这个人群正是能从馆藏资料受益最多的人群。对于美国境内的美洲原住社群而言,记载着本土历史、文化传统及本土居民母语的资料都是极其重要的资源。纽伯瑞希望通过创建这种档案与美洲原住社群之间的联系,能更好地促进美国原住民和学术界的联系与关系。

大家好,刚才我是在用莫霍克印第安语向大家问好。我的母亲要是知道我今天会在这里说上几句她的母语,她肯定会非常高兴。能获邀参加此次重要的文化盛会,与大家共享我们各自文化中的方方面面,我感到非常荣幸。我的母亲是一位美国土著居民,我的父亲是一位欧洲裔美国人,作为他们的儿子,我从小就意识到文化交流的概念已经成为我生活的一部分。我是在我母亲本族人的故土上,

即今天的纽约州长大的。当时我的父母居住在美国印第安人保留地的附近,我的外祖父母则在保留地居住,因此,在我成长时就体验到了我父母两边的不同文化。现在,我成了一家专门研究美国土著居民文化的中心的主任,这个中心就位于芝加哥的纽伯瑞图书馆。纽伯瑞图书馆是一家独立研究机构——也就是说它由私人资助,与州政府或大学院校无关。

今天我们共聚一堂探讨建立多元文化间的桥梁,我则希望谈谈建立美国与其境内本土民族之间的桥梁——我们可以将这些本土民族统称为美国印第安人或美国土著居民。我在这次文化对话中的工作主要是通过我所工作的档案馆完成的。任何一名档案管理员、图书馆员或研究中心主任,在研究一组关于美国土著居民的资料时,所要解决的一个首要问题就是明确建立这些资料与它所代表的群体之间的联系。这看似是个简单明了的问题,与其他研究文化敏感性资料的图书馆员所面对的问题没有什么不同。但我仍希望重点谈谈几个关键问题,这些问题曾经是而且仍然是研究美国印第安人历史档案(如爱德华·E·亚逸的藏品)时面临的难题与挑战。如果这里有人对纽伯瑞图书馆及其拥有的不同寻常的收藏不太熟悉,那么我在这里简要介绍一下。亚逸(1841—1927)捐赠了超过17000件与早期接触美国印第安人和欧洲人有关的藏品。他是纽伯瑞图书馆第一任董事会的成员，同时也是第一位捐赠者，为纽伯瑞图书馆捐献了一份伟大的藏品。自此，亚逸基金已经为图书馆收集了130000多册图书、超过100万页的手稿、2000多幅地图、500多部图册、11000多张照片和3500幅绘画，涵盖了美国印第安人和西半球土著居民研究的所有主题。

亚逸是一位热衷于美国印第安人艺术品和工艺品的收藏家，今天我们仍可在自然历史博物馆参观他的部分藏品。但是，从文化层面上讲，档案馆和博物馆本身是一种过于武断的场所——在有关美国土著居民历史的探讨中它们常常具有争议性，而从未保持过完全中立的地位。作为一位研究美国印第安人的学界人士，以及一家致力于研究美国印第安人历史的研究中心的主任，我有幸与各领域的专业人士及民族成员进行交流。在纽伯瑞任职的这段相对较短的时期里，我为图书馆确定了两个需要重点关注的领域，以使其能扮演好监护人角色，保护好这份以纽伯瑞藏品为代表的灿烂无比的文化遗产。

第一个问题，恐怕显而易见，就是使用途径的问题。在纽伯瑞，我们自然有理由骄傲地宣称，图书馆对公众是免费开放的。但在当时，左右19世纪末的建筑师们建造这座图书馆的艺术思潮，却无疑显得不合时宜，它所面对的是另一个有着不同抱负和价值观的年代。如果您了解纽伯瑞图书馆，见过它那新浪漫主义风格的正门和它那令人生畏的白色大理石门厅，您就会明白尽管这种格局会营造一种永恒持久和高雅权威的气氛，但对另外一些人来说，似乎这座建筑本身就会让人望而却步。图书馆的入口通往规模庞大的大厅，厅里装饰着南北战争时期将军们的画像，大厅中央矗立着一个警卫岗——这样一个入口很难让人产生宾至如归之感；但恐怕这正是许多研究型图书馆的典型风格。对许多赞助者而言，这种风格可能会让他们联想起自己的大学图书馆，但对于那些有着截然不同背景的人们来说，这种风格似乎很缺乏吸引力。人们会产生一个明确的印象，就是自己不属于这里。要解决这个问题仅仅依靠修饰和改变室内设计是不够的，但我们仍需关注该问题。

访客完成注册后，即会受到工作人员的盛情款待，正是他们在冷冰冰的正门后为来宾营造出了一种温暖、热情的气氛。我认为或许可以制定出某种程序，使人们无须入馆就可参观我们的藏品。在这里，我必须再次声明，我们将竭尽全力履行对印第安群体的使命。书面文字从来不是美国土著文化的朋友：我们发现我们在文字中受到嘲讽，在文字中被所谓的权威所歪曲，并在无数条约中受到愚弄。那么档案馆受到印第安人的质疑和敌视，也并不让人意外。很长一段时期，非土著历史学家们以所有者的身份霸占美国印第安人的资料。至于博物馆，我们被问道："为什么我们的文化遗产保存在你们的档案馆里？"我当然从未这样看待过这些档案，这种观点未免太过简单化，但它却代表了一些土著居民的态度，因而值得我们做出审慎的回应和理解。

作为美国印第安人，我们与美国以及我们共同的历史的关系错综复杂，有时还比较紧张。在曾经被我们称为故土的区域，我们竟然代表的是少数民族——今天我们仅占美国总人口的2%，而且在过去，我们和殖民者的关系往往充斥着斗争和冲突。自共和国成立初期美国最高法院将美国印第安人确定为"国内依附族群"以来，我们始终与大多数人口及其制定的针对我们的政治和文化政策保持着一种自相矛盾的关系。要在美国的大背景下更好地理解美国印第安人的主权，你一定要去看看那段记载了我们共同历史的档案。

普通大众可能认为自己拥有使用研究型图书馆所必需的学术证明，但对于许多希望在档案馆里进行研究的土著居民而言，这种感觉更为强烈。信息技术已经取得了巨大的成功，并以多种不可思议的方法拓展了访问图书馆的途径，但我们仍然有义务对我们可能服务的群体保持文化上的基本认知与敏感性。我的一位亲爱的朋友，已故的塞内卡学者和活动家约翰·莫霍克曾和我探讨过目前信息所受到的重视。我指出，现今的大环境使得"知识"受到了某种程度的贬低，约翰叹息说："你只需要想象一下，智慧已经远行。"当时我意识到了自己的责任，我应当将我们智慧的保管者请进图书馆，向他们展示我们的藏品，并向他们学习怎样充分地利用这些藏品。我希望纽伯瑞图书馆成为这样一个地方，在这儿印第安群体能带着一种轻松舒适的感觉前来聆听一场讲座——由学识渊博的学者主讲，或是由部落长者主讲。纽伯瑞也可以成为一个开展传统的讲故事活动或举办当代文学活动的场所。这有助于图书馆成为一个充满活力的地方，而不是埋葬书本的陵寝。

我要致力解决的另一个问题是，加强图书馆对其所拥有的资料的理解，这些资料大都涉及当代美国印第安人的政治和文化问题。为此，我们同样需要邀请土著居民到档案馆帮助我们确定这些资料的重要性，并使他们深入了解我们拥有的宝贵资源。我们有一部分资料是土著语的，这算是我们的藏品中最迫切需要解决的问题。在516种逼近灭绝的世界濒危语种列表中——这里的濒危是指有可能在我们有生之年濒临灭绝，有170种来自美洲。这是一件亟待解决的大问题。

几十年前我的研究工作正式开始，当时我未能预见到的一个发展领域就是新媒体和数字技术的崛起。这听起来实在有些自相矛盾：新媒体和数字技术这种现代生活的象征，同时也最有可能保护我们的本土语言和传统智慧，这些语言和智慧已濒临灭绝，但却通过数码复制和万维网得以恢复和复兴。几个世纪以来，欧洲和美洲的档案馆里收藏了浩瀚的文化资料，这些资料对于美洲的土著种群具有极其重要的价值。但这些档案馆却苦于无法与这些种群——信息的发源点——分享这些信息。主要问题是：这些档案馆通常坐落在远离部落族群的地方，许多部落成员没有钱长途跋涉到这些档案馆。这即是说，文化资料与其产生源头被分离了。但新技术可以帮助我们将档案馆中宝贵的文化和历史资料带给那些希望研究它们的偏远群体。这一趋势被称为"数码遣返"，已经有几家档案馆开始着手复制这些资料，这当然是个漫长的过程。它们还与美国印第安群体密切合作，以将这些资料归还其原始主人。

爱德华·亚逸主要为其所在群体——芝加哥群体收集藏品。他不相信自己为美国印第安群体所作出的贡献远远超过了他的想象，他所创建的档案有一天竟能为墨西哥和拉丁美洲的土著居民提供资源——尽管他也收集了这些地方的资料。我们芝加哥群体仍然是这笔伟大捐赠的受益者——但亚逸的遗产同时也能使另一个群体受惠——这个群体就是整个美国印第安人群体。当然，芝加哥印第安人群体在任何时候都不可忽视，他们在20世纪的生活在一定程度上塑造了美国印第安人的政治生活：从卡洛斯·蒙特祖玛及其政治刊物 Wassaja 之类的知识分子和活动家的兴起，到1950年随着被我们后来称为"终止与重新安置法"的联邦政策的颁布而成立的美国印第安群体，再到20世纪60年代"红色权力"运动的崛起和呼吁美国政府解决社会、教育和政治不平等问题的要求不断被提出。但是，这些芝加哥美国土著居民的运动只是全国乃至国际范围内的土著权力运动的一部分。

亚逸的遗产使图书馆得以继续在这些具有重要历史意义的领域收集资料——这也保证了美国印第安人的生活不会被一个被美化的过去所掩

饰，而记载了美国印第安人公民权利运动的宝贵资料也将被永久保存在纽伯瑞图书馆。但是，能从纽伯瑞图书馆受益的土著居民远不止于芝加哥群体——印第安群体分布在全国各地超过561个保留区里。我相信，许多美国土著居民学者都有兴趣了解中国是如何保护其少数民族群体文化的。

除了各种传教资料和殖民资料，我们还拥有美国印第安人创建的丰富资料和关于我们自己的资料。过去几十年来，我们看到人们对美国印第安文学的兴趣与日俱增，对藏品表现出的政治行动主义、视觉艺术及其他所有方面都表现出了浓厚的兴趣。纽伯瑞所面临的挑战便是，如何将其影响力扩展至美国印第安人群体中去——并使其成为学界人士和非学界人士的资源宝库。为此，我们将亚逸先生的遗产保存在麦克尼克尔中心供公众参观。此外，人们还可以通过中心主办的面向外地学者和部落成员的各种项目接触这些遗产。我们非常愿意与中国学者分享我们在美国土著居民研究领域的知识和资源，我还希望能在不久的将来亲自在图书馆迎接他们的到来。我最大的愿望是，通过利用新技术和加深对古代土著信仰及语言的理解，使当代美国印第安人转变观点，将纽伯瑞及其他类似的档案馆视为延续其文化遗产、保护其濒危语言的宝贵资源。

Bridging the Divide between the Archive and American Indians

Scott Manning Stevens

Director of D'Arcy McNickle Center for American Indian and Indigenous Studies, Newberry Library

Abstract: My paper addresses several of perennial issues facing libraries and other cultural institutions with collections focused on American Indians. Primary among those issues is how best to build a relationship between a research facility like the Newberry Library and the American Indian community it represents. In 1911, Edward E. Ayer (1841-1927) donated more than 17,000 items relating to American Indian history to the Newberry. Since then, the Ayer endowment has enabled the Library to become one of the leading archives of American Indian history and culture in the world.

As an American Indian scholar and director of a research center for American Indian studies, I interact with a variety of professional and ethnic constituencies. I quickly realized the need to address several issues facing the library. The first issue is access to our collections. At the Newberry we are rightly proud that the library is free and open to the public. But the building is located in a major American city – far from many of the remote reservation communities on which many American Indians live. By creating innovative programs that bring Native American scholars to the Newberry and by reaching out to the urban American Indian population we can create a mutually beneficial relationship for both the library and American Indians. The library has a duty to make sure the cultural materials held in its collections are not alienated from the peoples that would most benefit from them. Materials that record indigenous histories, cultural traditions, and their native languages are vital resources to Native American communities across the United States. By creating relationships between archives and American Indian communities, the Newberry hopes to foster better relations between Native Americans and the academic world.

Hello in the Mohawk Indian language. My mother will be pleased to know that some words of her people's language were spoken here today. I am honored to have been invited to participate in this important cultural gathering that allows us to share aspects of our respective cultures. As the son of a Native American mother and a Euro-American father I feel the notion of cultural exchange has been a part of my life since childhood. I grew up in the traditional homeland of my mother's people in what is now

called New York State. My parents lived near the American Indian reservation on which my grandparents lived and I was exposed to both my parents' different cultures as I grew up. Now I am the director of a center dedicated to the study of Native American cultures that is housed in the Newberry Library in Chicago. This library is an independent research library – meaning that it is privately endowed and not connected to the state or a university.

We are here to discuss the bridging of cultures and I would like to speak about bridging cultures between the United States and the indigenous nations within the United States – those people we have come to refer to collectively as American Indians or Native Americans. My part in this cultural dialogue is done largely through the archive at which I work. One of the primary issues for any archivist, librarian, or research center director to address when working with a collection focused on Native America is to articulate the relationship between the archive and the community it represents. This might seem like a straightforward issue and not unlike that facing other librarians of culturally sensitive materials. But I wish to examine a few key issues that have been, and remain, part of the challenge of working with an archive such as the Edward Ayer Collection in American Indian History. For those not familiar with the Newberry Library and it's remarkable holdings a bit of back-story: in 1911, Edward E. Ayer (1841-1927) donated more than 17,000 pieces on the early contacts between American Indians and Europeans. Ayer, a member of the first Board of Trustees, was the first donor of a great collection to the Newberry Library. Since then, the Ayer endowment fund has enabled the Library to collect in excess of 130,000 volumes, over 1 million manuscript pages, 2,000 maps, 500 atlases, 11,000 photographs and 3,500 drawings and paintings on the subject all on the subject of American Indians and the indigenous peoples of the Western Hemisphere.

Ayer was also an avid collector of American Indian art and artifacts and much of that collection can be visited today at the Field Museum. But the archive and the museum are themselves culturally over-determined sites – often contested and never completely neutral in the debates over Native American history. My position as an American Indian academic and director of a research center for American Indian history allows me to interact with a variety of professional and ethnic constituencies. In my relatively short time at the Newberry I have identified two main areas of concern for our library as a custodian of the extremely rich cultural legacies represented by the Newberry's collection.

The first is, perhaps obviously, access. At the Newberry we are rightly proud that the library is free and open to the public. But the ethos that guided the architects in the late nineteenth century is definitely one that speaks to a different age with different aspirations and values. If you know the Newberry Library, with its solid neo-Romanesque façade and august white marble foyer, you know that while the layout may give an air of permanence and cultivated authority; for others the building itself may seem forbidding. The entry into its oversized hall with portraits of Civil War generals and a guard's station in the center of the room is hardly welcoming; this I fear is typical of many research libraries. For many patrons it may remind them of their college libraries but those folks coming from a very different experience it hardly seems inviting. One can be given the distinct impression that one doesn't belong here. This is a problem that will not be solved with mere cosmetic changes to the interior and it still demands our attention.

Once one has signed in there is, because of our truly exceptional staff a warm and welcoming presence behind the cold façade. I do believe that perhaps certain protocols be developed for assisting people with the content of our collection beyond access. This is where I must do the hard work of continuing my efforts to articulate our mission to the Indian community. The written word has not always been the friend of Native American cultures: we find ourselves caricatured in it, misrepresented by so-called authorities in it, and duped in countless treaties. Not surprisingly the archive may be viewed with suspicion or even hostility. For too long non-Native historians have maintained a proprietary relationship to American Indian materials. As with museums, we are left asking, "Why is OUR culture in your archive?" That is not how I see the archive, that would be a very reductive view, but it is represents the attitude of some Native peoples and it should be responded to with thoughtfulness and understanding.

As American Indians, we have a complex and often difficult relationship with the United States and our shared history. We represent ethnic minorities in the regions that we once called our homelands – today we comprise barely 2% of the general population of the United States and our past relationships with settlers were often marked by conflict. Ever since the early period of the Republic, when the Supreme Court of the United States designated American Indians as comprising "domestic dependent nations," we have had a paradoxical relationship with the majority population and its political and cultural policies towards us. Much of the key to better understanding the nature of American Indian sovereignty, within the context of the United States, lies deep in the archive of our shared history.

The general public may feel that they possess the necessary scholarly credentials to use a research library but that feeling is intensified to many Native people who wish to do research in the archive. While tremendous gains have been made in information technology, thus extending access in ways hitherto unimagined, the onus remains on us to be both culturally literate and culturally sensitive toward the specific communities we may serve. A dear friend of mine, the late Seneca scholar and activist, John Mohawk and I were discussing the emphasis currently put on information. I pointed out that 'knowledge' seemed somewhat denigrated in the current atmosphere, John sighed and said, "Just imagine how wisdom is faring." I see my duty then as one that can bring our wisdom keepers into the library. To show them our holding and learn from them how they may best be used. I want the library to be a space where the Indian community feels comfortable coming to hear a lecture – by either an accomplished scholar or a tribal elder. We can also be a place that hosts traditional story-telling and contemporary literary events. This helps make the library a vital place and not a mausoleum of the book.

The other area I am committed to serving is to better our library's understanding of the materials that we have as they relate to contemporary American Indian political and cultural issues. This likewise means that we have a need to bring the Native people into the archive to help us determine the significance of our materials and on the way make members of the community more aware of our great resources. A number of our materials are in Native languages: this represents perhaps the most urgent aspect of our collection. On the list of world endangered languages, endanger of going extinct in our lifetimes, of the 516 languages worldwide in immediate danger, 170 of them are from the Americas. This is of tremendous concern.

One area of development I had not anticipated when I began my studies, decades ago, was the rise of new media and digital technologies. It seem a great paradox that such a symbol of modernity also represents the best hope for preserving our languages and traditional wisdom that have been on the verge of being lost only to be recovered and revitalized by digital reproduction and the world-wide web. For centuries European and American archives have held a wide range of cultural materials of tremendous importance to indigenous communities in the Americas but these same archives have had limited means of sharing that information with the communities in which they had their origin. The problem often being that archives are typically housed in place remote from tribal nations and many individual members of those communities lack the financial resources necessary to travel to those archives. This meant that cultural materials were essentially alienated from their sources of origin. But new technologies allow our archives to bring precious cultural and historical materials to those distant communities who wish to study them. This trend has been called "digital repatriation" and several archives have begun the long process of copying materials and working closely with American Indian communities so as to help reintegrate this knowledge into their populations of origin.

Edward Ayer collected for his community – Chicago. He did not likely believe that he was serving the American Indian community any more than he imagined that he was creating an archive that might someday act as a resource to the indigenous peoples of Mexico and Latin America – even though he collected these materials as well. We in the Chicago community remain the beneficiaries of that great donation – but Ayer's legacy serves another community – the American Indian community at large. Of course there has always been a Chicago Indian community and their experiences in the twentieth century have helped shaped much of American Indian political life. From such intellectuals and activists like Carlos Montezuma with his political journal Wassaja, to the American Indian community that grew in the 1950 with the introduction of the federal policy we have come to call "termination and relocation", to the late 1960s with the Red Power movement and increased demands that the US government address social, educational, and political inequalities. But these Chicago based Native Americans were part of national and international movements in the field of indigenous rights.

Ayer's bequest made it possible for the library to continue to collect in these historically significant areas – thus guaranteeing that American Indian life was not consigned to a romanticized past and the invaluable records of the American Indian civil rights movement would be preserved in perpetuity at the Newberry Library. But the Newberry is a cultural resource for native peoples well beyond the Chicago community – our communities are spread across the nation in over 561 reservations. I am sure that many scholars of Native America would be interested in how China protects and promotes its ethnic minorities and the preservation of their cultures.

Aside from various missionary and colonial documents we are rich in materials by American Indians as well as about us. We have seen increased attention to American Indian literature in the last decades, as well as political activism, and the visual arts and are all represented in the collection. The challenge for the Newberry is to increase its reach into AmericanIndian communities – and make itself a resource for both scholar and non-scholars alike. To this end Mr. Ayer's legacy can be felt in the establishment of the McNickle Center and its programs with their outreach to scholars and tribal members from any miles away. We would welcome the opportunity to share our knowledge of Native American culture and our resources with Chinese scholars and I hope to welcome them personally in the not too distant future. It is my greatest hope that through a combination of new technologies and a deeper understanding of ancient indigenous beliefs and languages that the contemporary American Indian people will come to view archives, such as the Newberry's, as invaluable resources for their people's continued cultural legacies and linguistic survival.

中国当代艺术：
在全球与本土之间

范迪安

中国美术馆馆长

内容提要： 伴随着中国社会的历史性变革，中国艺术呈现出多元的发展态势，"当代艺术"成为新的社会文化现象。与20世纪以来西方现代艺术发展的文化逻辑不同，中国当代艺术在经济与资本的作用下、在全球化的文化条件下，呈现出新的生态结构，艺术博物馆、艺术市场、艺术空间、艺术传播几个方面的蓬勃发展，构成了艺术从创造到消费的文化格局。这种"后现代"（Post-modern）的中国模式在某种程度上也表现出"后西方"（Post-West）的文化特征。中国当代艺术在全球与本土文化矛盾冲突所构成的张力中面临挑战与机遇。依靠改革时代的中国社会现实所提供的丰富资源，中国当代艺术在"现实主义"与"参与性艺术"（Participatory Art）方面形成了与西方当代艺术中的"美国模式"不同的表现方式；通过对本土艺术传统的转换，中国当代艺术的观念更加凸显了东方文化的内涵。在中美艺术交流中，如何克服以"符号化"的视角观察和评价中国当代艺术，如何在信息时代与全球文化语境中认识中国艺术的当代特征与文化价值，是一个急迫的问题。

我今天很荣幸在这里和大家一起来探讨中国当代艺术这个话题。中国当代艺术，不仅在中国，在国际上也是一个备受关注的热点话题，有时候甚至成为焦点。说到中国艺术，首先要了解的是中国艺术有着不曾间断的历史，通常认为早在五千年前中国的艺术，包括绘画、雕刻和建筑等均已呈现出了具有东方文化特色的端倪。近几十年来，随着考古的新发现，实际上已经把中国艺术起源的时间结点不断往前推溯。更为重要的是，中国艺术历史的不间断性使得它无论是在观念上还是形式上都拥有自己自主的体系，同时也具备了借鉴、消化、融汇其他文化的能力。早在公元前2世纪的两汉时期，中国艺术，尤其是最基本的艺术形式——绘画，已经形成了

稳定的样式,那就是以中国的纸、中国的笔、中国的墨为媒介的绘画样式,同时对绘画自觉地进行理论上的把握,并提出品评标准。人们通常认为,欧洲要到13世纪,也就是文艺复兴萌芽之初才开始具备艺术,更具体地说是绘画的自觉。艺术的自觉实际上是艺术家的自觉。中国在公元3世纪,也就是魏晋南北朝时期的画家就开创了强调"气韵生动",讲究内在精神营造的独特而成熟的绘画境界。

在中国绘画的观念中,艺术家作为人,与天、地之间的关系是一个非常重要的文化结构,人不是去主宰天和地,而是尽可能地使自己融汇于天地之间,因此天人合一作为中国的代表性哲学,或者观念思想,也主导了中国艺术观念的发生。这样一个观念系统有其自主性,同时也造成了它的封闭性。所以几千年来中国艺术总体来说是在一个相对封闭的系统下发展的。但毋庸置疑,这是一个伟大的传统。

我今天主要探讨的是中国艺术在进入20世纪之后所遇到的状况。美国《纽约时报》记者罗伯特·休斯曾著有一本关于西方现代艺术的重量级艺术史著作《The Shock of the New》,讲述20世纪初西方艺术遭遇的"新的震撼"。而对于20世纪的中国艺术来说,它遭遇的可以说是西方的震撼(the shock of the west)也就是西方文化、西方艺术进入中国以后引发的强烈震荡。在20世纪的100年里,中国艺术开始大规模、系统性地向西方学习。20世纪上半叶,主要是向欧洲或者通过日本间接向欧洲学习;在50、60年代特殊的政治语境下,主要是学习继承苏联的系统;到了80年代,中国向世界打开大门之后,依然是向世界各国学习,但主要还是

向西方学习,特别是这一时期,美国现代艺术对中国艺术的影响相当大。但今天我并不想讨论这种影响带来的后果,相反,我想提出的是,处在21世纪第一个10年之后,中国艺术,也包括美国艺术共同面对的是什么呢? 就如同这次论坛的主题,我们面对的其实是全球化的挑战,由此,我们就可以在这个新的起点上找到共同的话题。

　　近年来,国际社会对中国艺术,特别是当代艺术的兴趣与日俱增。中国当代艺术不仅在重要的国际艺术事件中频繁亮相,比如威尼斯双年展、卡塞尔文献展,也在世界各地的重要艺术机构中展出,包括纽约的MoMA、伦敦的泰特现代馆等。但是较长时间以来,无论是西方的评论界、专业领域,还是大众媒体领域,包括报纸、杂志、电视等,对中国当代艺术的理解和阐释均存在两个问题:一是了解不够充分,有时候甚至有点盲目;二是有一种文化上的偏见,这种偏见可能部分源自一种固有的文化中心主义,也可能是长期以有色眼镜过滤他文化的习惯遗传到了对中国艺术的认知当中。这就导致长时间以来,中国当代艺术在西方媒体,甚至专业刊物上总是呈现为一些非常政治符号化的图像,一些以抵抗特定意识形态为姿态的产物。这就简单地甚至是粗暴地把中国当代艺术的整体展开,乃至它的一些重要的内在文化价值弱化、约化为政治的内涵。当然政治与艺术永远是有关联的,艺术也的确是反映政治的。狭义的政治符号化,固然包含部分中国当代艺术家对一段特定的国家历史,乃至自我成长史的真诚反思,也不排除有一部分功利的中国艺术家渴望以容易识别的符号为西方快速消费。但是中国当代艺术作为一个整体的内涵,

要远远大于这种符号化的呈现。因此我们在观察、理解中国当代艺术时，如果仅仅从一个褊狭的角度展开，很容易导致各种误读，尤其是忽视了中国当代艺术的整体展开，是中国社会在改革开放时代，特别是进入21世纪以来的一种整体的文化表征。它的整体力量和复杂性，与中国近年来的综合国力上升，中国社会目前所形成的复杂、多元态势其实是非常默契，相互对应的。正如中国当代社会发展中蕴含着矛盾、困惑，甚至强烈的危机一样，中国当代艺术中所发生的各种现象亦可被视为这种社会现象在艺术上的映射。所以我们面临一个问题，在讨论中国当代艺术的时候，是以一种简单、固化的惯性文化思维，还是以一种更开放、更客观的态度，更多地把中国艺术放到人类文明发展进程的高度下来审视？我想不同的观察方式会得出不同的结果。

在今天短暂的时间里，我只跟大家谈谈中国当代艺术两个方面的情况。第一，是中国当代艺术的整体生态。众所周知，艺术不仅仅是艺术家的创造，而是整体艺术事件的发生，这个事件包括了从艺术生产到社会传播、从艺术评价到艺术消费等一系列复杂的价值生产链条。当然，在过去几十年里，中国艺术的生态结构是不完整的，有时候甚至是缺链的。但是进入21世纪之后，这种状况有了根本性的变化，我指的是整个艺术生态目前已经形成了一个非常具有中国文化特点的结构，我列举三个方面的情况。

首先，近年来中国的美术馆正在飞速发展，我们称为一个"美术馆时代"正在到来。我们知道，美国的博物馆，包括美术馆有较长的发展史，无论是体制还是管理上都相当先进。中国的美术馆建制较晚，但是近年来也有了长足发展，一是政府加大财政投入，在各地兴建了许多新馆；二是政府整体出台了一系列扶持政策，帮助美术馆更好地发挥作用。以我所在的中国美术馆为例，现在每年可以吸引上百万的观众，也多次举办像"美国艺术三百年"等重要大型展览，向公众进行不间断的艺术推广和

教育。美术馆作为一个知识生产、价值传递、体验交流的场所正逐渐成为新的文化活动中心。比如杭州的浙江美术馆、江苏南京的江苏美术馆等，都成为当地新的文化地标。现在，在中国许多城市，一般都有四个建筑构成的一个新的文化中心——图书馆、博物馆、音乐厅、美术馆。这四座建筑所构成的文化中心或综合文化区自然是各级政府为丰富公众的文化生活而设立的公共设施。此外还有一些大学也在经营自己的美术馆。比如北京的中央美术学院美术馆，杭州的中国美术学院美术馆，这些美术馆依托学院的学术资源优势，成为美术馆学术研究的重要阵地，也能主动关注并积极参与到当下正在发生的艺术动态之中。中央美术学院美术馆目前正在展出一个"未来展"，关注的就是年轻艺术家的动态。除了公立美术馆之外，还有许多私立美术馆。例如北京的今日美术馆，它也非常关注新艺术的发展。如今在中国各地有大量的美术馆，我初步统计了一下，在未来3年内，中国将出现包括公立和私立在内的至少80座美术馆，现在在建的还有一大批重要的城市美术馆，包括上海的 MoCA。

　　上个礼拜我到了上海。各位朋友如果到上海将会发现那里有一座新的文化设施——中华艺术宫。上海世博会之后，上海市政府把世博会的中国馆改造成一个美术馆。中华艺术宫有16万平方米的空间，它可能成为全世界最大的美术馆。目前展览已基本就绪，将于10月1日——中国的国庆日之前面向公众开放。值得一提的是上海在考虑世博遗产的利用方面有长远的考虑，同时还注意到其他建筑的潜力。比如上海当年的一个发电厂，在世博会期间成为世博会的未来馆，世博后则改造成了上海的当代艺术博物馆。这个当代艺术博物馆也将于一个月后开放。在我5天前去的时候，它的内部还是这样的，整体还在修建。我作为一个同行，也有些怀疑在30天后，甚至不到30天的时间里，它是不是能够面向公众开放，但我想，这就是中国的速度，它完全能够以"上海双年展"的形式实现。有意思的是这个美术馆不叫MoCA，一般当代馆就叫MoCA。人们给它起了一个全新的名字，POWER STATION OF ART，因为它原本是发电厂（Power Station），但是Power Station这个词似乎不仅仅是为了纪念它原来的功能，它似乎更要透出中国当代艺术的力量。

以上是美术馆，在中国当代艺术结构里还有另一个重要组成部分——艺术区。我们知道，在美国有著名的Soho，也有Chelsea等后起的艺术区。中国发展速度之快、规模之大，也催生了一批非常活跃的艺术区，比如众所周知的北京798艺术区、宋庄等。这些艺术区的一个重要特征是艺术机构、商业画廊、艺术家工作室形成了一种混合的生态，一种原发生态和文化生态之间的对话，这就使得艺术越来越近距离，甚至零距离地走向社会，而且走向消费。这些艺术区为艺术家的创作、传播以及艺术讨论提供了一个非常宽松、自由的氛围。宋庄是北京东部的一个小村子，现在这个村子成为了一个艺术家村落，目前有将近6000位艺术家居住，这个数字几乎是不可想象的，是全世界最大的艺术家村。宋庄同样形成了自己内部的小型艺术生态，包括宋庄美术馆等。全国各地还有其他艺术区，在此不一一介绍。

体现这个生态结构的第三方面是大家最关心的艺术市场。艺术市场是一个很大的话题，我不可能在这里展开介绍。中国艺术市场呈现出三个方面的特点：一个是总体成交量在市场上不断提高。首先是画廊的数目在增加，大家可以看到这是各地画廊的比例，最大的画廊区在北京（画面上蓝色的部分）；其次是上海。艺术品成交量的指标在过去10年内提高得非常快，2000年的时候大概只有12.5亿元人民币，去年已经达到了974.5亿元，可以说是翻了几十倍。在这些过程中，我们可以把中国艺术市场和全球的市场进行比较，很多具体的数据表明中国的市场在急剧地上升。中国艺术品市场中当然又有不同的类别，比如传统艺术、当代艺术，当代艺术里面不同类型的比例也可以作进一步细分。当然在这里我们不讨论这个专题。有很多数据，如果大家有需要的话，我都可以提供。

总而言之，就当代艺术而言，目前也在艺术市场上呈现出越来越火热的趋势，这是毋庸置疑的。这就是我想谈的第一大点，即中国当代艺术已经拥有了自身完整的生态结构。

第二个要讨论的是中国当代艺术的创作观念。我们知道，当代艺术不仅是一个外环境的问题，更本质的是艺术自身的文化问题，也就是艺术观念、艺术语言形式的发展等。这方面有什么新情况呢？长时间以来，中国当代艺术受西方，特别是美国艺术的影响特别大，那么今天的艺术家如何应对这个挑战呢？当然中国当代艺术家都知道，一味地追随显然是没有出路的，他们必须找到一种本土的经验。其实正如黄平先生上午讲的，这种本土经验又是和全球文化有关联的本土经验，所以在本土与全球之间，中国艺术有了自己新的增长点。而中国改革开放的社会现实所产生的丰富性是中国艺术最重要的助力。

在这里我想向大家解释两位艺术家。一位艺术家叫张路江。今年春天他在广州画了一幅大画，是从广州的一座高楼上去观察这个现代都市。他画的就是这一片，叫作《城中村》——因快速的城市化发展而被城市包围的村庄。他面对这片风景，画了35天，我想一个艺术家在构建一个如此庞大的场景时，不是凭借照片去画，而是直面实际现场，这本身就蕴含了一种新的意识，一种整体观察和观照现实的在场意识。这个村后来成了一片废墟，一块新的城市地王。张路江不仅画了这个村的整体，还勾勒了许多细部。他甚至在作画过程中和当地的老百姓生活在一起。另外一位是画家刘小东，他在一些重大的社会事件或者自然事件发生后总是奔赴现场去作画。比如汶川大地震后，他就到了现场写生，看上去是在现场描绘一个客观的现实，实际上他是把对现实的思考，以及一种人文的关怀带到了创作现场。他在各种现场留下了许多作品，同时也留下了艺术家自己参与现实的印证。这是他在画完之后一起祭奠地震中逝去的生命。他还到过太湖，当时太湖有很严重的绿藻污染。后来作品展出的时候引起了许多讨论。这是他最新的作品。今年夏天在新疆的和田，他画了那里的工人。这幅作品现在正在新疆首届当代艺术双年展里展出。艺术家之所以需要这样一个现场，就是艺术家不愿意去重复历史的图像，也不愿意重复别人的图像，而是更多地尊重自己的感受，来反映中国社会的一些现实。这种参与型的艺术，实际上就是我们讲的艺术最本质的批判，这种批判不是否定，而是通过研究、通过体验找到与你心灵相撞击的那些真实。中国当代艺术家的另外一种明显取向，是更多地挖掘自身的文化资源，并对其进行语言的转换。这里有今年获得普里兹克建筑奖的王澍，他的建筑不是去分离城乡的关系，而是更多地把乡村的资源，包括乡土建筑的材料用于新的建筑，因此他获得了这个奖项。他没有做过更大的建筑，他自己甚至不认为自己是名建筑师，而称自己是位工匠。而他要做的事从某种程度来说是批判越来越过分的现代主义，乃至后现代主义建筑。除此之外，还有许多当代艺术家也采取了类似的路径，比如这位艺术家叫展望，他不断以金属翻模中国文人艺术里面富有代表性的太湖石造型，把传统置于当代中国的空间里，形成一种古今的对话。还有，大家可能知道，蔡国强做了很多焰火作品，他的做法也是一种向传统的回归，把山水画的大千意象通过具有中华文明象征性的火药爆破出来。

最后一分钟我要讲的是，中国传统的山水画，也通过这位叫徐东升的艺术家被带到更广阔的公共空间里，使得这种传统资源——完全是中国自身的材料和形式——能够与更广大的公众相遇，使得传统不再是一个封闭的传统，而成为一个开放的传统。他的许多展览都是在大型博物馆和大型公共空间内展出的，由此能构成更广泛的对话。我想，今天的艺术创作就是明天的遗产，我们对当代艺术的讨论实际上就是对未来文化遗产的讨论。

Fan Di'an
Director of National Art Museum of China

Contemporary Chinese Art: Between Globalization and Localization

Abstract: With historical changes happening in the Chinese society, Chinese art began taking on a climate of diversity, with "contemporary art" becoming a new social and cultural phenomenon. Unlike the cultural logic in the development of modern Western art since the beginning of the 20th century, contemporary Chinese art established a new ecological structure under the combined action of economy and capital and in the cultural context of globalization, and the thriving development of art museums, art markets, art space and art diffusion brought about a cultural picture of art from creation to consumption. This "post-modern" Chinese model shows to a certain degree some "post-West" cultural features. Contemporary Chinese art is facing challenges and opportunities amid tension arising from global and local cultural collision. With plentiful resources the Chinese society provides in an era of reform, contemporary Chinese art has established a new form of expression different from the "American model" in Western contemporary art in terms of "realism" and "participatory art"; through transformation in local art tradition, contemporary Chinese art shows more of an Oriental culture. How to overcome a "symbolic" perspective from which contemporary Chinese art is observed and appraised and how to understand contemporary features and cultural values of the contemporary Chinese art in an information age and in the context of global culture is a pressing issue to be addressed in Sino-U.S. art exchanges.

I feel honored today to be here with you talking about contemporary Chinese art. Contemporary Chinese art, not only here in China but also elsewhere in the world, is a hot topic, and sometimes even in the spotlight. The first and foremost thing to know about Chinese art is its uninterrupted history. It is generally accepted that, as early as 5,000 years ago, Chinese art, including painting, sculpture and architecture, already showed some initial features of Oriental culture. With new archaeological discoveries made over the latest several decades, the Chinese art can be dated back to a much earlier period. More important, the continuity of Chinese art in its history brought about its own independent system, whether conceptually or in form, and made it able to learn from, absorb and incorporate with other cultures. As early as the Western and Eastern Han Dynasties of

the 2nd century BC, Chinese art, especially painting – the primary form of it – already established a stable form, that is, painting with Chinese paper, brush and ink as media, and at the same time, looked consciously into the theoretical aspect of painting and established criteria for appreciation and appraisal of painting. It is generally believed that there had been no art, more specifically self-consciousness of painting, in Europe until the 13th century, when the Renaissance initially started. Self-consciousness of art is in fact artists' self-consciousness. In the 3rd century, or during the Wei, Jin, Southern and Northern Dynasties in China, Chinese painters inaugurated the unique style of painting that highlights spirit resonance.

In Chinese painting ideas, the relationship between an artist as a human being with heaven and earth (namely, nature) is a very important cultural structure, in which the artist, rather than dominating heaven and earth, tries to make himself part of haven and earth. Therefore, "Tianren Heyi", or unity between man and nature, as a representative Chinese philosophical notion, also played a dominant role in producing Chinese art ideas. Such a conceptual system, autonomous in itself, also led to its closeness. In thousands of years, therefore, Chinese art on the whole evolved in a relatively closed system. But it is undoubtedly a great tradition.

My focus today is mainly on what has happened to Chinese art since the start of the 20th century. Robert Hughes, New York Times reporter, wrote a heavyweight book on Western modern art, The Stock of the New, which gave an account of "the new shock" that Western art experienced during the early 20th century. To Chinese art in the 20th century, what it encountered could be said to be "the shock of the West", that is, the strong shock arising from Western culture and art after their introduction to China. Throughout the century, Chinese artists learned from the West extensively and systematically. In the first half of the 20th century, they learned mainly from Europe or indirectly from Europe through Japan; in the 1950s and 1960s with the special political context, they learned mainly from traditions of USSR; in the 1980s after the beginning of the reform and opening-up, they continued to learn from countries worldwide, but mainly from the West, and during this period in particular, modern American

art exerted considerable influence on Chinese art. I'm not going to talk about what consequences such influence brought about; instead, I'd like to put forward a question: What Chinese art, in common with American art, will face after the first decade of the 21st century? Just like the theme of this forum, what we are facing is actually the challenge of globalization, and from this new starting point we can find topics in common.

In recent years, the international community has showed a growing interest in Chinese art, especially contemporary art. Contemporary Chinese artworks have not only been displayed frequently in major international art events like Venice Biennale and documenta in Kassel, but also been exhibited in major art galleries worldwide, including Modern Museum of Art in New York and Tate Modern in London. But there have long been two problems about the comprehension and interpretation of contemporary Chinese art, whether in the Western critic and art fields or in mass media like newspapers, magazines and TV. One problem is inadequate, and sometimes even blind, understanding, and the other is cultural prejudice – which probably originated in part from inherent ethnocentrism or inherited from a habit of looking at other cultures with tinted spectacles. That's why contemporary Chinese art has long been presented as a politically symbolic image, a product of an ideologically resisting posture, by Western media and even professional publications. As a result, the whole of contemporary Chinese art has been simply and even rudely interpreted, and even some of its important inherent cultural values have been belittled or simplified as something political. Politics and art are, of course, always associated one way or another, and art indeed mirrors politics. Narrow political symbolism contains, as it is, some Chinese artists' heartfelt reflection of some particular parts of the state history, and even their own past experiences, and it doesn't rule out the possibility that some utilitarian Chinese artists yearn for instant recognition from the West through easily recognized symbols. But contemporary Chinese art as a whole is far more than the presence of such symbolism. Therefore, if we look at and understand contemporary Chinese art merely from a narrow point of view, it is quite likely to cause misinterpretations of various sorts and to neglect the fact that the whole of contemporary Chinese art is a cultural representation of the

Chinese society as a whole since China's beginning of reform and opening up, especially in the new century. The power and complexity of contemporary Chinese art as a whole coincides with the present complex and diverse situation of the Chinese society due to China's growing comprehensive strength in recent years. Just like the contradictions, perplexities and even crises existent in development of the contemporary Chinese society, phenomena of all sorts that occur in contemporary Chinese art may also be seen as a reflection on art of those social phenomena. So we face a problem: In what manner should we look at contemporary Chinese culture, with a simple, habitual way of thinking, or with a more open-minded and more objective attitude and seeing it as part of the process of human civilization development? Different ways of thinking, I think, result to different conclusions.

Below I will talk about two aspects of contemporary Chinese art. The first is about the holistic ecology of contemporary Chinese art. As everyone knows, art is not merely about creation by artists, but concerns a complex value creation chain from art creation to social dissemination, from art appraisal to art consumption and so on. In the past several decades, the ecological structure of Chinese art was not complete, and sometimes faulty. But in the new century, the situation has changed fundamentally, by which I mean that the entire art ecology has formed a structure strongly characteristic of the Chinese culture. Now I give some examples.

China has seen rapid development in art museums in recent years. We call it the advent of "an art museum era". It is understood that American museums, including art museums, are quite advanced whether in regime or in management, due to a long history of development. Though fairly late in establishment, Chinese art museums have developed rapidly in recent years, as the government increased financial investment to build a great many new art museums throughout the country and introduced a series of support policies to help art museums work more efficiently. National Art Museum of China, for example, now attracts millions of visitors each year and has staged large-scale exhibitions such as the "Art in America: 300 Years of Innovation", promoting art to the public. As a place dedicated to knowledge production, value transfer and experience exchange, National Art Museum of China is gradually becoming a new center of cultural activity. For another example, Zhejiang Art Museum in Hangzhou, and Jiangsu Provincial Art Museum in Nanjing, have become new cultural landmarks in the local region. At present, many cities in China have a new cultural center that comprises four buildings – library, museum, concert hall and art museum. These cultural centers or integrated cultural areas are

public facilities that governments at various levels have established to enrich the cultural life of the public. Some universities also have their own art museums, for example, CAFA Art Museum in Beijing, and Art Museum of China Academy of Art in Hangzhou. With academic resources of the school as support, these art museums have become important bases for art research and can actively pay attention to and take part in current art developments. CAFA Art Museum now is staging an exhibition on the theme of "Future", which is about art developments and trends of young artists. In addition to public art museums, there are also many private ones, for example, Today Art Museum in Beijing, which pays close attention to developments of new forms of art. By far, there have been a large number of art museums throughout China. In three years to come, according to my rough estimate, there will be at least 80 public and private art museums in China. There are also a large number of city art museums under construction, including Museum of Contemporary Art Shanghai.

Last week I went to Shanghai, where one will find a new cultural establishment – China Art Museum, transformed from China Pavilion by Shanghai government after the closing of World Expo 2010 in Shanghai. China Art Museum covers an area of 160,000 sq meters, and probably is the largest one of its kind in the world. Preparations for exhibitions have been made and it will be open to the public by October 1, the National Day of China. It is worth mentioning that Shanghai is far-sighted in considering the use of World Expo legacies and has also paid attention to the potential of other buildings; for example, a power station in Shanghai was turned into the Pavilion of Future during World Expo 2010, and after the Expo, it was transformed into a museum of contemporary art, to be opened a month later. When I went there five days ago, the interior was still as it had been during World Expo 2010, and the entire building was still undergoing transformation. As a counterpart, I doubt whether it can be open to the public in 30 days or less. However, that is "China speed", and it can be completely implemented in the form of "Shanghai Biennale". It is interesting that this art museum is not called a MoCA, or Museum of Contemporary Art, by convention. Instead, it has a novel name – Power Station of Art, after what the building used to be – a power station. But the phrase "power station" seems not to be used merely in memory of its previous function, but more to show the power contemporary Chinese art.

Besides art museums, another important part of contemporary Chinese art is Art District. It is known that the United States has the famous art districts of SoHo and Chelsea. Rapid and large-scaled development of China also gave rise to a batch of art districts of great vitality, most notably 798 Art Zone and Songzhuang in Beijing. One important feature of these art districts is that art institutions, commercial galleries and artists' studios form a mixed sort of ecology, a dialogue between primary and cultural ecology which makes art increasingly close to society and consumers. These art districts provide a quite loose and free atmosphere for artists' creation, dissemination of their artworks, and art discussion. Songzhuang is a small village in eastern Beijing, the home to nearly 6,000 artists – a figure making it the world's largest artist community. It has also formed its own small art niches including Songzhuang Art Museum. There are other art districts elsewhere in China, which I will not talk about here.

The third aspect of this ecological structure is what we are most concerned about, the art market. The art market is a big topic, which it is impossible for me to introduce here. The Chinese art market has features in three aspects: firstly, it has seen a growing trade volume. The number of art galleries has been increasing. This diagram shows the numbers of galleries in China, with Beijing ranking first (in blue), followed by Shanghai. The volume of trade in artworks has increased rapidly over the past decade; it stood at only about RMB1.25 billion in 2000, and reached RMB97.45 billion last year. If we compare the Chinese art market with the global market, we can find that a lot of specific data show that the Chinese art market has been growing fast. There are of course different types of art in the Chinese art market, such as traditional art, and contemporary art that can be further divided. Of course we don't talk about this here. If you like, I may provide you with a lot of data in this regard. In a word, as far as contemporary art is concerned, it tends to be increasingly popular in the art market, which is unquestionable. The above is the first major point I wanted to talk about; that is, contemporary Chinese art already has a complete ecological structure of its own.

The second aspect is about creative ideas of contemporary Chinese art. It is understood that contemporary art is not merely about external environments, but more essentially about the cultural aspect of itself, i.e. the development of art ideas and forms of art language. Have there been some new developments in this aspect? As contemporary Chinese art has long been influenced by Western, especially American, art, then how should artists today cope with this challenge? Contemporary Chinese artists certainly know that there's no way out if they blindly follow others; they must find a sort of local experience. Just like what Mr. Huang Ping said this morning, this local experience is such that is associated with global cultures, so Chinese art has its new growth point between local and global cultures. And the richness arising from China's beginning of reform and opening-up provides the most important support to Chinese art.

Here I'd like to introduce two artists to you. One is Zhang Lujiang, who created a massive painting this spring in Guangzhou. This painting is a bird's-eye view of the modern metropolis from a high-rise Guangzhou building, entitled Urban Village, a village in a city as a result of rapid urbanization. It took Zhang 35 days to complete the work, staring at the scene every day. Constructing such a massive painting on the spot, rather than gazing at a photograph, I think, implies a new form of consciousness in itself, consciousness of presence for observing reality. The village in question later fell into ruin and became the most expensive land for housing development in the city. Zhang not only gave a panoramic view of the village but also brought about many details of it, and, in the process of painting, he even lived together with local residents. The other artist is Liu Xiaodong, who creates paintings on site of major social events or natural disasters. After the Wenchuan Earthquake in 2008, for example, he went and painted from life on the scene; it seemed that he portrayed the objective reality on the spot, but actually he brought his thought about reality and his sympathy for victims of the quake to the site of his creation. Liu created a great many works on various scenes, together with them his participation in reality as an artist. This picture shows him in a memorial ceremony for the dead in the quake. He also went to Lake Tai for painting when the lake was in severe green algae pollution, and his relevant works provoked considerable discussion later. This is his latest work, created in this summer in Hotan, Xinjiang, which portrays workers there. This work is on display at the 1st Contemporary Art Biennale of Xinjiang which is ongoing at present. An artist needs such a scene because he/she is unwilling to repeat pictures of history, pictures of others, but pays more respect to his own feeling so as to reflect realities of the Chinese society. Such participatory art is actually what we say the most essential criticism of art, which is not to negate, but to find through research and experience those realities that collide with the heart. Another noticeable tendency of contemporary Chinese artists is tapping more into cultural resources and effecting language transformation of them. This is Wang Shu, the Pritzker Prize winner of this year, whose architectural works highlight the application of more rural resources, including materials used in vernacular architecture, to new buildings, rather than weakening the urban-rural relationship. He has never design bigger buildings, and he doesn't even consider himself an architect, but an artisan. What he does is, in a sense, the criticism of more and more excessive modernist and even post-modernist architecture. Besides Wang, there are also many artists who take a similar path. This artist called Zhan Wang, for instance, keeps using metal to duplicate representative Taihu rock design of Chinese scholarly art, placing tradition in spaces of contemporary China to form an ancient-modern dialogue. Perhaps you know about Cai Guoqiang, who has created a lot of artworks about fireworks, and his practice is also a return to tradition – producing images of landscape painting through blasts of gunpowder, a symbol of the Chinese civilization.

For the last minute, I'd like to mention an artist called Xu Dongsheng, who has brought traditional Chinese landscape painting into broader public spaces so that these traditional resources – material and form utterly produced in China – could be shown to more people, thus making the tradition open to the public. Many of his exhibitions are held in large museums and public spaces to create broader dialogue. Our art creation today, as I see it, is heritage tomorrow, and our discussion about contemporary art is actually about cultural heritage in the future.

文化与教育交流

阿瑟·泰
"美中学术交流委员会"
北京办事处主任

内容提要： 当前，中国和美国在经济上已经建立了前所未有的密切关系。随着经济关系的深入扩展，美国教育机构及美国学生对中国的兴趣也空前高涨。在未来几年，我们可以预测美中之间将会产生更多更为广泛、深入的学术合作，这一切都得益于经济、制度和科技变革，这些变革正在改变教育和文化的全景。

首先，我希望对中方文化部各位东道主的盛情款待和精心安排表示感谢，同时，我还要感谢美国国家人文基金会的利奇主席和各位同事。今天非常荣幸能够代表美国人文学会理事会和美中学术交流委员会发言，我将在全面回顾过去三十多年美中文化与教育交流复兴概况的基础上谈论"文化与人类"这一主题。

美国前国务卿基辛格曾经问过周恩来总理对法国大革命的观点，当时周总理回答说"现在评价还为时过早"。想到这里，我不免对担起回顾过去30年的这份重任感到忐忑不安。虽说如此，本领域的同事和朋友们常常引诱我、逼迫我，要求我提出一个回顾和审视这一时期的架构，并重点关注在寻求推动文化与教育交流——尤其是人文领域的文化与教育交流的同时，我们作为专业人士应该如何调整研究活动，拨正方向。

在此，我想特别重申一下赵部长和利奇主席今天早些时候提出的观点，即美中双边关系是当今世界上最为重要的双边关系。对今天的会议而言，美中双边关系也是今天最为重要的双边教育交流关系。

回想这些年中国各领域发生的变化，可谓日新月异，让人惊叹不已。我们今天欢聚一堂的大厅就是一个很好的例子。20世纪70年代末美中刚刚恢复邦交时,人们简直难以想象能在这里竖立起一座如此具有文化特色的建筑。前不久,我还在另一座大厅欣赏了由中外演员用普契尼的母语意大利语演唱的歌剧《托斯卡》——这充分说明了文化与人文研究正在产生日益深远的影响!

当然,美中交流恢复伊始,国际宏观环境也是迥然不同的。我还记得美中邦交正常化后不久我造访北京时的情景,那时的北京是一个完全不同的世界,因为当时中西方世界观之间存在较大差异,这种感觉显得更加强烈。这就是那段时期文化交流开始增多的时代背景。

我准备了几幅幻灯片来说明两国交流关系的转变。第一幅幻灯片展示了过去30年来中方出国人员和来访中国人员的总数。我们可以看到,总人数的增长是十分惊人的,现在中国每年输出约二十万留学生和交流人员,每年来访中国的国际交流人员将近十五万人。

第二幅幻灯片介绍了来自中国的交流人员及其背景,"背景"是指他们是政府资助的、单位资助的,还是自费的。我们发现一个有趣的现象,自20世纪90年代以来,由政府和单位资助的出国人员总数基本持稳,由

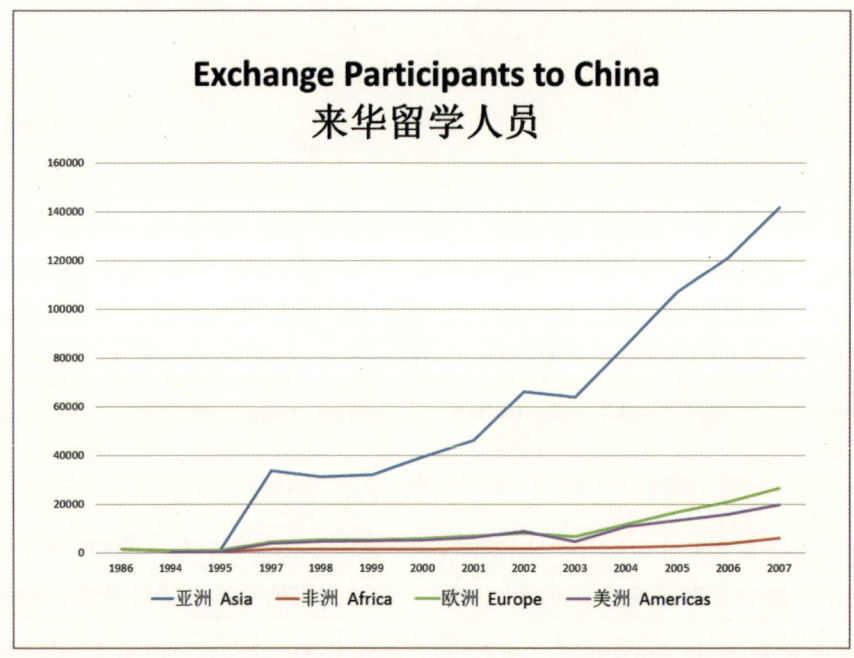

此可知，过去17年来出国交流总人数的增长直接来自自费出国人员的增长。"自费"即自筹经费出国，或者由政府或单位之外的其他机构资助。

第三幅幻灯片显示了在中国的外国留学生的地理分布，如亚洲、非洲、欧洲和美洲。我们注意到一个很有趣的现象，来自亚洲的留学生人数最多。很明显，中国在国际上占据着越来越重要的地位，这一现象正是中国直接影响力的反映。此外，更早时期亚洲留学生人数的增加也反映了这种影响力。

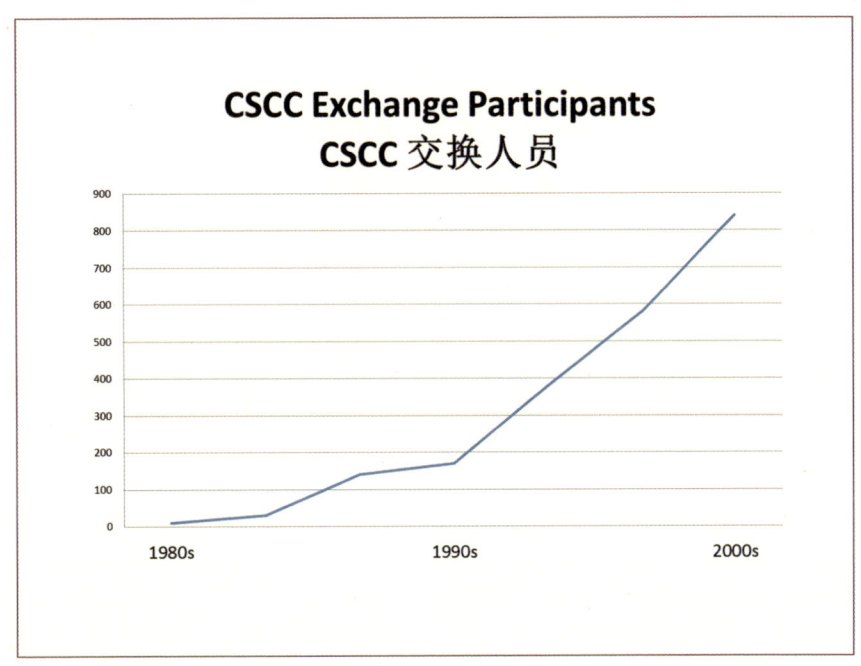

第四幅幻灯片展示了同期 CSCC 派遣的交流人员，从最开始每年不到十人，增长到现在每年的数百人、近千人。这张图与显示过去三十多年交流人数增长的总图所揭示的趋势一致。这段时期 CSCC 总共花费了超过三千万美元，包括由美国国家人文基金会的关键资金，以派遣美国学者造访中国。

观察结论

那么，通过观察这一时期中美文化与教育交流领域的变化，我们可得出哪些结论呢？

1. 数字——涨势惊人，但某些重大事件时期（如1997年亚洲金融危机时）除外。众所周知，资助方和资金的健康运营与交流总人数密切相关，但这些图表甚至能反映出全国层面上也存在这种影响。我们注意到一个有趣的现象，就活动层面而言，危机并不会对美中交流产生切实影响，这可从总交流人数层面和CSCC层面上看出，但对中方交流人数产生了影响，并非常直接地影响到了亚洲的交流。但是，从参与度上看，"非典"和一些其他事件的确对美中交流产生了不利影响。

从这些图表我们可以得出一点结论，尽管美中交流的增长趋势和重要性不容忽视，但其也直接受到财政因素和其他宏观因素的影响。从根本上说，美中交流的发展与中国政府的政策直接相关，并体现了中国在世界上日益增长的重要地位。另一个影响交流人数激增的直接因素不仅体现了当今的现实因素和发展状况，还与20世纪80年代以来复兴美中交流的"复兴"有关。实际上，美中文化与教育交流的历史源远流长，可追溯至19世纪。学者们认为，美中交流的源头可追溯至两国交流早期建立的教会学校、教会大学、教会医院和其他机构。得益于这一历史基础，两国交流迅猛发展，这与没有此类历史基础的国家交流形成了鲜明反差。

的确，正是这种复兴促成了我们的ACLS项目：20世纪90年代派遣交流人员到北京郊区通县的潞河中学。潞河中学的前身是杰斐逊学校，1860年由美国教会兴办。

2. 早期的美中交流主要以双边的、官方的交流为主——政府对政府，只允许指定的机构参与。CSCC可以说是一个很好的例子，当时里根政府与州政府共同合作，宣布设立CSCC北京办事处。有了这一先例，社会科学研究委员会和美国国家科学院及其直属机构也相继主办了交流项目。

从数字上我们可以看出，这种官方机构对官方机构的交流如今在文化与社会交流总数中仅占很小的一部分，绝大部分是自费人员，不管是对美方还是中方而言，均是如此。因此，这种与官方派遣联系最小的个人对机构和机构对机构的交流的重要性，如今已超过了官方交流的重要性，并成为整个文化与教育交流活动的主体。

3. 多边交流、跨领域交流和多利益相关方的交流——这些交流不仅增加了个人对机构以及机构对机构的交流，交流本身也在更深层的结构上发生了变化。现在多边交流项目日益增多，不仅包括传统的双边交流，还延伸至三方交流和/或多学科和领域的研究，以涵盖那些必须从多学科领域角度进行研究的问题。此外，利益相关方的数量也更多：学者、大学、出资方、政府机构、非政府组织以及职业人士。

我们负责的一个项目就涉及三国间的交流，涵盖了社会科学和人文领域的课题，并由跨国机构和国际出资人共同合作，工作时需要使用多国语言。

另一个项目——由卢斯基金会主办的"早期考古学项目"，尽管只有一个出资方，但参与的学者来自多个国家和多个专业，他们需要共同合作，抓住极其有限的机会之窗来鉴定、记录和保护文化遗产。

在这类项目中，官方指定机构的作用不断减少，越来越多的项目开始由多个具有合作关系的机构或由多个合作机构共同主办，团队建设技能的重要性与日俱增。

4. 交流人员也有所变化。早期从中国派遣出去的交流人员和现在一样，大多为汉族。但来华人员方面正在发生变化。早些年，来访人员主要是在中美恢复正常邦交之前出国的、受过美国教育的中国专家。几十年过去了，越来越多来自亚洲各地的华裔学者在美国学术界的地位不断上升，然后，中国大陆的学者纷纷到来。近些年，除纯科学和工程机械领域的人员外，来自人文领域的学者日益增多。

在这一时期，CSCC 也经历了同样的模式变化。首先，来自散居在亚洲各地的华裔交流人员数目开始增长。20 世纪 20 年代，一位主修中国现代艺术的香港人首次来到美国，此后，他又以一个交流项目美方代表的身份来到这里。如今，已有不计其数的中国学者来到 CSCC，成为我们的校友。

华裔学者（尤其是祖籍大陆的）——如今，他们是美国访华人员的主流——的人数增长如此之快，以至于我经常听到负责交流项目的中方人员问我们是否"可以派遣一些真正的美国交流人员过来"。如此看来，我们当中土生土长的真正的美国人是太少了。

这种状况反映出当今美国的三个非常有趣的方面：1) 美国社会的流动性（今天早些时候，利奇主席在开幕致辞时提到过这一观点，巴尔杰博士在她的演讲中也有所论述）；2) 在美国，与中国有关的研究和机会日益增多；3) 语言精通程度的重要性以及哪些人能满足这一需求。

5. 对专业语言的要求——交流双方对语言的要求越来越高。中国已经在全国范围启动了一项艰巨的项目，即使英语成为第二语言，如今英语已经成为小学的必修课。

而在美国，学习语言的动力主要在私有领域，与过去相比，越来越多的人希望发展和提高自己的中文能力。几年前，我们的国家测试机构开始提供高级别的普通话等级测试服务，现在全国各地都有学区增设普通话课程，该课程甚至还成为此类学校的卖点。一些学区甚至完全采用中国学校的授课模式，有的从幼儿园阶段就开始教授中文。

我想重点谈谈两个与语言有关的项目：关键语言教师项目和ACLS翻译项目。这两个项目不仅反映了广泛意义上的增长，还体现了学术深度上的增长。最近，我看到一家精英机构的教材中使用了"charisma（魅力）"一词的术语音译。语言的要求已经上升到了很高的程度，以至于高级软件包也无法满足一些基本的要求，例如理解特定领域的专业术语。

人文领域的展望

1. 双边关系——当今最为重要的双边关系

今天，中国和美国在经济上已经建立了前所未有的密切关系。随着经济关系的深入扩展，美国教育机构及美国学生对中国的兴趣也空前高涨。在未来几年，我们可以预测美中之间将会产生更多更为广泛、深入的学术合作，这一切都得益于经济、制度和科技变革，这些变革正在改变教育和文化的全景。

在现今的美国大学院校，中国项目——尤其是人文领域——正在繁荣发展起来，学生更迫切地希望深入了解中国，到中国求学。

在中美两国，这种势头都愈发明显。1979—1989的短短10年间，到美国求学的中国学生人数甚至超过了1860—1950年间的人数。被美国大学院校录取的中国学生人数达到惊人的近十万人（最新统计），此外，参加美国交流项目和中方办校点的人数同样出现大幅增长，这些都充分展现了学术交往的蓬勃发展。

现在每年约有15000名美国留学生来中国学习，我国政府希望该数目能增长到至少10万人/年。

2. 扩大交流仍需官方双边联系保驾护航

尽管过去30年间的交流增长主要源于自费交流人数的大幅增加，但我们依然需要建立官方双边联系。在美国，像孔子学院这样的机构非常多，而且它们都可以公开注册和自由发展，但在中国境内就没有类似的美方机构。

3. 美中双方都需要认识到中国源远流长的人文历史

中国科举考试对历史的考察主要建立在人文研究的基础上。直到中国封建帝制结束，进入国民时期，这种重心才得以改变。甚至到1928年，世界上最大的出版社也并非在纽约、伦敦、巴黎，或者是柏林，而是在上海。

一位"美国学术团体协会"（ACLS）的前主席曾经说过，"放眼世界，没有哪种文明能像中国文明那样，知识本身能在如此长的时期内发挥如此重要的作用。"这段着重强调人文研究的漫长历史可以被更加有效地推广到大众层面，使之成为人文研究整体发展的一部分。

4. 环顾四周，人文研究需求高涨

最近，我曾经和一位负责解决社会保障制度资金不足——这一问题在大洋两岸同样备受关注——的政府官员有过谈话。很明显，决策权不应只集中在保险精算领域，要解决该问题，还需要考虑一些建立在伦理学和其他人文领域基础上的基本预设。我们不能放弃参与决策的责任，因为单纯依赖数学模式是远远不够的。

5. 长远发展

社会学家南希·卢瑟曾经提出过一个较大的论点："高等教育（当然也包括文化与人文研究——这一句是我自己添加的）是地下蓄水层，而不是水龙头；建立大学不能仅为了满足短期需求，不能像拧开水龙头那样只顾满足当时的知识需求。应将大学看作是社会的地下蓄水层，应当不急不缓地建立，以便维持长远需求。"

参与这些论题的一个最好的方法，就是始终铭记我们的核心价值标准。美国国家科学院的国家研究委员会曾经发表过一份支持长远发展提议的报告，以反驳另一份关注人文研究领域的短期目标的报告。这份报告称："联邦政府对语言和地域研究的资助可能会在未来带来无法估量的效益。"因此，"坚持在那些眼下不存在战略意义的领域教授语言和文化必将在未来显示出其重要价值。"我还希望加上一句，这一立场对于美国和中国都非常重要，我们衷心期待美中文化与教育交流复兴迎来第四个10年。

Cultural and Educational Exchanges

Arthur Tai

Director of the Beijing Office of the US Committee on Scholarly Communication with China

Abstract: Today, China and the US are economically entwined as never before. As business connections have expanded, so has interest in China among American educational institutions and their students. In the years ahead we can foresee an even more extensive and intense academic partnership, thanks to economic, institutional and technological changes that are transforming the landscape of education and culture.

I'd like to begin by thanking our Chinese ministerial hosts for their kind hospitality and gracious arrangements and also Chairman Leach and colleagues at the National Endowment for the Humanities. It is an honor to be speaking today on behalf of the American Council of Learned Societies and the Committee on Scholarly Communication with China on the topic of Culture and People as seen through the renewal of cultural and educational exchanges between the US and China over the past 30 plus years.

I undertake this task of reviewing the immediate past 30 years with a degree of trepidation knowing that when asked his opinion of the French Revolution, Premier Zhou Enlai responded to Secretary Kissinger that "It's too soon to tell." Nonetheless, I am frequently being cajoled and pressed by colleagues and friends in the field to provide a framework for looking at this period with an eye to how we should, as practitioners, adjust our activities and re-focus our vision as we seek to encourage cultural and educational exchanges particularly in the Humanities.

Echoing the statements of the Minister Madam Zhao and our Chairman Leach from earlier today among other observers, the U.S-China bilateral relationship is the single most important bilateral relationship in the world today. Specific to this conference, it is the single most important bilateral educational exchange relationship today.

It is amazing to think about the speed of changes that have taken place with almost anything related to China. The hall in which we are gathered is a case in point. It would have been difficult to imagine a structure so culturally distinctive being erected at this location when the renewal of exchanges was just starting in the late '70s. I was recently in a different hall enjoying Tosca sung in Puccini's native tongue by a company of international and Chinese performers with electronic subtitles translated into Chinese and an English program – how's that for an example of the expanding influence of cultural and humanities studies!

Similarly, when the renewal of exchanges was just getting started the macro-environment was so very different. I recall arriving in Beijing soon after the normalization of relations between our two countries and it was a very different world, accentuated more so by an even greater distance in world views. That was the background of the increases in exchange participants over this period.

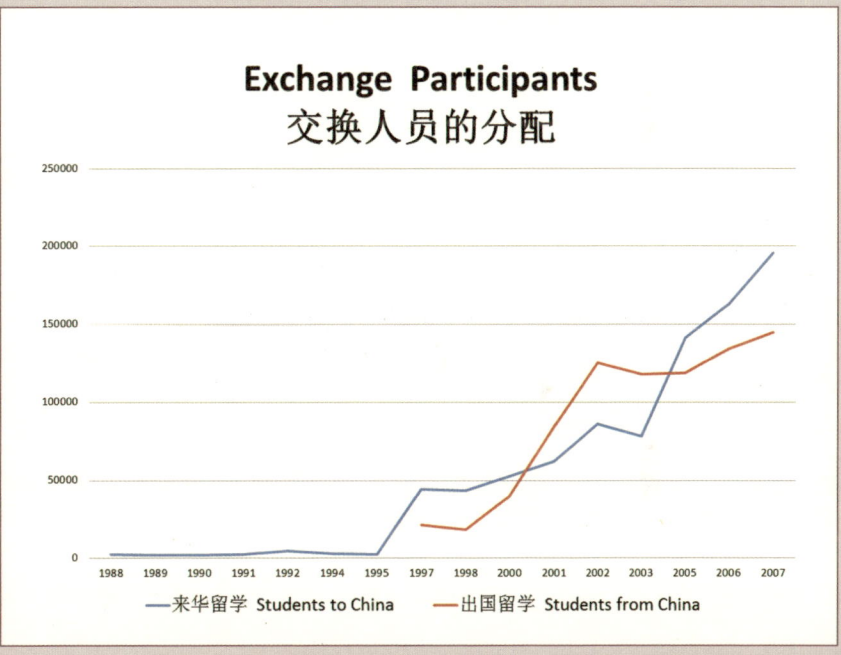

To illustrate the transformation of the exchange relationship, I've prepared a few slides. Slide one shows the total number of participants going out from and coming to China over the thirty year period. As you can see, the increase in total numbers is rather staggering with now nearly 200,000 Chinese students and exchange participants going abroad annually and nearly 150,000 international participants coming to China.

Slide two shows exchange participants from China and their backgrounds, whether government sponsored, danwei sponsored or independently sponsored. It is interesting to note that since the 1990s that the number of government and danwei sponsored participants has remained largely flat, so the increase in overall numbers is directly related to independently sponsored participants, defined as self-sponsored or with support institutionally and/or financially from

other than government or danwei sources, over the course of the past seventeen years.

Slide three shows geographical distribution of exchange students coming to China: Asia, Africa, Europe, and Americas. It is interesting to note that greatest number of inbound participants is from Asia, itself. Clearly, the direct impact of China's increasing importance is mirrored and is reflected earlier in the increase in numbers for the Asian region.

Slide four shows CSCC participants during this same period starting from fewer than 10 to now in the high 100s, at just under 1,000 participants annually. This graph corresponds to the overall graph showing the growth of exchange participants over the thirty years. The CSCC has over its history expended more than $30 million, including critical funding from the NEH throughout this period, bringing American scholars to China.

OBSERVATIONS

What are some observations that can be made about changes in cultural and educational exchanges over this period of time?

1. Numbers – tremendous increase with the exception of some notable events like the 1997 Asian financial crisis. We've always known that the health of funders and funding has a very direct relationship in volume, but these graphs show the impact even at a national level. It is interesting to note that that crisis did not actually affect the level of activity between the US and China as shown in the overall participant level or at the CSCC level, but affected Chinese national figures and very directly Asian exchanges. The SARS epidemic and other events did, however, negatively affect exchange participation levels between the US and China.

One point we can take away from these graphs is that though U.S.-China exchanges are growing and important we are not immune, but directly related to financial and other macro-level factors. More fundamentally, the increase is directly related to governmental policy in China and reflects the growing importance globally of the country. A direct factor influencing the tremendous increase in participant numbers reflects not just current at-the-time factors and developments, but is related to the "re" in the renewal aspect of US-China exchanges from the 1980s. Extending back to the 19th century there has been a long history of cultural and educational exchanges between the US and China. Scholars trace the origins back to the many Christian institutions of schools, universities, hospitals and other institutions that developed in those early days of such exchanges between the two countries. Having that foundation put expansion of exchanges on a fast track as opposed to between societies where there has previously been no such historical foundation.

Indeed renewal is particularly apropos as one of our ACLS programs placed participants at Luhe School in Tong Xian, now a suburb of Beijing, in the 1990s. Luhe was originally American church-sponsored, the Jefferson Academy, when it opened in the 1860s.

2.The early period of exchanges is characterized by bilateral, official exchanges – government to government with participation by designated institutions. The CSCC would be a good example when the Reagan White House working with the State Council announced the opening of the Beijing Office. Under its auspices, the ACLS, Social Science Research Council and National Academy of Sciences with its directly affiliated institutions administered programs.

As we can all see by the numbers, this form of official institution to official institution exchange now makes up only a very small part of the overall numbers of cultural and educational exchanges. Independently sponsored participants now account for the great majority of participants and that is for both directions of exchange. So the importance of individual to institution and institution to institution, most unrelated to any official designation, has outpaced that of official exchanges and now account for the majority of all cultural and educational exchanges.

3.Multi-lateral, multi-disciplinary and multi-stakeholder exchanges – Not only have exchanges transitioned numerically to more individual to institution and direct institution to institution relationships, but they have also changed at a deeper structural level. There are increasingly programs that are multi-lateral, involving more than the traditional two-way exchange, expanding into third jurisdictions and/or going beyond a single discipline or area study to encompass issues that necessarily require a multi-disciplinary perspective. Increasingly there are also more stakeholders: for example scholars, universities, funders, governmental agencies, non-governmental organizations, and career professionals.

One of our administered programs involved exchanges among three countries. There were social science and humanities issues. Cross-border institutions and international funders worked together using multiple languages.

Another program, the Luce Foundation sponsored Early Archaeology Program while solely funded by a single funder involved scholars from several countries and different specialties working together to identify, record and preserve cultural heritage during a very small window of opportunity.

In these types of programs, officially designated institutions are playing a decreasingly exclusive role. More and more programs may be divided and co-administered, with entities collaborative and teaming skills increasingly important.

4. The participants have changed as well. In the early years, participants going abroad from China were as they are today largely ethnic Han Chinese. But a change has taken place on the incoming side! The early years were populated by American educated China specialists from before normalization. As the decades progressed an increasing number of ethnically Chinese scholars from various Asian regional areas started to move up the ranks of the American academy and then came the arrival of their mainland Chinese counterpart. These individuals were in the later years not just from the pure science and engineering areas, but increasingly from the humanities.

At the CSCC, we experience a similar pattern over the period. There was an increase first among ethnically Chinese participants from the diaspora in Asia. One Hong Kong participant first went to the US, specialized in modern Chinese art of the 1920s, and then came here as an American representative of an exchange program. Numerous mainland Chinese examples now are counted among our alumni.

The numbers of ethnically Chinese, especially with mainland roots, who now represent incoming American participants has increased to the point that I have heard more than one Chinese counterpart in the area of administering exchanges wonder if we might "send some real or authentic American participants!" There seems to be a dearth of corn-fed, non-Asian faces among the ranks.

This situation reveals three very interesting aspects of America: 1) mobility in American society (This aspect was described earlier today by both our Chairman in his opening remarks and Dr. Bulger in her presentation), 2) expansion of studies and opportunities related to China in the US, and 3) the increased importance of language proficiency and who are the individuals filling this need.

5. Professional language requirement – In both directions, language requirements are increasing. China has embarked on an ambitious nationwide program of making English the second language with English now being mandatory at the elementary school level.

While in the US initiatives are primarily in the private sector, the greater interest in developing Chinese language capability and capability at a higher level than in the past is evident. A few years ago, our national testing service began to offer advanced placement tests in Mandarin, and now school districts all over the country are adding Mandarin programs, which have become selling points for the schools. Instruction in some school districts is even mirroring their Chinese counterparts and beginning as early as kindergarten.

I'd like to mention two programs related to language: Teachers of Critical Languages Program and ACLS Translation Project. Both of these programs evidence not just the growth in a broad sense, but the growth in depth of the discipline. Use of transliterations for terms like 'charisma', which I noticed was used in a text at an elite institution just recently. Language requirements have moved past what a sophisticated software package can provide for basic requirements like scheduling to the level of specialist understanding in specialized sectors.

Looking Forward in the Humanities

1. Bilateral relationship – the single most important bilateral relationship today

Today, China and the US are economically entwined as never before. As business connections have expanded, so has interest in China among American educational institutions and their students. In the years ahead we can foresee an even more extensive and intense academic partnership, thanks to economic, institutional and technological changes that are transforming the landscape of education and culture.

Chinese programs—exceptionally among the humanities—are growing and thriving in American universities today, and students have already increased demand for opportunities to learn more about China and study there.

The traffic has grown in both directions. In the single decade between 1979 and 1989, more students from the People's Republic of China studied in the US than did so between 1860 and 1950. The impressive numbers of Chinese students enrolled in American institutions – nearly 100,000 by the most recent count - and of American exchange programs and university centers in China provide evidence of a vigorous academic traffic.

Approximately 15,000 American students now study in China each year, and our government would like that number to increase to at least 100,000.

2. Expansion still requires official bilateral ties

While growth over the past thirty years has been driven by independently sponsored exchange participants, that does not diminish the need for official bilateral ties. Unlike in the US where organizations like Confucius Institutes abound and are openly able to register and flourish, there is no comparable American counterpart in-country in China.

3. Recognition of the long humanities history in China both in China and in the US

Chinese history of civil examinations was based entirely on humanities studies. It was not until after the end of the imperial period, in the nationalist period, when this emphasis changed. Even in 1928, the largest publishing house in the world was located not in New York, or London, or Paris, or Berlin, but in Shanghai.

A former president of the ACLS has said that, "In none of the world's civilizations has knowledge for its own sake played so prominent a part over so long a time as in that of China." This long history of emphasis on humanities studies can be more effectively brought to the general public as part of an overall development of humanities studies in both China and the US.

4.Seeing the need for humanities studies all around us

In a recent discussion with a government official responsible for the underfunded social security system – a topic apropos to both sides of the Pacific – it was apparent that decision-making ought not be just the domain of actuaries, but it required fundamental pre-suppositions requiring a foundation in ethics and other humanities disciplines. We cannot abrogate responsibility for decisions because sole reliance on mathematical models is insufficient.

5.Long Term Development

Sociologist Nancy Ruther has made the broader point that "higher education (and indeed cultural and humanities studies – my addition) is an aquifer, not a spigot; universities cannot be built in response to immediate needs, as the spigot someone can turn on for the expertise they need at the moment. Universities should be conceived as a deep reserve, built up slowly and sustained over the long term."

The best way to engage with these discussions is to keep our core values firmly in mind. The National Research Council of the National Academy of Sciences produced a report supporting a long term approach as opposed to one focused on immediate results related to humanities studies. The report asserts, "federal funding for language and area studies may have future benefits that are difficult to quantify." Thus, "[m]aintaining capacity for the teaching of languages and cultures in areas that are not of current strategic importance to the United States but may be in the future is important." I would add that such a position is essential for both the US and for China as we look forward to the fourth decade of the re-newal of cultural and educational exchanges.

利玛窦的发现

余秋雨

著名文化学者

内容提要： 人类分为很多不同的文化族群。不同的文化，有着明显的差异。这种差异，曾被亨廷顿教授解释为冲突的根源；而我们则否定这种观点，认为文明的敌人不是别的文明，而是野蛮，因此文化和文化之间不应该冲突，而应该互相包容、互相理解，甚至互相欣赏。利玛窦神父早在五百年前就解决了"人类与文化"、"人类与历史"中的一个大难题。他的文化判断，高于亨廷顿教授。

本届中美文化论坛的中心议题是"文化与人类"。这个议题很大，容易掉入漫无边际的概念游戏，因此我要在今天的演讲中把它缩小，定位成这样一句话：文化差异不应该导致人类冲突。

我认为，这是近十五年来全世界最重要的文化命题。记得2004年我应联合国开发计划署之邀，参加了当年《人类发展报告》中文化问题的研究和讨论，这句话也就成了那份报告的主线。6年后，2010年5月，联合国教科文组织总干事博科娃女士到上海世博会发布联合国历史上第一份以文化为主题的"世界报告"，我和她一起主持了发布仪式，当时我的发布演讲也围绕着这个主题。

为什么这个主题那么重要？因为亨廷顿教授在1994年发表了《文明的冲突》，影响巨大。这个理论，与最近十几年世界上越来越激烈的冲突产生了强烈的呼应关系，至少造成很多人的误会，都纷纷在文明和文化的差异上寻找着冲突的理由。

我们既要阻止以文明差异的理由发生冲突，又不能为了防止冲突而导致文明的单一。因此，必须提倡以谦虚和欣喜的态度来面对各种自己不熟悉的异态文化。这种文化态度，正是当代世界最急需、最紧缺的精神风范。

我想以400年前一位来中国的欧洲人的目光说起。这位欧洲人刚来中国时,处处感到陌生和不理解,因此按照欧洲思维产生了种种猜测。其他来到中国的欧洲人也产生了类似的猜测,但后来证明,几乎所有的猜测都错了。因此,这个欧洲人就产生了警惕,他觉得,问题可能出在自己固有的逻辑和目光上。因此,他花费漫长的时间进行了从头考察,终于把自己心中的欧洲逻辑改换成了世界逻辑。

这个欧洲人,就是意大利天主教耶稣会传教士利玛窦(Mattew Ricci,1552—1610)。

一

与马可·波罗不同的是,利玛窦在中国逗留了整整30年,深入研究了中华文明的历史和经典,与许多中国学者有充分的交往。他在晚年所写的《利玛窦札记》第一卷第六章中,表述了他几十年研究的一个重要答案。

利玛窦说:虽然中国人有装备精良的陆军和海军,很容易征服临近的国家,但他们的皇上和人民都从来没有想过要发动侵略战争。他们很满足于自己已有的东西,没有征服的野心。在这方面,他们与欧洲人很不相同。

利玛窦说,当时有一些欧洲学者写的文章中认为,中国曾经或必然会征服邻国,扩张自己的势力范围。与他同行的一些西方传教士,也有类似的观点。他认为,这种说法是不真实的。他的结论是:我仔细研究了中国长达四千多年的历史,不得不承认我从未见到有这类征服的记载,也没有听说过他们扩张国界。

他还说,他经常拿着这个问题询问中国博学的历史学家。他们的回答完全一致:从来没有发生过侵略和扩张的事,也不可能发生这样的事。

对于成吉思汗的大范围征服,利玛窦认为,当时中华文明的主体部位也是"被征服者",而不是"征服者"。

利玛窦的这部札记,由一位比利时籍的传教士从中国带回欧洲,1615年在德国出版。后来有拉丁文本四种,法文本三种,德文、西班牙文、意大利文和英文本各一种。

为了在广泛的对比中研究利玛窦论述的可靠性，我本人经历了长期的研究和考察。甚至冒险穿越了从北非、中东到西亚这一现今充满恐怖主义的"古文明发祥地"。在这过程中，我还阅读了大量的书籍，仔细分析中华文明和其他文明在这些问题上的思维异同。

我发现，古代的希腊人、波斯人、罗马人、阿拉伯人，近代的西班牙人、葡萄牙人、荷兰人、英国人、德国人、日本人，都在一系列历史文献中留下了征服世界的计划。但在中国浩如烟海的各类典籍中，却怎么也找不到类似的计划。

古代中国虽然对世界了解不够，但也早已通过一些使节、商人、僧人和旅行者的记述，知道外部世界的存在。在唐代，通过丝绸之路，中国对外部世界的了解已相当充分。但是即便如此，中国在实力很强的情况下，既没有参与过中亚、西亚、北非、欧洲之间的千年征战，也没有参与过近几百年的海洋争逐。

这实在太让人惊讶了。大家都在伸手，它不伸手；它有能力伸手，还是不伸手。大家因此不理解它，不信任它，猜测它迟早会伸手。猜测了那么多年，仍然没有看到，大家反而有点慌乱和焦躁。

是啊，这究竟是怎么回事？

产生这种情况的根本原因，是中华文明的本性决定的。

中华文明的主体是农耕文明，与海洋文明和游牧文明很不相同。海洋文明和游牧文明大多具有生存空间上的拓展性、进犯性、无边界性。它们的出发点和终点，此岸和彼岸，是无羁的，不确定的。相反，中国农耕文明的基本意识是故土自守、热土难离。它建立精良军队的目的，全都在于集权的安慰和边境的防守。农耕文明的"厚土观念"、"故乡情结"，上升为杜甫所说的"立国自有疆"的领土自律，结果，中国历代朝野压根儿对"占领远方"不感兴趣。

万里长城作为中华文明的象征，便是防守型而不是进攻型的证明。我在中东和欧洲见到不少进攻型的城墙，总是围成一个大圈，用的材料是刚刚被破坏的古典建筑残片，里边造了很多马槽，只等明天一开城门，蹄如箭发。经过反复对比，我终于强烈感受到，中国的万里长城是干什么的了。

即使具有马背上的尚武精神，中国军人也主要是为了守护疆土、排除干扰，偶尔有一些边界战争，但也仅止于此。即使有些使者远行万里，也是为了《尧典》中所说的"协和万邦"。明代的大航海家郑和七次大航海也是为了这个目的，对于所到之地并无领土要求。从郑和本人到每一个水手，一丝一毫都没有这种念头。而且正如大家知道的，他七次大航海结束后，朝廷又是长期的闭关自守。这与晚他60年的欧洲航海家哥伦布等人发现新大陆相比，就完全不同了。不同在行动，但行动的背景是文化。

这种非侵略性的特点，也护佑中华文明成为所有人类古文明中传之今日的唯一者。因为在古代，一切军事远征都是文明自杀，或迟或早而已。

这个观点也获得了现代国际学术界的支持。三十多年前美国学者爱德华·麦克诺尔·伯恩斯（Edward McNally Burns）和菲利普·李·拉尔夫（Philip Lee Ralph）合著的《世界文明史》（*WORLD CIVILIZATIONS*）第一部分第七章第一节写到中国文明时，曾经这样说：

> 它之所以能长期存在，有地理原因，也有历史原因。中国在它的大部分历史时期，没有建立过侵略性的政权。也许更重要的是，中国伟大的哲学家和伦理学家的和平主义精神约束了它的向外扩张。

这两位美国学者的说法，很接近利玛窦的观点。漫长的历史，沉淀成了稳定的民族心理。中华文明的内部，为了争权夺利发生过大量的血腥争斗；但是对外，基本以和平自守的方式相处。它大体上是一种非侵略性的内耗型文明。国际社会一次次产生的"中国威胁论"，只是一种被利玛窦神父早就否定过的幻觉。

二

今天我在这里，不是想借利玛窦来说明中国，而是想借利玛窦来说明一个文明人对待异态文化的态度。利玛窦是一位杰出的示范者，值得当代世界各国的人文学者敬仰和效仿。

利玛窦在中国30年的经历还证明，人类文化的差异，是彼此欣赏之源，而不是冲突之源。

这就可以跳过几百年，来说说亨廷顿先生了。

亨廷顿先生的《文明的冲突》，发表于1994年。一发表，就在世界上产生了极大影响，这是为什么？

那是因为，当时全世界的智者们都开始回顾和总结20世纪，以便更好地走向21世纪。大家一回顾总结，无穷无尽的枪炮血泊又回到了眼前。20世纪太可怕了，不仅发生了两次世界大战，而且又持续了严重的"冷战"。但是，到了20世纪最后10年，似乎一切都烟消云散。什么同盟国、协约国、法西斯同盟、反法西斯同盟，什么社会主义阵营、帝国主义阵营，都已成过眼烟云，就连后来匆忙提出的"三个世界"划分，也很快发生了变化。总之，一切作为20世纪冲突根源的政治依据，眼看着都很难延续。但是，这并没有给人们带来心理上的安全感，反而，由于不知道新的冲突根源，人们更慌乱了。大家不喜欢冲突，但更不喜欢那种不知道冲突由来的无准备、无逻辑状态。因此，地球的各个角落，都在期待一种判断、一种预测。否则，就不知如何跨入21世纪了。

正是在这种情况下，美国哈佛大学的政治学教授亨廷顿先生出场了。他说，21世纪的冲突，将以"文明"为坐标。他预言，所有古往今来所积聚的不同文明群落，在摆脱别的种种归类后，将以自己的文明为皈依，然后与其他文明对弈、纠缠、冲突。在所有的文明群落中，21世纪最重要的冲突将发生在最重要的三大文明之间，那就是西方文明、伊斯兰文明、中华文明。

这种解释和划分，乍一听，理由比较充分，具有文化含量，又有现实证据，因此一发表便轰传各国，万人瞩目。

有人说，亨廷顿先生的厉害，就是从政治划分回归到了文化划分，而文化确实比政治更稳固、更长久。这就无怪，"文明冲突论"成了20世纪晚期最重要的人文理论。

但是从一开始，就有学者指出了这种理论的弊端。

我作为一名东方学者，就从1999年开始连续地批评亨廷顿先生的理论："以对立、对抗思维解析文明格局，淡化了比冲突更普遍的文明交融和文明互置，实际效果令人担忧。"

在几国学者的共同坚持下，2004年的《人类发展报告》在序言中就加了一个结论：本报告否定文化差异必然导致文明冲突的理论。

更让我高兴的是，2010年5月21日发布的联合国有关文化的"世界报告"中，明确指出了"文明冲突论"的"三大错误假设"。

在发布会上，我对于这"三大错误假设"向与会的各国朋友进行了简单的理论阐释。我说——

亨廷顿先生的"文明冲突论"，就像历史上很多轰传一时却站不住脚的理论一样，立足的基础是一系列假设。学术研究是允许假设的，但亨廷顿先生未能诚恳地表明是假设，显然是一种理论错误。

"文明冲突论"的第一个假设，是粗糙地设想人类的每一个文明群落在文化归属、文明选择上，只能是单一的。事实上，全部世界史证明，这种归属和选择都是多重的、叠加的、互相依赖的。因此，那种看似"正宗不二"的单色、单线、单层、单调，只是一种假设，一种出于幼稚而懒惰的思辨方便而进行的"想象式提纯"，与实际情况相距甚远。

"文明冲突论"的第二个假设，是武断地设想不同文明之间的边界是一条条水火不容的封闭式断裂线。事实上，所有这样的边界都是多孔的、互渗的、松软的。文明的边界不像战时国界那样壁垒森严，而是混沌地包括着风俗、语言、婚姻、祭祀、歌舞等生态文化的不可分割元素，即使某些地方出现了区划，仔细一看也是异中有同、同中有异，甚至大同小异。因此，那种以邻为壑式的所谓文明边界，其实也只是一种不真实的理论切割，为的是使冲突双方"到位"，并找到"冲突的身份"。这很不应该，因为绝大多数"冲突的身份"，是自欺欺人的虚构。

"文明冲突论"的第三个假设，是鲁莽地设想每种文明的传承都是保守的、凝固的、复古的。事实上，世界上的多数文明都在忙着创新、改革，广采博纳、吐故纳新。我走遍全世界，看到一切活着的文明都很不确定，一切健康的文明都日新月异。因此，它们都不可能拿着千年不变的模式去与别的文明冲突。在学术上，把不确定的活体说成是僵化的实体，那就是在为冲突制造理由。

以上所说这三个"错误假设"，是"文明冲突论"所隐藏的三个理论支柱。今天发布的"世界报告"明确指出了这一点，我很希望世界上有更多的人能够看到。如果大家都明白了各种文明之间归属的叠加性、边界的模糊性、内容的变动性，那么，信奉和执行"文明冲突论"的人群就会大大减少。

三

最后，我还想就这个问题，谈谈个人的感受。

前面提到，我在20世纪末就对"文明冲突论"提出异议。这种异议，较系统地见之于我在考察世界各大文明后写的书籍《千年一叹》和《行者无疆》中，也见之于我花了两年时间在香港凤凰卫视的谈话专题《秋雨时分》中。

照理，我贴地考察了当今世界冲突最严重的中东、北非、中亚、南亚地区，最能呼应"文明冲突论"，为什么却反对了呢？

我在那两本书里写道，看来看去，确实到处都在发生冲突。但是，所有的恶性冲突都发生在文明和野蛮之间，而不是发生在文明和文明之间。因此，当今世界应该划出的第一界限，是文明和野蛮的根本区别。

那么，什么是"当代野蛮"呢？我在书里一再指出的是七项，那就是：恐怖主义、核竞赛、环境破坏、制毒贩毒、极端霸权、极端民粹，以及面对自然灾难和传染病无所作为。从事这些"当代野蛮"的人和反对这些"当代野蛮"的人，散布在不同的族群里。如果有人硬把文明和野蛮的冲突解释成文明与文明之间的冲突，那么，他们就有掩饰自己野蛮行径的嫌疑。

我在几本书里反复表述了这样一个意思——

几万里历险告诉我，"文明"之所以称为"文明"，互相之间一定有共同的前提、共同的默契、共同的底线、共同的防范、共同的灾难、共同的敌人。这么多"共同"，是人类存活至今的基本保证。如果有谁热衷于文明族群之间的挑唆，那就势必会淡化乃至放弃这么多"共同"，最后只能导致全人类的生存危机。

在这么多"共同"下，文化差异就必须被保护、被欣赏了，并由此产生文化的多样性。

对于守护文明的共同底线，我们的态度是严峻；而对于保护文明范围内的多样差异，我们的心情是喜悦。

可惜，由于文明与文明之间的差异被一批学者和政客夸张成了你死我活，我们听到最多的还是那种激烈的文化自守言论。对此，我还是只能以自己为例来作一些分析。

我在华文读者中的形象，是中华文化的搜寻者和捍卫者，因此中国国内的那些民族主义情绪激烈的人士也总是在我身边活动，希望由我进一步来带头强化。但是，只能让他们深深失望了，因为我的看法完全不同。我写道——

一个人的文化结构，可以透视全世界的文化结构。不错，我是中华文化的忠诚阐释者，但是，我完成这些思考的基础逻辑，是欧几里得几何学给予我的；我文化思维的美学基础，是黑格尔（G.F.Hegel）、康德（I.Kant）给予我的；我的现代意识，是荣格（C.G.Jung）、爱因斯坦（A.Einstein）、萨特（J.p.Satre）给予我的。我从来没有觉得，这些来自欧洲的精神资源，曾与我心中的老子、孔子、屈原、司马迁产生过剧烈冲突。

既然一个小小的心灵都能融汇那么多不同的文明成果而毫无怨隙，那么，大大的世界又会如何呢？

确实，我一直认为，当我们在讨论文化与人类、文化与历史、文化与文化之间关系的时候，真不如把自己的内心储备，当作一个参照范本。

世界文化为什么能多元并存、多样并欢？依据就是我们每个人的内心。我们的内心，往往远比我们的言论更宽阔。这也可以倒过来说，凡是当我们用狭隘的观念在制造文化对立时，我们的内心其实并没有同意。

说到内心储存，我想到一件有趣的事，可能与我们今天的中美文化论坛有关。我在几十年的文化教学生涯中发现，一般中国学生对于美国文化的内心储存，远远超过美国学生对于中国文化的储存。仅就西方文学论，在中国，大多数文科学生都会更熟悉欧洲，但至少也都知道美国的惠特曼（Walt Whitman）、马克·吐温（Mark Twain）、欧·亨利（O.Henry）、杰克·伦敦（Jack London）、赛珍珠（Pearl Buck）、海明威（Ernest Hemingway）等作家，美国戏剧家奥尼尔（Eugene O'Neill）、阿瑟·密勒（Arthur Miller）的名字也不陌生。但相比之下，美国学生对中国文化的了解，实在是少得可怜。而且这中间还有一个时间上的巨大落差。美国文学史，满打满算也就是200年吧，但中国文学多少年？那位全世界华人都在纪念的屈原，今年应该是2352岁了。对200年如此熟悉，对2000年知之甚少,这个对比,说明了中美文化交流的重要性和迫切性。

如果对于对方的文化并不了解,那就只能随意猜测了,而以自己的立场猜测自己不熟悉的对方,一定笑话百出,南辕北辙。因此,我们又不能不想起利玛窦。

Matteo Ricci's Discovery

Yu Qiuyu
Famous cultural scholar

Abstract: Human beings have been divided into many distinct cultural groups. Obvious differences exist between cultures. Such differences have been explained by Professor Samuel Huntington as the causes for conflict. However, we do not agree with him. We think what runs counter to civilization is barbarism rather than other civilizations. Therefore, there should not be any conflict between different cultures, but mutual tolerance, understanding and even appreciation. Priest Matteo Ricci had solved the conundrums in "humanity and culture" and "humanity and history" as early as five hundred years ago. His argument on culture-related issues was superior to Professor Huntington's.

The theme of this CHINA-U.S. Cultural Forum is "Culture and Humanity". This is a very broad theme, and our discussion may become too discursive to be a concept game only. Therefore, I'll limit my topic to a specific one—Cultural differences should not cause human conflicts.

I think this is the most important cultural theme in the past fifteen years. In 2004, at the invitation of the United Nations Development Program, I participated in the research and discussion of the cultural issues in the Human Development Report of the year. My topic today is precisely the theme of the report. Six years later, in May 2010, Ms. Irina Bokova, UNESCO Director-General, went to the Shanghai World Expo to release a "World Report" on culture, the first of its kind in the history of the United Nations, and she co-chaired the report release ceremony with me. My speech made on that occasion was also on this theme.

Why is the theme so important? It has to do with publication of the very influential book The Clash of Civilizations by Professor Huntington in 1994. The intensifying conflicts in the world in the past decade seem to have proved the theory reflected in the book title which has caused misunderstanding among many people. They have been trying to ascribe the causes for the conflicts to the differences in civilizations and cultures.

On the one hand, we must prevent conflicts caused by the differences in civilizations; and on the other hand, we should not bring about the singleness of civilization on the pretext of preventing conflicts. Therefore, we must face the unfamiliar and different cultures with modesty and readiness. Such an attitude is exactly what contemporary world most demands and most desires.

I want to begin with the viewpoints of a European who came to China four hundred years ago. When the European first came to China, everywhere he went he found nearly everything was strange to him. So he made many speculations in his European way of thinking. Other Europeans in China had the same speculations, but it turned out that all the speculations were wrong. Therefore, the European became discreet. He thought that the problem lay in his inherent logic and stereotyped views. So he spent much time in making a study of China all over again, and finally he converted his European logic to a world logic.

The European is Matteo Ricci (1552-1610), a missionary of Italian Catholic Jesuit.

I

Different from Marco Polo, Matteo Ricci stayed in China for a good 30 years. During that time, he made an in-depth study of the history and classics of Chinese civilization, and had sufficient contact and communication with many Chinese scholars. In Chapter Six of the first volume of The Journals of Matthew Ricci written by himself in his declining years, he summarized a remarkable achievement of his own made over years of research.

As pointed out by Matteo Ricci, although Chinese had well-equipped army and navy, with capacity to conquer the neighboring countries, their emperors and people had never intended to launch an aggressive war. They were very contented with what they already had, and had no ambition for conquest of others. In this respect, they were completely different from Europeans.

According to Matteo Ricci, some articles by his contemporary European scholars held that China did or would certainly conquer its neighboring countries to expand its sphere of influence. Other western missionaries to China, Matteo Ricci's peers, held similar viewpoints. However, Matteo Ricci thought otherwise. And his conclusion is as follows:

I have carefully studied China's history of over four thousand years, and I have to admit that I have never come upon any record of such conquest. Moreover, I have never heard that it has ever expanded its national border.

He also said that he often inquired of Chinese learned historians about the related question, and their answer was the same: China never invaded other countries, nor launched war of expansion, and would never do so.

As to the large-scale conquest of Genghis Khan, Matteo Ricci thought that the Chinese civilization was challenged rather than "the conqueror".

The Journals of Matteo Ricci was brought back to Europe by a missionary from Belgium and published in Germany in 1615. Later, they came out in four Latin editions, three French editions, and one edition in German, Spanish, Italian and English respectively.

To confirm the reliability of Matteo Ricci's accounts through broad comparison, I have made research and exploration on a long-term basis. I even ventured through the "cradles of ancient civilizations" in North Africa, the

Middle East and West Asia, which are plagued by terrorists today. Still, I have had extensive reading and carefully analyzed the similarities and differences in thinking between the Chinese civilization and other civilizations on these issues.

I've found out that ancient Greeks, Persians, Romans, Arabians, and modern Spaniards, Portuguese, Dutch, Britons, Germans, and Japanese all have plans of conquering others in their historical documents. But in China's voluminous ancient books and records, we can not find such plans.

Although ancient China had less than a clear idea about the outer world, it got to know about it through the accounts of the missionaries, merchants, monks and travelers. During the Tang Dynasty, China gained a good knowledge about the outer world through the Silk Road. However, even at the crest of its power, China had never participated in the wars between the Central Asia, West Asia, North Africa, and Europe in the past 1,000-plus years, and had never had a part in the scramble on the seas in the past centuries.

It is really surprising. All others were aggressive, but it wasn't; and it didn't invade other countries though it had the capacity to do so. So some countries didn't understand it, and became suspicious of it, speculating that sooner or later it would launch an aggressive war. Things turn out to be opposite to their speculation, so they became somewhat panicky and fretful.

Uh, why?

Fundamentally, this can be attributed to the inherent nature of Chinese civilization.

Chinese civilization is a characteristic cultivation civilization, far different from the marine civilization and the nomadic civilization. Most marine and nomadic civilizations are characteristically expansive, aggressive, and with no definite national border. Their starting point and the destination are indefinite. Contrarily, the fundamental consciousness of Chinese cultivation civilization clings to the land. The purpose of the establishment of a well-equipped army is to protect the centralized power and to defend the border. The concept of "attachment to local land" and the "complex of homeland" of the cultivation civilization have been sublimated to the concept of territorial confinement, as indicated by a line by Du Fu—"the expansion of of a country's territory should be kept within a limit". As a result, the rulers and the subjects throughout Chinese history have no interest in "encroaching on remote land".

The Great Wall, a symbol of Chinese civilization, is an embodiment of the defensive rather than offensive character of our civilization. I saw many offensive ramparts in the Middle East and Europe. They are in circular formations, and built from the debris of the destroyed ancient buildings. Within the rampart are many mangers; when the city gate was opened at daybreak, all the horses would dash out like arrows. After repeated comparative studies between the Chinese and other civilizations, I finally fully understand the role of the ten-thousand-li Great Wall.

Even though Chinese military men showed martialism on horseback, the motivation behind that was to protect the territory and to defuse outside interferences. Occasionally, wars broke out on the border, and that was all. Even some messengers traveled over ten thousand li, their purpose was to "negotiate a harmonious relationship with various Nations" according to Emperor Yao.

The Ming Dynasty's great mariner Zheng He made seven voyages on the same purpose, and he made no territorial claim wherever he went. Both Zheng He and all of his fellow sailors had no such intention. As we all know, after the seven voyages of Zheng He, the subsequent dynasties again adopted the closed-door policy. Zheng He's voyages are totally different from the discovery of the New World by Columbus and other European navigators 60 years later. The differences lie in the actions, and the backdrop of the actions is culture.

The non-aggressive character props up the Chinese civilization, the only civilization that has survived and thrived in the world since the ancient times. Actually all military expeditions led to suicidal of civilizations, only sooner or later.

The viewpoint has been confirmed by the contemporary international academia. A quotation about Chinese civilization from Section One of Chapter Seven in the First Part of World Civilizations coauthored by US scholars Edward McNally Burns and Philip Lee Ralph thirty years ago reads as follows:

It has existed for long for both geographical and historical reasons. For most part of its history, China has never established any aggressive regime. Perhaps more importantly, the pacifism advocated by China's great philosophers and ethicists constrains its outward expansion.

The two US scholars share nearly the same view with Matteo Ricci. Over the long history, Chinese people have developed a stable national psyche. Within the Chinese civilization, a great number of bloody struggles for power and interests have occurred. However, it gets along with the outer world in a peaceful and defensive way. It's basically a non-aggressive civilization. The international community again and again raises the bogey of "China threat", but it is simply an illusion that has been denied by Matteo Ricci.

II

Here, by quoting Matteo Ricci I don't intend to introduce China, but illustrate the attitude that civilized people should take toward a different culture. Matteo Ricci is a distinguished exemplar, worthy of respect and imitation by today's scholars from across the world.

The thirty-year living experience of Matteo Ricci in China also proves that the differences of human cultures are source of mutual appreciation rather than the root of conflict.

Now we come to Mr. Samuel Huntington who lived hundreds of years after Matteo Ricci.

Mr. Huntington's The Clash of Civilizations came out in 1994. It evoked enormous repercussions worldwide upon publication. Why?

It was because that at the time insightful people from across the world were beginning to look back on and take stock of the 20th century, so as to be better prepared for the 21st century. In retrospect, they were again confronted with the relentless roar of the guns and bloody scenes. The 20th century was horrible: two world wars broke out, which was followed by the protracted Cold War. But during the last decade of the 20th century, it seemed nothing was left of the wars. Things like the allied powers, the Triple Entente, the fascist alliance, the anti-fascist alliance, the socialist camp, and the imperialist camp all were gone. Even the later hastily proposed division of "three worlds" changed soon. In a word, all the political rationale claimed to be the root of the conflicts in the 20th century became increasingly untenable. However, that did not bring a sense of security to the people. Instead, they became more panicky because they had no idea about the root for potential conflicts. People hate conflicts, and they hate even more the illogical state brewing conflicts which they are unprepared for. Therefore, at every nook and corner of the world, people are expecting a certain judgment and prediction. Otherwise, they would not know how to go ahead into the 21st century.

It was under such conditions that Mr. Huntington, a Professor of political science at Harvard University came into the focus of people's attention. He said that culture would be the primary axis of conflict in the 21st century. According to Huntington, different civilizations evolving from the ancient times will fall back on themselves once they break away from various classifications, and will confront, entwine and conflict with other civilizations. Among all the civilizations, the gravest conflicts in the 21st century would happen among the three key civilizations, i.e., the Western, Islamic and Chinese civilizations.

Apparently, the explanation and division sound reasonable in that it is of cultural content, and has realistic evidence. Therefore, it has attracted wide attention of the world once published.

It's said that Mr. Huntington distinguishes himself in the fact that he has returned from the political division to the cultural division. And the culture is indeed more stable and permanent than politics. It's no wonder that the theory of the clash of civilization has become the most influential theory in humanities in the late 20th century.

However, from the very beginning, some scholars have pointed out the weaknesses of the theory.

As an oriental scholar, I began to continuously criticize the theory of Mr. Huntington from 1999. I pointed out that he "interprets the pattern of civilizations more in opposition and antagonism; and he ignores the integration and communication of the civilizations which are more widespread than conflicts. The actual effects of his theory are troubling. "

With the joint efforts of the scholars from several countries, one conclusion had been added to the preface of 2004 Human Development Report——the report denies the theory that cultural differences will definitely lead to the clash of civilizations.

To my gratification, the UN "World Development Report" on culture released on May 21, 2010 articulately pointed out the "three mistaken hypotheses" in Mr. Huntington's theory of the clash of the civilizations.

At the report release ceremony, I briefly talked about the "three mistaken hypotheses" to the friends present from various countries. I said:

Mr. Huntington's theory of the clash of civilizations is based on a series of hypotheses, just like the other theories in history that were popular for some time but actually untenable. Hypothesis is allowed in academic research, but Mr. Huntington failed to state earnestly that his study was based on hypotheses. It is evidently a theoretical mistake.

The first hypothesis underlying the theory of the clash of civilizations roughly assumes that each cultural community has a single identity and sticks to unvaried civilization selection. In fact, the entire history of the world has proved that the identity and civilization selection are multi-faceted, with diverse alternatives overlapping and interdependent. Therefore, the apparently "authentic" solid-color, unilinear, monotonous development of civilizations is simply a hypothesis. It is an "imaginative refinement" done for the convenience of a childish and lazy speculation, which is far from the reality.

The second hypothesis of the theory of the clash of civilizations arbitrarily assumes that the borders between different civilizations are a series of incompatible and closed fault lines. In fact, all such borders are "porous, mutually permeable, and soft". The borders of civilizations are not as heavily fortified as the national borders during wartime. Instead, they largely contain the inseparable elements of ecological culture, such as customs, languages, marriage, sacrifice and songs and dances. Although in some places there are administrative divisions, if we look carefully, we can find similarities in differences, differences in similarities, and even almost the same cases only with slight differences. Therefore, the so-called borders of civilizations which tend to shift the troubles to the neighboring countries are actually a kind of untrue theoretical division. The purpose of such division is to place the conflicting parties "in place", and find out the "conflicting identities". Scholars should not do like this, because most of the "conflicting identities" are simply a self-deceiving hypothesis.

The third hypothesis of the theory of the clash of civilizations recklessly assumes that the inheritance of each civilization is conservative and fixed, and tends to return to the ancient ways. In fact, most civilizations in the world are busy in innovating and reforming. They are also extensively taking in the positive experience of other civilizations, and are reinvigorating themselves by getting rid of the outdated things and adopting the new ones. As I traveled around the world, I found that all the existing civilizations are ever-changing, and all the healthy civilizations update themselves with each passing day. Therefore, they can not come into conflict with other civilizations with an unchanged pattern over a thousand years. In the academic field, taking the uncertain living organism as the rigid object is none other than making excuses for the conflicts.

The above three "mistaken hypotheses" are the three latent theoretical pillars of the theory of the clash of civilizations. The World Development Report published today has made the point clear which I hope that more people in the world can get. If all of us understand the overlapping ascription, the fuzziness of borders, and the ever-changing content of different civilizations, the number of people who embrace and implement the theory of the clash of civilizations will dramatically decline.

III

Finally, I wish to share with you my own opinions on this problem.

As mentioned above, I began to question the theory of the clash of civilizations in late 20th century. My dissenting opinions can be found systematically in my books A Sigh in Thousand Years (Qian Nian Yi Tan) and The Endless Journey (Xing Zhe Wu Jiang) written after my examination of the key civilizations in the world. And they can also be seen in the talk show series of Qiuyu Time on Phoenix TV based in Hong Kong, which took me over two years to make.

Normally, since I have studied the Middle East, North Africa, Central Asia, and South Asia which are most gravely plagued by conflicts in the world, and the reality in these regions seem to verify the theory of the clash of civilizations, why do I oppose it?

You will see in my above two books that conflicts really erupt here and there. However, all the violent conflicts occur between civilization and barbarism, not between civilizations. Therefore, the contemporary world should, for the first thing, draw a line between civilization and barbarism.

Then, what constitutes "contemporary barbarism"? I've repeatedly pointed out the following seven items in my books: terrorism, nuclear arms race, environmental damage, drug making and trafficking, extreme hegemony, extreme populism, and passive response to natural disasters and epidemics. The people who perpetrate the "contemporary barbarism" and those who oppose "contemporary barbarism" are scattered among different ethnic groups. If someone intentionally defines the conflict between civilization and barbarism as conflict between civilizations, he probably is covering up his own barbarism.

In my books, I repeatedly try to express my following thinking:

My venture over tens of thousands of miles tells me that among the civilizations there must be common premises, tacit understanding, bottom line, precautions, disasters, and foes. So many commonalities constitute the fundamental guarantee for the survival of the human beings until today. If someone is enthusiastic in instigating the conflicts between different civilizations, he will definitely minimize and ignore the commonalities, which can only precipitate the survival crisis of the human beings.

With so many commonalities, cultural differences must be protected and appreciated, and so comes the cultural diversity.

We unswervingly guard the common bottom-line of the civilizations, and we are happy to protect the diversity of civilizations.

Regretfully, the differences between different civilizations have been exaggerated by some scholars and politicians to be "life or death" problems. We've also heard much more about the vehement opinion of cultural self-defense. On this point I'd like to share with you my personal experience.

In the eyes of the Chinese readers, I'm a seeker and custodian of Chinese culture. So some Chinese people with a strong sense of nationalism always attempt to persuade me to take the lead to reinforce nationalism. But I may have deeply disappointed them, because I entirely disagree with them. So I wrote:

The cultural structure of a person gives a hint to the cultural structure of the whole world. Yes, I'm a faithful interpreter of Chinese culture. However, the basic logic behind my thinking comes from Euclid's geometry; the aesthetic foundation of my cultural thinking comes from G. F. Hegel and I. Kant; my modern consciousness comes from C. G. Jung, A. Einstein, and J. P. Satre. I have never thought that the spiritual resources from Europe have been ever in violent contradiction with Laozi, Confucius, Qu Yuan, and Sima Qian.

A small soul can hold so many achievements of different civilizations. How about the big world?

True, I have been thinking that when we are talking about the relationships between culture and humanity, between culture and history, and among cultures, we'd better refer to our innermost thoughts.

Why diverse cultures in the world can coexist? It depends on our innermost perception. We are far more accommodating than we sound. Conversely, whenever we create cultural antagonism based on our own narrow concepts, our inner self actually may not approve.

When it comes to understanding each other, I think of an interesting phenomenon, which has something to do with today's China-U.S. Cultural Forum. As I've found out in my career of culture teaching in the past decades, generally speaking, Chinese students know far more about US culture than their US counterparts about Chinese culture. Take western literature as an example. In China, most of the students in liberal arts are more familiar with European literature, and they at least know about such US writers as Walt Whitman, Mark Twain, O. Henry, Jack London, Jack London, Pearl Buck, and Ernest Hemingway, and the US playwrights Eugene O'Neill and Arthur Miller. In comparison, US students have much little knowledge about Chinese culture. And there is also a gap in time between Chinese literature and US literature. The history of American literature is two hundred years at most. How about Chinese literature? This year, we will celebrate the 2352nd anniversary of the birth of Qu Yuan. The fact that the Chinese students are familiar with the 200-year-long US literature and US students know little about Chinese literature with a history of more than 2000 years history necessitates China-US cultural communication of which the importance and urgency is evident.

If you don't know much about the culture of the other party, you have to speculate at will. And if you speculate on the unfamiliar party from your own perspective, you'll definitely make mistakes and be farther away from the truth. Therefore, we can not help thinking of Matteo Ricci.

中国非物质文化遗产保护的创造性实践

李新风

中国艺术研究院·中国
非物质文化遗产保护中
心常务副主任

内容提要： 人类创造的丰富多彩的非物质文化遗产，是文化多样性的生动体现，也是人类可持续发展的重要保证。中国是非物质文化遗产资源极为丰富深厚的国家。在中国，保护非物质文化遗产已经成为全社会的普遍共识和国家文化发展战略的重要组成部分。中国的非物质文化遗产保护，十分重视认真学习、积极汲取世界其他国家在非物质文化遗产保护方面的有效做法和宝贵经验。与此同时，中国的非物质文化遗产保护还特别注重从中国非物质文化遗产保护工作的具体实际情况出发，尊重中国非物质文化遗产的自身发展规律和特殊性，根据保护工作的实际需要，充分发挥各个方面的积极性、主动性，在非物质文化遗产保护方面进行了一系列宝贵的、富有创造性的探索和实践。

人类创造的文化遗产，主要可分为两大类：一是物质文化遗产，即文物，包括可移动与不可移动的文物；二是依靠传承人的活态传承的非物质文化遗产，即无形文化遗产。人类创造的丰富多彩的非物质文化遗产，是文化多样性的生动体现，是文化创新、文化创造取之不尽用之不竭的宝贵源泉，是人类可持续发展的重要保证。中国是非物质文化遗产资源极为丰富深厚的国度。在中国，保护非物质文化遗产已经成为全社会的普遍共识，也已经成为国家文化发展战略中的一个重要组成部分，受到空前关注和高度重视。

为了在世界范围内全面推动非物质文化遗产的保护工作，联合国教科文组织于2003年通过了《保护非物质文化遗产公约》(以下简称《公约》)。该《公约》对于全世界范围内的非物质文化遗产保护工作，起到了十分重要的作用。中国早在《公约》通过的第二年即2004年便加入了该《公约》。而且，如大家所知，目前，世界上的绝大多数国家均已加入了该《公约》。但是,让我们颇感困惑的是,据我们所知,美国等少数国家,至今好像仍未加入该《公约》以及对于保护世界文化多样性具有重要意义的另一个重要的国际文件《保护和促进文化表现形式多样性公约》(联合国教科文组织于2005年通过)。

中国的非物质文化遗产保护,努力遵循联合国教科文组织2003年通过的《保护非物质文化遗产公约》的基本精神和基本规范,十分重视认真学习、积极汲取世界其他国家在非物质文化遗产保护方面的有效做法和宝贵经验。与此同时,中国的非物质文化遗产保护还特别注重从中国非物质文化遗产保护工作的具体实际情况出发,尊重中国非物质文化遗产的自身发展规律和特殊性,根据保护工作的实际需要,充分发挥政府、专家、传承人、社会、企业等各个方面的积极性、主动性,在非物质文化遗产保护方面进行了一系列宝贵的、富有创造性的探索和实践。

1. 努力建设符合中国实际的、富有实效的非物质文化遗产保护制度。中国的非物质文化遗产保护在制度建设上的创造性实践是系统的、多方面的,主要包括:

——非物质文化遗产保护工作部际联席会议制度。

——非物质文化遗产保护工作专家委员会制度。文化部和各省、市、自治区分别成立的非物质文化遗产保护工作专家委员会制度,建立了有效的专家咨询制度,以保证非物质文化遗产保护工作的科学性、专业性。

——非物质文化遗产的调查制度。在政府的组织下,开展了全国性的非物质文化遗产普查工作,全面了解到非物质文化遗产的资源情况。

——非物质文化遗产代表性项目名录保护制度。建立包括国家级与省级、地市级、县级在内的四级非物质文化遗产代表性项目名录体系。其中,最为重要的是国家级非物质文化遗产代表性项目名录的评审与管理机制。到目前为止,国家已公布三批国家级非物质文化遗产项目名录,共有国家级非物质文化遗产代表性项目1219项。对于进入国家级名录的项目,努力探索实行"有进有出"的动态管理,以保证进入国家级名录的项目真正具有代表性。

——非物质文化遗产代表性项目代表性传承人保护制度。对国家级、省级、地市级和县级代表性项目的代表性传承人进行评审、认定、扶持、资助。目前已公布三批国家级非物质文化遗产代表性项目代表性传承人共1488名。

——将每年6月的第二个星期六设立为"文化遗产日"。在文化遗产日期间举办丰富多彩的非物质文化遗产展示、展演、宣传、讲座等活动,让更多的人参与非物质文化遗产保护。

——将除夕、端午、清明、中秋等传统节日纳入国家的法定假日。各个国家、各个民族的传统节日是一种重要的传统文化表现形式,也是非物质文化遗产中的一种特殊而重要的类型,在非物质文化遗产保护中受到格外的关注。2008年之前,我国的传统节日中,只有春节被列入了国民法定的假日体系,放假三天,而且还不包括除夕在内。自2008年元旦开始,清明、端午、中秋这三个中华民族重要传统节日被增设为国家法定假日。原春节放假三天不变,但放假时间由原来的农历正月初一至初三修改为从除夕开始到正月初二,即是说,农历的除夕这一重要传统节日也被纳入了国家法定假日。这次国家法定假日的调整,对于提高公众的文化自觉,更好地保护传统节日文化,产生了非常好的效果。

——在国家文化部专门设立非物质文化遗产保护的行政管理机构——非物质文化遗产司。各省、自治区、直辖市也分别建立了各自的非物质文化遗产行政管理机构。

——成立国家级的非物质文化遗产专业学术咨询机构——中国非物质文化遗产保护中心。各省、自治区、直辖市乃至一些地级市,也成立了各自的非物质文化遗产保护中心之类的专业机构等。

上述一系列高效、有力的制度建设,为中国非物质文化遗产保护事业提供了最基本的刚性的制度化保障。

2. 积极探索、实践各种有效的、符合中国非物质文化遗产实际的保护方式。中国的非物质文化遗产保护,十分重视探索和实践各种各样行之有效的保护方式。主要包括:

——以国家级项目为中心的项目保护方式。

——以国家级项目代表性传承人为保护重点的传承人保护方式。

——生产性保护方式,即在具有生产性质的实践过程中,以保持非物质文化遗产的真实性、整体性和传承性为核心,以有效传承非物质文化遗产技艺为前提,借助生产、流通、销售等手段,将非物质文化遗产及其资源转化为文化产品的保护方式。

——文化生态区的整体保护方式(详下)。

——抢救性保护方法,即对某些濒危的非物质文化遗产采取的各种抢救性的保护措施。

——运用现代数字技术手段对非物质文化遗产进行数字化的记录、收集、整理、存档的数字化保护方式。

——对一些非物质文化遗产产品生产的减、免税办法的探索。

——探索鼓励、吸引社会尤其是有实力并崇尚文化的企业积极参与非遗保护的方法等。

3. 特别注重整体性的保护，大力推进文化生态保护区的建设。国家对非物质文化遗产代表性项目集中、特色鲜明、形式和内涵保持完整的特定区域实施整体性保护，积极推进文化生态保护区的建设。目前已建立国家级文化生态保护区或文化生态保护实验区如闽南文化、徽州文化、热贡文化、羌族文化、客家文化（梅州）、武陵山区（湘西）土家族苗族文化、海洋渔文化（象山）、晋中文化、潍水文化、迪庆民族文化、大理文化、陕北文化等文化生态保护区或文化生态保护实验区12个。

4. 高度重视非物质文化遗产保护的法律建设。2011年，中国非物质文化遗产保护领域最重要的一部法律《中华人民共和国非物质文化遗产法》诞生并开始施行。这为中国的非物质文化遗产保护提供了根本的法律保障。在一个国家的法律体系中，专门建立一部《非物质文化遗产法》，这是中国人的首创，对于中国的非物质文化遗产保护意义重大，对于人类的文化遗产保护也具有重大意义。除此之外，国家及地方还十分重视非物质文化遗产保护其他相关的、配套的法律、法规、条例等的建设，努力构建一个比较完备的法律体系。

5. 积极申报联合国教科文组织"人类非物质文化遗产代表作名录"（最初叫作"人类口头和非物质遗产代表作名录"）和"人类急需保护的非物质文化遗产名录"。至去年年底为止，我国入选联合国教科文组织"人类非物质文化遗产代表作名录"的项目已达29项，它们分别是：昆曲（2001）；古琴艺术（2003）；蒙古族长调民歌（与蒙古国联合申报）、新疆维吾尔木卡姆艺术（2005）；中国蚕桑丝织技艺、福建南音、南京云锦、安徽宣纸、贵州侗族大歌、广东粤剧、《格萨尔》史诗、浙江龙泉青瓷、青海热贡艺术、藏戏、新疆《玛纳斯》、蒙古族呼麦、甘肃花儿、西安鼓乐、朝鲜族农乐舞、书法、篆刻、剪纸、雕版印刷、传统木结构营造技艺、端午节、妈祖信俗（2009）；中医针灸、京剧（2010）；中国皮影戏（2011）。入选"人类急需保护的非物质文化遗产名录"的项目共有7项。

6.重视非物质文化遗产基础理论的研究与学科的建设。非物质文化遗产保护是一项实践性很强的事业,但也是人文社会科学的一个独特的研究对象、研究领域,有其深奥复杂的规律性、学理性,需要深入开展对它的基本理论研究,进行非物质文化遗产学的学科建设。在这方面,中国较早上升到理性的自觉,多年来积极探索,产生了一大批学术研究成果。如由王文章先生主编的《非物质文化遗产概论》,便是国内第一部系统探讨非物质文化遗产基础理论研究方面的系统著作,同时也是第一部非物质文化遗产学领域的高校教材。该书于2006年由文化艺术出版社初版,被人们称为"学术版"。此后,又于2008年,根据高校教学需要,增补、修订为一部高校教材重新出版。今年,又根据《中华人民共和国非物质文化遗产法》的基本精神以及近年来中国非物质文化遗产保护领域的一些新的创造性的探索和新产生的实践经验,再一次对该著作做了全面的修订,重新再版,以满足社会上和高等学校对于非物质文化遗产基础理论研究及高校教学的需求。基础理论研究与学科建设方面的成就,为非遗保护工作提供了宝贵的理论上的指导与智力上的支持等。

当然,中国的非物质文化遗产保护,在具体的实践和探索的过程中,也会遇到一些问题,面临一些无法回避的挑战。比如,一些地方的政府官员和部分公众对于保护非物质文化遗产的意义的认识及行动上的自觉意识还有待提高;一些地方还存在着颇为明显的"重申报,轻保护"的现象;各地在非物质文化遗产保护工作中,还普遍存在着人才匮乏、资金不足的现象等。这些都是需要在未来的保护实践中不断加以解决的问题。对于中国非物质文化遗产的保护,我们依然任重而道远。

各国、各民族创造的杰出的非物质文化遗产,不只属于各自的国度和民族,它们也是属于全人类的共同精神财富。今天,中国人已经自觉地认识到,努力保护中国的非物质文化遗产,就是对整个人类文化作出的重要贡献。我们将与包括美国在内的各国加强非物质文化遗产保护领域的交流与合作,认真学习、借鉴世界各国非物质文化遗产保护方面的成功经验,也愿将中国在非物质文化遗产保护方面所进行的探索与实践、所获得的有益经验,与世界各国共同分享,愿与世界各国共同努力,积极协作,竭尽全力保护属于全人类的文化遗产和精神家园。

Creative Practice of China's Intangible Cultural Heritage Protection

Li Xinfeng

Executive Deputy Director of China Intangible Cultural Heritage Protection Center, Chinese National Academy of Arts

Abstract: Rich and colorful intangible cultural heritage created by humans vividly demonstrates cultural diversity and provides important guarantee for mankind's sustainable development. China boasts rich intangible cultural heritage. In China, protection of intangible cultural heritage has become the consensus of the whole society and a significant part of the national culture development strategy. China has attached great importance to earnestly studying and actively drawing on the effective practices and valuable experiences of other countries in intangible cultural heritage protection. Meanwhile, special attention has also been paid to the specific conditions of intangible cultural heritage protection in China and the law of development and uniqueness of China's intangible cultural heritage has been respected. Moreover, the initiative and enthusiasm of all sides has been brought into full play according to the actual needs of protection, and a series of valuable and creative explorations and practices have been conducted in intangible cultural heritage protection.

The cultural heritage created by mankind can be roughly divided into two categories: tangible cultural heritage, i.e., cultural relics, including movable and non-movable cultural relics; intangible cultural heritage, referring to the heritage passed down by the inheritors. The rich and colorful intangible cultural heritage created by humans vividly demonstrates cultural diversity, represents inexhaustible and valuable resources for cultural innovation and creation, and important guarantee of humankind's sustainable development. China is rich in intangible cultural heritage. In China, protection of intangible cultural heritage has become the consensus of the whole society and an important part of the national culture development strategy. It has received unprecedented attention.

To comprehensively advance the world-wide protection of intangible cultural heritage, the UNESCO adopted the Convention for the Safeguarding of the Intangible Cultural Heritage (hereafter referred to as the Convention) in 2003. The Convention has played a very important role in the protection of intangible cultural heritage throughout the world. China acceded to the Convention in 2004, the next year after it was adopted, and it's well-known that most of the countries in the world have joined the Convention. However, it's strange that a small number of countries, including the United States, so far have not joined this Convention and the Convention on the Protection and Promotion of the Diversity of Cultural Expressions (adopted by the UNESCO in 2005), another international document of enormous significance to protection of the cultural diversity worldwide.

China has endeavored to follow the essential spirit and fundamental norms of Convention for the Safeguarding of the Intangible Cultural Heritage adopted by UNESCO in 2003. Moreover, it attaches great importance to earnestly studying and actively drawing on the effective practices and valuable experiences of other countries in intangible cultural heritage protection. Meanwhile, special attention has also been paid to the concrete conditions of intangible cultural heritage protection in China, and the law of development and special characteristics of China intangible cultural heritage have been taken into account. Furthermore, the initiative and enthusiasm of the government, experts, inheritors, society and enterprises have been brought into full play according to the actual needs of protection, and a series of valuable and creative explorations and practices have been conducted in intangible cultural heritage protection.

1.We will strive to build an effective intangible cultural heritage protection system that conforms to China's reality. The creative practices of China's institutional construction for protection of intangible cultural heritage are systematic and multifaceted. They mainly include:

—Inter-departmental joint conference system of intangible cultural heritage protection.

—Expert committee system on intangible cultural heritage protection. The expert committees are formed at the Ministry of Culture, and in all the provinces, cities and autonomous regions. Effective expert consultancy system has been established to ensure scientific and professional protection of intangible cultural heritage.

—Intangible cultural heritage survey system. Under the auspices of the government, nation-wide surveys of intangible cultural heritage have been conducted to gain an all-round view of the distribution of intangible cultural heritage.

—Representative intangible cultural heritage directory system. We have established representative intangible cultural heritage directory systems at the national, provincial, municipal, and county levels, among which the most important is the national evaluation and management mechanism of representative intangible cultural heritage directory. Until now, China has published three batches of national representative intangible cultural heritage lists with 1219 items. Over the programs on the national list, we have been exploring dynamic management to ensure the real representativeness of those listed in the directory. It means that the intangible cultural heritage if found to be not representative enough may be taken off the list.

—Protection system of representative inheritors of representative intangible cultural heritage. The representative inheritors of representative intangible cultural heritage at the national, provincial, municipal, and county levels are evaluated, verified, supported and financed. So far, the government has verified a total of 1488 representative inheritors of representative intangible cultural heritage in three batches.

—The second Saturday of each June is designated as "Cultural Heritage Day". During the Cultural Heritage Day, a rich variety of activities have been held, including exhibitions, shows, publicity activities, and lectures, to involve more people in the protection of intangible cultural heritage.

—The traditional festivals such as the Lunar New Year's Eve, the Dragon Boat Festival, the Tomb-sweeping Day, and the Mid-autumn Day have been designated as national public holidays. The traditional festivals of all countries and all nationalities are important cultural expressions, which constitute a special and important category of intangible cultural heritage. Therefore, they have drawn wide attention. Before 2008, among traditional Chinese festivals, only the Spring Festival had been designated as a three-day national public holiday, excluding the Lunar New Year's Eve. Starting from the New Year's Day of 2008, the Tomb-sweeping Day, the Dragon Boat Festival, and the Mid-autumn Day have also been listed as national public holidays. The Spring Festival still has three days of leave, but the time has been changed from January 1-3 to between the Lunar New Year's Eve and January 2nd on the lunar calendar. It means that the Lunar New Year's Eve, an important traditional festival, has been included into the national public holidays. The adjustment in the national public holidays has had very positive effect on improving the cultural awareness of the public, and on better protecting traditional festival culture.

—An administrative institution for protection of intangible cultural heritage has been established under the Ministry of Culture—The Department of Intangible Cultural Heritage. Administrative institutions for protection of intangible cultural heritage have also been established in the provinces, autonomous regions, and municipalities directly under the central government.

—Establishment of a state-level professional academic and consultancy institution for protection of intangible cultural heritage—China Intangible Cultural Heritage Protection Center. Such centers have also been founded at the levels of provinces, autonomous regions, municipalities directly under the central government, and the prefecture-level cities.

The above highly-efficient and powerful institutional construction has provided the most fundamental and solid institutional guarantee for the protection of China's intangible cultural heritage.

2.Other protection methods are actively explored and practiced. In light of the actual conditions for intangible culture protection, China has attached great importance to seeking for and practicing various effective methods of protection. They mainly include:

—Protection driven by state-level programs.

—Implementation of cultural heritage inheritor protection mode with protection of representative inheritors of the state-level programs as the focus.

—Production-based protection: It is a protection method adopted in the production process, focusing on keeping the authenticity, integrity and inheritability of intangible cultural heritage, taking the effective inheritance of the workmanship of intangible cultural heritages as the premise, and resorting to the means of production, circulation, and sale, to transform the intangible cultural heritage and related resources into cultural products.

—Overall protection of cultural ecological reserves (see below for details).

—Rescue protection method—taking rescue protection measures over some endangered intangible cultural heritage.

—Digital protection method—utilizing modern digital technology to document, collect, sort through, and file intangible cultural heritage;.

—Seeking the method of tax reduction and exemption for products featuring intangible cultural heritage.

—Seeking the method of encouraging society, especially the competent enterprises that hold culture in high regard, to actively participate in the protection of intangible cultural heritage.

3.Special attention has been paid to overall protection, and vigorous efforts have been made to promote the construction of cultural ecological reserves. China implements overall protection over certain regions where the representative programs with distinct characteristics of intangible cultural heritage are concentrated, and where the forms and connotations of the intangible cultural heritage are kept intact, and actively promotes the construction of cultural ecological reserves. So far, China has established 12 state-level cultural ecological reserves or cultural ecological protection experimental areas, which cover Minnan culture, Huizhou culture, Regong culture, Qiang Ethnic group culture, Hakka culture (Meizhou), Tujia and Miao Nationalities culture in Wuling Mountainous Area (Western Hunan Province), marine fishing culture (Xiangshan), Jinzhong culture, Weishui culture, Diqing ethnic culture, Dali culture and Shanbei culture.

4.Great attention has been given to the legislation for protection of intangible cultural heritage. In 2001, the Intangible Cultural Heritage Law of the People's Republic of China, the most important law in the field, was promulgated and came into effect. It has provided fundamental legal support for protection of China's intangible cultural heritage. China's enactment of this law is the first attempt of the kind in the world, which is of great significance for the protection of intangible cultural heritage both in China and the world at large. Besides, the state and the local governments have attached great importance to the enactment of other relevant laws and regulations so as to construct an all-round legal system for intangible cultural heritage protection.

5.We actively apply for entering China's intact cultural heritage into UNESCO's Representative List of Intangible Cultural Heritage of Humanity (originally Masterpieces of the Oral and Intangible Cultural Heritage of Humanity) and List of Intangible Cultural Heritage in Need of Urgent Safeguarding. By the end of 2011, we had 29 items of intangible cultural heritage listed in the UNESCO's Representative List of the Intangible Cultural Heritage of Humanity, including Kunqu opera (2001); guqin and its music (2003); Uyghur Muqam of Xinjiang, Mongolian long tuned songs (jointly applied with Mongolia) (2005); sericulture and silk craftsmanship of China, Fujian Nanyin music, Craftsmanship of Nanjing Yunjin brocade, traditional handicraft for making Xuan paper of Anhui, grand song of dong Nationality, Yue opera, gesar epic tradition, traditional firing technology of Longquan celadon of Zhejiang, Regong art of Qinghai, Tibetan opera, Manas of Xinjiang, Mongolian art of singing Khoomei, Hua'er, Xi'an wind and percussion ensemble, Farmers' dance of China's Korean ethnic group, Chinese calligraphy, art of Chinese seal engraving, Chinese paper cut, China engraved printing technique, Chinese traditional architectural craftsmanship for timber-framed structures, Dragon Boat Festival, Mazu belief and customs (2009); acupuncture and moxibustion, Peking opera (2010) and Chinese shadow puppetry (2011). Seven programs have been entered into the List of Intangible Cultural Heritage in Need of Urgent Safeguarding.

6. Importance has been attached to the basic theoretical research and discipline construction on intangible cultural heritage. Intangible cultural heritage protection is a practice-dominated undertaking, and it's also a unique subject of humanities and social sciences. Basic research in this field involving profound knowledge and complicated reasoning should be conducted in depth. And the discipline construction of intangible cultural heritage should be promoted. In this respect, China has made active explorations in recent years, and has produced a large number of academic achievements, such as the Introduction to the Intangible Cultural Heritage edited by Mr. Wang Wenzhang, China's first book to systematically study the basic theories of intangible cultural heritage and the first textbook compiled for the higher institutions about intangible cultural heritage. The book was first published by the Culture & Art Publishing House in 2006, and it is known as the "academic edition". In 2008, it was republished as a college textbook after supplementation and revision according to the demand of the higher institutions. This year, according to the spirit of the Intangible Cultural Heritage Law of the People's Republic of China and the new and creative explorations and the new experience in the field of intangible cultural heritage protection, the book was revised comprehensively and published again, to meet the demand for the basic theoretical research of intangible cultural heritage by society and the higher institutions. The achievements in the basic theoretical research and discipline construction have provided valuable theoretical guidance and intellectual support to the intangible cultural heritage protection.

Of course, in the process of practices and explorations, China's protection of intangible cultural heritage may encounter some problems, and face some unavoidable challenges. For example, the understanding and awareness of the significance of the protection of intangible cultural heritage of some local government officials and part of the public need to be further improved. In some places, there exists the phenomenon of putting emphasis on application and neglecting protection. The problems of the lack of competent professionals and fund for the protection of intangible cultural heritage are widespread. These problems should be solved in the future protection practice. We still have a long way to go in intangible cultural heritage protection.

The distinguished intangible cultural heritage created by all the countries and nations belongs not simply to the countries and nations of its origin. In fact, it is the common spiritual wealth of all humankind. Today, Chinese people have realized that efforts made for the protection of China's intangible cultural heritage are important contributions to the human culture. We will strengthen communication and cooperation with people of all countries in the world in intangible cultural heritage protection, including the United States, earnestly study and draw on the experience of other countries, and share with all the countries the beneficial experience we have acquired in the experimental attempts and practices of intangible cultural heritage protection. We'd like to work together with all the countries and make utmost efforts to protect the cultural heritage and spiritual homeland of the mankind.

UNIT TWO: CULTURE AND HISTORY

第二单元 文化与历史

中国社会科学院荣誉学部委员，民族文学研究所研究员刘魁立做主题发言
《保护文化遗产，践行国际公约》
Liu Kuili, Honorary Academician of Chinese Academy of Social Sciences,
Research Fellow of the Institute of Ethnic Literature
"Safeguarding Cultural Heritage and Implementing International Conventions"

"杰出贡献教授理事会"成员，历史学教授，
罗格斯大学纽华克分校"种族、文化与现代经验"学院院长克莱门特·普莱斯做主题发言
《纪念一种新的美国史和美国文化》
Clement Alexander Price, Board of Governors Distinguished Service Professor of History and Director,
The Rutgers Institute on Ethnicity, Culture, and the Modern Experience, Rutgers University
"Commemorating a New American History and Culture"

中国艺术研究院艺术创作研究中心及陶瓷艺术研究中心主任朱乐耕做主题发言
《论中国社会发展背景下的陶瓷艺术创作》
Zhu Legeng, Director of Art Creation Center and Ceramic Art Center, Chinese National Academy of Arts
"Artistic Creation of Ceramics in the Context of Social Development in China"

中国艺术研究院中国文化研究所研究员摩罗做主题发言
《文化权利是国家主权和国家利益的组成部分》
Mo Luo, Research Fellow of Institute of Chinese Culture , Chinese National Academy of Arts
"Cultural Right is an Integral Part of National Sovereignty and National Interests"

美国现代语言学会学术传播部主任，
美国波莫纳学院媒介研究教授凯思琳·菲茨帕特里克做主题发言
《我们怎样阅读与写作：社会网络与文学社群》
Kathleen Fitzpatrick, Director of Scholarly Communication,
Modern Language Association; Professor of Media Studies, Pomona College
"How We Read and Write: Social Networks and Literary Communities"

中国艺术研究院院长助理，文化发展战略研究中心主任贾磊磊做主题发言
《中国电影表述的文化价值观》
Jia Leilei, President Assistant of Chinese National Academy of Arts, Director of Cultural Development
Strategy Research Center, CNAA
"Cultural Values Presented in Chinese Movies"

保护文化遗产，践行国际公约

刘魁立

中国社会科学院荣誉学部委员，民族文学研究所研究员

内容提要： 长期以来，人们常常特别关注文化的物质层面，而轻视物质中蕴含的思想和精神以及整个非物质文化的重要意义和价值，对蕴藏在广大民众中间的最普遍、最常用、最基础的非物质文化反倒视而不见。这种对于文化的偏见，容易造成文化的民族性、广泛性及其深厚历史底蕴的丧失，使文化日益趋同化，缺乏应有的生命力和创造力。本文分析非物质文化遗产的可共享性特点，这一特点无疑会对文化多样性的充分实现、对推进整个人类的文化发展，提供强大助力。联合国教科文组织关于非物质文化遗产保护的设计理念之一，在于正确处理民族文化与人类文化的关系，在于确认特定民族文化的人类文化地位；其意义在于借助这个文化规律，为人类社会寻求一个超越物质独占、消弭由之而造成的人与人、社会与社会之间的纷争，并推进人类文化的持续的繁荣发展。

  自从联合国教科文组织2001年公布首批"人类口头和非物质文化遗产"代表作以来，特别是自联合国教科文组织于2003年发布《保护非物质文化遗产公约》以来，"非物质文化遗产"这一新鲜的术语，在短短数年时间里，在我国各地、各民族以及各阶层中成为最热门的词汇。这说明非物质文化遗产是一项具有重大意义，与广大民众生活密切相关，受到大家特别关爱的宝贵的精神财富。作为文化领域中的一项重要举措，非物质文化遗产保护问题的提出以及受到广泛关注，有着深刻的历史文化背景。

  广义上说，文化是人类所创造的一切物质产品和精神产品的总和。那些被人类创造或改造过的、满足人类某种需求、表达某种意图的"物"，通常被称为物质文化。非物质文化是指人类创造的不以物质载体形式呈现的成果。人生下来，不单单靠物质存在于世。物质仅仅提供人作为生物体生存的基础性条件。更重要的是，人要靠非物质文化的习得和传承，才能不断成长，才能成其为人。从学说话、学走路，到懂得道理、丰富知识、掌握技艺，一天天、一年年都在和非物质文化打交道。对于社会群体来说，尤其如此。有宝贵发达的非物质文化作为基础，才有丰富的物质文化以及幸福和谐的社会生活环境。

长期以来，对文化的认识存在一定程度的偏差：人们常常特别关注文化的物质层面，而轻视了物质中蕴含的思想和精神以及整个非物质文化的重要意义和价值。同时，在关注非物质文化的时候，又特别重视精英文化和主流文化，对蕴藏在广大民众中间的最普遍、最常用、最基础的非物质文化反倒视而不见。这种对于文化的偏见，容易造成文化的民族性、广泛性及其深厚历史底蕴的丧失，使文化日益趋同化，缺乏应有的生命力和创造力。

国际社会为了人类的整体价值和长远利益，联合国教科文组织于2003年通过了《保护非物质文化遗产公约》，并且提出保护人类文化多样性的主张。因为保护和继承优秀文化传统，坚持文化发展多元性和多样性是人类创造力持续发展的必要条件。联合国教科文组织2001年通过的《世界文化多样性宣言》指出："文化表现形式，包括传统文化表现形式的多样性，是个人和各民族能够表达并同他人分享自己的思想和价值观的重要因素。"2005年10月20日，联合国教科文组织大会第33次会议通过的《保护和促进文化表现形式多样性公约》指出："文化在不同时间和空间具有多样形式，这种多样性体现为人类各民族和各社会文化特征和文化表现形式的独特性和多元性。"

《保护和促进文化表现形式多样性公约》还特别指出："文化多样性是人类的一项基本特性"，"文化多样性创造了一个多姿多彩的世界，它使人类有了更多的选择，得以提高自己的能力和形成价值观，并因此成为各社区、各民族、各国可持续发展的一股主要推动力。"

在认真践行国际性公约和文件的过程中，中国广大民众和各级文化行政领导部门根据自己的实际状况，创造了一系列保护和传承非物质文化遗产的有效方法和实际经验。

人总是生活在一定的社会群体当中，非物质文化规范着这一群体的生活方式、价值取向。因此，它是维系和巩固群体团结和谐的黏合剂，是一定群体、一定民族凝聚力的载体。无论你的政治态度如何，无论你的年龄、性格如何，无论你有怎样不同于其他人的经历，无论你处在如何异样的生活环境中，本民族历史传承的非物质文化总会无形地把你同自己的社会群体、同自己的民族牢牢地联系在一起。因此，非物质文化也是每一个人的民族身份的标识，是一个民族的所有成员文化认同的依据。

同时，每个民族善待自己的传统文化，继承和弘扬自己优秀的民族文化传统，也是关乎人类文化如何发展的大事。我们越来越清楚地认识到，民族的立场和全人类的立场并不是截然对立的。保护自己的优秀文化传统不仅仅是单纯地涉及一个国家、一个民族文化建设的重要问题，也是人类文化多样性发展的基础和保证。

严格地说，物质文化和非物质文化是彼此相依密不可分的，正如一件产品和这件产品的制作技术不可分开一样。但同时，它们又是截然不同的两种事物。为了表述方便，我们只有在同与物质文化的比较中，才可以更清晰、更深刻地体验到非物质文化的本质特点。

首先，每一个物质文化对象，是不能够被不同主体所共同持有、共同享用、共同传承的。而非物质文化对象则是可以共享的。这里我所说的"可共享性"，不是指不同的人对同一文化对象能够共同感知、共同感受、共同欣赏、共同品味等，而是指不同的人，不同的社群、族群，能够共同持有、共同享用、共同传承同一个文化成果。这种非物质文化的可共享性不受时空的限制。文化共享的历史与人类文化发展的历史共短长。人类文化发展的历史，是文化创造的历史，同时也是不同人群、社群、民族、国家相互间文化共享的历史。与非物质文化遗产可共享性相关联的一个重要的基本概念就是前面已经提到的"文化多样性"。如果没有这种非物质文化遗产的可共享性，就无从实现人类文化的多样性发展。

非物质文化遗产的可共享性无疑会对文化多样性的充分实现、对推进整个人类的文化发展，提供强大助力。以我个人的理解，联合国教科文组织关于非物质文化遗产保护的设计理念之一，在于正确处理民族文化与人类文化的关系，在于确认特定民族文化的人类文化地位。

教科文组织推动非物质文化遗产保护的意义，恰恰在于借助这个文化规律为人类社会寻求一个超越物质独占、消弭由之而造成的人与人、社会与社会之间的纷争，并能推进人类文化繁荣发展的有效途径。因此针对非物质文化遗产的保护，我们不仅要有民族的视角，还要有全人类的视角。用人类的视角来认识和保护我们各自民族的非物质文化遗产，将使我们的保护工作具有更广泛、更长久、更深刻的意义。

如果说，物质文化成果一旦被人创造出来，它便脱离开人而独立存在；那么，非物质文化则以人为载体，以人的观念、人的知识、人的技能、人的行为作为其表现形态。

上述这些特点，对于我们认识作为非物质文化一部分的"非物质文化遗产"的本质，同样具有重要意义。

我们认识到，现在所谈的"非物质文化遗产"并不囊括非物质文化的全部。"非物质文化遗产"的概念源于我国于2004年8月28日业已批准的联合国教科文组织2003年《保护非物质文化遗产公约》。该公约对"非物质文化遗产"的定义是：

"'非物质文化遗产'指被各群体、团体，有时被个人视为其文化遗产的各种实践、表演、表现形式、知识和技能及其有关的工具、实物、工艺品和文化场所。各个群体和团体随着其所处环境、与自然界的相互关系和历史条件的变化不断使这种代代相传的非物质文化遗产得到创新，同时使他们自己具有一种认同感和历史感，从而促进了文化多样性和人类创造力的发展。"

在这个定义中，不仅明确指出了非物质文化遗产的主体、对象、功能等重要因素，同时还包含了主体对对象的价值判断。

在我国推行非物质文化遗产保护工作的多年实践中，特别强调非物质文化遗产在民众生活当中的生命力、历史的传承性和在现实当中的实际功能。传统只有在对当今社会生活发挥积极作用时，才能体现其自身的价值，否则是没有实际意义的。所以说，非物质文化遗产保护不是为了回忆昨天的历史，发思古之幽情，而是为了今天广大民众的生活和明天的美好未来，是为了人类文化的多样性发展。

进入当代社会历史阶段以来，我们在民间传统文化的搜集、整理方面，做了大量工作，但是"非物质文化遗产"的概念的提出，使这项活动走向一个新的阶段。"非物质文化遗产"的概念同以往"民族民间文化"、"传统文化"、"传统习俗"、"民间艺术"、"民间手工艺"等一系列概念，有了本质的区别，体现了新的视角，获得了新的意义和内涵：

1. 获得了新的价值评估。非物质文化遗产是民族文化的精华，

是民族智慧的象征，是民族精神的结晶，是民族文化之根、民族精神之魂。

2. 对它的功能有了新的理解。认为它可以激发文化的生命力和创造力，建设精神家园。

3. 使地方文化、群体文化获得了全人类意义。将文化由民族的视角提升到全人类的视角。我国各民族的非物质文化遗产是人类文化的优秀成果和宝贵财富。同样地，世界其他族群和人群的非物质文化遗产成果也是人类共同的宝贵财富。我个人有幸三次赴马来西亚做过关于中元节的考察，我也深入西伯利亚俄罗斯旧礼仪派当中，考察他们的古老民歌和文化空间，分别写过推介马来西亚和俄罗斯非物质文化遗产的文章。

综上所述，"非遗"保护便不再是学界或部分人感兴趣的对象，而是受到全民的前所未有的关注和参与，保护"非遗"成为民族文化建设的有机组成部分。

联合国教科文组织公布了人类非物质文化遗产代表作名录，由于我国民族众多、人口众多，所以建立了相应的四级名录制度，形成了有序的体系。

由于非物质文化遗产的载体是传承人，历代的非物质文化遗产传承人同样也是值得我们高度尊重、高度评价的文化历史的伟大创造者。所以在评选和公布代表作名录之外，我国又建立了评选和公布非物质文化遗产代表性传承人的制度。这是对相关国际公约等文件的发展。代表作名录和代表性传承人的名录是保护非物质文化遗产的重要途径。这两个名录的主旨不是光荣榜，不是广告，也不是著作权性质的依据，而是保护单位和传承人的庄严承诺，是他们在人民大众、在民族乃至国际社会面前立下约言，要为广大民众今天的福祉和明天的文化建设承担起保护和传承自己所代表的非物质文化遗产的责任。在这方面我亲自观察到很多可歌可泣的生动事例，很多传承人把保护非遗项目看成是自己生命的最高价值和意义。在传承和弘扬方面也创造出不少好的经验。例如，古琴进校园，通过积木游戏的方法介绍和传播中国传统木结构营造技艺，再如通过建桑基鱼塘为蚕丝纺织技艺创造一个良好的生态链系统。

另外，我们知道，如果没有好的社会环境，非物质文化遗产项

目也罢,代表性传承人也罢,都难以单独地传承和保护非物质文化遗产,显然需要有相应的有利于保护和传承的社会条件和社会氛围。于是,中国文化行政领导部门又提出文化生态保护区的建设问题。所谓"文化生态保护区"就是指"以保护非物质文化遗产为核心,对历史文化积淀丰厚、存续状态良好,具有重要价值和鲜明特色的文化形态进行整体性保护,经文化行政领导部门批准设立的特定区域"。文化生态保护区的建设还带有某些实验的性质,正在摸索实践,创造经验。

在非物质文化遗产的保护工作中,以我的了解还有一些有待改进的地方。例如,在某些地方特别关注非物质文化遗产项目的申报和选定,而缺少有力的措施,从而影响有效地保护非物质文化遗产。其次,有个别地方和部门,片面追求旅游的效益,而忽视非物质文化遗产的文化性质和非物质文化遗产保护的根本要求,对这些项目的真实性、完整性和传承性等特点缺乏应有的关注。在以往的实践中,我们看到了一些文化产业与"非遗"保护相辅相成、共存共荣的典型范例,同时也看到一些只顾短期经济效益而危害非遗保护的事例。有些事例,从长远的角度看既危害"非遗"的传承,也影响文化产业的长期发展。

这里有很多需要思考和探讨的问题。在践行各项国际公约和文件的基础上,需要我们各国人士共同努力,以使保护和传承人类非物质文化遗产这项重要的文化事业,达到能令今人生活康乐,能为后人创造幸福的美好愿景。

Safeguarding Cultural Heritage and Implementing International Conventions

Liu Kuili

Honorary Academician of Chinese Academy of Social Sciences, Research Fellow of the Institute of Ethnic Literature

Abstract: For a long time, people usually pay special attention to the material level of culture, and despise thought and spirit contained in the material as well as the significance and value of intangible culture which is the most universal, common and fundamental in people's life. This cultural prejudice could result in the loss of cultural nationality and universality, as well as deep historical background, thus leads to increasingly converged culture which lacks of the due vitality and creativity. The paper analyzes the shared characteristic of the intangible cultural heritage, which undoubtedly provides powerful boost to the full realization of the cultural diversity and cultural development of the entire humankind. One of UNESCO's design concepts of intangible cultural heritage protection lies in correct treatment of relationship between national culture and human culture and the confirmation of the human cultural status of specific national culture. Its significance lies in that with the help of this cultural law, transcendence of material exclusive can be sought for human society and the caused disputes between peoples or between societies can be eliminated, moreover the continued prosperity of human culture can be promoted.

Since UNESCO published the first batch of masterpieces of the "Oral and Intangible Cultural Heritage" in 2001 and the Convention for the Safeguarding of the Intangible Cultural Heritage in 2003 especially, the "intangible culture", a fresh term, has become a catchword in all ethnic groups and all walks of life across China in just a few years. This phenomenon indicates that the intangible cultural heritage is the precious spiritual wealth of great significance and concern, and closely related to common people's life. As an important measure in the cultural field, the safeguarding of intangible cultural heritage has been put forward and attracted widespread attention against a profound historical and cultural background.

In a broad sense, culture is the sum of all material and spiritual goods created by humankind. Those "objects" created or transformed to meet some kind of human needs or express some intentions are often referred to as material culture. Intangible culture refers to the achievements created by humankind but not presented in the form of material carriers. Everyone born in the world cannot live by simply relying on materials. Materials only provide the basic conditions for the human survival as living beings. More importantly, people can only be growing and become the real human beings by acquiring the intangible cultures and pass on them to new generations. From learning to speak and walk to understanding the truth, acquiring more knowledge and mastering skills, people are dealing with intangible cultures day by day and year by year. It is the same case especially for social groups. It is the developed and valuable intangible cultures that provide a basis for the rich material cultures and happy and harmonious social environment.

For a long time, there has been a deviation in the recognition of culture to some extent: people usually pay special attention to the material level of culture, and despise thought and spirit contained in the material as well as the significance and value of intangible culture. When attention is paid to intangible culture, special emphasis is laid on the elite culture and the mainstream culture. The most universal, common and fundamental intangible culture contained in common people's life, however, has been neglected instead. This cultural prejudice could result in the loss of cultural nationality and universality, as well as deep historical background, thus leads to increasingly converged culture which lacks of the due vitality and creativity.

For the overall value and long-term interests of human being, UNESCO passed Convention for the Safeguarding of the Intangible Cultural Heritage in 2003, advocating the protection of the diversity of human culture. Protection and inheritance of excellent intangible cultural heritage and insistence of culture pluralism and diversity are the necessities of the sustainable development of human creativity. The Universal Declaration on Cultural Diversity adopted by UNESCO in 2001 points out, "The diversity of cultural expressions, including traditional cultural expressions, is an important factor enabling individuals and nations to express and share their ideas and values with others." The Convention on the Protection and Promotion of the Diversity of Cultural Expressions adopted by the 33rd session of the UNESCO General Conference on October 20, 2005 states, "Culture takes diverse forms across time and space and this diversity is embodied in the uniqueness and plurality of the identities and cultural expressions of the peoples and societies making up humanity."

In particular, the Convention on the Protection and Promotion of the Diversity of Cultural Expressions also points out that "cultural diversity is a defining characteristic of humanity", and "cultural diversity creates a rich and varied world, which increases the range of choices and nurtures human capacities and values, and therefore is a mainspring for sustainable development for communities, peoples and nations".

While seriously implementing the international conventions and documents, the majority of Chinese people and the cultural administrative departments at all levels, according to their actual situations, have created a series of effective methods and summed up practical experience in protecting and passing on intangible cultural heritage to new generations.

People live in a certain community, of which the way of life and value orientation are normalized by the intangible culture. Therefore, the intangible culture is the adhesive maintaining and strengthening the unity and harmony of the community, and a cohesion carrier for a certain community or a nation. Necessarily, the historically inherited intangible culture of a nation will invisibly but firmly link people with their community and their own nation regardless political attitude, age, temperament, experiences or the environment where they live. The intangible culture, therefore, is the national identification for everyone, providing a basis of cultural identity for all members of a nation.

Meanwhile, it is of great significance to the development of human culture for every nation to properly treat their traditional culture, and inherit and carry forward outstanding national cultural traditions. More and more clearly we have understood that the standpoint of a nation is not completely opposed to that of the mankind. Safeguarding excellent cultural traditions is not just an important issue to the cultural construction of a country or a nation, but also the foundation and guarantee for the diverse development of human culture.

Strictly, the tangible and the intangible cultures are inseparably dependent on each other as a product cannot be separated from the technology used to produce it. However, they are two things totally different. For the convenience of expression, we cannot experience the essential features of the intangible culture more clearly and more profoundly unless it is compared with the intangible culture.

First of all, an object of the intangible culture cannot be jointly possessed, enjoyed and inherited by different key actors, while that of the intangible culture can. That does not mean the same cultural object is felt, sensed, enjoyed and appreciated by different people, but means the same cultural achievement can be possessed, enjoyed and inherited by different people or different communities and groups. Such a characteristic transcends the spatiotemporal constraints and its history is as long as the development history of human culture, a history of cultural creation, and a history of different people, communities, races and countries sharing the culture. One of the important basic concepts associated with the shared characteristic of intangible cultural heritage is the abovementioned"cultural diversity". Without such a characteristic, there would be no way to achieve the diverse development of human culture.

The shared characteristic of the intangible cultural heritage undoubtedly provides powerful boost to the full realization of the cultural diversity and cultural development of the entire humankind. I think one of UNESCO's design concepts of intangible cultural heritage protection lies in correct treatment of relationship between national culture and human culture and the confirmation of the human cultural status of specific national culture.

The significance of UNESCO promoting the protection of intangible cultural heritage lies in that it is with the help of this cultural law that we can find an effective approach to transcend the material exclusive, eliminate disputes between peoples and between societies thus incurred, and promote the prosperity of human culture. Therefore, the intangible cultural heritage should be protected not only from the national perspective but also the perspective of the entire humankind, the latter of which will lead to more extensive, lasting and significant protection.

If the achievements of the material culture exist independently away from human being once there are created, then the intangible culture, with human beings as the carrier, is expressed by the form of man's concepts, knowledge, skills, and behaviors.

The above-mentioned characteristics are also very important for us to recognize the nature of the "intangible cultural heritage" as a part of the intangible culture.

We are aware that the discussed "intangible cultural heritage" does not include all of the intangible culture. This concept stems from UNESCO's Convention for the Safeguarding of the Intangible Cultural Heritage in 2003 approved by China on August 28, 2004 which defines the "intangible cultural heritage" as:

"The 'intangible cultural heritage' means the practices, representations, expressions, knowledge, skills – as well as the instruments, objects, artifacts and cultural spaces associated therewith – that communities, groups and, in some cases, individuals recognize as part of their cultural heritage. This intangible cultural heritage, transmitted from generation to generation, is constantly recreated by communities and groups in response to their environment, their interaction with nature and their history, and provides them with a sense of identity and continuity, thus promoting respect for cultural diversity and human creativity."

This definition not only clearly specifies the important factors of the intangible cultural heritage such as key actors, objects, and functions, etc, but also includes the key actors' evaluation over the objects.

In years' efforts of protecting the intangible cultural heritage, China has particularly emphasized on the heritage's vitality among people's lives, historical inheritance and actual function in reality. Only through playing an active role in current social life, can the tradition present its own value; otherwise it is of no practical significance. In this sense, the intangible cultural heritage is protected not for the memories of the past history, or to meditate on the remote past, but for people's current life and their brighter future, as well as the diverse development of human culture.

China has done a lot of work on collecting and sorting out the traditional folk culture in the contemporary era, but the proposal of the concept of "intangible cultural heritage" ushered in a new phase of this activity. Essentially different from a series of concepts in the past such as "national folk culture", "traditional culture", "traditional customs", "folk art", and "folk handicraft", etc, this concept presents a new perspective and acquires new meanings and connotation:

1. It acquires the new evaluation that intangible cultural heritage is the essence of national culture, symbolizing the national wisdom. It is the root of the national culture, the crystallization and the soul of the national spirit.

2. It acquires the new understanding of its functions. It is believed that the intangible cultural heritage can stimulate the cultural vitality and creativity, and thus build the spiritual home.

3. The local and community cultures acquire the significance of

the entire humankind. The culture is regarded from the perspective of the entire humankind instead of the national perspective only. The intangible cultural heritage of all ethnic groups in China is the outstanding achievements and precious assets of the human culture. Likewise, that of other ethnic groups and communities in the world is also shared wealth by the entire mankind. It is my honor to have personally investigated the Ghost Festival in Malaysia three times, and visit the Russia Old Believers in Siberia to make an in-depth study of their ancient folk songs and cultural space. Later I have written articles introducing and popularizing the intangible cultural heritage of Malaysia and Russia respectively.

In brief, the intangible cultural heritage protection has no longer interested the academia or some people, but an activity unprecedentedly concerned and joined by all, and an integral part of the national culture construction.

UNESCO has released the Representative List of the Intangible Cultural Heritage of Humanity, and China, due to its magnitude of ethnic groups and the large population, has established four-level lists correspondingly, thus forming an orderly system.

The carrier of the intangible cultural heritage is the successive inheritors, who are great creators of the cultural history deserving our high respect and evaluation. Therefore, in addition to the selection and announcement of the Representative List, China has established a system of selection and announcement of representative inheritors of the intangible cultural heritage. This is the development of relevant international conventions. The Representative List and the Representative Inheritors List are the important way to safeguard the intangible cultural heritage. These lists are not the hall of fame, advertisement, or the basis of the nature of copyright, but the solemn commitment made by the protection units and inheritors to the the public, the nation and even the international community that they will, for the well-being of the general public today and the cultural construction in future, take on the responsibility for safeguarding the intangible cultural heritage they represent and pass it on to new generations. I was touched in many occasions in which inheritors attached highest value and importance in their life to protecting intangible cultural heritage. There are many good experiences in inheritance and promotion. For example, the guqin, a traditional Chinese music instrument, is introduced to school; the Chinese traditional architectural craftsmanship for timber-framed structures is introduced and transmitted by the method of block play; and a well-run ecological chain system is created for the sericulture and silk craftsmanship by building mulberry fish ponds.

In addition, we know that favorable social conditions and atmosphere are needed; otherwise, neither intangible cultural heritage project nor the representative inheritors can separately inherit and safeguard the intangible cultural heritage. Thus, cultural departments of the Chinese government put forward the construction of eco-cultural protection area which refers to "the specific area established upon the approval of administrative departments in change of culture. Centering on the intangible cultural heritage, such areas are intended to protect in an all-round way well-preserved cultural forms with profound historic and cultural accumulation, significant value and distinctive features." As such areas are still experimental, the construction is on the way of exploration so as to accumulate experience.

As far as I know, the intangible cultural heritage protection is yet to be improved. For example, some places pay special attention to the nomination and selection of intangible cultural heritage projects, but the absence of powerful measures impedes effective protection. In some other cases, local governments and specific departments blindly pursue the benefits brought by tourism, but disregard the cultural nature of the intangible cultural heritage and the fundamental requirement of protecting it, and fail to pay due attention to the authenticity, integrity and inheritance of these projects. The past practice shows us some typical examples of interconnection, coexistence and co-prosperity between the cultural industry and the intangible cultural heritage protection, but there are also some examples in which the short-term economic benefits are pursued at the price of the intangible culture heritage protection. Some instances, from the long-term perspective, not only harm the intangible cultural heritage protection, but also affect the long-term development of the cultural industry.

There are many issues for consideration and discussion. Based on the implementation of the international conventions and documents, people of different countries need to work together for the important cultural cause of safeguarding and inheriting the intangible cultural heritage of humanity, thus realizing the beautiful vision that the people of our era live healthily and happily and our offspring will enjoy the happiness created by us.

纪念一种新的美国史和美国文化

克莱门特·普莱斯

"杰出贡献教授理事会"成员，历史学教授，罗格斯大学纽华克分校"种族、文化与现代经验"学院院长

内容提要： 一年多以来，美国一直沉浸在一场史无前例的纪念活动中。早在150年前的1861年4月，美国出人意料之外地进入了一个史无前例的革命时代。这个时代最首要的标志就是一个新政府即南方美利坚联盟国（简称邦联）的建立，以及由此导致的美利坚合众国（简称联邦）政府的分裂。可能在今天许多美国人看来，这个新政府以及它声称所代表的人民看待美国独立战争意义的方式是不可接受的，甚至令人反感。继政治势力一分为二后，一场漫长的噩梦般的内战随即打响。这场战争的野蛮与残酷也是世人公认的。事实上，据最新的学术研究表明，内战的死亡人数已经从1868年所估计的618000人上升到一个更加难以想象的数字：今年最新公布的752000人。在战争时代，甚至在现在，我们都应该扪心自问：到底是什么使如此多的生命丧生。

这场战争的中心争议在于一系列旨在回顾过去几次重大动荡中的开发活动，以及几项从根本上改变了美国进程并进而改变了现代世界历史的决议。从我的学术研究领域——非洲裔美国历史领域——的总体视角看来，战争的恐怖已经是举世公认的事实，此外，还存在另一个与当时美国人经历的恐惧息息相关的命题，即400多万美国黑人开始获得自由。

在"文化与历史"议题期间，本报告将探讨在何种意义上，美国南北战争的150周年纪念和所谓的黑奴大解放与对美国历史文化意识的一次重大调整相重合。这次重大调整的发展是美国南北战争和黑奴大解放的重要遗产之一，也是对世界范围内历史文化叙事的一次贡献。

我们先从两幅图像说起吧，这两幅图像同时创作于美国内战时期。第一幅是一张照片，照片的主人公是一位刚从战争中摆脱奴役的年轻非裔美国女性。这场大规模内战从1861年一直持续到1865年，而这张照片就是在1865年战争尾声时拍摄的。除了知道她住在弗吉尼亚州里士满（原南部邦联首府），靠给支持联邦政府的士兵洗衣服为生，我们对这位年轻女性一无所知。

我们应如何看待这张照片呢？为什么当美国历史学家以及其他人谈到美国内战和黑奴大解放时，这张照片极具代表性呢？这张照片又如何能够见证黑人在美利坚共和国地位的提升呢？首先，这位普通的洗衣工充满自信地面对镜头，我们现在认为这正是美国黑人重获自由的结果。自1865年照片拍摄之时到现在，时光荏苒，这位女性见证了美国的成长

洗衣妇（1865）

与发展。她的上身缝了一面美国国旗，胸前还别了一枚纽扣，或是胸针？上面刻着字母"US"，显然代表着"美国"。可以说，这位无名洗衣工正在以崭新的姿态走进美国，走进这个在邦联和罕有的奴隶制（4年前正是奴隶制催生了邦联）土崩瓦解后重获新生的国度。这张照片将出现在黛博拉·威利斯和芭芭拉·克劳萨姆尔的新作《解放的愿景：美国黑人和奴隶制时代》一书的封面上。该书是一本有关美国内战期间以及战后重获自由的黑奴的图像集。美国即将迎来庆祝黑奴大解放150年纪念，在这个具有纪念意义的时刻，这张洗衣妇照片以及其他许许多多有关重获自由或尚未获得自由的黑奴照片必将引起人们对黑人的同情与尊重，这标志着美国文化的重大变革。

第二幅是美国著名艺术家温斯洛·荷马于1865年创作的画——《安

德森维尔旁》或名《木屋门口》，描述了一位头裹非洲头巾的黑人女性走出破旧的木屋，迎接自由之光的情景。屋外的庭院长满了葫芦，房屋周围的木板错综交织。画中的妇女几乎位于画布正中，吸引着我们多半的注意力。在画的背景，我们能够隐约看到被俘的邦联军队被押往臭名昭著的邦联监狱——安德森维尔。画中的士兵或许有其存在的意义，但在荷马看来，其意义远不及这位摆

《安德森维尔旁》/《木屋门口》（1865）

脱奴役、走向自由的女奴重要。2011年，美国历史学家大卫·罗迪科尔在罗格斯大学举办的第三十届玛丽恩·汤普森系列讲座中表示，作为一名奴隶，她就是美国内战的症结所在，而她的命运也将预示着美国的未来。

这幅《安德森维尔旁》或《木屋门口》，直到20世纪60年代才展现在公众面前，此前一直被掩没在新泽西州一座旧房子的阁楼上。如今，此画被公认为是描述美国19世纪有关黑奴大解放的典型画作。不久，它将从拥有此画的纽瓦克美术馆运往华盛顿特区史密森尼学会的美国艺术博物馆进行展览，之后还将被运往纽约大都会艺术博物馆。也许荷马早就意识到，解放奴役、为自由而战才是美国内战冲突的根本，而美国却花了一个多世纪才认识到这一点。①

我以此开篇是因为，美国人民已重新审视美国历史和文化发展进程中那段转型时期的经历，使得这些令人联想起残酷的内战、无道的奴役，以及奴隶制瓦解的图像，乃至其他艺术品、历史古迹、无名的人物和事件，都上升到一个新的层面，成为具有纪念价值的珍品。

让我们来思考一个问题，为什么美国内战爆发150年后，人们对美国历史的感触会有如此大的提升？19世纪接近尾声之际，美国

民众对内战（上一代人之间发生的）的记忆全被更紧迫的任务——民族和解所淹没。美国为这一和解付出了近乎最大的代价，因为在此后一个世纪甚至更长时期内，美国不失时机地混淆了内战本身和废除奴隶制的深层意义，以及美利坚合众国需要怎样做才能彻底终结奴隶制。为原黑奴及其后代寻找正确位置的努力被搁置下来，留待后人解决，这就是我们这一代历史学家经常提到的"第二次重建"。

换言之，美利坚共和国对内战的深层含义选择了遗忘，它当时只是幻想着一个美国白人共和国，这使得其在战时治愈了旧伤，却为战后留下了新伤。②最重要的是，美国黑人，特别是那些住在奴隶制根深蒂固地区的黑人，仍旧过着穷困潦倒的生活，他们没有社会地位，无法改变自身及其后代的低下地位。尽管他们获得了自由，但仍不过是一个受人轻视、遭人讥讽的群体，徘徊在美国历史和国家未来发展的边缘地带。

1963年，即美国总统亚伯拉罕·林肯签署《奴隶解放宣言》100年后，马丁·路德·金在华盛顿大游行中发表"黑人尚未自由"的言论，这一言行让"二战"后的美国人——包括曾经受过奴役的黑人和未经历奴役的美国人的后代，重新反思起存在于这个民主共和国中的历史健忘症和种族主义悖论。

显然，1963年，受奴役的美国黑人后代已获得自由，但同时，人们对美国历史的研究方向和编写方式发生了重大改变，使得美利坚共和国对自由标准的令人可耻的定义遭受了严重挑战。事实上，在美国内战150周年这一相当长的纪念时期，真正标志历史领域和美国历史叙事发生关键性转变的，正是对美国内战和黑奴大解放的深入剖析。

1963年金博士发表著名演讲时，美国的史学研究便开始了一场新的转变。最先转变的是，受过良好教育的黑人也有资格获得奖学金，这一转变是在美国学校仍在实行种族隔离的环境下开始的，在当时算是影响深远，一直延续下来。那时，黑人学者和少数白人学者不受重视，他们在被称作"黑人历史"的葡萄园辛勤劳作，而不被承认。随着时间的推移，到第二次世界大战结束后，他们找到了新的方式谈论美利坚共和国的历史和黑人的地位问题，即通过繁复的仪式讲述有关美国过往的故事。③

有关黑人历史运动的第一部重要作品是由乔治·华盛顿·威廉姆斯撰写的。1884年，威廉姆斯完成了《美国黑人的种族问题》，该作品共分为两卷，威廉姆斯也因为这部作品被荣称为"黑人历史之父"。威廉姆斯并非专业的历史学家，用今天的历史学术标准来衡量的话，他的作品实属晦涩难懂。但他的确为黑人历史的探究作出了贡献，为后人的研究工作提供了可信的依据。威廉姆斯在该作品的前言部分这样写道：

> 我在散乱纷杂的记录美国历史的文章中努力寻找我的同胞，寻找我的流血流泪的同胞。我听到了他们的哀嚎呻吟，听到了他们脚链划过地面时发出的当啷声，听到了他们催人泪下的祈祷声，直到黑人种族遭受苦难、几个世纪痛苦挣扎的残酷现实死死裹住我的灵魂。描写这段历史的章节浸满了我的泪水；即使只过了一个时代，但我却觉得几经世事。

人们一直以崇敬的心情审视美国历史和文化，而威廉姆斯和追随他的两代历史学家却提供了新的视角。这标志着美利坚共和国"新历史"研究的开始，民权运动时期，新历史研究进入高潮。④

美国内战和黑奴大解放运动即将迎来150周年纪念，我们看到了有关美国史和美国文化的全新认识。如今，黑奴大解放被视为美国内战和动乱的最重要产物。曾几何时，美国黑人命运悲苦，一直渴望摆脱奴役，但在压迫面前却无能为力。而如今，他们被视为这场具有标志性的重大运动的积极参与者，他们将内战的导火索指向了奴隶制。对美国内战和黑奴大解放这段历史的重新认识，是逐渐走向成熟的民主社会的宝贵馈赠，尽管还存在一些不满的声音。对我的中国人文学科同行来说，这一认识的转变是如何发生的，将成为他们研究历史和文化的有用素材。

从知识和道德的层面上提升美国内战和废除奴隶制的这段历史给纪念时期造成了深重的影响。1963年，金博士站在林肯纪念碑前谈到了勇武、胆量、气魄，和长久笼罩美国历史的受人膜拜的美国白人历史人物以及这个国家对其自身的记忆，在当时掀起了一股思潮。而如今，各大会议、座谈会、影集，以及纷至沓来的新书都在向公众传达各种信息，可这同时又为新时期的美国带来了前所未有的复杂局面。眼下，美国社会对文化和社会多样性表现出前所未有的包容性，在这样的背景下，我们也许有理由相信即将到来的纪念活动可能会更加符合主流历史观点和民权运动的理念，这可是上一代人始料未及的。

从美国历史研究的模式及其丰富多样的文化景观中我们可知，纪念能够有效地帮助人文研究重启被历史健忘症封存已久的辩论话题。记忆是人类独有的天赋，存在争议的记忆又使我们成为有思想的人类，将我们置身于历史的兴衰起伏中,无论现在还是未来,激励我们不断反思,重新认识历史。

---

①详见彼得·H·伍德,《〈安德森维尔旁〉:温斯洛·荷马眼中的美国内战》(马萨诸塞州坎布里奇:哈佛大学出版社,2010年)。
②详见大卫·W·布莱特,《〈种族与团圆〉:美国人记忆中的内战》(马萨诸塞州坎布里奇:哈佛大学出版社,2010年)。
③详见奥古斯特·迈耶和艾略特·洛德韦克,《黑人历史和历史专业研究,1915—1980年》(伊利诺伊州乌尔班纳:伊利诺伊大学出版社,1986年)
④详见乔治·胡伯·富兰克林,《乔治·华盛顿·威廉姆斯传》(北卡罗来纳州达勒姆:杜克大学出版社,1998年)。

Clement Alexander Price

Board of Governors Distinguished Service Professor of History and Director, The Rutgers Institute on Ethnicity, Culture, and the Modern Experience, Rutgers University

Commemorating a New American History and Culture

Abstract: For more than a year, the United States has been immersed in a commemorative season like none other. Over 150 years ago, beginning in April, 1861, the nation entered, quite unexpectedly, a revolutionary era, an era like none other. It was marked, first and foremost, by the coming apart of the Union as the result of the establishment of an alternative Government—the Confederate States of America. That government, and those it claimed to represent, looked upon the meaning of the American Revolution in ways that many Americans today find unacceptable, possibly repugnant. A long, nightmarish Civil War soon followed the breach. The brutality of that War is widely acknowledged. Indeed, the most recent scholarship on the human costs of the War has increased the grim death toll from an 1868 estimate of 618,000 dead to the even more inconceivable number of 752,000, given to us this year. At the time of the War, and even now, we must ask ourselves: for what reasons were so many lives lost.

The War encircled a series of developments that in retrospect underscored significant upheavals and several transformative decisions that fundamentally changed the course of the American Republic and, as result, the evolution of modern world history. From the vantage point of my field of study, African American History, the horrors of the War are acknowledged, and yet there was an important corollary to the horrors Americans at that time lived through—the beginning of freedom for well over 4 million black Americans.

This presentation during the Culture and History session will explore how the sesquicentennial of the American Civil War and the so-called Great Emancipation coincides with a remarkable realignment of sensibilities about the history and culture of the United States. The evolution of this realignment is at an important legacy of the American Civil War and the Great Emancipation and a contribution to a useful historical and cultural narrative beyond the United States.

Let me begin with the screening of two images created around the same time in the United States, during the era of its Civil War. The first is a photograph taken of a young African American woman emancipated from slavery by the end of the War. That war raged from 1861 to 1865, when the photograph of this unknown American woman was taken. We know far too little about her, other than her occupation and that she lived in Richmond, Virginia, once the capital of the Confederate States of America. She was a washer woman for soldiers fighting to preserve the Union.

What are we to make of such a photograph? Why does it now symbolize a significantly important paradigm shift in the way American historians and others think of the American Civil War and the ending of slavery? How does this photograph acknowledge the ennobled status of black people in the history of the American Republic? First and foremost, the woman, who is identified simply as a Washer Woman,1865 Photographer unknown washer woman, is looking into the camera with a confidence we now associate as an attribute of black freedom in the United States. Over the vast number of years from 1865, when the photograph was taken, until now, she is looking

Washerwoman (1865)

at and into America. Sewn onto her garment is an American flag and attached to her garment is a buckle, or is it a brooch?, bearing the letters US, obviously symbolic of the United States. It is fair to say that the anonymous washer woman was entering the United States as a newly imagined person at a time when the nation was becoming a new nation, reinvented because of the collapse of the Confederacy and the peculiar institution of slavery that had brought the Confederacy into existence four years earlier. The photograph will appear on the dust jacket of a new book by Deborah Willis and Barbara Krauthamer. Their Envisioning Emancipation: Black Americans and the Era of Slavery is a compilation of images of emancipated blacks during and after the Civil War. During the present commemorative season, when the United States will observe the 150th anniversary of the Great Emancipation, the image of the washer woman, and scores of other images of black Americans on and beyond the threshold of freedom, will be looked upon with empathy and a respectfulness toward black Americans that marks a change in American culture.

The second image is a painting, also from 1865, by the distinguished American artist, Winslow Homer. Titled Near Andersonville, or At the Cabin Door, it depicts a black woman stepping out of her humble dwelling, into the sunlight of freedom, wrapped in an African headdress, and into a yard scattered with gourds and complicated by a boardwalk heading in opposite directions. The woman commands our attention as she is positioned near the center of the canvas. In the background, almost faintly, we can see captured Union troops being marched off to the infamous Confederate prison, Andersonville. The soldiers matter to us, of course, but in Homer's imagination they should not matter as much as the enslaved woman stepping into the light of freedom. As the American historian David Roediker observed in 2011, at the thirtieth anniversary of the Marion Thompson Wright Lecture Series at Rutgers University, she, as a slave, is at the center of the cause of the War and what becomes of her will be at the center of America's future.

Near Andersonville (1865)

Near Andersonville/At the Cabin Door was until the 1960s far out of the public domain, virtually sequestered in the attic of an old New Jersey family. It is now considered to be the quintessential emancipation painting of America's nineteenth century, and will soon travel from the Newark Museum, which owns the painting, to the Smithsonian Institution's Museum of American Art in Washington, DC, and then to the Metropolitan Museum of Art in New York. It is likely that Homer realized what it would take the nation over a century to realize: that freedom from slavery and those about to claim it were at the center of the conflict.[1]

I begin this way because these images and other artifacts, historic places, anonymous figures and events that remind Americans of their starkly brutal Civil War, of slavery, and of the ending of slavery have increasingly grown in commemorative stature over the last generation as a cross section of Americans have reconsidered what was once believed about that transformative period in the nation's history and culture.

Let us consider what might explain the evolving sensibilities about American history 150 years after the beginning of the American Civil War. As the nineteenth century drew to a close in the United States, the nation's collective memory of its Civil War, waged just a generation before, was dispatched in favor of the daunting task of national reconciliation. It was as costly a reconciliation as the nation would ever make, because over the next century and beyond the nation conveniently misplaced the deeper meaning of the Civil War —the ending of slavery—and what the ending of slavery required of the American Republic. Efforts to find an honorable place for former black slaves and their progeny were systematically shelved, left for another generation to wage in what my generation of historians often refers to as the Second Reconstruction.

In other words, the American Republic's historical amnesia about the deeper meaning of the Civil War helped it, imagined at the time as a white American Republic, to bind its wounds while other wounds were created after the War.[2] Most importantly, black Americans, especially those who lived in regions where slavery had taken root, remained impoverished and without the legal and social status to improve their elevated condition or that of their progeny. They were free, but not much more than a caste of despised, ridiculed, and maligned Americans on the sidelines of the nation's history and vision of its future.

Post-World War II Americans, those whose ancestors were once enslaved and those whose journey in America were unencumbered by enslavement, were reminded of this convergence of historical amnesia and the paradox of racism in a democratic republic when, in 1963, at the March on Washington, Dr. Martin Luther King, Jr. pronounced that one hundred years after President Abraham Lincoln signed the Emancipation Proclamation, "the Negro is still not free."

Obviously, in 1963 the progeny of the enslaved were free, but it is equally obvious that over time what shamefully stood as an acceptable standard for freedom in the American Republic was challenged by significant changes in the way the nation's history was researched, written, and consumed. Indeed, it might be argued that this over long commemorative season, when a cross section of Americans are observing the 150th anniversary of the Civil War, what is known about the War and the Emancipation mark extraordinary transformations in the history profession and in the American historical narrative.

In 1963, when Dr. King made his famous declaration, American historiographical sensibilities had already begun a transformation. First and foremost, the transformation resulted in part from a strong and persistent tradition of scholarship by well-educated blacks begun at a time when the American academy was segregated space, when black and a few white scholars labored largely under-recognized in the vineyards of what was called Negro History. Over time, certainly after World War II, what they had to say about the history of the American Republic and the place of black people in the Republic found its way into the complicated rituals of telling the story of America's past.[3]

The first major opus in the Negro History Movement was penned by George Washington Williams. In 1884, Williams completed his two-volume study The Negro Race in America, which made him the titular "father of Negro History." Williams was not a professionally trained historian and what he wrote is arcane by contemporary standards of historical scholarship. Yet, he was instrumental in giving Negro History a believable framework that resonated in the work of those who followed in his footsteps.

In the preface of his book, Williams wrote:

I have tracked my bleeding countrymen through the widely scattered documents of American history. I have listened to their groans, their clanking chains, and melting prayers, until the woes of a race and the agonies of centuries seem to crowd upon my soul as a bitter reality. Many pages of this history have been blistered with my tears; and, although having lived but a little more than a generation, my mind feels as if it were cycles old.

Williams and the two generations of historians that were to follow him chipped away at the monumentalized view of American history and culture. This marked the beginning of the so-called "new history" of the American Republic, which flowered around the years of the Civil Rights Movement. [4]

Fast forwarding to the sesquicentennial of the American Civil War and the Great Emancipation, we see a remarkable realignment of sensibilities about the history and culture of the United States. Emancipation, not only the preservation of the Union, is now seen as the most important consequence of the War and its horrors. The enslaved blacks, once seen as hapless, anonymous figures on the sidelines of the long season of their deliverance from slavery, are now seen as active participants in the symbolic and dramatic events that turned the tide of the War against slavery and positioned slavery as its cause. The evolution of this realignment is an important legacy of the way the American Civil War and the Great Emancipation have been viewed in society that, despite its multiple discontents, is a maturing democracy. How that realignment has occurred is a useful historical and cultural narrative to my humanities colleagues in China.

The intellectual and moral elevation of the historical narrative on the Civil War and the ending of slavery powerfully influences this commemorative season. Conferences, symposia, film presentations, and a spate of new books inform the general public and complicate the beginning of a new American Republic far beyond what was once in vogue, when Dr. King spoke on the steps of Lincoln Monument in 1963: the valor, courage, manhood, and iconic historical white figures that long overshadowed American history and the nation's memory of itself. It may be that this

commemorative season—unfolding at a time when cultural and social diversity in the United States is accorded an unprecedented level of tolerance—will be more in line with settled historical scholarship and the ideals of the Civil Rights Movement than could have been imagined a generation ago.

Within the rhythm of American historical scholarship and the complicated cultural landscape it has sought to explain, commemoration is one important way for humanities scholarship to open up debates long shelved by historical amnesia. Our memories distinguish us as humans.

Contested memories distinguish us as more thoughtful humans, engaged in the ebb and flow of what needs to be known about a past that is constantly being reinvented for the present and the future.

---

① See Peter H. Wood, Near Andersonville: Winslow Homer's Civil War (Cambridge, Massachusetts: Harvard University Press, 2010).
② See David W. Blight, Race and Reunion: The Civil War in American Memory (Cambridge, Massachusetts: Harvard University Press, 2002).
③ See August Meier and Elliott Rudwick, Black History and the History Profession, 1915–1980 (Urbana, Illinois: University of Illinois Press, 1986).
④ See John Hope Franklin, George Washington Williams, A Biography (Durham, North Carolina: Duke University Press, 1998).

论中国社会发展背景下的陶瓷艺术创作

朱乐耕

中国艺术研究院艺术创作研究中心及陶瓷艺术研究中心主任

内容提要： 改革开放30年，中国社会发生了巨大的变化，这种变化不仅体现在经济的发展上、城市的发展上等，同样也体现在人们的心理变化、精神追求，还有审美价值的选择等方面。本文试图以笔者自己陶瓷艺术创作的几个阶段的变化，来说明这一变革时期的种种特性。

我原定要讲的题目是《中国陶瓷的审美精神》，后来考虑到我是一位艺术家，以自己的艺术创作来讨论改革开放以来，中国人的价值观审美观以及社会的文化思想变化，也许会更有意义。艺术是文化的一个部分，是文化最活跃和最敏感的部分。纵观人类的发展史，我们可以看到每一次人类社会新的文化运动都是以艺术为肇始的，最为典型的例子就是欧洲的文艺复兴。

同样，改革开放以来，中国社会发生了巨大的变化，这种变化不仅体现在经济的发展上、城市的发展上等，同样也体现在人们的心理变化、精神追求，还有审美价值的选择等方面，而这些方面常常是通过艺术来体现的。我是一位艺术家，主要是从事陶瓷艺术，我希望通过自己的艺术创作的不同阶段，来讨论中国改革开放以来，折射在艺术家身上的种种变化。通常学者们一般认为文化有三大系统，第一是技术系统；第二是制度系统；第三是思想意识系统。陶瓷艺术的发展需要这三个系统的互动，因为陶瓷艺术和其他的艺术不一样的就是，它不仅仅是一项创造性的精神活动，同时也是一项技术劳动，是需要有一套社会组织系统为其服务的，同时又是具有观念性的，它需要表现人的意识形态和价值追求。

在我三十年陶瓷艺术创作过程中，经历了两个大的历史阶段，一个是计划经济时期；另一个是改革开放以后的市场经济时期。这两个时期，中国经历了从相对封闭走向开放、包容，从相对本土性走向相对国际化，从经济相对贫乏走向经济高速发展的社会变迁的过程。下面我想以我自己的艺术创作为例，来体现这样一种社会变迁过程。

一、计划经济时期相对单一的艺术创作风格

在中国的计划经济时期，所有的陶瓷工厂都是国营的、国家的。那是一种大工业化生产的模式，陶艺家普遍没有自己的工作室，因为陶艺家跟一般的艺术家、绘画家不同，他需要有窑炉，有一系列的设备条件，所有的创作原来都是在国营工厂完成的，我读研究生的时候，需要创作作品，都是由学校开一张介绍信，带到工厂去制作。所以在那个时候，陶瓷艺术家们很难在材料上和自身特殊语言上来表达、来探索自己的独特艺术风格。当时的陶瓷艺术作品主要是在釉上进行彩绘。没有条件拥有自己的窑炉和工作室，也就没有条件尝试在泥性、釉料、烧成等方面做实验。作品主要是在工厂现成的白瓷上做彩绘装饰，表现手法比较单一，也很难体现陶瓷艺术自身的火与土的语言。

二、新的技术条件带来的新的艺术风格

随着中国改革开放的发展，市场经济的活跃，中国的陶瓷艺术家的创作条件有了一定的改善，艺术家们开始建立自己的工作室，而我本人也一样，有了自己的工作室和窑炉。当时中国窑炉是从澳大利亚进口的，后来我们借助他们的技术，开始自己建造，现在这个技术已经很成熟很普遍了，建一个窑炉不贵，很多陶艺家都能拥有它。新的技术条件和工作环境让许多陶瓷艺术的想象力以及创造力都得到了充分地发挥，并开始运用不同的陶瓷材料以及窑温来进行新的陶瓷艺术语言的探索。有了窑炉以后，陶瓷艺术的烧成就不像国营工厂那样都是一个温度，可以根据作品效果的需要控制温度，还可以在泥土的肌理上进行一些探索。这样的探索使中国的现代陶艺进入了一个风格多样的活跃期，并在国际舞台上受到关注。

三、新生活的需求促进新的陶瓷艺术的产生

改革开放以后，中国开始处于工业化发展的高峰期，国家经济处于恢复发展期，但工业文明带来的负面影响也在不断地显现。出于对工业文明的反思，本人试图将陶艺的创作拉回生活的原点，让现代陶艺与现代人的生活发生关系，让人们在用的时候重新体悟物的珍贵性，从而尊重物质的创造，从尊重物到尊重生命，同时新的生活需要新的艺术形式和新的艺术器物。这是一些对陶瓷在新生活中用的思考。当然，自古以来，陶瓷艺术就是为生活、为用服务的。但在近代社会，现代陶瓷艺术的产生，使陶瓷艺术家的作品远离了用。而中国新的城市生活的发展，需要我们艺术家重新思考，艺术与生活的关联性。所以在这个时期，我做了许多与生活有关联的陶瓷艺术品，如："审视的晚宴"、"蓝色的梦"、"炊

烟·人家"等都是以餐具、茶具等生活用具呈现的。而且从这个时候开始我开设了一门生活陶艺的课程,并招收这方面的研究生。

四、现代陶艺在现代环境空间中的运用

在现代工业文明的推进下,中国城市化进程在加速,城市越来越成为水泥的森林,需要有一种更具艺术感染力、更具自然亲和力的材料来缓解现代生活空间给人们造成的压力,同时也需要考虑陶瓷材料与其他领域的运用关系,与建筑室内环境空间的关系,让陶瓷艺术与人类的生活空间形成有机的联系,于是在本人的陶瓷艺术创作中,就越来越关注陶瓷艺术与现代生活环境空间的

关系,创作了一系列与建筑相结合的大型环境陶艺,并且开设了一门有关环境陶艺的课程。在这些作品中最有代表性的有:九江市民广场的"莲"系列陶瓷雕塑与装置壁画,规模很大,装置壁画沿着一口长满荷花的湖有一百多米长。2010年世博会时,我还为上海浦东机场做了一个陶艺装置壁画,这是因为上海市政府希望在世博会期间,面对世界通过机场建筑有很好的文化艺术的表达,这个题目是叫"惠风和畅",是以蓝天白云为题材做成的,很有中国意境。2011年,我还在天津的"瑞吉"酒店大堂做了一幅大型的陶艺装置壁画,题目叫"流金岁月",这个酒店是天津最好的、超五星的酒店,是美国的国际品牌。以上许多城市重要的建筑物和重要的公共环境空间,都让类似我这样的艺术家来做艺术品,一方面是城市发展的需要;另一方面也让我们看到,中国的发展不仅是经济的发展,也包括了文化的发展,包括了对艺术作品的需求和重视,这是新的

国家形象所带来的新的审美追求。

五、国际合作背景下的艺术创作

随着改革开放的发展，中国越来越成为一个国际化的国家，成为世界大家庭中的一员，这不仅体现在经济上、文化上，也体现在艺术的相互交流与合作上，而且这种合作不仅是国与国之间，也包括不同区域之间的合作，跨地区、跨专业、跨文化的合作几乎成为一种世界的发展趋势。以我自己的创作经历为例，2002—2006年我被邀请为韩国首尔麦粒音乐厅做系列的陶艺装置壁画。麦粒财团的负责人希望将这座建筑用陶艺作品建成一座陶瓷艺术的宫殿。开始他是想邀请美国著名的陶艺家来做。后来一次偶然的机会，他到中国美术馆买书，正好看到了我个人的陶瓷艺术展。他觉得我的作品更有东方特点，所以临时改变注意，邀请我来做。当时和我合作的是韩国著名的建筑师于杰博士，还有韩国汉阳大学音响设计系的全正龙教授。这是世界上第一例用高温瓷做成的音乐厅，不仅是艺术效果，就是音响效果也是世界第一流的，其音响实验是在韩国的汉阳大学做的。音乐厅落成后，在世界音响界引起很大的反响。2004年，我和全正龙教授一起参加了在韩国济州岛举行的国际音响研讨会，会议结束后，所有的与会者到首尔麦粒音乐厅聆听了音乐会，反响非常好。现在这座音乐厅在韩国非常有名，成为了当地的一个文化景点。这不仅是一个跨国家的，也是一个跨专业、跨学科的合作项目。

六、国家的力量给艺术的发展平台

国家的力量是艺术家发展的重要条件之一。回忆起自己第一次在中国美术馆办展览是在1997年，当时我还是景德镇陶瓷学院的老师，展览是景德镇陶瓷学院和中国美术馆共同举办的。后来我调到中国艺术研究院工作，又在中国美术馆、上海美术馆、法国巴黎中国文化中心、德国柏林中国文化中心、中国妇女儿童博物馆等地方举办个人展览，都得到了中国艺术研究院和文化部的大力支持。是国家的力量有效地推动了中国当代艺术的发展。

七、国际交流带来的新视野

全球一体化给中国的艺术界带来的是更加开放的国际视野和更加频繁的国际交流,通过国际交流不仅让中国艺术家学到了不同国家的文化艺术,也让世界更了解中国的文化和艺术。改革开放让中国的艺术家有机会走出国门到世界不同的国家参加展览会,举办个人陶艺展,参加各种陶艺研讨会,并被邀请到各个不同国家的大学做讲座。从1995年我第一次到新加坡举办个人陶艺展至今,我曾到过韩国、日本、法国、德国、美国、加拿大、中国香港等国家和地区举办个人陶艺展览,还到不少国家参加国际陶艺联展。2009年,我还被邀请到美国肯塔

基大学做访问学者,期间被美国哈佛大学、阿佛雷德大学、纽约城市大学、加拿大拉瓦尔大学做讲座。同时还曾被日本东京艺术大学、韩国弘益大学、圆光大学等邀请做讲座。这样频繁的国际交流,是在中国艺术史上从未有过的,它代表中国已经成为一个开放的、多文化包容的、具有国际化视野的泱泱大国。

八、结束语

以上我的发言让我们看到了陶瓷艺术不仅是贯穿理念,产生视觉审美,也有物质和材料本身的效用,还包括了如何引领当代人的生活潮流,在日常生活中渗透一种新的哲学精神,以及对环保的关注,对当代生活方式的关注,对生命的珍爱等。当今的中国已经进入全球经济一体化,不仅是完成了对工业文明的推进,而且文化产业和信息产业也在蓬勃发

展。而中国的现代陶瓷艺术的创作也应该参与其中,这也是中国社会发展到现今对我们中国陶瓷艺术家提出的要求与责任。同时艺术家命运和国家的社会发展是紧密相依的,其艺术创作必然会打上社会和时代的烙印,不同文化之间、不同文明之间的相互交流与相互理解也是非常重要的,我们可以不懂得不同国家的语言、文字甚至宗教活动,但是我们都能欣赏不同国家的艺术,因为艺术不需要文字、语言,其实可以用心灵来沟通和感受的,艺术是可以超越国界的,所以我希望在未来的世界里我们可以以艺术来搭起一座座友谊的桥梁,让不同的文明得到相互的理解和尊重,真正做到费孝通所讲的"各美其美,美人之美,美美与共,天下大同"。

Artistic Creation of Ceramics in the Context of Social Development in China

Zhu Legeng

Director of Art Creation Center and Ceramic Art Center,Chinese National Academy of Arts

Abstract: Over the past 30 years of reform and opening-up, great changes have taken place to the Chinese society. These changes are manifested not only in economic development, city development and so on, but also in the people's psychology, cultural pursuits, aesthetic values etc. This paper gives us a glimpse into that period of change through several phases of change in the author's own artistic creation of ceramics.

I originally planned to give a speech titled "The Aesthetic Spirit of Chinese Ceramics", but later I discarded the topic, considering that perhaps it might be more meaningful for me, as an artist, to talk about the change of the Chinese people's values and aesthetic standards and of the change of culture and philosophy in the society, through my own experiences of artistic creation. Art is the most energetic and most sensitive part of culture. In the entire history of human development, every new cultural movement of human society started with art, most notably the Renaissance in Europe.

Similarly, since the beginning of the reform and opening-up, the Chinese society has seen tremendous changes, not only in economic development, city development and so on, but in the people's psychological dimension, cultural pursuits and selection of aesthetic values – the aspects usually manifested through art. I'm an artist, mainly in ceramics, and I'd like to talk about various changes in artists since the beginning of the reform and opening-up in China, through several different stages I've undergone in my artistic creation. A culture is generally accepted to have three main systems, a technological system, an institutional system and an ideological system. The development of ceramics, or the ceramic art, entails the interaction of all the three systems, as it differs from other arts in that it is not only a mental activity of creation, but also a form of technical labor that requires services from a set of social organizations and systems, and is conceptual and needs to reflect human ideologies and

pursuits of value.

In my 30 years of artistic creation of ceramics, I have experienced two major historical periods. One is the planned economy period and the other is the market economy period, the two periods through which China underwent a process of change from relative closeness to openness and tolerance, from relative localization to relative internationalization, and from economic insufficiency to rapid economic growth. Below I'll use my own experiences of artistic creation to mirror this process of social changes.

I. A Monotonous Art Style during the Planned Economy Period

During China's planned economy period, all ceramic factories were run and owned by the state, and followed a pattern of mass industrial production. Ceramic artists at large had no studios of their own, no kilns, no equipment necessary to complete their creation, and all the work of creation had to be done in state-owned factories. When I was a postgraduate student, I had to get a letter of introduction from the school and took it to the factory, where I would complete my creation. At that time, therefore, ceramic artists could hardly express and explore their own particular styles of art, whether in material or in their special languages of art. It was dominantly colored drawing that was made on glaze for ceramic works then. Without their own kilns and studios, ceramic artists then had no conditions for making experiments in such aspects as properties of clay, glaze and firing. Finished works were mainly white porcelains decorated with colored drawing, which were produced by the factory and monotonous in techniques of expression and could hardly embody the fire-and-clay language of ceramics.

II. New Art Styles Brought about by New Technical Conditions

With the deepening of the reform and opening-up and the thriving of markets, Chinese ceramic artists saw certain improvements in their creation conditions. They began building their own studios, and I, too, had my own studio and kiln. Kilns in China then were imported from Australia. Later we began building kilns ourselves by using their technology, which now is very mature and widely applied. Many ceramic artists could afford to build their own kilns since it costs not much. New technical conditions and working environments brought into full play the imagination and creativity of ceramic artists, who began explorations of a new ceramic language through different ceramic materials and kiln temperatures. With his/her own kiln, a ceramic artist could fire ceramics at controlled temperatures required to achieve particular effects, rather than at a constant temperature as in a state-owned factory, and make explorations on the texture of clay. Such explorations brought about a great variety of styles in Chinese modern ceramics, which began drawing attention from the international arena.

III. Birth of New Forms of Ceramics from Needs of New Life

Since the beginning of reform and opening-up, China has reached the peak of its industrial development with the national economy in a phase of restorative growth, but negative effects arising from industrial civilization also emerged continuously. Out of reflection about industrial civilization, I attempted to put ceramic creation back to its origin, so that there could be interaction between modern ceramics and the life of modern people, and people – while using ceramics – could become aware of their preciousness and thus respect creations and life as well. Moreover, a new life needs new forms and objects of art. These are some thoughts of mine about the utility of ceramics in a new life. Of course, ceramics have been used to serve people's life since ancient times. In modern society, however, the birth of modern ceramics made ceramic artists' works separate far from utility. The development of a new city life in China required

us artists to have a rethink of the relationship between art and life. In this period, therefore, I created a great many ceramic works of art linked to life, for example "An Evening Banquet of Examination", "A Blue Dream" and "Kitchen Smoke and Family" – all of them rendered in the form of domestic utensils like tableware and tea sets. And from this time on, I began offering a postgraduate program concerning domestic ceramics.

IV. Application of Modern Ceramics in Modern Environment

Driven by modern industrial civilization, China's process of urbanization accelerated, and cities more and more became forests of cement. This made it necessary to have a material more artistically appealing and with a stronger affinity with nature used to relieve human pressure from modern living spaces. It was also necessary to consider the relationship that the ceramic material has with applications in other fields and with interior spaces of buildings, so as to bring about an organic connection between ceramics and living spaces of man. I thus paid more and more attention in ceramic creation to the relationship between ceramics and modern living spaces, and created a series of large-sized ceramic works in combination with buildings. I also launched a curriculum concerning environment ceramics. Among those works, the representatives included: the massive lotus-themed ceramic sculptures and fresco – more than 100 meters long around a pond that abounds with lotus flowers – at People's Plaza in Jiujiang; a ceramic fresco – titled "Refreshing Breeze" – created during Expo 2010 Shanghai at Shanghai Pudong International Airport, which, according to the intention of Shanghai Government, displays the Chinese culture and art to the world through the airport architecture, and highlights white clouds in a blue sky, rich in Chinese elements; and an enormous ceramic fresco – titled "Golden Days" – created in 2011 at the entrance hall of The St. Regis Tianjin, a five-star rated hotel of American brand and the best hotel in Tianjin. The fact that artists like me are commissioned to create artworks for landmark buildings and major public spaces in many cities reflects the needs of city development on the one hand, and on the other let us see that China's development not only lies in its economic growth, but also in the cultural progress, and the demand for and importance given to artworks. That is a new aesthetic pursuit brought about by a new image of the country.

V. Artistic Creation in the Context of International Collaboration

With the deepening of the reform and opening-up, China has become more and more important in the international community as a member of the world family. This is manifested not only economically and culturally, but also in art exchange and collaboration; such collaboration takes place not only between countries but also between regions, with cross-regional, cross-disciplinary and cross-cultural collaboration nearly becoming a world trend. Take one of my own experiences of creation as an example. From 2002 to 2006, I worked on a series of ceramic frescos for the Ceramic Palace Hall in Seoul of ROK, whose president wished to make the building a palace of ceramic art by using ceramic works. The president had originally wanted the job done by an eminent American ceramic artist, but he happened to catch sight of my personal ceramic exhibition while buying books at National Art Museum of China. He felt my works had more of Oriental features, and so changed to invite me for the job. I then began to work in collaboration with Dr. Yoo Kerl, a famous architect in ROK, and Prof. Chun Jin Yong, at Department of Voice, Hanyang University. It is the world's first concert hall made of high-temperature porcelain, with world-class artistic and sound effects. Sound experiments were made at Hanyang University. Upon its completion, the concert hall drew great attention from the sound field in the world. In 2004, Prof. Chun Jin Yong and I attended an international sound forum held in Jeju Island, ROK; after the meeting, all the participants went to the Ceramic Palace Hall and listened to a concert, which was highly acclaimed. This concert hall is very famous now in ROK and has become a tourist attraction of cultural interest. It was a collaborative project both cross-border and interdisciplinary.

VI. State-supported Platforms for Art Development

One of the important conditions for the development of artists is support from the state. My first exhibition at National Art Museum of China took place in 1997, when I taught at Jingdezhen Ceramic Institute. It was jointly held by the two institutions. Later I was transferred to Chinese National Academy of Arts, and staged my solo exhibitions at National Art Museum of China, Shanghai Art Museum, China Cultural Centers in Paris and Berlin, Chinese Museum of Women and Children and so on, all of those exhibitions vigorously supported by Chinese National Academy of Arts and the Ministry of Culture. It is the national support that has effectively promoted the development of contemporary arts in China.

VII. New Horizons from International Exchange

Global integration has widened the horizons of the Chinese art community and brought more international exchanges which enable Chinese artists to learn the cultures and arts in different countries and deepen the world's understanding of the Chinese culture and arts. The beginning of the reform and opening-up has offered Chinese artists opportunities to attend exhibitions in other countries, hold solo ceramic exhibitions, participate in ceramics forums and give lectures at universities in different countries. Since 1995 when I held a solo ceramic exhibition for the first time in Singapore, I have staged many

exhibitions in ROK, Japan, France, Germany, the United States, Canada, Hong Kong and some other countries and regions, and participated in international ceramic exhibitions in a great many countries. In 2009, I was invited as a visiting scholar to University of Kentucky in America, and meanwhile I was invited to give lectures at Harvard University, Alfred University, The City University of New York, and Laval University of Canada. Besides, I was also invited to give lectures by Tokyo University of the Arts, Hongik University, Wonkwang University of ROK and so on. Such frequent international exchanges never happened before in the Chinese history of arts, suggesting that China has become an open and culturally tolerant country of international vision.

VIII. Conclusion

My statement above suggests that ceramics, as an art, is not only productive of visual aesthetics, but also involves the utility of materials used, and embraces such aspects as how to set trends for contemporary people, how to develop a new philosophy that is pervasive in everyday life, and how to arise concern about the environment and modern ways of life, and love for life. Already part of global economic integration, China has not only advanced the development of industrial civilization, but also is seeing rapid growth in its cultural and information industries. The Chinese modern ceramic art also should play a part in this process, which is the requirement and responsibility that the present Chinese society raises to us Chinese ceramic artists. As the fate of artists is closely connected with their countries' social development, their artistic creations are bound to have an imprint of society and age. The exchange between and mutual understanding of different cultures and civilizations is also crucial; we might not understand the language, words and even religion of other countries, but we all can appreciate arts of different countries, because arts can actually be understood and felt by hearts without the aid of words or language. Therefore, I wish we can build bridges of friendship in the future through arts, so that different civilizations can be understood and respected and in great harmony with each other, just as what Mr. Fei Xiaotong highlights – respect for cultural diversity.

文化权利是国家主权和国家利益的组成部分

摩罗

中国艺术研究院中国文化研究所研究员

内容提要： 在近代以来形成的"民族国家"文明形态中，一个国家的文化权利，就是国家主权和国家利益的组成部分。民族国家不是一个空壳，它是由人群、领土、政权、社会组织、生产方式、历史传统、文化等共同组成的综合性实体，国家主权就体现在对这一切因素的正当性和主体性的坚定维护，并确保这一正当性和主体性受到国际社会的尊重，而不允许其他国家以任何理由任何方式对其正当性和主体性予以否定、侵犯或摧毁。文化是构成民族国家实体的因素之一，理所当然也是国家主权的组成部分。对国家主权的认可与尊重，必定包含着对于其人群、领土、政权、社会组织、生产方式、历史传统、文化等方面的认可与尊重。

由于各国综合实力不同，它们在国际社会所拥有的影响力和话语权远非均等，强势国家与弱势国家的不同权力、不同地位构成了国际框架中的等级秩序。各国在政治、经济、军事各个领域既相互合作、相互依存，又有或隐或显的相互博弈、相互遏制。合作是相对的，竞争与博弈是绝对的。这是我们讨论国与国之间文化关系的基本语境。

在这种既合作又博弈的国际关系体系中，不同国家的文化地位、文化影响力，具有天壤之别。如何对待他国他族文化，如何与文化传统相异的他国他族相处，是国际交往中一个非常重要的问题。强势国家常将自己的文化描述为唯一合理、唯一正当的文化，甚至树立为标准，以此批评弱势国家的文化，否定其文化正当性，并进而按照自己的利益改造之。弱势国家如何看待强势国家的文化权利和影响，如何在认可其优势和影响的同时，坚信本土文化的正当性，坚守本土文化的权利，坚持以本土文化资源与强势文化相竞争、相博弈，是一个世界性的难题。

百余年来，中国为应对强势国家的文化压力付出了艰辛的努力，在一些特定的阶段取得了某种程度的成功，积累了一些经验，在另一些特定的阶段则遭遇失败，留下深刻教训。我们遭遇失败的原因相当复杂，对于文化的价值和功能缺乏准确的理解，是原因之一。

通常一个民族有大体一致的文化认同，也就是说创造文化的主体大体上可以认定为"民族"，世界上每一种文化，都是由某个特定的民族创造的。

每个民族都是在与其他民族的征战、冲突、博弈、妥协中成长的，因而不可能在歌舞升平的仙境中创造文化，而是在与其他民族争夺生存资源和发展空间的紧张关系中创造文化的。每个民族都希望通过创造自己的神灵（比如耶和华）、自己的神话（比如伊甸园神话）、自己的学说（比如白人优越论）、自己的学术体系（比如欧洲中心主义）论证自己的优越性，增加自己的竞争优势和制胜力量，帮助自己实现利益最大化。所以，文化从其起源上，就是创造主体用以建构自身正当性、维护自身权利、增加自身利益、扩展自身影响的工具，是进可以攻击他者、退可以护卫自身权益的武器。总之，民族文化是民族利益的表达形式。

在近代以来形成的"民族国家"文明形态中，一个国家的文化权利，就是国家主权和国家利益的组成部分。民族国家不是一个空壳，它是由人群、领土、政权、社会组织、生产方式、文化传统等共同组成的综合性实体，国家主权就体现在对这一切因素的正当性和主体性的坚定维护，并确保这一正当性和主体性受到国际社会的尊重，而不允许其他国家以任何理由任何方式对其正当性和主体性予以否定、侵犯或摧毁。

文化既是构成民族国家实体的因素之一，理所当然也是国家主权的组成部分。对国家主权的认可与尊重，必定包含着对其文化的认可与尊重。现代国际社会处处以尊重他国主权相标榜，这种尊重也应该相应地坐实为既尊重其利益诉求，也尊重其文化传统及文化权利。

如果甲国宣称尊重乙国的国家主权，却对乙国的历史传统和文化予以否定、批评、妖魔化描述，那只能说明，甲国对乙国的国家主权的尊重是不真实的，不过是在做表面文章。它对乙国文化主权的蔑视与否定，才是其内在的态度。这种格局发展下去，必定会导致甲国对乙国国家利益的否定与损害。

在这种情况下，乙国就应该以维护国家主权和国家利益的态度，抵制甲国对其文化传统的否定、批评、妖魔化描述，并且针锋相对地对甲国提出同样的批评，因为进攻就是最好的防御。

最近几百年的东西方交往，虽时有合作与互助，但也经常出现征战与其他冲突。由于西方是强势一方，东方是弱势一方，东西方交往的主动权一直掌握在西方手中。西方强国大多数时候都宣称尊重东方国家的主权，但是对东方国家的文化传统和文化主权，一直缺乏应有的尊重。西方国家大多数时候都在强调，基督教是世界上唯一正确的宗教，西方制度是世界上唯一正确的制度，西方观念是世界上唯一正确的观念，对于包括中国在内的东方国家的宗教、文化、制度、观念展开全面的批评与否定，企图用西方文化覆盖东方文化。这种文化侵略和文化覆盖的倾向，对东方国家的文化主权和国家主权构成压力和威胁。

百余年来，中国社会在国际交往中最为沉痛的教训，就是没有认识到每个民族的文化都是用来维护本民族利益的，没有认识到文化主权是国家主权和国家利益的组成部分。从辛亥时期和"五四"时期的蔡元培、胡适、鲁迅，到今天知识界的一些活跃人物，几乎都全面认可西方国家对中国历史传统和文化的否定、批评、妖魔化描述，并在此基础上，以自虐狂心理，对自身的文化传统、文化资源进行比西方人更彻底、更脱离事实真相的否定、批评、妖魔化描述。

事实上，一个民族和一个群体的核心利益，就深深隐藏在其文化密码之中。漠视自己的文化，将他者文化放在神龛里顶礼膜拜，结果就会将他者的标准看作高于自己的标准，将他者的利益诉求看作高于自己的利益诉求，最终导致对自身利益的损害与放弃。百余年来，中国几代知识分子对文化的错误认识，对文化安全和文化主权的漠视，给中国的发展与崛起，带来了负面影响。

历史已经翻开了新的一页，世界格局正在产生变化，东西方的力量对比正在朝着均衡化的方向发展。力量的均衡将可能导致文化地位、文化影响力的均衡。所以，东西方国家在文化方面相互尊重、平等相处的那一天，有可能不是遥远的梦想。

为了迎接那一天的到来，东方人和西方人、中国人和美国人，都需要在频繁互动中调整自己的文化心态，需要学会既尊重自己的文化传统，也尊重对方的文化权利。中美文化论坛是一个可以在这方面发挥积极作用的平台。

Cultural Right is an Integral Part of National Sovereignty and National Interests

Mo Luo

Research Fellow of Institute of Chinese Culture, Chinese National Academy of Arts

Abstract: According to the civilization pattern of the nation-state that formed in modern times, a country's cultural right is an integral part of the state sovereignty and national interests. The nation-state is not an empty shell, but an integrated entity jointly composed of the people, territory, regime, social organization, mode of production, history and tradition, culture and so on. The national sovereignty is to firmly protect these factors' justification and subjectivity and guarantee the respect to the justification and subjectivity from the international community, never allowing any country to deny, infringe or destroy the justification and subjectivity in any way for any reason. Culture is one of the factors that constitute the national entity, and is taken for granted the constituent part of the national sovereignty. The ratification and respect of the state sovereignty is bound to contain the ratification and respect of the people, territory, regime, social organization, mode of production, history and tradition, culture and so on.

Influence and right of speech due to their different overall national strength. Different powers and statuses of the powerful and disadvantaged countries form the hierarchical order of the international framework. Countries cooperate with each other and coexist in political, economic and military fields, but meanwhile compete with and constrain each other explicitly or implicitly. The cooperation is relative while the competition is absolute, which is the basic context to discuss the cultural relations between nations.

In such cooperative and competitive international relations, the cultural status and influence of different countries differ a lot. How to treat other cultures and get along with people with different cultural traditions is an important issue in the international exchange. The powerful country usually regards its own culture as the only reasonable and righteous culture, or even set it as the standard, whereby criticizing disadvantageous cultures, denying their justification and renovating them to serve its own interests. It is a worldwide problem how the disadvantaged countries view the cultural power and influence of the powerful countries and how, recognizing their advantages and influence, the disadvantaged countries firmly believe the justification of their local cultures, stand fast to its cultural rights, and keep competing with the powerful cultures based on their local cultural resources.

The past 100 years has witnessed the arduous efforts China has made to withstand the cultural pressure imposed by powerful countries. China has succeeded to some degree and accumulated some experience in some certain stages, and failed with bitter lessons in other stages. The reasons for these failures are quite complex, one of which is the inaccurate understanding of the cultural value and functions.

Usually a nation has an almost consistent cultural identity. That means people creating a culture can be regarded as a nation. Every culture in the world is created by a particular nation.

Every nation develops through campaigns, conflicts, competitions and compromises with other nations, so a culture can by no means be created in the peaceful wonderland but in the fight with other nations for subsistent resources and development space. Every nation wishes to demonstrate its superiority, enhance its competitiveness and winning power, and maximize its interests by creating its own gods (e.g. Jehovah), myths (e.g. the Garden of Eden), doctrines (e.g. white supremacy) and academic systems (e.g. Eurocentrism). Therefore, in the light of origin, culture is the tool of its creator to construct its justification, safeguard its own rights, enhance its own interests, and expand its own influence; and it is also a weapon to attack others on the one hand and defend its own rights and interests on the other hand. In short, a nation's culture is an expressive form of the national interests.

According to the civilization pattern of the nation-state that formed in modern times, a country's cultural right is an integral part of the state sovereignty and national interests. The nation-state is not an empty shell, but an integrated entity jointly composed of the people, territory, regime, social organization, mode of production, history and tradition, culture and so on. The national sovereignty is to firmly protect these factors' justification and subjectivity and guarantee the respect to the justification and subjectivity from the international community, never allowing any country to deny, infringe or destroy the justification and subjectivity in any way for any reason.

Culture is a constituent part of the nation state, and of course a part of the state sovereignty. The ratification and respect of state sovereignty is bound to contain the ratification and respect of a country's culture. The modern international community often boasts of respecting the sovereignty of other countries, and such respect should also be showed to the appeal for interests and the cultural tradition and rights as well.

If country A claims to respect the state sovereignty of country B but denies, criticizes and demonizes the latter's historical tradition and culture, this only shows that country A's seemingly respect for country B's state sovereignty is merely lip service. Its scorn and denial of county B's cultural sovereignty is its real attitude. If things go on in this way, country B's national interest will undoubtedly be denied and damaged.

Under this circumstance, country B should resist country A's denial, criticism and demonized description of its cultural tradition to protect its state sovereignty and national interests, and fight back in the same way, because offense is the best defense.

The past centuries have witnessed wars and other conflicts between the East and the West despite occasional cooperation and mutual assistance. The West is strong while the East is weak, so the West has kept the initiative of the East-West exchanges. The western powers mostly have claimed respect to the sovereignty of the eastern countries, but they have never shown enough respect to the latter's cultural tradition and cultural sovereignty. The western countries usually stress that Christianity is the only correct religion in the world, the western system is the only correct system in the world, and the western concept is only correct concept in the world. They criticize and deny the eastern (including Chinese) religions, cultures, systems and concepts, in an attempt to cover the eastern culture with the western culture. Such a tendency of cultural invasion and cultural coverage constitutes pressure and threat to the cultural and national sovereignty of the eastern countries.

The most painful lesson the Chinese society has learned in international exchanges in the past 100 years is the failure to realize that a nation's culture is used to safeguard its own interests and the cultural sovereignty is an integral part of state sovereignty and national interests. Almost all scholars, from Cai Yuanpei, Hu Shi, Lu Xun in the periods of the Revolution of 1911 and May Fourth Movement to activists in the intellectual circles today, have recognized the overall denial, criticism and demonized descriptions of the western countries to Chinese historical tradition and culture. They even masochistically go further than the westerners did.

In fact, the core interests of a nation and a group are deeply hidden in the codes of their cultures. If a nation disregards its own culture and enshrines the culture of others, it will regard the standard and interest expression of others as higher than its own, thus damaging and discarding its own interests in the end. Misunderstanding the culture and disregarding the cultural security and sovereignty for generations by Chinese intellectuals have laid a negative impact on China's development and rise in the past century.

As we are ushered in a new era, the global layout is changing towards the balance between the East and the West, which is likely to result in a balance of cultural status and cultural influence. It may not take very long to see cultural mutual respect and equality between Eastern and Western countries.

To greet that day, Easterners and Westerners, including Chinese and Americans, need to adjust their cultural mentality in the frequent interactions, and learn to respect the cultural traditions of their own and the cultural rights of others. China-U.S. Cultural Forum serves as a conducive platform in this regard.

我们怎样阅读与写作：
社会网络与文学社群

凯思琳·菲茨帕特里克

美国现代语言学会学术传播部主任，美国波莫纳学院媒介研究教授

内容提要：过去的几年里，包括尼古拉斯·卡尔和杰伦·拉尼尔在内的美国作家都认为互联网影响并干扰了现代人的感知能力，几项广受关注的研究结果也提出证据，证明在媒体高度饱和的现代文化中，阅读的重要性不断下降，而阅读正是一种可能改变了美国历史进程的主要严肃认知形式。此类论点和研究均使我们对文化在未来的发展，以及今天的青年将能为文化的未来作出何种贡献产生重大忧虑。

然而，另有证据表明，这些下降的消息并不全面，阅读和写作在当代美国生活中继续占据着重要地位，因为现在的图书销售量比以往任何时候都高。事实上，互联网建立在书面文字交流的基础上，这样看来，事实上现在读者的阅读量超过以往任何时候。或许更重要的一点在于，有更多的人在从事写作。新的在线社交网络有助于推进这种读写上的增长趋势，因为不同的人群可以聚集在网上讨论他们所阅读的小说；同样的，在线社区的成员还可以分享各自的作品。本报告将会探讨几个在线文学群体的范例，并论述这种阅读与写作的相互促进如何推动新文化和新群体的形成。

今天我要与你们分享的关于文化和历史的观点一直以来都明显受到这一事实影响：即我所有这方面的工作的重点都是当代，尤其是当代美国人对媒体转变的观点。事实上，我从事书籍与其他媒体形态之间关系的写作已有15年之久。有人会想，这种关系在这么长的时间跨度内肯定已开始稳定，或者至少可以这么说，如果书籍与新媒体之间关系的故事讲述了书籍的重要性在当代美国文化中有所滑落，那么这一叙述至少应该是明确的。毕竟，美国人对于书籍和阅读可能出现衰落的焦虑在很早之前就已出现。

在我的第一本书《衰退的焦虑》中，我主要探讨了这些焦虑的形成，特别是当20世纪后期人们再次对电视以及电视对书籍在美国文

化生活中的作用的影响产生担忧时。照我的理解，人们对这些影响的焦虑取决于这样的前提条件，即两种不同而又同样具有深远影响的事实夸大效果：首先，很多人认为阅读曾经是一种主导性的文化实践形式——他们认为过去曾存在过那样一种宁静的时刻：人人都活跃地、经常性地致力于严肃的阅读活动，这一观点实际上是基于一种枉然的空想，是人们对一种从未存在的过去的渴望。事实上，严肃阅读，尤其是阅读文章而非神圣作品一直都是那些受过教育的社会中坚分子在闲暇时的主要活动。第二种夸大效果是电视以及电影（电视面世之前）造成美国人更少参与书籍阅读的程度。这种夸大从某种程度上说是有意的，旨在暗示书籍成为了一种濒危形式，进而鼓动其准保护者们创造出一个我将之看作是"野生文化保护区"的空间，在这个空间里濒危形式会受到保护，从而不受那些明显视图破坏它的侵略式大众媒体影响。这种保护主义者姿态又会带来更进一步的影响，促使那些对书籍逐渐失去重要性感到忧虑的人（一群文化层次较高的文艺创作者和消费者）重新将自己想象成社会边缘人群，称自己已经被挤到主流文化生活的门外。这一群体的所作所为转移了人们对当代文化中其他种族的、性别的、经济的边缘化形式，反之将大众媒体视为文化问题的主要原因。

当然，我早前研究的人们对电视的焦虑现在很大程度上都转移为对较新媒体形式，如视频游戏或互联网的焦虑。评论家杰伦·拉尼尔在《你

不是机器》、尼古拉斯·卡尔在《浅水区》中分别指出：互联网及伴随它的体系和技术，正对我们的认知能力造成干扰，导致我们不再拥有持续的注意广度和个人主义取向，此二者是传统书籍阅读这一严肃活动中所需要的。但这两种言论均以书的形式出版过而且还卖得很火，这似乎说明了实际情况比拉尼尔和卡尔所说的要复杂很多。

换言之，"现如今已经没有人读书了"这句话从某种程度上说已经成了一种我们在美国文化中得知的世俗认知，但即使是说出这句话的人，他/她所表达的意思通常也是更为具体和私人的，而"现如今已经没有人读我认为好的书了"应该是人们普遍认同的观念。许多评论家认为阅读这种严肃的实践在现代生活中的重要性逐渐降低。而且现实中也存在能够支撑这一设想的证据。2004年，国家艺术基金会发布了一篇《阅读危机》报告，这是从一项针对美国阅读实践的系统研究中得出的结论；2007年，该基金会又发布了一篇名为《读还是不读》的报告。这些报告所要表达的观点很明确：文学阅读以及书籍阅读整体而言在所有年龄阶层、种族和教育水平的群体中的重要性正在加速衰退。虽然我们不能把这种衰退归咎于人们对其他媒体形式的消费，但这些报告确实失望地提到人们将大量时间花在了电影、电视、视频游戏和互联网上。报告称，人们对阅读的关注不断减少将对美国公民生活产生深刻影响，同时表明阅读对培养社群感、归属感以及社会责任感的重要性。

尽管这些研究有着深远的意义，但能够证明阅读正处于衰退的证据还不清楚。首先，过去70年来，出版业的数据表明每年的图书销量在不断上升，而且现在的销量要高出以前的销量。实际上，许多畅销书籍针对的读者群正是那些被视为最有可能不读书的群体：儿童，而儿童的媒体消费习惯似乎与他们对书籍的热爱互不干扰。网络技术和设备也使我们能够与书籍互动的平台迅速扩展。Kindle电子书和其他电子阅读器的销售势头尤为强劲，而电子书销量也在迅猛发展，这意味着对书籍能够提

供的内容的投资也在不断发展当中。

甚至连全国教育协会都在第三次对美国人阅读情况进行的研究（2010年"阅读呈上升趋势"）中看到了转机。在某种程度上说，这种转机至少源于该研究中所用的对"阅读"的定义发生了细微的变化。2004—2007年期间，"阅读"仅用于描述闲暇时间阅读大量全篇印刷的小说和诗歌。2010年的研究开始审视其他阅读形式，包括非小说书籍以及短篇文章，其中一些还是网上的。在第三次研究中，我们可以看到人们首次意识到互联网也主要由文字构成而且网上阅读实际上也是一种阅读。如果我们（作为一个文化群体）在网上花费更多的时间，我们也有理由认为活跃互联网用户在一天当中可获取的阅读量要比以往多得多。

也许更重要的是，互联网在过去10年内创造了各种不同的技术和站点，读者通过这些技术和站点能够彼此沟通、分享并探讨他们所阅读的内容。互联网从只读环境转变为读写环境使这一切成为可能。如今，活跃在互联网上的读者期待不仅能够消费出版的读物，同时也能够对这些读物做出回应并与他人分享自己的作品。这种从被动消费向主动奉献转变的期望也许能够对2004年原始报告《阅读危机》中已提到但未经核实的罕见资料做出一些解释：即使阅读作为一种休闲活动的重要性看似在迅速衰减，但写作在各个年龄阶层和经济群体中正处于上升趋势。而且自2004年以来，随着博客搜索引擎和其他便于操作的网上发布方式的传播，能够与他人分享的非专业作品也迅猛增加。

当然，大部分的博客和其他网上出版物的阅读率很低，但在某种程度上说是有意而为的；大部分博客并非为读者本身而设，而是为一群共同阅读和写作的朋友而设。比如，早期的博客网络 LiveJournal 使用户能够进行"朋友锁定"发布，以便只有作者认可的读者才能看到发布的内容。因此，该网站就开发出了许多个小型且亲密的读者和作者群体，这些人因共同的兴趣而结集在一起。这些兴趣通常包括是某些电影或电视剧的影迷，或甚至是某些书籍的书迷，而这些登录 LiveJournal 的人可以在自己的网站上探讨并扩展自己的小小宇宙。围绕这些在社交网络中发展形成的虚拟世界的作品被描述且常常被嘲笑为"粉丝小说"。粉丝们创作的富有想象力的新作品对他们所热爱的作品进行了延伸扩展或修改，虽然里面的人物和场景可能不是原始的，但他们作品的性质与学者们的作品有着很多共同之处：他们从批判的角度将原作品中他们认为存在问题的方面推翻，他们与志同道合的人分享作品，对团体评论方式进行实践并在作品发布之前进行"beta 测试"。

其他在线书籍互动形式也在增加。例如，我们可以看到社交网络 Goodreads 越来越流行，目前它的注册会员数量已超过1000万人次，这些会员们丰富着自己的书架、创建愿望清单、分享评论并通过其他方式对书籍发表自己的见解。他们在同一个社交网络内参与作者的问答环节、建立并加入讨论组、浏览朋友的书架，而这个社交网络是围绕同一个浓厚的兴趣建立起来的。目前有超过1000万的读者引导着他人阅读自己喜爱的书籍。

其他网络社区也不断发展并将重点放在引导读者寻找书籍。举一个具体的例子：作家大卫・福斯特・华莱士2008年8月逝世后，博客使用者马修・鲍德温决定在接下来的夏天专门阅读《无尽的玩笑》这部庞大的小说，而且他还会利用互联网来寻求帮助。这个由鲍德温利用博客发起的集体项目——"无尽的夏天"成为了网络热点，使世界各地成千上万的读者聚集到一起，共同在"无尽的夏天"这个网站和分支网站上对这部小说进行探讨。主流媒体人物也迎接了这一挑战，其中包括主流报刊，如《华盛顿邮报》和《卫报》的作家们。众多参与"无尽的夏天"的人在自己的博客上发布了相关帖子，还有许多读者举行了面对面的聚会来探讨这本书。博客帖子和讨论表明人们从更深的层面诠释和理解这部小说、并与其他参与这一过程的读者进行互动的愿望。

所有这些社会活动均受到《无尽的玩笑》启发绝非偶然现象。华莱士英年早逝这一事实使许多读者觉得自己需要从他的作品中寻求某种慰藉。而正如华莱士在1996年接受采访时所提到的那样：他写严肃小说的目的就是让读者"通过想象来接触到其他的本我"，而这最终的结果便是"如果一部小说能够让我们感受到人物的痛苦，那么我们会很容易地想到其他人也能够感受到我们自己的痛苦。这种结果会不断繁衍且具有救赎性；而我们的内心也不再那么孤独。"换言之，读者在阅读时通常会将自己与人物或作者联系到一起；在没有作者介入时，与其他读者联系到一起也许会更可取。华莱士在《无尽的玩笑》这部小说中还探讨像匿名戒酒会这样有意义的社区以及社区成员的社交网络，怎样才能帮助当代美国人脱离他们在日常生活中所经历的痛苦的孤独和自我怀疑。从这一点来说，这一特定小说的读者为了对所读内容进行探讨而寻求与他人建立联系便不足为奇。

但读者通过网络，而非一般意义上的本地组建的读书俱乐部来建立联系这一点可能有点出乎人意料。当然，《无尽的夏天》这样的网上读书社区与以前的线下读书小组有着一定的共同点，但网络社群的网络结构不受本地设置影响，使志趣相投的读者能够在各个地点建立联系，不用担心受到地理位置限制。网上读书社区同时也因其读写定位而有别于欧普拉读书俱乐部这样大规模的阅读社群。像我前面所说的那样，网上读书社区，如LiveJournal不仅注重在独立的环境下阅读或倾听他人，尤其是专家的见解以及对内容进行探讨，同时也注重对所读的内容进行反馈和评论。但"无尽的夏天"这样的社群与其他传统读书社群的共同点是阅读之间具有紧密联系，这种活动既是孤立的，又是团体的，而这种联系强调了读书体验与理解并回应他人（而不是我们自己）的体验的感性愿望之间的密切关系。即使在孤立的情况下阅读，阅读也能让我们与他人建立联系；以团体形式阅读，尤其是在能够就读写体验进行分享的团体中阅读时，创造新型社群的可能性又会增加。

通过这些例子，我认为我们可以承认这一点：那就是虽然阅读在不断向网络形式发展，但它在当代美国人生活中的重要性根本没有减退。虽然《阅读危机》一文对于阅读的重要性衰减的担忧预示我们要将公民生活牢记在心，但同时也暗示我们要勇于寻求新的公民生活方式、寻找新的网上社区，并思考这些社区在新的读写能力方面向我们传达了怎样的信息，以及书籍在21世纪会有怎样的未来。

Kathleen Fitzpatrick

Director of Scholarly Communication, Modern Language Association, Professor of Media Studies, Pomona College

How We Read and Write: Social Networks and Literary Communities

Abstract: In the last several years, American authors including Nicholas Carr and Jaron Lanier have argued that the Internet is interfering with contemporary cognitive abilities, and several well-publicized studies have presented evidence that reading -- perhaps the primary form that serious cognition has taken over the course of U.S. history -- is declining in importance in today's media-saturated culture. Arguments and studies such as these have resulted in significant anxiety about what is becoming of our culture, and how today's youth will be able to contribute to its future.

However, other evidence suggests that these stories of decline do not present a full picture of the continuing importance of reading and writing in contemporary American life, as book sales are higher than ever. In fact, given that the Internet is founded on the exchange of written text, it appears that if anything more readers are in fact reading more than ever today. Perhaps more importantly, more people are writing as well. New online social networks have helped to facilitate this increase in reading and writing, as diverse groups come together to discuss the novels they are reading; similarly, members of online communities are able to share the work that they are writing with one another. This talk will explore some examples of literary groups online and the ways that the interconnected acts of reading and writing together are encouraging the formation of new kinds of literacies and new kinds of communities.

The perspective on culture and history that I will share with you today has been significantly shaped by the fact that all of my work to this point has focused on the contemporary, and in particular on contemporary American perspectives on media change. In fact, I have been writing about the relationship between the book and other media forms for more than 15 years now. One would think that, over such a span of time, this relationship would have begun to stabilize — or at least, one would think, that if the story of the relationship between the book and newer media forms were a narrative of the book's decline in importance in contemporary American culture, that narrative would at least be unambiguous. After all, anxieties

about the decline of books and reading have been evident in the United States for quite a long time.

In my first book, The Anxiety of Obsolescence, I explored the history of these anxieties, particularly as they recurred in late twentieth-century concerns about television and the effects that it was having on the role of the book in American cultural life. In my understanding, these anxieties about those effect were premised on two different but equally profound overstatements: First, the idea that reading was ever as dominant a cultural practice as many seem to suggest it once was — that there was some halcyon moment in the past when everyone was engaged actively in regular, serious reading — is based on an unabashedly utopian longing for a past that never was. In fact, serious reading, especially of texts other than the sacred, has always been an activity dominated by a relatively elite, educated segment of the population with leisure time at its disposal. And the second overstatement is the degree to which television — and before television, film — has produced a decline in American engagement with books and reading. This overstatement has been at least in part intentional. Suggesting that the book is an endangered form allows its would-be protectors to create what I like to think of as a "cultural wildlife preserve," a space within which the endangered form can be kept safe from the predatory mass media that are apparently seeking to destroy it. This preservationist stance has the further effect of allowing those who are anxious about the book's declining importance — a comparatively elite group of cultural producers and consumers — to recast themselves as a marginalized group, claiming that they are being pushed out of the mainstream of cultural life. In so doing, this group deflects attention from other forms of racial, gendered, and economic marginalization in contemporary culture, and instead points to the mass media as the primary cause of cultural problems.

Those anxieties that I earlier studied with respect to television, of course, today largely take newer media forms such as video games or the Internet as their objects of concern. Commentators including Jaron Lanier in You Are Not a Gadget and Nicholas Carr in The Shallows have argued that the Internet and its attendant systems and technologies are interfering with our cognitive capacities, that we no longer have the sustained attention span or the individualist orientation required to engage with the kinds of serious work that have traditionally been done in book form. That both of these arguments were published in book form, however, and that both sold extremely well, seems to indicate that the situation is more complex than Lanier and Carr acknowledge.

That "no one reads anymore", in other words, has become a bit of the conventional wisdom that we frequently hear about American culture, and even if the speaker who utters this phrase usually means something much more specific and personal by it — "No one reads anything I think is good anymore" — it's nonetheless a commonly accepted notion. Many commentators assume that reading as a serious practice is in decline in contemporary life. And there's evidence to back that assumption up. In 2004, the National Endowment for the Arts released "Reading at Risk", a systematic study of reading practices in the United States; in 2007, they followed up with "To Read or Not to Read". And these reports were quite clear: Literary reading, and book reading in general, were in sharp, and sharply accelerating decline, among groups of all ages, races, genders, and education levels. While this decline was not blamed on the consumption of other media forms, the reports did note with dismay the significant increase in time spent with movies, television, video games, and the Internet. This decline in attention to reading, the report argued, would have profound implications for American civic life, indicating the deeply felt importance of reading in the development of a sense of community, of belonging, and of public responsibility.

But despite the far-reaching nature of these studies, the evidence for this decline in reading is far from clear. First, publishing industry sales figures have shown an increase in book sales, year after year, for the last several decades, and those sales are higher today than they have ever been. In fact, many of the top-selling books are selling precisely to the demographic popularly considered to be most at risk for not-reading today: kids, whose media consumption habits seem not to be interfering with their devotion to books. And our networked technologies and devices are rapidly expanding the platforms on which we can engage with books. Kindle and other e-reader sales are extremely strong, and e-book sales are growing quickly, suggesting an ongoing investment in the kinds of content that books provide.

Even the NEA saw a turnaround in its third study of reading in America, 2010's "Reading on the Rise". In part, at least, that turnaround came from a slight shift in the definition of "reading" used in the study. In 2004 and 2007, "reading" was used to describe only the leisure-time consumption of full-length printed and bound works of fiction and poetry. The 2010 study began to examine other forms of reading, including non-fiction books, as well as shorter texts, some of which were online. In this third study, we can see the first hints of a recognition that the Internet is largely composed of text, and that reading online is in fact reading. If we are, as a culture, spending more hours online, it remains arguable that active Internet users do more reading in the course of a day than has ever before been possible.

Perhaps even more importantly, the Internet has in the last ten years produced a range of technologies and venues through which readers can connect with one another, sharing and discussing what they're reading. This is made possible by the transformation of the Internet from a read-only to a read-write environment. Readers who are active on the internet today expect to be able not simply to consume published texts, but to respond to those texts, and to share work of their own as well. This shifting expectation, from passive consumption to active contribution, might go some distance toward explaining a curious bit of data that was mentioned but unexamined in the original 2004 report, "Reading at Risk": even as reading as a leisure-time activity seemed to be in precipitous decline, writing, across all age and economic groups, was on the rise. And since 2004, with the spread of blog engines and other user-friendly means of publishing online, the non-professional production of writing meant to be shared with others has grown astronomically.

Of course, it is true that most blogs and other web publications have very low readership levels, but this is in part by design; the majority of blogs are produced not for an audience per se but for a community of friends who are reading and writing together. The early blog network LiveJournal, for instance, allowed users to "friends-lock" posts, such that they could be read only by readers the author admitted to her circle. As a result the site developed many small, tight-knit communities of readers and writers bound by common interests. Often those interests included being fans of particular movies, or television series, or even books, whose universes the LiveJournalers discussed and extended  on their own sites. The mode of writing about, around, and against a fictional universe that developed in these social networks has come to be described, and often derided, as "fan fiction." Fans produce new imaginative work extending or revising the texts that they love, and while their characters and settings may not be original, their work bears much in common with that of scholars: they push back critically against aspects of the original texts they find problematic, they share their work within a community of equally invested fans, and they practice a form of community review, "beta-testing" work before they consider it published.

Other forms of critical interaction with books have grown online as well; one can see, for instance, the growing popularity of Goodreads, a social network that recently surpassed 10 million registered members, all of whom are collecting their bookshelves, creating wish lists, sharing reviews, and otherwise writing about books. They participate in Q&As with authors, they start and join discussion groups, they browse their friends' shelves, all within a social network built around a passionate interest in reading. More than ten million readers, guiding one another to the books they love.

And other online communities have developed with a focus on guiding readers as they work their ways through books. To take one particular example: after the death of author David Foster Wallace in August 2008, blogger Matthew Baldwin determined that he would devote the following summer to reading, at last, the mammoth novel Infinite Jest, and that he would draw on the Internet for support. The group blog-based project that Baldwin started, "Infinite Summer", became something of an Internet sensation, pulling together thousands of readers around the world in order to discuss the novel online, both on the "Infinite Summer" site and on offshoot websites. And mainstream media figures picked up the challenge, including writers for mainstream newspapers such as the Washington Post and The Guardian. Numerous participants in "Infinite Summer" posted about it their own blogs, and many readers held in-person meetups to talk about the book. And the blog posts and discussions reveal both a desire to interpret and understand the novel at a deep level and a desire to connect with other readers engaged in the same process.

It's not accidental that all of this social activity was inspired by Infinite Jest. Wallace's untimely death left many readers feeling as though they needed to seek some kind of comfort in his writing. And, as Wallace noted in a 1996 interview, his sense of the purpose of serious fiction is to give the reader "imaginative access to other selves", with the end result that, "if a piece of fiction can allow us imaginatively to identify with characters' pain, we might then also more easily conceive of others identifying with our own. This is nourishing, redemptive; we become less alone inside." Readers, in other words, have always read for connection, with a character or an author; in the author's absence, a connection with other readers might be that much more desirable. Even more, in Infinite Jest, Wallace explores the ways that intentional communities such as Alcoholics Anonymous and the social connections that they require of their members might present possibilities for helping contemporary Americans escape the painful isolation and self-doubt that they experience in their day-to-day lives. It is little surprise, then, that readers of this particular novel sought connections with others in order to discuss it as they read.

It might, however, be a little bit of a surprise that readers sought those connections online, rather than in a more conventionally understood, locally organized book club. Of course, online reading communities such as Infinite Summer bear something in common with earlier, offline reading groups like these, but the networked structure of online groups free them from local settings and allow connections to be forged among like-minded readers in widely dispersed locations, rather than being restricted by physical proximity. Online reading communities also differ from large scale reading projects such as Oprah's Book Club in their read-write orientation, being focused, like the LiveJournal groups I discussed earlier, not just on consuming a text in isolation, or on listening to others — and especially experts — discuss the text, but on actively writing back in response to what is being read. What groups like "Infinite Summer" bear in common with older forms of reading groups, however, is a close tie between reading — an activity we think of as solitary — and community, a tie that highlights the intimate relationship between the experience of reading and the empathetic desire to understand the experiences, and the responses, of other people than ourselves. Even when conducted alone, reading connects us to others; when reading happens in a group — and even better, when reading happens in a group that is able to share both their reading and writing practices — the possibilities for creating new kinds of community arise.

Given these examples, I would suggest that we might begin to acknowledge that reading is not at all in decline in contemporary American life, though it has moved increasingly online. And while the concerns expressed in "Reading at Risk" about what a decline in reading might mean for civic life are worth bearing in mind, it's also important for us to be willing to look for new kinds of civic life, for new kinds of communities developing on the Internet, and to think about what those communities might tell us about the new kinds of literacy, and the possible futures for the book in the twenty-first century.

中国电影表述的文化价值观

贾磊磊

中国艺术研究院院长助理，文化发展战略研究中心主任

内容提要：不论是人们对某种商品的购买，还是对于不同生活方式的选择，乃至于对精神信仰的恪守，都是基于人们所持有的文化价值观。所以，文化价值观实际上是决定人类生存方式与社会发展方向的精神导向系统。作为一种在长期实践活动中逐渐形成的主流社会意识形态，文化价值观并非只是躺在经典文献中的文字符号，而是体现在艺术作品变化多端的表现形式之中，贯穿在商业贸易纷繁复杂的交易活动之中，它绵延在普通百姓衣食住行的日常生活之中，当然，它也呈现在电影这种炫目多彩的流行文化之中……

当前，中国本土电影的竞争压力日益凸显，好莱坞进口影片对我们的市场占有不断增加，海外电影对内地电影的影响不断加剧，在这种严峻的市场竞争中，我们对中国电影的总体设计上，必须要把提高电影的市场竞争力放在首位。一部电影如果没有市场的认可，没有能够吸引观众进入电影院进行观看的缘由，它的所有价值诉求都将归零。所以，增强中国电影的市场竞争力，在中国电影产业化发展的战略排序中应当居于首位。然而，市场竞争力并不仅仅是指一部影片的商业竞争力，而且还包括这部电影的文化竞争力。或者说，我们在考虑提升电影商业竞争力的时候，必须考虑将文化的因素"植入"商业的理念之中。所以，我们现在不论是讨论中国电影的艺术使命，还是研究中国电影的社会责任，以及中国电影的文化职能，都不能将电影的这些作用与电影的市场竞争力对立起来，即不能预先"搁置"了电影对市场的经济责任，然后再去奢谈它的艺术使命、社会责任与文化功能。同理，我们在为一部电影的市场胜利而欢呼的时候,除了总结电影的商业运作模式与成功的营销策略之外,我们还应当关注的是它的文化表达。特别是那些表现题材重大,资金投入巨大,市场反响强大的影片,对其电影文化经验的分析与对其商业经验的总结同样重要,如果一种正向的文化价值观在这些影片中得到有效的传播,那么,不仅对中国电影的历史发展贡献巨大,而且对于促进中国文化的长远发展同样功不可没。

一、心向仁爱

文化价值观是一个民族、一个国家、一种文化所体现的关于生活方式、社会理想、精神信仰的基本取向,它决定着人们在政治、社会、伦理、艺术领域对于是非、善恶、正邪、美丑的基本判断。什么样的东西值得珍惜,什么样的东西不值得珍惜?什么样的生活有意义,什么样的生活没有意义?什么样的思想能够被认同,什么样的思想不能够被认同,都与人们的价值取向密切相关。电影所表达的文化价值观,时常会由于选择的题材、类型、主题不尽相同,在精神旨向上也不尽一致,但是,就总体的价值取向而言,中国电影对于中国传统文化精神的取舍,对于传统文化价值的认同,是我们分析中国电影文化经验的重要内容。

作为一种普遍认同的文化价值观,"仁爱"思想贯穿在政治、哲学、伦理、艺术等不同的精神领域,它是整个中华民族核心价值体系的有机组成部分。千百年来,仁者所以为人所仰慕、仁学所以被人所敬奉,首先在于仁学就本质而言是一种"爱人之学"。据考:"仁"是人字的复体,与任、妊同源。古时怀孕称"仁"。"仁"即引申为育人、养人、助人、爱人之意。阮元说,"仁之意,人之也",就是说仁的本意即以符合人类普遍意愿的方式对待每个人。2012年,中国出品了一部刷新了中国电影历史最高票房纪录的影片《画皮2》。这部影片集爱情、魔幻、动作为一体。它共打破了中国电影史上五项历史纪录。这样一部典型的商业电影,支撑它的究竟是一种什么样的文化价值体系呢?易言之,中国电影创作者植入在这张"画皮"中的传统文化元素包括哪些呢?影片中小唯这个有着千年修行经历的妖狐,曾经为了救人而自毁妖灵,违反妖界的禁令,被冷冻在冰湖的寒冰之中达500年,这表明她在影片叙述的前史中已经站

在了与人类相同道德的基准线上。在神雀儿将她从冰天雪地中救出来后,她一直都梦想变成人,过一种人的生活。小唯曾经问雀儿:"你有过人的体温吗,有过心跳吗,闻过花香吗,看得出天空的颜色吗,流过眼泪吗,世上有人爱你、情愿为你去死吗?"这一切只有人才能够得到的感觉,是小唯最想得到的生活——就像在徐克电影中的青蛇一样,尽管在人类世界中眼泪是苦涩的,但是,那毕竟是一个绚丽多彩、芬芳四溢的世界。小唯最后不惜用自己美艳无比的皮肤,换得精公主的人心,替精公主下嫁到天狼国与虎狼为伍,就是想要体验到那种虽然短暂但却幸福的人类生活。对人类世界的神往成为影片极为突出的叙事主旨,同时也是这部影片表达的核心价值取向。

其实,小唯此前在人间生死之情的感召下,曾经含着眼泪弃恶从善,放弃了对人心的血腥争夺,把生的希望还给了自己心爱的人(把插在王生胸口的尖刀拔了出来),使王生再度回到人间。就在她看着心爱的人渐渐起死回生的时候,自己也缓缓地现出了狐的原形。此后她回到了山岩的洞穴边,默默地观望着人世间的一切……这难道应该是妖的所作所为吗?我们过去看到的妖孽也罢,鬼神也罢,它们不是被天意所惩治,就是被人类所正法,何时何地有这种"杀身成仁"的义举呢?在这种妖向人的转换机制中,最能够打动观众的并不是玄妙的数字技术,也不是魔幻的空间造型,而是妖道向人道的认同,是邪恶向仁爱的皈依。我们在总结一部电影骄人的票房业绩的时候,一定要注重它对于文化价值的表达方式。韩国电影和电视剧之所以在亚洲风行,它靠的是好莱坞电影那种炫目的数字技术吗?它有美国电影那么雄厚的制作资金吗?韩国电影最能够被亚洲观众接受的是其作品中体现的那种仁爱、忠诚的文化理念。可见,文化依然是驱动电影商业之轮的内在动力。

中国古代的仁爱思想不可能跨越千年的时光隧道直接进入当代观众的心中。它必须经过相应的文化传播载体,才能够被世人所认识、所理解、所接受。影片《5颗子弹……》的原名叫《仁枪》,这是别有寓意的。枪,原本是暴力的工具,是杀人的利器。把一个"仁"字置放在枪的前面,显然并不是在强化它的杀戮功能,不是突出它的物质威力,而是在强调它的文化喻义和道德力量。把枪命名为仁,枪即变得"出师有名",与此同时使持枪者具有一种仁者的风范,彰显出一种仁者的威慑力。纵观影片的整个叙事过程,一个即将退休的警察押解着四个犯人,他枪里的五颗子弹全都是为了保护人、救助人、帮助人而打出的——没有一颗子弹真的是要去杀人取命。顺便说的是,中国电影对暴力的呈现方式并不全像好莱坞电影那样,打起枪来就是鲜血四溅、血肉横飞,全然是机械暴力的崇拜。从这个意义上讲,影片《5颗子弹……》完整地体现出我们主流电影在文化价值取向方面的人道主义诉求。

社会学家迪耶戈·甘伯塔曾经讲述过一个黑手党头目回忆的故事。当他还是一个少年的时候,有一次他的父亲(黑手党人)叫他爬上一堵墙,然后又叫他跳下来,答应说会接住他。他一开始不肯跳,但在父亲的坚持下,他终于跳了下去,结果他的父亲并没有去接他,摔得他嘴啃泥。他父亲这样做,是为了让他明白一个道理:"你必须学会不信任别人,连你的爹娘也别信任。"[①]这个故事的中国版本在影片《赵氏孤儿》里复现过。就在赵孤从屋顶上纵身跳下的那一刻,屠岸贾收回了他张开的双臂,使赵孤重重跌在地上。屠岸贾这样做的目的是想用肢体的痛苦告诉赵孤,这个世界上谁都不能信——包括自己的干爹也不例外。他能够信的只有手中的刀剑,这就是屠岸贾灌输给赵孤的处世哲学。这种教育就是要在赵孤幼小的心灵里灌输一种冷酷的"丛林法则",让他崇尚实力与强权,并以此作为安身立命的处世之道。也就在赵孤重新回到屋顶上拿回宝剑再跳下来的时候,程婴走上前去紧紧抱住了他。程婴是在告诉孩子,在这个世界上还有比刀剑更可靠的力量,那就是仁爱。也许,正是从那一刻开始赵孤坚定了他的人生信念。在人生的路口上他没有选择强权，而是选择了人性。影片《赵氏孤儿》与传统戏曲最根本的区别就在于它放弃了那种"血亲之上"的复仇伦理，改变了那种"你杀了我全家，我也要杀了你全家"的以恶制恶的黑色逻辑。

在中国古代诸侯纷争的岁月里，柔如杞柳的人性怎么能够抵得住"争夺相杀"的刀枪剑戟，怎么能挡得住"驰骋疆场"的金戈铁马？所谓"终身之仁"和"救世之仁"只能是身处战乱中的人们对良辰美景的无限憧憬。就连孔子也不得不惊呼："君子之所谓仁者，其难乎！"孟子亦慨叹："今之为仁者，犹以一杯水，救一车薪之火。"正因如此，"仁爱"的理想境界才令人们备加珍惜，分外向往，"仁爱"精神也必然成为人类对现实世界进行文化救赎与道德重构的理想之途。

二、道法天意

在中国文化的价值谱系中，虽然没有一个主宰一切的上帝，却有着超然于万物之上的天意。天意，在中国古代被看作是超越于其他法度之上的最高道德范畴，是世界万物生死兴衰的主宰。正所谓"顺天意者，兼相爱，交相利，必得赏；反天意者，别相恶，交相贼，必得罚"。（《墨子·天志上》）墨子的意思是，顺应天意，就是要与别人相敬相爱，分享各自的利益，这样必定得到上天的赏赐；所谓违反天意，就是把别人和自己区分开，厌恶人家，致使大家相互伤害，这样必定遭到上天的惩罚。可见，在墨家的精神世界中天意与人伦是翕然相通的。特别重要的是墨子还将"强者不劫弱，贵者不傲贱，智者不欺愚"作为顺应天意的"义政"的标志，从而体现出中国传统文化思想中，从世俗生活到社会政治领域对天意的一致尊奉。由此可见，天意并不是一种超然物外的绝对精神，而是一种与人的伦理取向相同、相合的文化理念。中国著名的现代小说家老舍在他创作的文学作品中也说过："凡事都有天意，顺天者昌，逆天者亡。"（《神拳》第三幕）强调世间的万事万物冥冥之中都因循着善有善报、恶有恶报的伦理法则。

在以中国传统文化为创意素材的许多电影中，天意，时常被置于一种改变影片叙事结局的叙事者的地位。中国电影正是利用这种世俗冲突的非世俗化表述，弥合了处于从属性社会地位的普通观众对正义、对光

明、对善良的期待。特别是中国电影在处理人物命运的结局时,往往将其与某种"天意"联系起来。影片《武侠》(2011)在七十二地煞的教主(王羽饰)与刘金喜展开绝杀之时,刘家村的上空电闪雷鸣。其后,被刘金喜与徐百九重创的教主在倾盆暴雨中被一道来自天空的闪电击中,使这个恶贯满盈的恶魔,毙命于泥泞的场院中(遁入了地狱)。这种看似极其偶然的命运结局,实际上却表现出反派人物必然覆灭的天意。在《晚清

风云——独臂壮士》(1993)中奸贼袁世凯(赵长军饰)在生死搏杀中并没有死于义士的刀剑,而是死在从房梁上骤然坠落的大钟之下,使这个类历史的叛逆得到的是一种来自上天的惩罚。《新龙门客栈》(1992)中武艺高强的东厂鹰犬(刘洵饰)在客栈激烈的厮杀中,也没有死于金镶玉的利刃之下,而是死在客栈中两个石磨的挤压之中,金镶玉只是将这个罪有应得的刽子手送到了他的坟墓入口,使这个茹毛饮血的恶魔最终落得一个"自作自受"的下场。《晚清风云——邪教白莲》(1993)里的占承天(计春华饰)尽管有一身过人的武艺,就拳脚功夫而言,没有谁是他的对手,作恶多端的他最后从高台上跳下来时却被劈开的竹尖刺透心窝。《黄河大侠》里罪孽深重的段王,最后葬身于黄河的万顷狂涛之中,也喻示出历史巨流对这个逆贼的无情埋葬! 中国武侠电影创作者们这种不约而同的情节设计,其实都是想在精彩的武术演义背后,转述一种"善恶有报"的天理,不论你的武功何等强大,都不能够逃脱天意的定数。包括《画皮2》里那个浑身尽是巫术、妖术、道术和魔法的天狼国的巫师(费翔饰),不论是霍将军还是捉妖师,谁也不是他的对手。最后,被成千上万只从天而降的神雀啄食成一具骷髅。可见,恶势力就是再强大,最终决定胜负的依然是冥冥之中的天意,它不仅能够评定是非善恶,而且还能够定夺胜负成败。更具有道德劝诫旨意的是,小唯将自己美丽的外皮换取了靖公主的心脏之后,完成了她做人的心愿。可是,万万没有想到的是,就在小唯以靖公主的名义去与天狼国的王子成婚的时候,等待着她的是一个惊天的阴谋：天狼国要把精公主（小唯假扮）的心挖出来移植给天狼国的王子，让他起死回生，而这个天狼国的王子的心恰恰是当年被小唯和雀儿挖出来的！好像冥冥之中攫取了他人的东西，现在又要被他人拿回去。影片的循环的叙事逻辑似乎在启示观众，世间的事情往往就是这样，善恶有报，生死轮回，不论是人是妖谁也逃不出上天的旨意。如上所述，中国影片中的暴力美学历来也是道德的美学。现代电影不论是恐怖片还是神怪片，都越来越具有一种功能上的"互文性"，有时一部正儿八经的电影还不如一部神怪恐怖电影更有劝诫的道德作用。

三、魂归田园

在中国，宗教是一种"出世"的文化，在西方，宗教则属于一种"入世"的文化。中国佛教的圣地（寺院）大都建在远离世俗生活的名山大川之中。在这些人迹罕至的崇山峻岭间，恰恰是佛教僧人逃避现实苦难的理想居所。同时，也是他们在现实生活之外寻找人生意义的圣地。而基督教、天主教的教堂基本上都是建在繁华的都市内。他们要"管理"的是世俗生活。在美国，在俄罗斯，包括在韩国，推开宾馆的窗户，映入眼帘的时常是教堂高耸的尖顶和用霓虹灯装点的十字架。西方的宗教明显地具有入世的倾向。马克斯·韦伯在分析民族的文化精神和社会经济的发展之间的内在关系时曾经指出：新教的教义是把宗教的理想世俗化，其核心是苦行意识的大众化，即把宗教的戒律引入到现实的世俗生活之中，使大众的生活本身变成一种具有宗教意味的修行方式，以此来推进社会经济的发展。中国的佛教更注重的则是来世，其最高理想的实现过程都具有禁欲苦行的色彩，它是通过离开世俗的世界来完成个体的修行。

从理论上讲，两种不同的宗教形态，在电影中根本不可能呈现为同一种意义表述系统。我们对武侠电影的宗教伦理的分析，实际上是建立在这样一种假设和猜想之上——现在看来，在中国武侠电影的叙事机制中，宗教不仅时常会引导电影的精神取向，而且实际上还对观众起着相当重要的询唤职能。电影作为一种旨在满足大众心理欲望的叙事客体，只有建立符合大众伦理的叙事本文，才能求得观众的普遍认同。所以，中国电影并没有像好莱坞电影那样把宗教的教义直接转变成暴力的旗帜，而是将宗教的伦理与影片的叙事情节交融起来，宗教伦理在为正义提供

了合理的道德依据的同时,也通过叙事突出了宗教自身的"出世情结"。

在中国电影中尽管伸张正义、除暴安良的义举是在充满血腥的叙事进程中展开的,但是,作为一种对暴力叙事的"校正",中国电影在江湖的搏杀结束之后,时常会描绘出一种没有杀戮、没有血泪的田园世界。影片《独臂刀》(1967)中的独臂英雄方刚以其一身绝技,用独臂断刀战胜了金刀锁,为齐家化解了生死大患,此时他实际上已经登上武林霸主的显赫地位,最起码江湖上齐家刀法掌门人已非他莫属。可是,方刚无意在武林中争强称雄,他上前向师傅齐如风辞行,说今天报了师恩从此要远走天涯,与自己的救命恩人一起做一个种田的农夫,过一种田园生活。齐如风见此也将手中的金刀毅然折断,扔在地上!至此,张彻这位以暴力美学而著称的香港动作电影的导演,在银幕上完成了他对暴力终极意义的否定。胡金铨导演的《龙门客栈》(1967)善恶双方经过一场生死决战,东厂首领曹少钦恶有恶报、死于乱剑之下。获胜的义士萧少兹等也没有率领于家子女重入江湖寻机复仇,或是杀入官府去夺回失去的权力。他们选择的是远离了纷争不息的世界,归隐于茫茫的山林之间。可见,宗教作为一种叙事因素进入电影之中,不仅改变了影片的主题意义,而且也改变了人物的性格走向。

许多中国武侠电影的结局,获得胜利的主人公都不会留恋世俗的功名利禄,而是向往一个没有恩怨情仇的世外桃源。《少林寺》中的觉远为继承师傅"保护少林,匡扶正义"的遗志,割断了与牧羊女的生死情缘,

选择了对佛门的"皈依"。这与西方电影中那个重新获得了王位与美女的侠盗罗宾汉完全不同。中国的少林弟子在完成了自己的使命之后,时常会离开这个血泪横流的江湖。他们有时甚至宁愿以自己的性命来中止江湖上的仇杀。影片《少林达摩》(1990)中杀人无数的刀客面对着江湖上循环往复的杀戮,冤冤相报的因果,最后竟然选择了自杀来完成自己的忏悔!影片《五郎八卦棍》(1990)中杨五郎与众僧一起击退辽兵,血刃了奸贼萧天佐,报了国恨家仇之后,六郎曾经劝五郎再组杨家军,重整河山。但五郎决意皈依佛门,辞别了与自己生死相依的若兰,重入寺门,普度众生。影片《索命逍遥楼》(1990)主人公单娥杀进逍遥楼,击破了八卦阵。经过殊死拼杀,将杀父仇人白宠踢进万丈刀坑,报了深仇大恨。而单娥最后同样了却尘缘,隐迹山林。真正的武林志士是把抑恶扬善作为自己毕生的天职,对功名、对财富即便是得到了也会将它抛入九霄。《天剑绝刀之独孤九剑》(1993)的结尾,夏侯太子(刘锡明饰)和后唐公主(李嘉欣饰)在胜利之后,一个扔掉了象征着权力和暴力的宝剑,一个扔掉了象征着财富的玉箫,双双退出江湖。虽然这是一种虚幻的理想,但这种理想的流露表达的正是人们渴望世间永世安宁、不再征战的宿愿。在经过惊心动魄的生死搏杀之后,出生入死的侠士面对着如诗如画的田园,面对着曾经心心相印的知己(《刺客新传》,1993),时常会感慨万千!《新龙门客栈》(1992)的"闭幕式"同样也充满了对无休止的暴力的唾弃!一场血腥的屠杀终于结束了,大漠上一片寂静,金镶玉(张曼玉饰）用烈酒烧毁了自己苦心经营的客栈，也烧毁了那个充满血腥气味的处所，她远离了大漠，也远离了那个杀人取命的生涯。她向往的是一处没有欺诈的精神寓所，一个没有杀戮的情感的归宿。可见，中国武侠电影中的宗教职能与西方电影中那种完全介入双方的是非恩怨，强化世俗暴力冲突的职能显然有所不同。

在饱受专制统治的中国封建社会，归隐田园、皈依佛门曾经是许多文人墨客的人生理想。他们在深山古寺里参禅悟道，在庙宇青灯下戒色修行，从而远离了社会的纷争和暴力的冲突，为心的清静留出了一片净土。深受中国传统文化"浸染"的中国电影，对梦幻般的田园景色的神往，对那种没有杀戮、没有争战、没有流血的生活的祈望，更是极其突出的一种文化取向。它不仅仅体现在一个导演的作品、一个地区的电影之中，而是贯穿在不同时期、不同区域的电影之中。尽管，我们现在早已远离了那个封闭、愚昧的封建社会，电影的审美想象永远也无法抵御现实的风雨，影像世界的田园风光也不能兑现为真实的世界图景，但是，那种超然物外的审美境界毕竟为我们的心灵提供了一处可以栖息的境地。

综上所述，在电影艺术的语言形态中，文化价值取向是一种寄予在影像故事体系中的"潜在意义"，它更多地是通过麦茨所说的那种"含蓄意指"的方式来表达，而不是通过抽象的说教来实现的。一部影片在文化价值观方面的正确与否，对于这部电影的市场营销的成败其实具有非常重要的作用。包括如何引导观众对于电影明星的文化认同，如何设定一部电影的文化趣味，如何确定一部影片的文化主题，其实，都是影响一部影片市场盈亏的重要因素。电影，归根结底是一种要在商业市场上流通的流行文化产品，如果它在文化趣味上脱离了我们这个时代的审美风尚，在文化市场定位上悖逆于现实生活的消费取向，在文化心理上偏离了我们这个社会的普遍趋势，那么，其市场前景必定暗淡。所以，增强中国电影的市场竞争力，并不仅仅是一个电影经济的命题，同样也是一个电影文化的命题。

---

① [美]狄亚哥·甘贝塔，《西西里黑手党：私人保护企业》，第35页，哈佛大学出版社，1993。

Cultural Values Presented in Chinese Movies

Jia Leilei

President Assistant
of Chinese National
Academy of Arts,
Director of Cultural
Development Strategy
Research Center,CNAA

Abstract: Either the purchase of a certain kind of goods, or the selection of different ways of life, or even upholding one's faith is based on one's cultural values. Therefore, the cultural values are actually the spiritual orientation system that determines the existence mode of mankind and the development direction of society. As a mainstream social ideology gradually developing in the long-term practical activities, the cultural values are not just the written signs in classic literatures, but embodied in changing expressions of artistic works, penetrating through massive and complicated commercial transactions, extending into the basic necessities of common people's daily lives, and of course presented in the dazzling and colorful popular culture of movies.

At present, Chinese local movies have been facing increasing pressure of competition, as more movies imported from Hollywood have continuously enlarged their market share in China, and the overseas movies have exerted the growing influence on local movies in the mainland of China. In the severe market competition, top priority must be given to enhancing the competitiveness of movies in the master plan for the development of Chinese movies. Without recognition of the market and attractions to the audience, a movie is almost valueless. Therefore, to enhance the market competitiveness of Chinese movies should be the most important part in the strategies of the industrialization of Chinese movies. However, market competitiveness does not just refer to the commercial competitiveness of a movie, but also includes its cultural competitiveness. In other words, the cultural factors must be injected in the commercial concept when a movie's commercial competitiveness is improved. Therefore, we can by no means set the movie's functions and its competitiveness against each other whether when we discuss the artistic mission of the movie or the social responsibility and cultural function of Chinese movie. In other words, we cannot talk about a movie's artistic mission, social responsibility and cultural function by putting aside its economic responsibility.

Likewise, when we cheer for the victory of a movie at the market, we should not only summarize the movie's business mode of operation and the successful marketing strategy, but also concern about its cultural expressions. Especially for those with magnificent themes, huge capital investment and a strong market response, the cultural analysis is as important as the summarization of its business experience. If a positive cultural value is effectively disseminated in these movies, then it will not only make a magnificent contribution to the historical development of Chinese movies, but also contribute to the long-term development of the Chinese culture.

I. Yearning for Benevolence and Love

The cultural values are the basic orientation embodied in a nation, a country and a culture in respect of lifestyle, social ideals and spiritual beliefs, and determine the basic judgments of people upon right or wrong, good or evil and beautiful or ugly in the political, social and ethical and artistic fields. What should be valued and what should not? What kind of life is meaningful and what is not? What kind of ideas can be accepted and what not? All these are closely related to people's value orientation. The cultural values expressed in Chinese movies are not always consistent in spiritual aspect due to the difference in the subject matter, type and theme chosen; however, in terms of the overall value orientation, the representation of traditional Chinese culture and the recognition of traditional cultural value in Chinese movies is an important part of our analysis of the cultural experience of Chinese movies.

As a kind of universally recognized cultural values, the thought of "Love and Charity" exits in different spiritual fields such as politics, philosophy, ethics and art and it is the organic integral part of the Chinese core value system. For thousands of years, the benevolent have been admired and the science of benevolence been observed, because, first of all, the science of benevolence teaches people how to love others. Research shows that, the Chinese character "仁 (benevolence)", the composite of the other Chinese character "人 (human)", is the paronym of "任(responsibility)" and "妊 (pregnancy)", the other two Chinese characters. "仁" meant pregnancy in ancient times with the extended meanings as "giving birth to people", "cultivating people", "helping people" and "loving people". Ruan Yuan, an ancient Chinese, says: " '仁(benevolence)' means '人(human)'", that is to say, the essence of benevolence is to treat everybody in a way conforming to the universal will of mankind. In 2012, a movie called Painted Skin II bettered the box-office record in China. Integrating love, magic and action, the movie broke five records in the history of Chinese movies. As a typical commercial movie, what is the cultural value system behind it? In other words, what traditional cultural elements are injected into this movie? Xiaowei, a fox demon who had practiced for a thousand years, saved a mortal man's life by sacrificing herself, which violated the laws of the demon world, and she therefore has been imprisoned in an icy abyss for 500 years. It shows Xiaowei has stood on the same moral benchmark as human beings. After the bird demon rescued her from the abyss, she has been dreaming of becoming a human and living a human life. Once she asked the bird demon: "Do you have a human temperature

and heartbeat? Can you smell flowers? Can you tell the color of the sky? Have you shed tears? Is there anybody in the world loving you and prepared to die for you?"These senses only owned by human beings are what Xiaowei wants most—just as the Green Snake in the movie of Tsui Hark, for whom the tears in the human world are bitter, but it is after all a colorful and fragrant world. Finally, Xiaowei exchanges with her beautiful skin for the heart of Princess Jing and married to the State of Sirius on behalf of the princess, just to experience the short but happy human life. Yearning for the human world is both the theme of the movie and also its core value orientation.

In fact, Xiaowei, touched by the human feelings of life and death, forsook evil and abandoned the bloody fight for the human heart, leaving the hope of living to her beloved person. Watching her beloved person gradually recovering from death, she slowly assumes the image of a fox. She returned to the side of the rock cave later, quietly watching the human world ... Is it what a demon should do? The demons or ghosts we saw were either punished by gods or executed by human beings, but never died a martyr for a just cause. In this conversion from demon to human, the most touching part is not the incredible digital technology, nor the magical space modeling, but the humanitarian recognition of diabolism, the conversion from evil to benevolence. When talking about the impressive box office of a movie, we ought to pay attention to its expression of cultural values. Is the popularity of Korean movies and TV plays in Asia owing to the dazzling digital technology or the colossal production funds as the Hollywood movies? It is the cultural concept of benevolence and loyalty that make Korean movies popular among Asian audience. It shows that the culture is still the intrinsic power driving the wheel of the movie business.

It is impossible that the ancient Chinese thought of benevolence cuts across the time tunnel of thousands of years to directly penetrate into the hearts of contemporary audience. It can be recognized, understood and accepted only through the appropriate carriers. The movie Five Bullets ... is originally named as Gun of Mercy. The gun is a tool of violence, a killing weapon. "Mercy" with "Gun" is obviously not to strengthen the gun's killing function or highlight its material power, but to emphasize its cultural metaphor and moral strength. Named Mercy, it becomes a gun with just, and its holder shows a power of benevolence. In the movie, a policeman near the retiring age escorts four prisoners with a gun of five bullets, all of which have been shot in order to protect, save or help the people—none of them are really shot to kill. By the way, Chinese movies present violence not in the way as Hollywood movies, in which the blood splashes and flies about, showing a complete worship for mechanical violence. In this sense, the movie Five Bullets … fully reflects the humanitarian expression of China's mainstream movies.

Diego Gambetta, a sociologist, has ever told a story recalled by a head of Sicilian Mafia that, when he was young, his father (a member of Mafia) asked him to climb onto a wall and then jump down with the promise to catch him. At the beginning, he was reluctant; but with his father's insistence, he jumped, but his father did not catch him and he tumbled completely. By this his father intended to make him know: "You must learn not to trust others including your parents". [1] This story has reoccurred in the Chinese movie "The Orphan of Zhao". In this movie, when the orphan of Zhao jumps down from the roof, Tu Anjia withdraw his open arms and let the orphan fall onto the ground heavily. He intend to tell the orphan that nobody, with no exception of his foster father, was worthy of being trusted, and the only thing he can trust was the sword in his hand. Tu wanted to teach a philosophy, the brutal "rule of jungle", to the child, so that he could uphold strength and power. When the orphan go to the roof again and jump down with his sword, Cheng Ying catches him, which tells the child that in the world there is still something more important than sword, i.e. love and benevolence. Maybe from that moment, the orphan firms his life belief: he did not choose power but humanity. The most fundamental difference between the movie The Orphan of Zhao and the traditional operas is that it has abandoned the ethic of revenge based on the "blood relatives" and changed that "you killed my family, and I will kill yours", a black logic of returning evil for evil.

In ancient war times, how could the soft humanity resist the shining spears and armored horses battlefields? The so-called "lifelong love and benevolence" and "love and benevolence for salvation" are only people's anticipation for peace. Even Confucius sighed with regret, "Difficult is it to attain to what is called the perfect humanity of the superior man! " Mencius also regretfully sighed, "Those, however, who now-a-days practise benevolence do it as if with one cup of water they could save a whole wagon-load of fuel which was on fire" Therefore, benevolence and love is especially cherished and yearned for by people, and is bound to become the ideal way for mankind's cultural salvation and moral reconstruction of the real world.

II. Following the Will of Heaven

Despite no dominating God, there is the will of Heaven transcending everything on earth in the value system of the Chinese culture, which was was

regarded superior to other laws and regulations in ancient China and determine the rise and fall, life and death of all things in the world. As Mozi said, "He who obeys the will of Heaven, loving universally and benefiting others, will obtain rewards. He who opposes the will of Heaven, being partial and unfriendly and harming others, will incur punishment." (Mozi, Will of Heaven I) . It means that people who obey the will of Heaven shall respect and love others and share benefits, and thus will be rewarded; those who oppose the will of Heaven are to separate themselves from others, disgust others, and thus harm each other and incur punishment by Heaven. Obviously, the will of Heaven in Mohist

spirit world is harmoniously interlinked with human relations. It is particularly important that Mozi argues that the sign of the righteous standard to obey the will of Heaven is that "The strong does not plunder the weak. The honored does not demean the humble. The clever does not deceive the stupid", reflecting the compliance with the will of Heaven in secular life and social and political fields as well in traditional Chinese culture. It shows that the will of Heaven is not an insular absolute spirit, but a cultural concept with the same orientation as the ethic and a concept integrated with the ethic. Lao She, a famous Chinese modern novelist, says in one of his literary works, "Everything is dominated by the will of Heaven. Those who obey the will of Heaven will prosper, otherwise, perish" (Magic Boxer, Act III), emphasizing that everything in the world follows the ethical rule that one turn, good or evil, deserves another.

In many movies on the same of the traditional Chinese culture, the will of Heaven is often taken as the narrator to change of the outcome. The non-secular expression of secular conflicts in Chinese movies meets the expectation for justice, brightness and goodness of the general audience in the subordinate social status. In particular, Chinese movies often connect the fate of the characters with the "will of Heaven". In the movie Wu Xia (Martial arts, 2011), it was thundering and lightning when the villain fights a duel with Liu Jinxi (the protagonist), finally the villain was hit by a lightning. This seemingly accidental ending shows the will of Heaven that villains are doomed to destruction. In "Wind and Cloud in Late Qing—One Armed Hero" (1993), the traitor Yuan Shikai (acted by Zhao Changjun) was not killed by the righteous men, but died from the bell suddenly falling from the beam, indicating the punishment by the Heaven for his treason. In New Dragon Inn (1992), the thug (acted by Liu Xun) of Dongchang (an eunuch-led espionage agency in the Ming Dynasty) was not killed by a sword, but was squeezed to death between two millstones. He finally suffered the consequences of his own deeds. In "Wind and Cloud in Late Qing—White Lotus Cult" (1993), the villain named Zhan Chengtian (acted by Ji Chunhua) was spiked through the pit of his stomach by a split bamboo when he jumped down from a high platform; in Yellow River Fighter, the sinful Princess Wang died in the vast raging Yellow River, implying that the mighty current of history buried the usurper ruthlessly. Such plots tell that "good and evil will be rewarded", and no matter how powerful you are, no one can escape the destiny. It is also true of the sorcerer (acted by Fei Xiang) of the State of Sirius in Painted Skin Ⅱ, who was good at witchcraft, sorcery, Taoist and other magic. Neither General Huo nor the demon hunter can defeat him, but he was pecked into a skull by thousands of birds descending from the sky. It is obvious that no matter how strong the vicious power is, it is the Heaven that has the final say. It is of more moral suasion that Xiaowei becomes a human as she wished after exchanging her beautiful skin for the heart of Princess Jing, but a conspiracy is uncovered: her heart will be taken out to save her fiancé whose heart was once taken way by Xiaowei and Quer. It seems that thinks robbed from other are doomed to be returned back. The cycling narrative logic of the movie implies that either good or evil will be rewarded, life and death will recur, and neither human beings nor demons can escape the will of Heaven. As mentioned above, the violence aesthetics in Chinese movies has always been the moral aesthetics. Whether the horror movies or the ghost movies, the modern movies have increasingly become "intertextual" in function. Sometimes a serious movie is not as dissuasive as a ghost or horror movie.

Ⅲ. Returning to the Idyllic Spirit

In China, the religion is a "reclusive" culture while the Western religion is the "secular" one. Most Chinese Buddhist sanctuaries (monasteries) are situated in great mountains and rivers away from the secular life. These inaccessible mountains are exactly the ideal places for Buddhists to escape the suffering of reality. At the same time, they are the holy land for them to look for the truth of life beyond the reality. On the contrary, churches of Christianity and Catholicism are basically built in prosperous cities. They intend to "manage" the secular affairs. Looking through the window of the hotel, you often see towering spire of the churches and crosses decorated with neon lights in the United States, Russia, and even South Korea. The Western religion has an obvious secular tendency. Analyzing the intrinsic relationship between a nation's cultural spirit and the socio-economic development, Max Weber pointed out: The Protestant doctrines are to secularize the religious ideals and its core is to popularize the ascetic awareness, that is, the religious precepts are introduced to the secular lives so that the lives of the public become a way of religious practice, whereby promoting the socio-economic development. Chinese Buddhism pays more attention to afterlife and the realization of its highest ideals has the ascetic color. The individual practice is to be completed by leaving the secular world.

Theoretically, it is impossible for two different religious forms to assume the same meaning presentation system in the movie. Our analysis on the religious ethics of martial arts movies is actually based on such an assumption and conjecture—it appears in the narrative mechanism of Chinese martial arts movies that religion not only guides the spirit orientation of the movies,

but actually can appeal the audience. As a narrative object designed to meet the mental desire of the public, the movie can be universally recognized only by establishing the narrative texts conforming to the public ethics. Therefore, Chinese movies blend the religious ethics with the plots rather than directly convert them into violence as Hollywood movies do. The religious ethics, while providing the reasonable moral basis for justice, highlights its "reclusiveness".

Though the justice is promoted and the wicked are weeded out through bloody violence in Chinese movies, the movies usually present a pastoral world without killing and blood and tears after the fights are over, as a kind of correction of violence. In the movie One-Armed Swordsman (1967), Fang Gang, the one-armed hero, defeats Jin Daosuo with one arm and a broken sword and settles peril for Qi family. He actually becomes the overlord, or at least becomes the only one candidate for head of Qi Family. However, with no intention to rule, Fang Gang bids farewell to his master Qi Rufeng, saying that he will travel to the remote corner of the world after paying the debt of gratitude for his master, and lead a pastoral life together with his rescuer. At his words, Qi Rufeng decisively breaks the golden sword in his hand and throws it on the ground! At this point, Zhang Che, a Hong Kong action movie director known for the aesthetics of violence, has completed his ultimate denial of violence on the screen. In Dragon Inn (1967) directed by Hu Jinshuan, after a fierce fight, the villain called Cao Shaoqin, head of Dongchang is killed, but Xiao Shaoci who wins the fight does not lead the family of Yu to revenge or assault the local authorities to regain their lost power. Instead, they choose to withdraw from the world of endless strives and live in seclusion in the vast mountains. Therefore, as a narrative factor into the movie, religion changes the thematic significance of the movies and characters' personalities as well.

Many Chinese martial arts movies end up with that heroes yearn for an earthly paradise with no pains and sorrows rather than the worldly fame and

fortunes. In Shaolin Temple, Jueyuan sacrifices his love with the shepherdess and converts himself to Buddhism so as to fulfill the behest of his deceased master "protecting Shaolin and upholding justice". It is totally different from Robin Hood who regains the throne and the beauty in the western movies. After finishing their missions, the Shaolin disciples often leave the secular world, and even stop the revengeful murders by sacrificing their own lives. In the movie Shaolin Damo (1990), the swordsman who has killed numerous people, when facing the recurrent murders, commits suicide to complete his repentance in the end! In the movie Eight-Trigram Cudgel of Yang Wulang (1990), Yang Wulang, together with the monks, repels the Liao armies and kills the traitor Xiao Tianzuo. Having revenged for the hatred of the family and the state, Yang Liulang advises Yang Wulang to reorganize the troop of Yang and fight for the lost territory. But Wulang, determined to convert himself to Buddhism, left his lover Ruolan, and reenters the temple for the universal salvation. In the movie Suoming Xiaoyaolou (Fatal Fun Pavilion, 1990), the heroin Shan E enters the pavilion and destroys the Eight-Trigram Battle Array. After a desperate fight, she kicks her enemy Bai Chong, who killed her father, into the bottomless pit of swords in revenge. Similarly, she finishes all the earthly affinities and lives reclusively. The real noble men take repressing the evil and advocating the good as their lifelong mission, and ignore the fame and wealth even they have already got them. At the end of the movie Celestial Sword—Nine Swordsmanship of Dugu (1993), Prince Xiahou (acted by Liu Ximing) and the princess of Late Tang (acted by Michelle Lee), after the victory, respectively throw away the sword symbolizing power and violence and the jade flute symbolizing wealth. Though an illusory ideal, it expresses people's long-cherished wish for eternal peace in the world. After fierce fights, warriors always are full of complex feelings for picturesque pastoral and their confidants once closely attached to each other (New Biography of Assassin, 1993)! The "closing ceremony" of New Dragon Inn (1992) is also full of spurn to the endless violence! A bloody massacre finally comes to an end. On the silence deserve. Jin Xiangyu (Acted by Maggie Cheung) burns with spirits the inn she has made painstaking efforts to run, a place full of bloody smell. She goes far away from the desert and the career of killing. What she longs for is a shelter with no deception and killing. Religions function differently in Chinese and Western movies, the latter of which intensify the violent conflict in the secular world.

In China's despotic feudal society, it is a life-long pursuit for many men of letters to live reclusively or be converted to Buddhism. Meditating at old temples in mountains and practicing religion beside the green lamps in the monasteries, they lived far away from the social strives and violent conflicts, leaving a piece of pure land for the tranquility of the heart. Chinese movies, "dip" in the traditional Chinese culture, highlight people's dream for pastoral scenery and peaceful life without killing, war and bloodshed. Such cultural orientation is not only reflected in the works of a director, or the movies of an area, but can be seen in movies of different regions in different periods. Although we have already been far from that isolated and ignorant feudal society, the aesthetic imagination in the movies can be realized in the real world and the pastoral beauty on the screen cannot turn real, the transcending aesthetics has provided our soul with a place for rest.

In summary, in the language form of movie arts, the cultural value orientation is a "potential meaning"under the plot. It is more often than not expressed in the way of the "implicit signified" mentioned by Metz rather than the abstract sermons. Whether a movie is correct or not in terms of cultural values actually is quite important to determine the success or failure of its marketing. How to guide the audience to culturally recognize the movie stars, how to set cultural interests for the movie, and how to determine the cultural theme of the movie? In fact, they are all important factors influencing the profitability of a movie. The movie, in the final analysis, is a pop cultural product in the commercial market. If divorced from the aesthetics of the times, going against the consumption orientation in the cultural and market positioning, or deviating from the general trend in the cultural psychology, a movie is bound to have a bleak prospect in the market. Therefore, how to enhance the market competitiveness of Chinese movies is not just an economic issue, but also a cultural one.

---

① Diego Gambetta, The Sicilian Mafia : The Business of Private Protection (Cambridge : Harvard University Press, 1993), P.35.

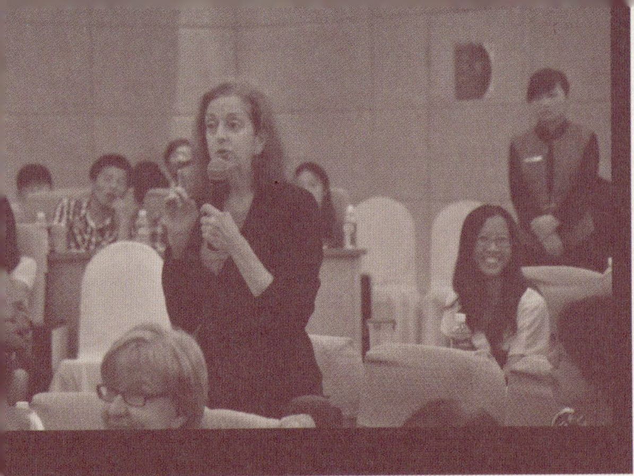
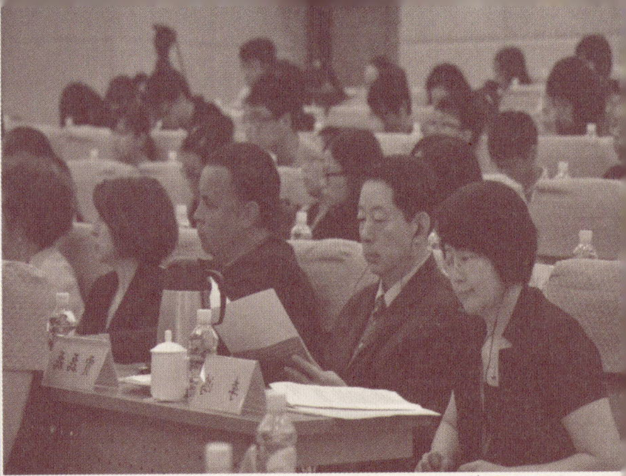
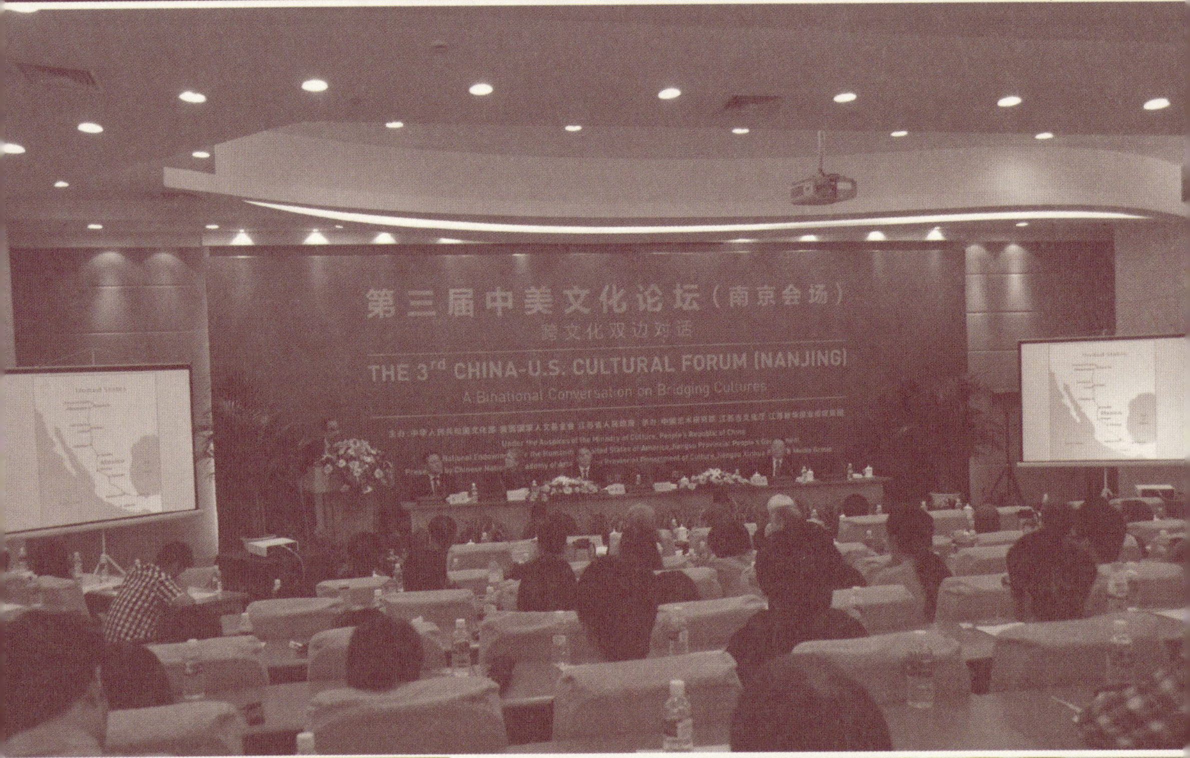
第三届中美文化论坛（南京会场）
THE 3rd CHINA-U.S. CULTURAL FORUM (NANJING)
A Binational Conversation on Bridging Cultures

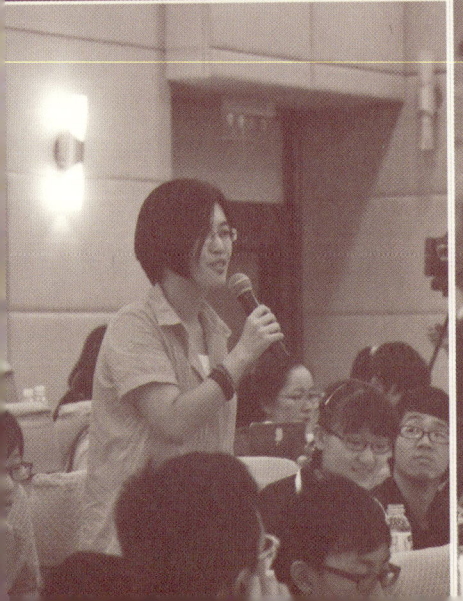

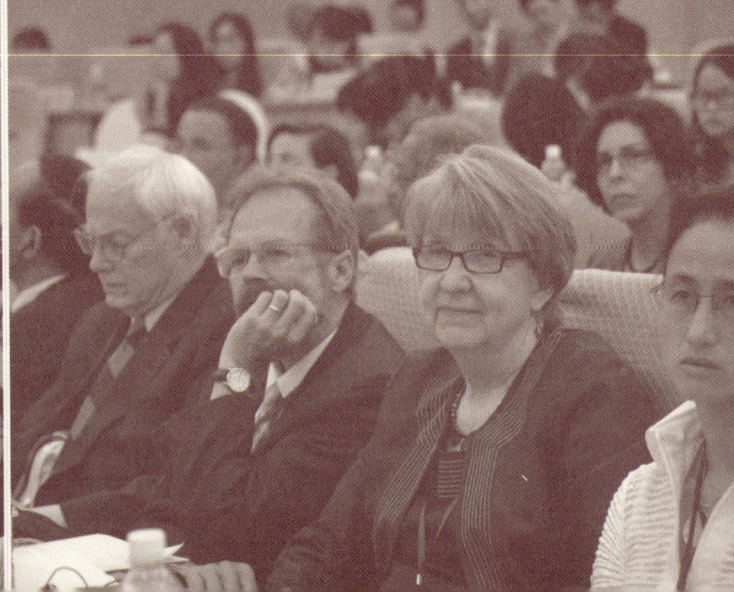

UNIT THREE: CULTURE AND PLACE

第三单元 文化与地域

江苏省人民政府参事室主任宋林飞做主题发言
《中国城市社会的来临与挑战——城市多元化及其融合》
Song Linfei, Director of Counsellors' Office of Jiangsu Provincial People's Government
"Arrival and Challenges of the Urban Society of China——Urban Diversification and Melting"

美国爱荷华大学国际写作计划主任克里斯托弗·梅瑞尔做主题发言
《窥视,沉醉,理解:论空间与文学》
Christopher Merrell, Director of International Writing Program, University of Iowa
"Peering, Absorbing, Translating: A Note on Geography and Culture"

江苏省作家协会副主席毕飞宇做主题发言
《地域文化的价值倾向》
Bi Feiyu, Vice President of the Writers' Association of Jiangsu Province
"Value Orientation of Regional Culture"

南京大学-约翰斯·霍普金斯大学中美文化研究中心
美方合作主任詹森·帕滕特做主题发言
《思维定势与世界观：对空间如何决定思想的反思》
Jason D. Patent, American Co-director of The Johns Hopkins University-Nanjing University Center for Chinese and American Studies
"Mindset and Worldview: Reflections on How Place Shapes the Mind"

南京大学外国语学院教授，当代外国文学与文化研究中心主任王守仁做主题发言
《美国文学教学与研究在南京》
Wang Shouren, Professor of the Foreign Language College of Nanjing University, Head of the Center for the Studies of Contemporary Foreign Literature and Culture
"Teaching and Study of American Literature in Nanjing"

江苏省文化厅厅长徐耀新做主题发言
《江苏及南京地域文化简述》
Xu Yaoxin, Director of Jiangsu Provincial Department of Culture
"On Regional Culture of Jiangsu Province and Nanjing"

美国斯坦福大学英语与比较文学系教授，
"人文与科学学院"霍格兰德家庭教授拉蒙·萨尔迪瓦做主题发言
《美国/墨西哥边境地区的文化与空间》
Ramón Saldívar, Professor of English and Comparative Literature and the Hoagland Family Professor of Humanities and Sciences at Stanford University
"Culture and Place on the US/Mexico Border"

南京大学-约翰斯·霍普金斯大学中美文化研究中心副主任蔡佳禾做主题发言
《全球化冲击下的文化融合与文化差异》
Cai Jiahe, Deputy Director of The Johns Hopkins University - Nanjing University Center for Chinese and American Studies
"Cultural Integration and Cultural Differences under the Impact of Globalization"

中国城市社会的来临与挑战
——城市多元化及其融合

宋林飞

江苏省人民政府参事室主任

内容提要：改革开放以来，中国最大的变化是越来越多的农民进城务工。目前，城镇人口已经超过总人口的一半，将中国从农业社会转变为城市社会。城市居民与文化多元化，同时也加快了融合的趋势。城市化面临新的难题："不完全城市化"，农民工还没有完全享受城镇居民的同等待遇；"城市病"，交通拥堵、污染、"陌生人社区"兴起等；"城乡二元结构"，城乡公共服务、社会保障水平与居民收入的差别比较显著。今后一个时期，城市化是经济社会发展的重要动力，中国将再创一个黄金发展期。发展思路是：进一步推进户籍制度改革；加快城市新老居民的融合；传承与创新城市文化，塑造充满人文精神和人文关怀的城市空间；加快城乡一体化，建立覆盖城乡的社会保障体系。

改革开放以来，中国最大的变化是越来越多的农民进城务工，城市化快速推进。这个过程，一直伴随着我的研究与思考。

1982年，我通过对江苏省南通县农村的实地调查，在《中国社会科学》杂志上发表了《农村劳动力的剩余与出路》。由于地少人多，当时农村存在大量的剩余劳动力。根据我的测定，当时农村劳动力剩余度达到60%以上。这种季节性的失业，既影响农民收入，又影响经济发展，还影响社会稳定，是一个不可忽视的大问题。

30年过去了，农民找到了出路，这个出路就是城市化。

一、城市居民与文化的多元化及其融合

经过快速的城市化，中国已经从一个农业社会转变为一个城市社会。2011年年底，全国城镇化率从1978年的17.92%迅速提高到

51.27%，江苏省城市化率达到61.9%；苏南地区城市化率达到70.3%，南京达到79.7%，进入"高度城市化"阶段。

这是中国社会结构的巨大进步，首先表现为城市的开放性与城乡人口的流动性。根据第六次人口普查，2010年，全国流动人口2.2亿，比2000年增长1倍，主要分布在东部沿海地区的城镇；全国流动人口对户籍人口的比率接近1∶3。外来流动人口与本地人口之比：长三角城市群的上海市为1∶1.6；珠三角城市群的广州市为1∶1.7；京津冀城市群的北京市为1∶1.8；部分地方出现"倒挂"现象，例如东莞市为3.3∶1。城市的新居民，不仅仅是进城的农民工，还有许多来投资与工作的外籍人员，城市人口的多元化十分显著。

多元城市居民的融合，是从就业、居住方面开始的。户籍制度改革不断推进，进城农民、外国合法移民，可以在新兴的城市中就业。同时，城市居民的居住条件普遍改善。2011年，江苏省城镇居民人均住房建筑面积为30.15平方米，已超过人均30平方米的小康标准。快速的城市化过程形成很多失地农民，失地农民都有住房的实物补偿，一般在原居住地附近建立集中居住点。从而，避免了世界城市化过程中普遍出现的大量贫民窟现象。外来务工人员一般分散居住在工作单位提供的住房内，也有一些人租住在城市居民、城郊结合部农民的出租房内。为了改善外来务工人员的居住条件，城市廉租房、公租房在内的保障性住房对他们开放。未来几年，随着城市保障性住房的大量竣工供应，外来务工人员的居住条件将有明显改善。

从城市外观来看，中国建筑文化与欧美建筑文化交融。城市新建的公寓、别墅，纷纷引进欧美建筑设计风格。数量之多、种类之繁杂、规模之宏大，在世界上是罕见的。法国文学家维克多·雨果曾经概括了东西方两大建筑体系之间的根本差别，他说："艺术有两种渊源，一为理念——从中产生欧洲艺术；一为幻想——从中产生东方艺术。"现在，不能这样绝对划分了，中西合璧的城市建筑文化在中国城市化进程中日趋发展。这反映了中国人日益开放的健康心态。

二、城市化面临的难题

对于越来越多的农民进城务工的潮流，我充满热情与期待进行了研究。1995年，我在《中国社会科学》杂志上发表了《"民工潮"的形成、趋势与对策》，认为"民工潮"给城市与社会带来的巨大冲击，"是摆在中国人面前的一个跨世纪难题"。这个"跨世纪难题"的解答任务至今没有完成，已经做出的答案需要进一步完善，同时还有许多方面需要找出新的答案。

第一，是"不完全城市化"。城镇人口中包括农民工，他们生活在城镇，但工资福利、子女教育、社会保障等方面还没有完全享受城镇居民的同等待遇。同时，"农民工"的文化素质、生活质量、消费行为、思想观念也没有完全跟上城市前进的步伐。2011年，在南京登记的181.6万流入人口，以具有初中、高中文化程度的男性为主，占69.9%；大专以上文化程度的占17.6%；小学以下文化程度的占12.5%。显然，比城市原住居民的文化水平低。

第二，是"城市病"。我国正在进入交通机动化时代，家庭小汽车不断增加。过去，我们说美国是"装在汽车轮子上的国家"。现在，我国不少城市也是这样的了。大城市普遍出现了交通拥堵现象，居民平均单行上班时间要花近40分钟，比欧洲大城市多12分钟左右。受重化工企业、机动车的废水废气排放的影响，城市普遍被污染。这个问题已经受到政府的重视，治理取得显著成果。2011年，在325个城市中，环境空气质量达标城市比例为89.0%，超标城市比例为11.0%。同时，城市中的"陌生人社区"兴起，熟人社会在解体，邻里互助的传统习惯在减少，居民自治与公众参与开始有效组织了起来，仍然需要进一步发展。

第三，是"城乡二元结构"。农村公共服务、社会保障水平逐步提高，但城乡差别仍然比较显著。同时，城乡居民收入差距比较大。2011年，全国城镇居民人均可支配收入与农村居民人均纯收入之比为3.13∶1，2010年该数值为3.23∶1，令人高兴的是，已经出现拐点。

三、加强城市社会文化建设的对策思路

城市化是中国过去发展特别是改革开放以来经济社会加快发展的动力，也是今后一个时期经济社会持续较快发展的动力。一个城市居民的消费，相当于3个以上农村居民的消费。今后，中国几个亿的农村人口进入城市，城市成为扩大内需的主要载体。从城市化率50%到70%以上的

发展阶段，中国将再创一个黄金发展期。

加快城市户籍制度改革。目前，农民工，特别是年轻一代农民工在城镇落户口的要求迫切。满足他们的要求，是维护他们合法权益的需要，也是扩大内需和维护稳定的需要。应进一步实行户籍制度改革，逐步放宽、直至放开城市户口的准入限制，实行按居住地管理的户籍制度。转变对外国人和中国人区别对待的思路，实行普遍的国民待遇，对于外籍人员实施登录制度和雇佣许可制度，严格查处非法滞留人员。

加快城市新老居民的融合。建立农民工的医疗、保障性住房与社会保障制度，解决农民工子女受教育、就业等问题。增强农民工对城市的归属感，实现农民工的"市民梦"。探索与建立农村土地使用权抵押机制，为农民进城或就地创业提供资金来源，实现农民的"创业梦"。鼓励政府和民间机构为合法移居的外籍人员提供服务，帮助他们尽早适应当地社会。

传承与创新城市文化。城市居民既要有"物质家园"，还要有"精神家园"，这是城市化的基本价值追求。文化是城市的生命和灵魂，应塑造充满人文精神和人文关怀的城市空间，建设"文化城市"。保护好文化遗产，留下个性化的城市记忆。进行跟上时代的文化创新，增强城市持久的活力。把文化创新与文化传承统一起来，把文化开发与文化保护统一起来。

加快城乡一体化。当前的重点是建立城乡一体的社会保障体系，这是公共服务体制改革最为艰难的环节。到2015年，江苏将率先建立城乡一体的社会保障体系，实现城乡基本养老、基本医疗保险和失业保险的全覆盖，城乡居民"老有所养、病有所医"。同时，推动交通、供水供电供气、信息网络等基础设施的城乡联网；基本实现城乡教育、卫生服务一体化，为城乡居民提供接受教育特别是享受优质高等教育资源的平等机会。

Song Linfei

Director of
Counsellors'
Office of Jiangsu
Provincial People's
Government

Arrival and Challenges of the Urban Society of China
——Urban Diversification and Melting

Abstract: The most remarkable change in China since the reform and opening up has been the increasing number of migrant rural workers in cities. At present, the urban population of China has exceeded half of the total, changing China from the agricultural society into urban society. As a result, the diversification of urban residents and culture accelerate the process of melting at the same time. The urbanization faces up a lot of new problems such as "incomplete urbanization", absence of equal treatment for migrant rural works as urban citizens, "urban disease": traffic jam, pollution, and "stranger community", etc.; "dualistic urban-rural structure": Different public services, social security level and rural-urban income gap become more and more remarkable. In a period to come, urbanization is an important drive for the economic and social development and China will open another golden era of development. The development thought for urbanization is to further promote the reform of household registration system, speed up the melting of new and old residents, carry forward and create urban cultures, build up the urban space full of humanity and humanistic concern, accelerate the rural-urban integration and construct the social security system covering urban and rural areas.

The most remarkable change in China since the reform and opening up has been the increasing number of migrant rural workers and the accelerated urbanization. I have kept researching and reflecting on this process.

In 1982, I published Rural Labor Surplus and the Way Out in Social Sciences in China in a journal named Social Sciences in China based on my field survey on the countryside in Nantong County, Jiangsu Province. Limited land and too many rural residents led to a large number of surplus labor forces. According to my determination, the surplus rural labor forces were more than 60%. The seasonal unemployment is a severe problem than cannot be ignored, as it influenced not only farmers' income and economic development, but also the social stability.

In the past 30 years, the farmers have found the way out: urbanization.

I. Diversification and Melting of Urban Citizens and Culture

After the rapid urbanization, China has changed from an agricultural society into an urban society. By the end of 2011, the rate of urbanization of the whole country has increased rapidly from 17.92% in 1978 to 51.27% with that of Jiangsu province up to 61.9%; in the figure of south Jiangsu reached 70.3%, and that of Nanjing was 79.7%, marking the start of a "high urbanization"stage.

This is the great progress of China's social structure, firstly reflected by the openness of the cities and the mobility of urban and rural population. According to the sixth census, there were 220 million floating populations in China in 2010, twice that of the year of 2000, mainly in the eastern coastal cities and towns; the ratio of floating population against the registered population was close to 1:3. The ratio of the floating population against the local population was: 1:1.6 in Shanghai in the Yangtze River Delta; 1:1.7 in Guangzhou in the Pearl River Delta; and 1:1.8 in Beijing in Beijing-Tianjin-Hebei area. The "upside down" phenomenon appeared in some places, such as 3.3:1 in Dongguan. The new city dwellers were not just rural workers, but many foreigners for investment and work. The urban population was remarkably diverse.

The melting of the diverse urban citizens started from employment and housing. Thanks to the progressive reform of the household registration system, farmers in cities and legal foreign immigrants can be employed in the emerging cities. At the same time, living conditions of the urban citizens have been generally improved. In 2011, per capita floor space in urban areas in Jiangsu Province was 30.15 square meters, more than the well-off standard of 30 square meters. Landless farmers made in the process of rapid urbanization were compensated in a way that they can move to collective settlements built in the vicinity of their former residences, whereby avoiding a large number of slums, a phenomenon universally appearing in the urbanization process across the world. Generally, migrant workers dispersedly lived in houses provided by their employers, and some others rent houses of the urban residents or farmers at the outskirts. In order to improve the living conditions of these workers, subsidized housing is accessible for them, including low-rent housing and public-rent housing. As many subsidized houses will be completed in years to come, migrant workers will enjoy much better living conditions.

As for the appearance of the city, Chinese architectural culture blends with European and American styles. New apartments and villas are built in European and American styles. It is rare to see in the world in terms of the colossal number, diverse types and the huge scale. Victor Hugo, a French writer, once summed up the fundamental difference between the Eastern and the Western architectural systems and said: "Art has two sources, one is the concept—which produces the European art; the other is fantasy—which produces the Eastern art." But they cannot be absolutely divided now, for the Chinese-Western urban architectural culture has increasingly developed in China's urbanization process, reflecting that Chinese people is growingly open-minded.

II. Problems Confronting Urbanization

With keen interest and anticipation, I have done research on the migrant rural workers inflow. In 1995, I published Formation, Trend and Countermeasures of Tide of Migrant Rural Workers in Social Sciences in China, arguing that the such a tide has laid a huge impact on the cities and the society and it "is a cross-century problem in front of the Chinese people". Having been not solved yet, this problem requires further improved solutions and new ones in many other aspects.

The first is "incomplete urbanization". Migrant rural workers, though included in the urban population, do not enjoy the same treatment as urban residents in wages and benefits, children's education, social security and other aspects. They have not kept up with urban development in education, living standard, consumption behaviors and concepts. In 2011, most of the 1.816 million registered inflow population in Nanjing were male workers which have received junior or senior high school education, accounting for 69.9%; those receiving college or higher education accounted for 17.6%; and those receiving primary school education accounted for 12.5%, obviously lower than original urban residents.

The second is the "urban disease". China is entering an era of motor-driven transportation, with increasing family cars. The United States is regarded as a country on wheels, and that is the same case for many Chinese cities. Traffic jams are common in big cities, and citizens spend an average of nearly 40 minutes on the one way to work, about 12 minutes longer than big European cities. Impacted by heavy chemical enterprises and waste emission of motor vehicles, cities are generally polluted. The government has paid attention to this problem and its efforts have reaped good results. In 2011, 89.0% of 325 cities reached the standard of ambient air quality, and the rest 11.0% failed. At the same time, the "stranger community" has emerged in cities while the acquaintance society has been disintegrated and the traditional habits of mutual assistance in the neighborhood have been decreasing. The citizen autonomy and public participation start to be effectively organized, but still need to be further developed.

The third is the "dualistic urban-rural structure". The rural public service and social security is gradually improving but still remarkably lag behind that of urban areas. Meanwhile, the urban-rural income gap is wide. In 2011, the ratio of per capita disposable income of urban citizens and that of their rural counterpart was 3.13:1, and this figure was 3.23:1 in 2010. It is delightful that the point of inflection has appeared.

III. Countermeasures to Strengthened Urban Cultural Construction

Urbanization was an important driving force for the rapid social and economic development, especially after the reform and opening up was launched, and will keep stimulating the fast development in a period to come.

The consumption of an urban citizen is equivalent to that of more than three rural residents. As tens of millions of rural residents will enter cities, cities will become the major carrier to expand domestic demand. China will greet another golden age of development when the urbanization rate increases from 50% to 70% and above.

Accelerate the reform of urban household registration system. At present, migrant rural workers, especially young ones, are eager to have the registered urban household. Their needs should be satisfied to safeguard their legal rights and interests, expand domestic demands and maintain social stability as well. The household registration system should be further reformed to relax the access control gradually and fully, and a domicile-based household system should be implemented. The universal national treatment should be implemented for foreigners and local people, rather than in a discriminatory way. Registration and work license system should be adopted for foreigners, and those illegally staying in China should be strictly punished.

Speed up the melting of new comers and original residents in cities. Efforts should be made to establish the medical, subsidized housing and social security systems for migrant rural workers, and provide access to education and employment for their children; enhance their sense of belonging in cities and realize their "dream of citizen"; explore and construct the mechanism to mortgage the rural land use rights so that they have funds to start their business in cities or in their local places to realize their "entrepreneurial dreams"; and encourage governments and civil societies to provide service to legal foreign immigrants and help them to adapt to the local communities soon.

Carry forward and create urban cultures. The urban citizens should have both "material homes" and "spiritual homes", which is the basic value pursuit of urbanization. Culture is the life and soul of the city, so the urban space should be full of humanity and humanistic concern and the "cultural city" should be constructed. The cultural heritage should be protected to leave personalized urban memories. Efforts should be made to keep up with cultural innovation of the times and enhance the lasting vitality of cities. The cultural innovation and the cultural inheritance should be integrated, so should the cultural development and cultural protection.

Accelerate the urban-rural integration. The current focus is to establish the integrated urban and rural social security system, which is the most difficult part in the reform of public service system. By 2015, Jiangsu will have firstly established the integrated urban and rural social security system and realized the full coverage of the urban and rural basic endowment insurance, basic medical insurance and unemployment insurance, to take care of old and sick urban and rural residents. At the same time, efforts should be made to promote the urban and rural infrastructure network construction in traffic, supply of water, electricity and natural gas, and information network; and basically realize the integration of urban and rural education and health service, providing the urban and rural residents with equal opportunities to receive education and especially enjoy quality resources of higher education.

窥视，沉醉，理解：
论空间与文学

克里斯托弗·梅瑞尔
美国爱荷华大学国际写作计划主任

内容提要：本文将探讨地理环境在沃尔特·惠特曼、亨利·戴维·梭罗和马克·吐温的作品中的主导地位。许多美国文学经典的鲜活生命力都源自一种场所精神——"场所精神"一词源于拉丁语 genius loci，即某地的守护神——在那些代表了美国现代文学的诗歌、小说和非小说作品中，一个地区的地理多样性往往在作品的多种创作手法中有所体现。惠特曼、梭罗和吐温被誉为赋予众多当代作家——尤其是自然作家——以灵感的守护神，本人将分析《草叶集》、《梭罗日记》和《密西西比河上》三部具有奠基意义的作品，借鉴作者再现这些地方的风土人情的方式。对大海、森林和河流这些场所的文学探索，都透露了我们在本土的栖居方式。在惠特曼激情澎湃的短诗中，在梭罗细微之至的观察中，在吐温对其作为河船领航员学徒生涯的回顾中，我们可以略略瞥见各种通过描述某地风土人情来培养想象力的方法。"小心翼翼地窥视着，沉醉着，理解着"，正如惠特曼在"从永久摇荡着的摇篮里"（一首描述他孩童时发现的一对筑巢鸟儿的诗歌）所写的那样，卓越的文学作品可能正是源于这种细致的观察，源于对某地的风向和天气的描绘中。

地理学与文化之间的关系，这个问题在中美文化论坛伊始就被提出，在我10年前第一次来到这里时，这个问题就对我呈现了新的意义。一天清晨，我沿着天安门广场不远处的一条大街跑步，突然对法国诗人、外交官圣-琼·佩斯的诗作恍然大悟，这位诺贝尔文学奖获得者的作品、独立的思想和勇气一直是我源源不断的灵感源泉。我不清楚哪股力量刺激了我——时差，还是眼前做着健身操的老头老太太们，他的一句诗：梦田！——让我突然领悟到其作品中的苍茫之感，他对空间的亲切感，这在法国诗歌里史无前例，这也许是他在1916—1921年间在中国任职的缘故。"我看到土地被分

成广袤的空间，"他在《远征》末尾处这样写道，这首鸿篇巨制的诗歌是他在北京郊外西山的一个道教寺庙创作而成，"而我的思想则跟随着我的引路人。"佩斯就是我的引路人之一；当我理解了他在中国逗留期间对其诗歌视野的发展所具有的重要性，更别提作为外交官的手腕，对我来说，我的审美眼界似乎也拓宽了——也许宽到足以重新评价我自身的文学传承，而为我提供这些评论内容的正是该文学传承。

场所精神赋予美国文学的许多伟大作品以生命力。河流、树林和海洋——这些对美国作家来说都是重要的借喻，我建议去沃尔特·惠特曼的诗歌、亨利·戴维·梭罗的日记以及马克·吐温的自传体小说《密西西比河上的生活》里去一探究竟。用历史学家弗雷德里克·特纳（Frederick Turner）的话说，他们开创了"发明和适应的过程，新来者通过这个过程最终占有了名义上早属于他们的土地"，其要点是看看真正摆在他们面前的是什么——是当下还是记忆。

"不经意地窥视、吸收、转化"——这是惠特曼对其诗歌里具有想象力作品的描述，"在不停晃动的摇篮外面。"他想起童年时一个夏天从南方飞来的一对小鸟。他每天观察它们，在无意识中日积月累的印象转化到诗歌当中；一天，雌鸟也许被杀了，没有返回鸟巢，他听到雄鸟的鸣叫，悲恸的叫声唤醒了他灵魂深处的某个东西。以下诗句表达了鸟儿的思念之情：

哦，海水猛烈地推向海岸，
充满爱意地——充满爱意地。

哦，夜晚！哦，我看到的难道不是我的爱人在浪花间翩翩飞舞吗？
在一片白茫茫中，我眼见的那个黑色小东西又是什么？

他看到的是死亡；他在这首诗歌里表达了自己对死亡的疑问，对他来说，这个问题与海洋有关，这是他童年时代所界定的地理特征。实际上，他的短诗，长短不一的有韵律的诗句源自他对《钦定版圣经》诗篇的阅读，时而汹涌澎湃，时而缓缓消退，如潮涨潮落，模仿着长岛海岸波浪的起起伏伏，而且他用印第安名字 Paumanok 来称呼长岛。尽管他花了多年时间才找到自己的声音，但就是在这里他在诗歌里找到了生命；在诗的最后两节，我们了解到他从海岸听到了什么——正是这个声音让他获得自由：

  于是就一个词语，（因为我将征服它）
  这最后的词语，胜过一切，
  捉摸不定，一直在上升——它是什么？——我洗耳恭听；
  是你在喃喃低语吗，一直都是，你海浪吗？
  它是否来自你流动的边缘和潮湿的沙滩？
  回答我，大海，
  不要犹豫，不要慌张，
  在黎明破晓前，整晚都对我明白地窃窃私语，
  不停地口齿不清地述说这个低俗而迷人的词语死亡，
  不停地，死亡——死亡，死亡，死亡，
  旋律优美的嘘声，既不像鸟儿的鸣叫，也不像被唤醒的我儿的心灵，
  但逐渐在靠近，仿佛只冲着我而来，在我的脚边飒飒作响，
  于是悄悄蔓延到我的耳边，
  死亡，死亡，死亡，死亡，死亡。

  我无法忘记，
  但将这两首歌融合在一起，
  这首歌在长岛灰色沙滩的月光之下对我唱起，
  上千首歌曲随意地在回应，
  我自己的歌，从那一刻苏醒，
  随着歌声从海浪传来曲调，词语，
  最甜美歌曲，和所有歌曲的词语，
  有力迷人的词语，悄悄地靠近我的脚边，
  低声地对我耳语。

  他在这首诗歌里融合平衡了生命与死亡、爱与遗失、过去与现在，在对未来的方向上，它体现了美国诗歌的首要原则：一个关注的行为可激发全世界反响热烈的诗歌，惠特曼的《自我之歌》约

五十种语言翻译便是最好的佐证。"我聆听鸟儿的华美华章,"他写道,"麦子竞相生长的熙攘喧闹,火焰熊熊燃烧的窃窃私语,灶炉柴火的哔剥作响"——我们也是如此。

与惠特曼同时代的梭罗对老普林尼称为"自然最微不足道的事情"也予以同样的细节关注。他备受颂扬的杰作《瓦尔登湖》依然是美国自然写作传统中极重要的文本。但我想要谈谈在他的日记(他本人认为这是其重要作品)里所记录的繁枝细节,这些日记由十六卷内容组成,七万页,约两百万字。我认识一位自然作家,他每天从阅读梭罗当天的日记记录开始,几乎堪比修道士每天在小房间里吟诵礼拜诗篇歌集。

梭罗最开始的记录是与一位未提名人士——拉尔夫·沃尔多·爱默生(Ralph Waldo Emerson)的简短谈话,实际上,这个人得知他想成为一个作家,便问他是否在记日记。于是便开始了。在相对短暂的有生之年,梭罗窥视、吸收,将他每天在马萨诸塞州康科德(Concord)散步时所见进行转化,他的野外记录从一名土地测量员的工作转变为对周围环境的动植物、季节更替、邻居习惯、自身阅读、创意过程——太阳、月亮和星星的下面一切的细致观察。从这些日记中,他将某些章节内容再创作为讲稿、散文以及为他赢得广泛赞誉的书籍——《瓦尔登湖》、《康科德和梅里麦克河上的一周》、《散步》、《不服从论》、《为约翰·布朗上校请愿》——但几年过去之后,他开始从更大的层面计划他的观察项目:他开始创作康科德诗歌,其中每一样元素都来自自然这本书,他决心学习如何去阅读自然。他对自己所在的地盘了如指掌——他研究这里的田野和森林,这里的春天和溪流,这里的天气和光线,如此心无旁骛——以至于他认为即便把他从外太空放在那里,在一两天之内他便能弄清楚日期。出于这种热爱,他不仅留下关于自然法则的记录,也记录下人类的思想,其中的点点滴滴都是他在康科德漫步时逐字逐句捕捉下来的。

学者劳伦斯·斯塔普顿在介绍梭罗写作记录的精选集时这样评论道:"事实的真实性得以确定不仅是事实本身的主要价值,也是由其作为线索随后而产生的事物的主要价值。'如果你对这一年[梭罗声明]的观察不准确,你在来年就有必要用实例去重复,季节和生命本身就被延长了。'""观察,"斯塔普顿总结道,"如同自然本身,是衍生的,纯粹始于看见。"关注的行为,实际上就是在对抗现代生活的忙乱。梭罗每天对周围环境的观察实则是迫使自己放慢脚步;将其所见、所闻、所听、所尝、所感、所想一一准确地记录下来；去探测自然界的无穷变化，这种变化又激励他更加深入、更加广博地去观察。事物层出不穷，为他带来文思泉涌，于是，文稿越积越多，正如154年前的今天的一条记录所透露："对自己的事情充满激情是一良策，"他这样提醒自己，"因为付诸行动和精力，就算未完成对自己声称的目标，也会有其他收获。因此，在我研究植物或自然历史的散步过程中，通常结果是，我为了一件事情而去，却得到另外一个结果。"的确，他的日记充满了对深邃大自然和美妙创造力的连连惊喜。

他在翌日前往瓦本悬崖散步时对这一主题做了进一步探讨："这需要在相同的地点具有不同的眼光去观察不同的植物，比如灯心草科和禾本科等；我发现，当我在寻找前者的时候，我在它们当中看不到后者。那么，这在多大程度上需要专注的目光和思维去关注不同的知识领域！诗人和自然主义者看待物体的眼光是何等不同！"但在其整个日记内容中，显而易见的是——他的眼力在于这位诗人与自然主义者始终在进行一场富有成效的对话，事实在对话中转变为诗歌，诗歌又产生深刻的见解。此刻，他以开玩笑的口吻记录一位职员在自家糖枫周围种了大豆，然后他又天马行空地想象晨曦冉冉升起又坠入水中的景象，此时他有了一个重要发现："在反射光中，你出现无数双眼睛，然后从每个观点去汇报事物的各个层面。"

梭罗尊重世间万物，将它们记录在自己的日记当中，直到它们散发出光芒，这为物体的诗情打下基础。这证明是我们时代最有影响力的文学发现之一，鼓舞了像莱纳·玛利亚·里尔克、聂努达和圣-琼·佩斯等不同作家的写作。它也为此次论坛首日所引用的威廉·卡洛斯·威廉姆斯的"本人再次声明"这首诗歌作品带来灵感（我想补充一下，这在某种程度上要归功于埃兹拉·庞德的唐诗英译本《中国》，这是美国现代诗史上一本有吸引力的作品）。眼见的一切都可成为一首诗歌：

> 我吃了
> 冰箱里的
> 李子
>
> 这也许

是你
留到早餐
才吃的

原谅我
它们太鲜美
香甜
而清凉

我希望你们原谅我诵读肯尼斯·考克的诗来介绍马克·吐温，因为，别忘了，幽默是美国实验精神的核心；如果没有喜剧演员，我们的生活该有多么贫乏：

威廉对同一主题的变异：

1
我砍掉你留到明年夏天居住的房子。
对不起，但现在是清晨，我无事可做
而且木制横梁又是如此诱人。

2
我们齐声嘲笑那些蜀葵
然后我朝它们喷洒碱液。
原谅我。我只是不知道自己在干什么。

3
我把你留作未来十年生活的积蓄都送给了别人。
要钱的人可怜寒酸
阳台上三月强劲的风如此潮湿而寒冷。

4
昨夜我们去跳舞我打折了你的腿。

原谅我。我动作笨拙而且
我希望你住院,因为我是这里的医生!

美国读者在这些诗句中听到了马克·吐温——这种过度的创造力,我们将其视为我们的文学和文化传承的一部分,这在库尔特·冯内古特的小说、理查德普赖尔的单人脱口秀以及无数的作家、电影制作人和那些让我们悲喜交加的喜剧中处处都有体现。这一传统的开创者就是马克·吐温,到他注意到什么会变成其真正的主题——密苏里州汉尼拔附近河上的生活(这是他生长的地方)时,他的幽默为他赢得了机会。如同许多男孩,他梦想成为一名汽轮领航员,而且他也的确在河上工作了近五年时间,这段经历为他提供了《密西西比河上的生活》的素材。他在这里不仅学会了如何在河上驾驶船只,而且也开始学习文学创作。"领航员必须不断地培养一种才能,一直到日臻完美,"马克·吐温这样写道。"未达到完美便不可以。这种才能便是记忆。他不停地思考一件事情的来龙去脉;他必须得弄清楚它。"这实际上是其写作的关键。他从记忆深处召集玩笑、故事和语言、色彩和枝节、质地和声响、荣耀和悲痛,这些在《哈克贝利·费恩历险记》中可见一斑,海明威认为它是美国小说真正的开山之作。

我现在想为大家引用一段,这段内容表面上在关心学习了解河流的艰难任务,但也对文学想象的培养进行描述:

河水表面不久成了一本内容精彩的书籍——这本书对未受训练的乘客而言是一门废弃的语言,但它却毫无保留地向我敞露心扉,仿佛一个声音将其珍贵的秘密在向我娓娓倾诉。这不是阅读一次就可扔至一边的书,因为它每天都讲述新的故事。整个一千两百英里,每一页都充满趣味,落下任何一页都会有所损失,任何一页你都不想掠过,而认为自己在别的地方可找到更大的乐趣。人类从未创作过如此精彩的作品;也从未有过哪一部作品如此引人入胜、如此兴趣盎然、每一次重新细读都会令人耳目一新。读不懂它的乘客也会为其水面特有的细微涟漪所吸引(在乘客无法俯瞰整条河流的少有情况下);但对领航员而言这是一段用斜体字写就的段落;实际上,还远非如此,它是用大写字母谱写的一个传奇故事,文末是一连串惊叹号;因为它意味着,潜藏在水面之下的船只残骸和岩石会将漂浮在水面之上的最坚固的船只四分五裂。这不过是河水最轻描淡写的表达,而在领航员的眼里却极为恐怖。实际上,读不懂河流这本书的乘客,除了光线的渲染和云朵的阴影等各种各样美妙的画面之外,他们什么都看不到,而在训练有素的眼睛里,看到的全然不是图画,而是极为阴森和一本正经的读物。

作为一名年轻的领航员,马克·吐温学习如何绕开密西西比河的浅滩和遇难船驾驶,而且也在自己的想象中学习如何认识和驾驭这些水流——而他的想象力就是一条活生生的语言河流,源源不断地滋养了美国文学这块三角洲。感谢上帝,我们可能要说,还好马克·吐温本人与神的关系并不确定。

想象力的培养形式多种多样,因艺术家而异。比如,惠特曼的记忆比马克·吐温更加严肃,虽然没有什么比玩笑更严肃。我从惠特曼、梭罗和马克·吐温身上学到不同的东西,他们每个人都建议我们要关注每件事物。因此,在我与已故克什米尔诗人阿里的友谊中,其中包括20年来几乎每天的电话交谈,我现在认识到,在我们的闲话、玩笑以及诗歌和政治问题的讨论中,我们时刻留意谁有没有不经意地说出可以写成诗歌的妙言。比如,当我向他朗读托马斯·德·昆西令人联想丰富的诗句——"这是粼粼波光的一年"——阿里很快就在一首诗歌里找到一种方式对其加以运用——最后我以写给我们的共同朋友、前美国桂冠诗人W.S.默温(W.S. Merwin)的诗歌作为答复,他已将其关注的行为有利地转化到诗歌当中,我将以这些诗句来作结:

> 西窗
> 献给W.S.默温
>
> 绿色棕榈轻拂山坡隐蔽了
> 山脚下的光辉,蜥蜴从棕榈叶
> 滑落或坠落到花朵,一颗雨滴消失在
> 树下的蕨类植物中。当北美红雀
> 从鸟巢飞向芒果树和远方,岛中的仿声鸟——

八哥和嘲鸫 —— 开始歌唱。

竹林嘎吱作响。门开了。无人在家。

在从印度尼西亚移植过来的棕榈林
在整理羽毛的北美红雀
既不是岛屿的
哨兵 也不是海洋的大使
风儿起伏摇曳 旋转 最后一扇门
关了 在悬崖峭壁之下
麻风病人聚居地 粼粼波光
在侵蚀 战争遗留下来的残骸

这位临终者仍在起草计划，这一次是为一个监狱。烛光闪烁，窗外，燕雀如雨点般坠落；唱诗班歌手用水箱捕捉它们，然后放在烤扦上烤制。一位牧师打开一本书，记录下这位政治家的临终遗言：法国的敌人是谁？德国亲王？他们的土地在燃烧。神圣的罗马帝国就是一个麻风病人聚居地。打开西边的窗户。我们将种子和羽毛留在各地。皇家烟火大师在庭院中品尝燕雀的酱汁。交际花们为唱诗班歌手倒上葡萄酒。剑伤容易痊愈，而言语的伤害则并非如此……牧师在空白页面涂写：已经开始说胡话了。烟火在城市上空纷纷坠落，如云雀一般。水箱里倒满了热油。很快，这个狂妄自大的帝国将一分为二。麻风病人就在门口。但就在他闭眼之前，红衣主教听到了这位诗人的声音：去年的雪在哪里？这就是为什么据说他在睡梦中平静死去的原因。

Peering, Absorbing, Translating: A Note on Geography and Culture

Christopher Merrell
Director of International Writing Program, University of Iowa

Abstract: This paper will explore the shaping role of geography in the works of Walt Whitman, Henry David Thoreau, and Mark Twain. Much of the best American literature is animated by a spirit of place—a term borrowed from the Latin, genius loci, the protective spirit of a site—and the physical diversity of the land is reflected in the variety of approaches to the writing of poetry, fiction, and nonfiction that marks modern American letters. Whitman, Thoreau, and Twain are tutelary spirits to a broad range of contemporary writers, especially nature writers; from three foundational works—Leaves of Grass, Thoreau's Journals, and Life on the Mississippi—I will draw lessons in the means by which places are evoked. Sea, woods, and river—these are the sites of literary investigation that inform how we inhabit our country. In Whitman's surging versets, Thoreau's meticulous observations, and Twain's recollections of his apprenticeship as a river boat pilot we glimpse ways to school the imagination in the facts of a place. "Casually peering, absorbing, translating," as Whitman writes in "Out of the Cradle Endlessly Rocking," describing a pair of nesting birds that caught his eye when he was a child; out of such acts of attention may come signal works of literature, inflected through wind and weather of a place.

The relationship between geography and culture, the question posed at the start of the China-U.S. Cultural Forum, took on new meaning for me during my first journey here, ten years ago. One morning on a run in Beijing, along an avenue not far from Tiananmen Square, I had a flash of insight into the work of St.-John Perse, the French poet, diplomat, and Nobel laureate whose writings, independent thought, and courage have been for me a constant source of inspiration. I am not sure what combination of forces—jet lag, the sight of elderly men and women doing their calisthenics, a line of his poetry: Plough-land of dream!—led me to the sudden realization that the sense of vastness in his work, his intimate feel for space, which has no precedent in French poetry, was perhaps a function of his tour of duty in China, where he was posted from 1916 until 1921. "I have seen the earth parceled out in vast spaces," he writes near the end of Anabasis, his book-length poem composed in a Taoist temple, in the Western Hills outside Beijing, "and my thought is not heedless of the navigator." Perse is one of my navigators; and when I grasped the importance of his stay in China to the development of his poetic vision, not to mention his skills as a diplomat, it seemed to me that my aesthetic horizons expanded—enough perhaps to measure anew my own literary inheritance, which furnishes the substance of these remarks.

A spirit of place animates many great works of American literature. River, woods, and sea—these are important tropes for American writers, which I propose to explore in the poems of Walt Whitman, the journals of Henry David Thoreau, and Mark Twain's memoir of his years as a river boat pilot, Life on the Mississippi. They inaugurated what the historian Frederick Turner describes as "the process of invention and accommodation by means of which the newcomers at last took possession of the land long since theirs in name," the key feature of which was to see what actually lay before them—in the moment or in memory.

"Casually peering, absorbing, translating"—this is how Whitman describes the workings of the imagination in his poem, "Out of the Cradle Endlessly Rocking." He is recalling a pair of birds, which arrived from the south one summer when he was a boy. He watched them day by day, unconsciously storing up impressions to be transformed into poetry; and when one day the female did not return to her nest, killed perhaps, he listened to her mate calling, a lament that wakened something in his soul. Here he gives voice to the bird's yearning:

O madly the sea pushes upon the land,
With love—with love.

O night! O do I not see my love fluttering out there among the breakers?
What is that little black thing I see there in the white?

What he sees is Death; and in this song he articulates his own questions about mortality, which for him is wrapped up in the sea, the defining geographical fact of his childhood. Indeed his versets, cadenced lines of varying length derived from his reading of the Psalms in the King James Version of the Bible, surge and ebb and flow in a tidal fashion, mimicking the action of the waves on the shore of Long Island, which he called by its Indian name, Paumanok. It was there that he was called to a life in poetry, though years would pass before he found his voice; in the last two stanzas we learn what he heard from the shore—what set him free:

A word then(for I will conquer it),
The word final, superior to all,
Subtle, sent up—what is it?—I listen;
Are you whispering it, and have been all the time, you sea-waves?
Is that it from your liquid rims and wet sands?
Answering, the sea,
Delaying not, hurrying not,
Whispered me through the night, and very plainly before daybreak,

Lisped to me constantly the low and delicious word death,
And again death—death, death, death,
Hissing melodious, neither like the bird, nor like my aroused child's heart,
But edging near, as privately for me, rustling at my feet,
And creeping thence steadily up to my ears,
Death, death, death, death, death.

Which I do not forget,
But fuse the song of two together,
That was sung to me in the moonlight on Paumanok's gray beach,
With the thousand responsive songs, at random,
My own songs, awaked from that hour,
And with them the key, the word up from the waves,
The word of the sweetest song, and all songs,
That strong and delicious word which, creeping to my feet,
The sea whispered me.

The song he fuses together balances life and death, love and loss, the past and the present, and in its orientation to the future it embodies a first principle of American poetry: that an act of attention can inspire responsive songs the world over, as the fifty or so translations of Whitman's "Song of Myself" attests. "I hear the bravura f birds," he writes, "the bustle of growing wheat, gossip of flames, clack of sticks cooking my meals"—and so do we.

Whitman's contemporary, Henry David Thoreau, was likewise meticulous in his attention to what Pliny the Elder called "the least things of nature." He is celebrated for his masterpiece, Walden, which remains the crucial text in the tradition of American nature writing. But I wish to speak about the minute particulars that he recorded in what he came to believe was his major work—his journals, which comprise sixteen volumes, seven thousand pages, roughly two million words. I know one nature writer who starts each day by reading all of Thoreau's journal entries for that date, the environmental equivalent of a monk chanting the Psalter in his cell.

Thoreau's very first entry consists of a short conversation with an unnamed man—Ralph Waldo Emerson, as it happens—who, upon learning that he wants to be a writer, asks if he is keeping a journal. So it begins. And for the rest of his relatively short life Thoreau peered, absorbed, and translated what he saw on his daily walks around Concord, Massachusetts, turning his field notes from his work as a land surveyor into polished observations on the flora and fauna of his surroundings, the succession of the seasons, the habits of his neighbors, his reading, the creative process—on, well, everything under the sun and moon and stars. From these journals he reworked passages for the lectures, essays, and books that earned him wide acclaim—Walden, A Week on the Concord and Merrimack, "Walking," "On Civil Disobedience," "A Plea for John Brown"—but as the years passed he began to envision his project of seeing in larger terms: he was writing the poem of Concord, every element of which had its place in the Book of Nature, which he was determined to learn how to read. He knew his home ground so well—he studied its fields and woods, its springs and brooks, its weather and light, so intently—that he believed he could be deposited there from outer space and discover within a day or two what date it was. Out of such love he left a record not only of the ways of nature but of the human mind, the motions of which he tracked, word by word and phrase by phrase, on his rambles around Concord.

The scholar Laurence Stapleton, introducing a selection of Thoreau's entries on writing, notes that for him "The veracity of the fact to be ascertained is the primary value not only of that fact but of its successors, to which it is the clue. 'If you make the least correct observation of nature this year [Thoreau declared], you will have occasion to repeat it with illustrations the next, and the season and life itself is prolonged.' Observation," Stapleton concludes, "like nature itself, is generative, and begins with simply seeing." An act of attention, that is, to counter the general pell-mell rush of modern life. What Thoreau's daily practice of observing his surroundings did was to force him to slow down; to make an accurate inventory of what he saw, smelled, heard, tasted, touched, and speculated about; to gauge some of the infinite variety of changes abroad in the natural world, which inspired him to look deeper, to see more. One thing led him to another, as one sentence drew from him the next, and so the pages accumulated, as an entry from this date 154 years ago reveals: "It is good policy to be stirring about your affairs," he reminds himself, "for the reward of activity and energy is that if you do not accomplish the object you had professed o yourself, you do accomplish something else. So, in my botanizing or natural history walks, it commonly turns out that, going for one thing, I get another thing." Indeed his journals teem with surprise about the depths of nature and the glories of creativity.

He develops this theme the next day, on a walk to Waban Cliff: "It requires a different intention of the eye in the same locality to see different plants, as, for example, Juncacaea and Graminea even; i.e., I find that when I am looking for the former, I do not see the latter in their midst. How much more, then, it requires intentions of the eye and of the mind to attend to different departments of knowledge! How differently the poet and the naturalist look at objects!" But what is apparent throughout his journals—the virtue of his eye, if you will—is that the poet and the naturalist are always engaged in a fruitful dialogue, in which fact turns into song and song yields insight. Now he notes that a clerk has planted beans in jest around his sugar maples, now he soars on a flight of the imagination about the ways in which twilight rises and fall in the waters, now he makes an important discovery: "In the reflection you have an infinite number of eyes to see for you and report the aspect of things each from its point of view."

Thoreau honors the things of the world by rendering them in his journals until they shine, laying the groundwork for a poetics of the object. This would prove to be one of the most potent literary discoveries of our time, which would animate the writings of figures as diverse as Rainer Maria Rilke, Pablo Neruda and St.-John Perse. And it inspired the poem by William Carlos Williams quoted on the first day of this forum, "This Is Just To Say" (which, I might add, owes a debt to Ezra Pound's translations of Tang poetry, Cathay, a magnetic book in the history of modern American poetry). Anything seen rightly can become a poem:

I have eaten
the plums
that were in
the icebox

and which
you were probably
saving
for breakfast

Forgive me
they were delicious
so sweet
and so cold

I hope you will forgive me for reciting Kenneth Koch's parody of this poem, by way to introducing of Mark Twain, for it is important to remember that humor lies at the heart of the American experiment; without our comedians our lives would be much impoverished:

Variations on a Theme by William Carlos Williams

1
I chopped down the house that you had been saving to live in next summer.
I am sorry, but it was morning, and I had nothing to do
and its wooden beams were so inviting.

2
We laughed at the hollyhocks together
and then I sprayed them with lye.
Forgive me. I simply do not know what I am doing.

3
I gave away the money that you had been saving to live on for the next ten years.
The man who asked for it was shabby
and the firm March wind on the porch was so juicy and cold.

4
Last evening we went dancing and I broke your leg.
Forgive me. I was clumsy and
I wanted you here in the wards, where I am the doctor!

American readers hear Mark Twain in these lines—the over-the-top inventiveness, which we recognize as part of our literary and cultural inheritance, coursing through the fictions of Kurt Vonnegut, the standup routines of Richard Pryor, and countless writers, film makers, and comics who make us laugh and cry. There at the start of the tradition was Twain, whose humor earned him a fortune by the time he turned his attention to what would become his true subject—life on the river by Hannibal, Missouri, where he was born and raised. Like many boys, he dreamed of being the pilot of a steamboat, and indeed he spent nearly five years working on the river, which provided him with the material for Life on the Mississippi. Here he not only learned how to navigate the river but also began to serve his literary apprenticeship. "There is one faculty which a pilot must incessantly cultivate until he has brought it to absolute perfection," Twain writes. "Nothing short of perfection will do. That faculty is memory. He cannot stop with thinking a thing is so and so; he must know it." This is in fact the key to his writing. From the depths of his memory he summoned jokes, stories, and language, color and incident, texture and sound, glory and heartache, which found their way into The Adventures of Huckleberry Finn—the true source of the American novel, according to Ernest Hemingway.

I wish to quote for you now a passage which on the surface concerns the difficult task of learning to read the river but which also describes the education of the literary imagination:

> The face of the water, in time, became a wonderful book—a book that was a dead language to the uneducated passenger, but which told its mind to me without reserve, delivering its most cherished secrets as clearly as if it uttered them with a voice. And it was not a book to be read once and thrown aside, for it had a new story to tell every day. Throughout the long twelve hundred miles there was never a page that was void of interest, never one that you could leave unread without loss, never one that you would want to skip, thinking you could find higher enjoyment in some other thing. There never was so wonderful a book written by man; never one whose interest was so absorbing, so unflagging, so sparklingly renewed with every reperusal. The passenger who could not read it was charmed with a peculiar sort of faint dimple on its surface (on the rare occasions when he did not overlook it altogether); but to the pilot that was an italicized passage; indeed, it was more than that, it was a legend of the largest capitals, with a string of shouting exclamation points at the end of it; for it meant that a wreck or a rock was buried there that could tear the life out of the strongest vessel that ever floated. It is the faintest and simplest expression the water ever makes, and the most hideous to a pilot's eye. In truth, the passenger who could not read the book saw nothing but all manner of pretty pictures in it, painted by the sun and shaded by the clouds, whereas to the trained eye these were not pictures at all, but the grimmest and most dead-earnest of reading matter.

As a cub pilot, Twain learned how to navigate around the shoals and shipwrecks in the Mississippi, and also how to recognize and ride the currents in his own imagination—a living river of words, which continually refreshes the deltas of American literature. Thank God, we might say, if not for the fact that Twain himself had an uncertain relationship to the deity.

The schooling of the imagination takes as many forms as there are artists. Whitman's memory is more serious than Twain's, for example, though there is nothing more serious than a joke. And I have learned in different ways from Whitman, Thoreau, and Twain, each of whom counsel us to pay attention to everything. Thus in my friendship with the late Kashmiri poet Aghah Shahid Ali, which included near daily telephone conversations over the course of twenty years, I realize now that in our gossiping, joke-telling, and discussions of poetic and political matters we were ever alert to stray bits of language which might be turned into a new poem. For example, when I read to him a suggestive line by Thomas de Quincy—"It was a year of brilliant water."—Shahid immediately found a way to use it in a poem—which eventually I answered in a poem for our mutual friend, the former U.S. Poet Laureate, W.S. Merwin, who has made a virtue out of translating his acts of attention into poems, the lines with which I will close:

West Window
for W. S. Merw

Green as the palm that fans the hill and hides
Flames at its base, the lizard slides or falls
From frond to flower, a raindrop disappearing
Into the ferns below. The island's mimics—
Mynas and mockingbirds—sing when the cardinal
Flies from the hutch to the mango and beyond.
The bamboo creaks. Doors open. No one's home.

―――――――

The cardinal preening in the palm transplanted
from Indonesia is not the island's
sentry nor the sea's ambassador
winds waves and wings whirl at the sound of the last
door closing in the leper colony
below the bluff where the brilliant water is
wearing down the wreckage from the war

―――――――

The dying man was still drawing up plans, this time for a prison. Candles flickered, and outside his window songbirds fell like rain; choristers trapped them in the cisterns to roast them over a spit. A priest opened a book and recorded the statesman's final words: Who are the enemies of France? The German princes? Their lands are burning. The Holy Roman Empire is a leper colony. Open the window on the West. We shall leave seeds and feathers everywhere. The Master of Royal Fireworks was in the courtyard, tasting sauces for the songbirds. Courtesans poured wine for the choristers. The blows from a sword are easily healed. Not so the blows of a tongue... The priest scribbled in the margins: Delirium has set in. Fireworks rained down on the city, like songbirds. The cisterns were filled with burning oil. Soon the swollen empire would split in two. Lepers were at the door. But just before he closed his eyes the cardinal heard the poet's voice: Where are the snows of yesteryear? And that is why it is said that he died peacefully in his sleep.

地域文化的价值倾向

毕飞宇

江苏省作家协会副主席

内容提要： 任何一种地域文化，只有有益于人类、有益于人类的发展与交流，这种文化才有生命力，才能成为人类文化的一个有机成分；相反，如果这种文化违背了基本科学常识、违背了人类文明的共同诉求、伤害了生命，无论这种文化具有多么华美的外表，多么具有煽动性和蛊惑力，它最终都会消失。我想说，任何一种文化都不该享有尊严，任何一种文化都不具备神圣不可侵犯的权利，只有文化内部价值才能使文化获得尊严。

1982年，也可能是1983年，我第一次读到了惠特曼，他的《草叶集》里有这样的一句诗："如果身体不适灵魂，那么灵魂又是什么？"

好吧，那我就从身体开始谈起。

我是1964年出生的，两年之后，"文化大革命"爆发了。从我懂事的那一天起，我就是伴随着"大概念"一起成长起来的，那些大概念包括"革命"、"人民"、"祖国"、"阶级"、"潮流"、"世界"，大概念盛行起来了，小概念的处境必然会艰难。我的羞耻感就是在小概念处境艰难的时候建立起来的。我的羞耻感大部分和人的身体有关，尤其是女性的身体。在相当长的时间里，"乳房"、"臀部"甚至"脖子"、"大腿"和"腰"都是不洁的，为了做一个好孩子，为了避免成为一个"小流氓"，我和我的小伙伴们在小学、初中和高中阶段没有和同班的女同学说过一句话。我们这样做是有依据的，正如大家所知道的那样，我们的样板戏里所有的英雄都没有配偶，女英雄没有丈夫，男英雄没有妻子。

"文革"里的一切都是极端的，但是，你不能说这样的极端就没有传统。六百多年前，在我的老家兴化诞生了一部伟大的小说，这部小说叫《水浒》。它描绘了108个好汉反抗压迫、争取自由的故事。108个好汉，每个人都有不同的遭遇，每个人都有不同的性格。但是有一点是一样的，这108个好汉都仇视并抵制女性的身体。这说明了什么呢？这说明了我们在1000年前就有了英雄的定义和要求：所谓英雄，除了充沛的体能，你不能亲近女人，你必须在女性面前表现出不屈不饶的克制力。

在今天，许多学者都已经达成了共识——我们的地域文化骨子里是一种"耻感文化"，这是和"快感文化"相对应的一个概念。耻感文化首先落实在我们对身体的感知和认识上，我们的身体是羞于见人的，我们的身体是难以启齿的。

但是，如果你考察一下当今的中国，你会高兴地发现，在我们的城市，到处都是健身房，到处都是美容中心和减肥中心，我们的年轻人正以一种自我欣赏的心态去选择自己的服装，他们沉迷于身体的线条与肌肤，他们的身体成了他们极为重要的审美对象。哲学上有一个很重要的概念，叫"自我观照"，用审美的心去看待自己，势必和用反省的心去看待自己一样重要。

我没有做过专门的调查，但是，如果我们企图选择这个时代的一些关键词，大概念依然是有的，这是不可或缺的，比如说，国家利益、GDP、宏观调控、环境保护、反恐，但是我要说，越来越多的小概念在我们的生活中散发出它们的魅力，这些小概念有一部分正是来自我们的身体，头发、指甲、刺青、三围和SPA。

现在的问题是，为什么我的演讲要从身体开始，再涉及一些大概念和小概念，我真正想说的还是文化问题。地域文化有其它的稳固性，同时，也有它的可变性。这种可变性往往来自不同文化的交流、渗透和彼此的化学反应。

3年前，我有幸读到过一本书，书的作者是乔治·维力雪罗，书的名字叫《洗浴的历史》。这是一本关于洗浴的书，一部关于身体的书，一部关于地域文化的书，一本有关文明的书。我吃惊地发现，就在200年前，法国人有一种顽固的认识，他们认为水是一种有害的东西，它能将病菌带入身体的内部。骄傲的法国人选择了不洗澡。在不得不洗的情况下，法国人必须先穿好衬衣、长裤和袜子，然后，再跑到浴缸里去。这是一种充满了喜剧色彩的文化形态，在这种文化形态里，法国人的鼻子最终没有能够忍受自己身体的气味，香水就这样诞生了。现如今，当我们在法国做客的时候，我们不仅可以洗上热水澡，我们还能在餐厅、咖啡馆、电影院享受到多种不同的香水所混合而成的气味，我要说，这气味是美好的，充满了生活的正面消息。

我相信法国人由穿着衬衣洗澡到光着身体洗澡一定会经历一个不愉快的过程。第一，法国人必须在科学这个层面上突破对水的认识。第二，在与其他文化的交流之后，法国人如何重新选择洗浴的法式。改变自己总是困难的，在文化上做出妥协和退让总是困难的。然而，这个世界从来就不存在不妥协、不退让的文化交流。文化交流的魅力就在于彼此渗透、相互影响，最终能够保持独立。

关于地域文化，伟大的鲁迅先生说过一句话："越是民族的就越是世界的。"这句话所有的中国人都知道。我承认，这句话有它的道理。但是，人类文化交流的历史告诉我，事实并不是这样。法国人穿着衬衣洗澡，全世界的人却是光着身体洗澡的，中国女人曾热衷于小脚，然而，小脚最终被天足替代了。我想说的是，越是民族的就越是世界的，这句话只看到了地域文化和世界文化的空间关系，它忽略了地域文化背后最为要紧的一个元素，那就是文化的价值。任何一种地域文化，只有有益于人类、有益于人类的发展与交流，这种文化才有生命力，才能成为人类文化的一个有机成分；相反，如果这种文化违背了基本科学常识、违背了人类文明的共同诉求、伤害了生命，无论这种文化具有多么华美的外表，多么具有煽动性和蛊惑力，它最终都会消失。我想说，任何一种文化都不该享有尊严，任何一种文化都不具备神圣不可侵犯的权利，只有文化内部价值才能使文化获得尊严。

鲁迅先生还说过一句话，他说："文学是叫人生的，不是叫人死的。"我非常喜爱这句话。我想把鲁迅先生的话改装一下，我想说："文化是叫人生的，不是叫人死的。"

我还想回到身体这个话题上来。关于身体，我想我们所有人都承认，它绝对不只是一个简单的生物组合，不只是蛋白质和维生素。身体的内部蕴含着人类文化的全部内容，它是政治，它是经济，它是教育，它是科技，它甚至还是军事——人类的军事行为都是以保存自己的身体、消灭对方的身体为前提的。我想强调的是，一切有益于身体的文化都是有价值的,无论它来自哪里。

中国人越来越珍惜自己、珍惜身体、珍惜生命,这样的共识已经成为我们民族文化的一个部分了。换句话说,文化交流改变了中国和中国人,文化交流让我们变得更好、更自信、更属于这个世界。我相信,从文化交流中获得好处的不只是中国人,而是这个世界上的每一个人。文化交流会让所有的身体更健康、更愉快、更美。

Bi Feiyu

Vice President of the Writers' Association of Jiangsu Province.

Value Orientation of Regional Culture

Abstract: Only if a regional culture is useful to humankind and the human development and exchanges can it have vitality and become an organic integral part of human culture; on the contrary, if a culture goes against the basic scientific knowledge and the common pursuit of human civilization or hurts the life of people, it will eventually disappear regardless of its magnificent appearance, agitation or delusion,. I want to say, no culture ought to enjoy dignity, no culture is sacred and inviolable, and only the internal value can bring dignity to the culture.

In 1982, or 1983, I read Whitman for the first time. In his Leaves of Grass there is such a poetic sentence: "If the body were not the soul, what is the soul?"

Well, let me start from the body.

I was born in 1964, and two years later the Cultural Revolution broke out. Ever since I could understand, I grew up with "big concepts", including "revolution", "people", "motherland", "class", "trend" and "World", etc.. When big concepts prevailed, it was inevitably difficult for small ones. My sense of shame was set up at the difficult times of small concepts. Most of my shames were connected with human body, especially the female body. In quite a long time, "breast", "buttocks", even "neck", "thigh" and "waist" were impure. In order to be a good boy and not to become a "hoodlum", my little friends and I did not say a word to female classmates in the elementary school, junior high school and senior high school. We were justifiable in doing so: as we know, all the heroes in our model operas are single, the heroine has no husband and the hero has no wife.

Everything in the Cultural Revolution was extreme, but such an extreme has its tradition. Over six centuries ago, a great novel called Outlaws of the Marsh was produced in Xinghua, my hometown. The novel depicts the story of 108 heroes fighting against oppression and for freedom. They are different with each other in experiences and personalities, but they have one thing in common: they are hostile to and reject the female body. What does it mean? It means we had a definition and requirements of hero a thousand years ago: a hero, in addition to his outstanding physical strength, shall not get close to a woman. He must demonstrate the indomitable willpower before a woman.

Today, many scholars have achieved consensus—our regional culture is in actuality a "shame culture", a concept corresponding to the "hedonic culture". The shame culture is first manifested in our perception and understanding of the body: it is ashamed to show people our body and even mention it.

However, a survey on China today will show you gyms, beauty salons and fat farms are everywhere in our cities, and the young people choose their own clothing with a mentality of self-appreciation. They are indulged in the skin and lines of the body, which have become the very important aesthetic object. There is a very important concept in philosophy, called "self-visualization". To look at oneself with an aesthetic mentality is bound to be as important as with self reflection.

I have not made a special investigation, but if we attempt to select some key words of this era, there are still some indispensable big concepts such as national interests, GDP, macro-control, environmental protection, and anti-terrorism, but I have to say, more and more small concepts show their charm in our lives and some of them come from our body: hair, nails, tattoos, measurements of our figure and SPA.

Now the question is why I started my speech from the body, involving some big and small concepts. What I really want to say is still the cultural issues. Regional culture is stable and variable as well. This variability often comes from the exchanges, infiltration and chemical reactions between different cultures.

Three years ago, I fortunately read a book History of Bathing, authored by Georges Vigarello, which talks about bathing, about body, about regional culture, and about civilization. To my surprise, I found two hundred years ago, the French stubbornly thought that water was harmful and could bring bacteria inside the body. The proud Frenchman chose not to bath. When they had to, they put on shirts, pants and socks before they went to the bathtub. What is interesting, French created perfume as they eventually could not bear the odor of their bodies. When we visit France today, we can not only have a hot water bath, but also enjoy the smell mixed by a variety of perfumes in restaurants, cafes and cinemas, etc.. I have to say that this odor is beautiful, full of positive messages of life.

I think it must an unpleasant process for French to change from bathing with the shirt to with nothing. First, they must have had a scientific breakthrough to the understanding of water; second, they must have changed their way of bathing after exchanges with other cultures. It is always difficult to change and make cultural compromises and concessions. However, there has never been the cultural exchange without compromises and concessions in this world. The charm of cultural exchanges lies in interaction, mutual influence, and independence in the end.

With regard to the regional culture, Lu Xun said: "the more national, the more international." Almost all Chinese people know this sentence. I admit that it is reasonable. However, the history of the human cultural exchanges tells me that it is not the case. The French had bath with the shirt on but other people bathed; and Chinese women were keen on bound feet, which have eventually been replaced by natural feet. What I want to say is that Lu Xun's argument pays attention only to the spatial relationship of the regional and the world cultures, but ignores the most important element behind the regional culture, that is, the value of culture. Only if a regional culture is useful to humankind and the human development and exchanges can it have vitality and become an organic integral part of human culture; on the contrary, if a culture goes against the basic scientific knowledge and the common pursuit of human civilization or hurts the life of people, it will eventually disappear regardless of its magnificent appearance, agitation or delusion,. I want to say, no culture ought to enjoy dignity, and no culture is sacred and inviolable; only the internal value can bring dignity to the culture.

Lu Xun also said: "literature gives life to people rather than killing them." I like it very much and would like to change it into "culture gives life to people rather than killing them".

I would like to come back to the subject of the body. I think we all agree that the body is definitely not just a simple biological combination, not just protein and vitamins. It contains all the contents of human cultures in terms of politics, economy, education, science and technology, and even military—all the military actions of human beings are premised on saving the bodies of one's own and destroying the bodies of the enemies. I want to emphasize that any culture useful to the body is valuable, no matter where it comes from.

Chinese people increasingly cherish themselves, bodies and lives. This consensus has become an integral part of our national culture. In other words, cultural exchanges have changed China and the Chinese people, and have made us better, more confident, and more closely attached to this world. I believe, not just Chinese people benefit from the cultural exchanges, but everyone in this world does. The cultural exchanges make all bodies healthier, more enjoyable, and more beautiful.

思维定势与世界观：
对空间如何决定思想的反思

詹森·帕滕特

南京大学－约翰斯·霍普金斯大学中美文化研究中心美方合作主任

内容提要：几个世纪以来，许多学科的学者一直在探讨和争论文化共性和文化相对主义的议题。各种学派此兴彼衰，各领风骚数年。20世纪20—30年代期间，相对主义在美国语言学家的论著中占主导地位，主要包括爱德华·萨皮尔和本杰明·李·沃夫的开山之作。到了20世纪60年代，共性主义又开始成为主流，这很大程度上是由于越南战争的影响：因为人们认为，如果所有人类在本质上是一样的，那么避免这种冲突应该是相对容易的。共性主义假设继续在社会科学中占主导地位，并引导了许多理论方法。譬如，理性选择理论认为人类理性是普遍的，因此空间最多是偶然的，这与人类生存的任何偶然因素一样。自20世纪70年代开始，人类学家、心理学家和语言学家的研究成果开始以具体精确的方式展示空间如何影响和决定人类体验。随着这一工作的进行，否认空间对不同文化群体的人的瞬间认知——甚至感知——的影响变得越来越难。在本次报告中，我将会简要列出近几十年来的主要研究成果，包括我自己在语言学领域的研究成果，这些成果都已经确定了空间作为一种关键决定因素在人类体验中的重要地位。此外我还将探讨人文学科的蕴含，以及此类研究成果的一些现实后果，供企业和政府参考。

  这次报告并非严格意义上的学术性演讲，而是有关个人经历的故事，随着故事的展开，我们将进入某些学术性和非学术性领域，它们主要集中在美国和中国。我的目的是向您介绍正在世界各地开展的我认为重要的学术性和非学术性工作，人们对此往往所知甚少。

  首先，谈谈我的个人情况。看到我的哲学博士学位，你会说我是一个语言学家；而我本科和硕士专攻东亚研究，你可能又会觉得我是个"区域专家"；从我以往的工作经历来看，你会更加不解，因为我不仅从事过学术研究，也曾在非营利私人部门工作过。

  贯穿我学习、研究和工作的主线就是"跨文化"。我实际上是一个跨文化学者（Interculturalist），无论从事什么工作，我总是从一种跨文化的视角去审视。跨文化学者遵循一套普遍公认的观点来观察人类群体，从中寻求增进理解和消除分歧的方法。这就不可避免地涉及诸多学科和方法，既包括学术性的，也包含应用性的背景（Context）。

1990年，我大学毕业，获得了东亚研究专业的学士学位。随后两年，我在一所著名大学学习了汉语以及许多有关中国历史与社会的课程。我觉得已经准备好了，于是，1991年9月，我踏上了前往中国的旅程。

但我错了，我实际上完全没有做好准备。在中国亲身经历的和我之前在头脑中盘算的简直有天壤之别。尽管我受过良好的教育，但依然疲于应付那些看似与我所学密切相联的状况。

我在中国的那一年过得惊心动魄，既不乏美好之处，同时又难免令人心生恐惧。我从没有在一年之中学到过那么多东西，这期间经历的点点滴滴都是我的最珍贵的财富。

当然，这都是后话了。我认为，我们实际上可以通过深刻而持久的方式汲取跨文化交流和消除思维定势（Mindset）方面的一些关键经验教训，而不至于像我在中国的第一年那样那么痛苦。现在想来，我就是在那一年决定投身跨文化交流事业的。

倒回到2000年秋天，当时我是加州大学伯克利分校语言学研究生的七年级学生。当时，我还没想好硕士论文的研究课题。我的一位指导老师乔治·雷克夫建议我从语言学的角度研究美—中关系上的一个关键问题。

在座各位如果有来自美国的"中国专家"，那有个情况你们肯定再熟悉不过：在与"非专家"闲聊时，人权问题经常被提起。就我个人而言，尤其是在非正式的社交场合，得知我是个"中国通"后，在场的美国人肯定会提出人权问题。人们认为我们应该非常了解这个问题，并能就此发表真知灼见。跟我交谈的那些人经常口若悬河，仿佛他们个个都是该问题的专家。

我经常遇到的问题是，美国人在谈论中国的人权问题时，夸夸其谈往往多于事实真相。在学术界，有关人权问题普遍性的争论不绝于耳，政治学者以及哲学家讨论得尤其热烈。所有这些谈话当然都很好，但我觉得，对这个问题进行一些实证研究才更能提升辩论的价值。我有幸接受了多年语言学分析方法的训练，有助于阐明该问题，因此，我决定将人权问题作为我的研究课题。

我对加州大学伯克利分校的中国研究生进行了几次实验性的采访（Pilot Interviews），但很快发现这样很难获得可靠的语言学资料。我遇到了两个问题：首先，在采访的情景下，受访者很难完全放松和自然。在回答访问者提出的问题时，他们给出的答案或多或少存在"表现"的成分。尤其是在这种被称为跨文化研究的课题中，中国受访者肯定会以一种特定的方式向外国提问者展示中国。

其次，受访者担心他们对这个话题的认识有限。谈到人权问题时，一种普遍观点是，"专家"知道得更多。因此，我的受访者在谈论人权问题时总是吞吞吐吐。结果，当我最后坐下来研究调查结果时发现，由于受这两个问题的影响，基本上无法从回答中了解受访者的信仰体系。

为确保获得有价值的语言学资料，不能让受访者感觉他们正在回答问题，也不能让他们对自身的专业知识产生怀疑。所以，我又回到问题的起点，思考怎样才能让他们忘记是在接受采访？我该问哪种问题，才能让他们始终保持自信？

为解决第一个问题，我征求了世界各地学界同仁的意见。埃默里大学语言学家艾伦·西恩基（Alan Cienki）提出了他的建议：将问题分别写到纸上，让两名受访者（一组）念出来，并一一回答。而我则坐在一旁，脸朝向一边，进行记录。他还建议受访的两人最好是朋友，这样可以避免与生人初次见面时的尴尬。我最终采用了这种方法，并取得了很好的效果。

对于第二个问题——该问哪些问题——我很自然地想到，一个人对人权问题所持的观点必然与个体对人的认知及其如何在某些环境下（最明显的就是国家和家庭）发挥作用有关。因此，我围绕这些主题设计了各种情境。

以下是我想到的一些问题：

假设你能创建一个新社会，你希望它是什么样子的？

假设一个人某天正走在街上，突然被警察逮捕了。警察没告诉他原因，直接将他逮捕，关了三天后又放了他。他并无违法行为。他该怎么想？怎么做？

政府未征求公民意见即通过了一项法律，将所得税增加了一倍。政府这样做合理吗？公民有何看法？他们会怎么做？他们应怎样做？

如果一个人很有钱,他/她应该如何处理这些钱?

汤姆即将高中毕业。他不顾父母反对,决定加入一支摇滚乐队,而不去上大学。他的家人彼此间会说什么? 结局会怎样? 谁是对的?

我采访了9组(两人一组)中国学生和13组美国学生,获得了大约200页(单倍行距)的语言分析资料,其中英语和汉语回答大约各占一半。

我由此发现了两种有关人类生活的截然不同的理想。美国人认为,人类生活包含两个方面:首先,是要成为人类全球村(Global Community)的成员。我们相互之间都负有义务。即使我们"得天独厚"或运气特别好,也有义务帮助他人。第二,每个人都拥有特殊的天赋,所以我们必须为了全人类的利益将这些天赋发挥到极致。

相比之下,中国人对人类生活的观点更为实际。他们认为,生活就是解决各种接踵而至的问题。你得不断进行鉴别排序,以便将真正迫切需要解决的问题与可以稍后解决或者根本无需解决的问题区分开来。总而言之,最为迫切的问题就是满足物质需求。其他问题都可以慢慢解决。

这两种观点都是理想化的观点,而且两个文化群体内部存在着巨大的分歧。然而,这种分歧确实存在,也正是因此,中国人和美国人从直觉上采取不同的方式看待世界,尽管每个群体内部都存在多元化。

但是,千万别被这种差异所左右。这两种信仰体系只是不同而已,并非毫无相通之处。无论是美国人还是中国人的回答,或多或少都能看到对方的影子。

直到完成博士论文后,我才发现心理学家们已经作了浩如烟海的研究,深入探索了文化在人们中间即时"发生"的方式。

20世纪50和60年代,美国社会科学的主流观点(至少在心理学、人类学和语言学领域)是,所有地方的人从本质上来说是相同的,文化只是某种"处理插件"(Processing Add-on),充其量只是装点门面的东西而已。人都是一样的,差异只是巧合。在这种模式下,空间——作为文化的首要决定因素——在对话中几乎很少被提及。

但如今,我看到的一些研究揭示出的人类的差别程度着实令人震惊。其中一个特别引人注目的实验是李俊基、彭凯平和理查德·E.尼斯比特在2000年开展的[①]。对于那些认为文化是某种认知性的"例外"(Extra)的人来说,这篇文章会改变他的看法。

学的本科生——接受了"棒框"(Rod and Frame)测验。研究对象沿着一条垂直线（棒）向下观察一个长长的方形管子（框）。框和棒都可以独立旋转。

棒框测验的用途之一是检测"场依存性"（Field Dependence）：即对棒的角度的认知在多大程度上受到了框的角度的影响？即人们在多大程度上能够摆脱框的影响，对棒的角度做出准确的判断。

如果我们用一个常见的比喻来理解"东方"和"西方"的区别，就可以说"东方人"的"场依赖性"比"西方人"更强，因为据说"背景"（Context）在东方国度重要得多；关系比个体更为重要。

当然这是一种荒唐的说法。幻觉终归是幻觉，千万别被这个比喻欺骗了。虽然中美两国文化不同，但真实知觉其实并不存在差别。

可这恰恰就是研究者们发现的情况：与中国人相比，欧洲裔美国人的场独立性较强。他们对棒垂直性的判断更为准确，较少受框的影响；当能够随意控制棒时，他们的判断更加准确。中国人则倾向于把"棒和框"作为一个整体来观察，即便在可以控制棒的时候，他们判断的准确性也不及美国人。

这个研究结果令我震惊不已。它表明，文化与我们——作为人——的个体身份紧密相连：如果我眼中的世界在一定程度上是我所处文化背景的产物，那么，我生命中的任何部分又怎能与文化相割裂呢？

身处陌生文化中的人更应时刻谨记该研究结果，以免想当然地认为只有我的观点是正确的，其他人都是错的。其实，中国人和西方人观察世界的方式是不同的。因此，暂时搁置自身的固有观念，深入了解这一残酷的事实将给予我们莫大的帮助。这种对"眼见为实"的新的驳斥不容置疑地证明：空间在个体对世界的认知方面影响巨大，至少在空间决定文化的情况中如此。

对这些研究成果的一种极端解释是：中国与美国完全不同，甚至毫无共通之处——这与普遍主义者的观点相左。但我认为真实情况绝不是非此即彼的，世界各地的人类群体可能存在天壤之别，但他们在本质上是相同的。实际上，这两种观点都可以服务于人类：由于人性相通，我们有着共同的兴趣；而我们之间的差别又为解决我们共同的问题提供了各种方法。

再回到我的故事上。阅读了大量有关文化差异的心理学著作后，我热切地希望进行一次不同于学术工作的尝试。我有了一个很棒的主意：开办一家企业，将这种知识销售给全球的公司。

但事实证明我并不是拥有这种想法的第一人。我发现这个行业已经悄然兴起，它们正在提供我所说的服务。我以为可以很容易地加入这一行业，但很少有企业愿意雇佣一位博士。

终于，在2009年，情况开始有了转机。我开始开展培训课程，对象是那些将要离开美国去另一个国家的人，或从其他国家被派驻到美国的人。其中一些培训涉及到中国，但大部分没有。期间，我发现了各种帮助人们适应外国生活的现成工具。让我印象最深的是，培训材料都是经过深思熟虑的，而且人们对这类学习的领悟力很强。

功夫不负有心人，我于2011年加入了约翰·霍普金斯大学－南京大学"中国与美国研究中心"。在这里，我每天都生活在两种语言和文化中。

所有这些学术界内外的经历都让我受益匪浅，我更深刻地了解到人类在建设一个和平世界的征途中所做的努力。

首先，我们要理解需要解决的问题。在许多情况下，我们不是生来就懂得如何与人相处；人类大脑进化过程中的最原始部分使人与人之间的相处极具挑战性。差异的存在会激发人类"要么战，要么逃"的应激反应。著名的跨文化专家米尔顿·贝内特（Milton Bennett）在其最负盛名的文章的开篇写道："跨文化的敏感性并非是天生的"，即人类历史上充斥着对异己者的暴力行为。我们绝不能被这种认识所左右，而须以好奇的思想和开放的心态研究我们自身。

其次，人类需要顽强的决心和巨大的努力才能学会尊重我们的"善良天性"（Better Angels）。如果在对一条垂直线的认知如此基本的事情上来自不同文化的人都会得出不同的结论，可想而知我们所面临的工作是多么艰巨。

再次，我相信这项工作是可行的，因为我们拥有友好相处所需的一切。我们拥有实现世界和平的认知架构（Cognitive Machinery），此外，得益于世界如此不同，我们可利用丰富多样的工具。所以，创建一个和平的世界是可能的。

最后，鉴于此次论坛是与美国国家人文基金会（National Endowment for the Humanities）合办的，我理应再谈谈人文学。这一切与人文学有何关系？你只要看眼这个词，答案不言自明。人文学是有关人类的学科，跨文化学者的工作也是围绕人展开的——克服偏见和打破陈规定型观念，促进不同的人类群体和民族之间生出同情与理解之心。尽管我这里谈到的方法属于社会学范畴，但是研究结果全都关乎人类。

然而，要使社会科学值得人们付出艰辛努力，其必须有助于实现人类的最大抱负。我很庆幸自己既能从事学术研究，又能开展应用实践，只有这样才能引导人类走向一个我们共同希冀的未来——那种我们在阅读文学名著、欣赏伟大的艺术作品、观看优秀的电影或舞蹈或者聆听震撼人心的音乐时分明能够感受到的未来：到那时，世界将不再有分离和隔阂，共同的人性会将我们紧紧相连。

---

① 《文化、控制与环境中的关系的认知》(Culture, Control and Perception of Relationships in the Environment)，《个性与社会心理学杂志》(Journal of Personality and Social Psychology)，2000年，第78卷，第5期，第943-955页。

Jason D. Patent

American Co-director of The Johns Hopkins University-Nanjing University Center for Chinese and American Studies

Mindset and Worldview: Reflections on How Place Shapes the Mind

Abstract: For centuries scholars from many disciplines have debated questions of cultural universality and relativism. Various trends have waxed and waned. Relativism dominated the work of American linguists in the 1920s and '30s, which included the seminal work of Edward Sapir and Benjamin Lee Whorf. In the 1960s universalism became dominant, largely as a response to the U.S. war in Vietnam: if all humans were inherently the same, then such conflicts, it was held, would be easier to avoid. Universalist assumptions have continued to dominate many theoretical approaches in the social sciences. To take one example, rational choice theory holds, among other tenets, that human rationality is universal — and therefore that place, as any contingency of human existence, is at best incidental. Beginning in the 1970s, research by anthropologists, psychologists and linguists began to demonstrate precise ways in which place influences and shapes human experience. As this work continued, it became harder and harder to deny the influence of place on the moment-to-moment cognition — and even perception — of people belonging to different cultural groups. In this talk I present a summary of key findings over recent decades, including my own research in linguistics, which have established place as a key determinant of human experience. I will also discuss implications for the humanities, as well as some of the practical consequences of these findings for business and government.

This talk is not strictly academic. Instead it is the story of a personal journey, which leads us through some academic and non-academic territory, mostly revolving around the U.S. and China. My intent is to introduce you to what I consider to be important work, both academic and non-academic, being done throughout the world, but about which few people know.

First, some remarks about the perspective I aim to bring. If you look at my Ph.D., you would say I am a linguist. If you look at my M.A. or B.A., which are in East Asian Studies, you could say I am some sort of "regional expert". If you look at my job history, you will be even more confused, since I've worked not only in academia but also in the non-profit and private sectors.

One unifying theme in my study, research and work can be described by the term "intercultural." I am at heart an interculturalist, and I bring an interculturalist's eye to all that I do. Interculturalists look at groups of humans with a broadly shared set of perspectives, and look for ways to understand and to bridge difference. This inherently involves many academic disciplines and methods, and both academic and applied contexts.

In September 1991 I found myself headed to China. I had graduated from college in 1990, with a B.A. in East Asian Studies. Equipped with two years of Chinese language study and a bevvy of courses on Chinese history and society from a reputable institution, I thought I was ready.

I was wrong. I was completely unprepared. The gap between what I thought I was ready for and what I actually experienced was enormous. Somehow my fancy education had completely failed to prepare me for something with a seemingly close connection to what I had studied.

My year was challenging and wonderful and horrible. I learned more than I had ever learned in a year. I wouldn't change a thing about it.

I only say that in retrospect, though. I think a number of key lessons in bridging cultures and mindsets can be learned in impactful and long-lasting ways without being nearly as painful as my first year in China was. Looking back now, I see that year as when I first became a committed interculturalist.

Fast-forward to fall 2000. I was beginning the seventh year of my graduate program in linguistics at the University of California, Berkeley. I still didn't know what I wanted to research and write about for my dissertation. One of my advisors, George Lakoff, suggested I do a linguistic study of a key issue in U.S.–China relations.

For those of you who are American "China experts," I don't need to tell you that human rights comes up a lot in casual conversations with "non-experts." In my experience, especially at informal social functions, not long after hearing that I'm a "China hand," Americans will raise human rights. It's something we're expected to know about. We're supposed to have something intelligent to say on the matter. Also, my interlocutors often felt free to speak as if they were experts on the matter.

The problem I always had was that there was always so much more bluster than fact when it came to Americans' views on human rights vis-à-vis China. And in the world of the academy — political scientists and philosophers in particular — there was no shortage of debates about how "universal" human rights "really are." All good conversations, no doubt, but I couldn't help but feel that some empirical investigating could add much to the debate. I had the good fortune of having been trained for several years in methods of linguistic analysis that promised to shed light on the issue, and so I decided to take on human rights as my topic.

I conducted several pilot interviews with Chinese graduate students at U.C. Berkeley, and quickly discovered that it was hard to get robust linguistic data. There were two problems. First, in an interview setting it's hard for the interviewees to be completely relaxed and natural. With an interviewer asking questions, there's always a "performance" aspect to the answers, especially in a study like this that had been advertised as cross-cultural: Chinese interlocutors were surely eager to present China in a particular way to the foreign interviewer.

Second, interviewees lacked confidence in their knowledge of the topic. One idea that people have about human rights is that it's something that "experts" know more about than they do. So when my interviewees discussed human rights, they hemmed and hawed. Ultimately these two problems yielded data which, when I sat down with it, didn't have much to offer in terms of revealing the interviewees' belief systems.

In order for linguistic data to be meaningful, speakers can't be thinking about the fact that they're answering an interview question, and they can't be doubting their own expertise. I went back to square one and thought: how can I get them to forget they're being interviewed, and what sorts of questions can I ask that can circumvent the confidence issue?

On the first question I reached out to colleagues the world over to ask what advice they had. One reply came from Alan Cienki, a linguist at Emory University. He advised writing the questions out onto separate sheets of paper, and having pairs of interviewees read them and answer them one by one, while I sit off to the side, facing away, taking notes. He also suggested that the pairs be friends, so that there wouldn't be any awkwardness around people meeting each other for the first time. This is the method I ended up using, and it worked well.

On the second question — figuring out which questions to ask — it seemed logical that beliefs about human rights are connected to beliefs about individuals and how they function in certain contexts — most obviously the state, but also the family. So I devised scenarios revolving around these themes.

Here are some of the questions:

Suppose you could create a new society. What would it be like?

Suppose a citizen is walking down the street one day when the police arrest him. They don't tell him why; they simply arrest him and keep him locked up for three days before letting him go. He has done nothing illegal. What will this person think? What will this person do?

The government passes a law doubling the income tax without consulting the citizens. Is the government right to do this? What would citizens say? What would they do? What should they do?

If a person is rich, what should he/she do with his/her money?

Tom is about to graduate from high school. He decides he doesn't want to go to college, despite his parents' wishes. Instead, he wants to join a rock band. What will the family members all say to one another? What will happen in the end? Who is right?

I conducted interviews with nine pairs of Chinese students and thirteen pairs of American students, yielding around 200 pages of single-spaced language for analysis — about half English and half Chinese.

What I discovered were two deeply contrasting ideals about what a human life is about. According to the American view, human life is about two things. First, it's about being a member of a global community of humans. We all have duties towards one another. To the extent that we've been "blessed," or had especially good luck, we're obligated to help others. Second, each individual has been given special talents, and it's vital that we maximize the use of these talents for the betterment of the species.

The Chinese view of human life is quite a bit less ethereal. According to this view, life is a series of problems to be solved. People have to do ongoing triage in order to sort the truly pressing problems from the ones that can wait a bit, or the ones that won't be addressed at all. In general the most urgent problems are around meeting material needs. The other stuff can wait.

These two views are idealizations, and there is massive variation within each cultural group. Yet the distinction is real — something has to account for the intuition that Chinese and Americans view the world differently, despite all the diversity internal to each group.

It's still important, though, not to get carried away by the differences. The two belief systems are just different, not incommensurable. Throughout the data there are reflections and refractions of the Chinese belief system in the American responses, and vice versa.

It was only after I finished my Ph.D. that I became aware of a vast body of research by psychologists into the moment-to-moment ways in which culture "happens" for people.

In the 1950s and 1960s the predominant view in the social sciences in the U.S. — at least in psychology, anthropology and linguistics — was that humans are inherently the same everywhere, and that culture is some sort of processing add-on, almost window-dressing. People are just all the same. Differences are coincidental. In this model, place — as the primary determinant of culture — is almost absent from the conversation.

But now I was discovering research that revealed sometimes shocking findings about the degree of difference out there. One particularly striking experiment was conducted in 2000 by Li-Jun Ji, Kaiping Peng and Richard E. Nisbett.[1] For anyone who might have thought that culture is some sort of cognitive "extra," this article should change your mind.

Two groups of subjects — European Americans and Chinese (from Taiwan), all undergraduates at the University of Michigan — took the "rod and frame" test. Subjects look down a long, square-shaped tube (the frame) at a straight line (the rod). The frame and rod can rotate independently of each other.

One of the uses of the rod and frame test is to measure "field dependence": to what extent is perception of the rod's orientation affected by the orientation of the frame? That is, how able are people to "factor out" the frame and make accurate judgments about the orientation of the rod?

If we take a common metaphorical understanding of how "East" and "West" differ, we might think that "Easterners" would be more field-dependent than "Westerners", since "context" is said to matter so much more in the East. Relationships matter more than individuals.

At the same time it's an absurd claim. Vision is vision, right? Let's not be fooled by the metaphor. There's no way actual perception could differ culturally.

Except that's exactly what the researchers found: the European Americans were less field-dependent than the Chinese. Not only were their judgments of rod verticality more accurate irrespective of the frame, but they got even more accurate when given control of the rod. The Chinese tended to see "rod and frame" together, and gave less accurate judgments when given control over the rod.

To me this finding is absolutely astonishing. It shows that culture goes to the very root of who we are as human beings: if how I literally see the world is partly a product of my cultural background, then how could any part of my life not be touched by culture?

It also serves as a stark reminder to anyone operating in an unfamiliar culture that we'd best be on guard against assuming our own perceptions are right and others' are wrong. Chinese and Westerners actually see the world differently. Knowing that brute-force fact can help us immensely if we're willing to distance ourselves from our own perceptions. This new spin on "seeing is believing" shows definitively that place — to the extent that place determines culture — matters tremendously in how each of us understands the world.

One extreme interpretation of these findings would be that China and America are hopelessly different, even incommensurable — the opposite of the universalist view. I don't see that it has to be one way or the other. It can be true that groups of humans the world over are both wildly diverse and inherently the same. And in fact both perspectives can be brought to bear in service of humanity: our common humanity shapes our common interest, and our differences provide an overflowing abundance of ways to solve our shared problems.

Returning now to my story: having familiarized myself with much of the psychological literature on cultural difference, and anxious to try something other than academia, I had what I thought was a brilliant idea: start a business selling this knowledge to global companies.

It turns out I wasn't the first person to have this idea. In fact I found that a small but thriving industry already existed doing just this. I thought it would be easy to get a foot in the door, but few in the business world were interested in hiring someone with a Ph.D.

Finally, in 2009 I caught a break and began conducting trainings with people who were either about to relocate to another country from the U.S., or who had recently arrived in the U.S. on assignment from another country. Some of the trainings involved China, but many didn't. I discovered an entire range of well-established tools for equipping people for life in a foreign land. I was struck by how well thought-out the training materials were and by how receptive people were to this kind of learning.

Eventually in 2011 I ended up at the Hopkins–Nanjing Center, where we have the chance to live a bilingual and bicultural reality day in and day out.

All of these experiences, inside and outside the academy, have taught me important lessons in the human struggle for a peaceful planet.

First, we need to start by understanding what we're dealing with. In many ways we aren't designed to get along: the evolutionarily primitive parts of our brains make it especially challenging. The "fight or flight" response feels threatened by difference. In fact one of the most influential interculturalists, Milton Bennett, led off his most famous essay by stating, "Intercultural sensitivity is not natural." He meant to point out that human beings have a long history of violence toward those perceived as different. We can't afford to let this aspect of our cognition rule us. We must study ourselves, with curious minds and open hearts.

Second, it takes dogged determination and tremendous commitment for human beings to honor our "better angels" .If something as basic as perception of a vertical line can differ cross-culturally, then we have our work cut out for us.

Third, I believe that this work is doable: we humans have all that we need in order to get along. We have the cognitive machinery for world peace, and we have an infinitely rich variety of tools to draw from, thanks to the diversity of the world's cultures. A peaceful world is possible.

Finally, because this forum was co-organized by the National Endowment for the Humanities, some words on the humanities are in order. How does all of this relate to the humanities? All we need to do is to look at the word. The answer is right there. The humanities are about humans, and the work of interculturalists — overcoming prejudices and default interpretations in order to arrive at a compassionate understanding of people who differ from us — is about humans. Though the methods I've discussed here are those of the social sciences, the findings are human through and through.

Yet if the social sciences are to be worthy of the efforts of humans, then they must serve the greatest aspirations of humans. I am grateful to have been exposed as I have to work, both academic and applied, that has the potential to guide humans toward a future we all want — the kind of future we can taste when reading great literature, or viewing great art or film or dance, or listening to great music: a future in which we are bound, not separated, by our shared humanity.

---

① Culture, Control and Perception of Relationships in the Environment, Journal of Personality and Social Psychology, 2000, vol. 78, No. 5, 943-955.

美国文学教学与研究在南京

王守仁

南京大学外国语学院教授,当代外国文学与文化研究中心主任

内容提要:包括美国文学在内的外国文学与中国现代化进程、与中国现代文学和文化的演进有密切关系。南京与美国文学有不解之缘。1921年,赛珍珠随丈夫来到南京,在多所大学任教。她在南京大学的小楼里创作了诺贝尔文学奖获奖小说《大地》。南京大学是国内为数不多的较早进行美国文学教学与研究的高校。小说家的职责是挖掘、揭示人物的内在心理和情感。在现实生活中,人与人之间无法完全地互相了解,只能通过对彼此的外部行为的观察来做一个大致的勾勒,而在小说中,小说家向我们展示小说人物的内心世界,"读者可以完完全全地了解小说人物",其生命的一切,从内心世界到外在言行,都可以把握。在这个意义上,小说比历史更真实。文学是人学,是描写人性。这正是美国文学吸引力之处:它帮助我们认识作为普通人的美国人,认识美国民族,洞悉超越了国别、政治、意识形态、肤色限制的普遍人性,而这是连接中美两国人民最根本的纽带,也是我们讲授和研究美国文学的价值所在。

　　南京地处中国东部沿海,一直是中国南北交汇、东西融通、内外交流的中心城市之一。六百多年前,伟大航海家郑和从这里走向世界。在历史上,南京是中国最早对外开放的城市之一。1911年,孙中山先生领导辛亥革命,推翻满清统治,南京成为民国政府首都。南京作为一座城市,有许多精彩故事,一方面聚集着中国文化的丰裕与繁华;另一方面又注重吸收融合西方文化,形成既传统又现代的特色。

　　外国文学作为外国文化的重要组成部分,在中国的翻译、传播和接受过程与中国的现代化进程、与中国现代文学和文化的演进有密切关系。外国文学曾先后作为反传统的话语、政治革命的工具、观看外部世界的窗口，参与中国社会变革。中美两国人民交往有许多渠道，其中一个非常重要的方式便是通过文学来实现文化交流。

美国诗人朗费罗的《人生颂》于1864年由英国使臣、汉学家威妥玛和户部尚书董恂译为汉语，这是中国翻译美国文学的最早尝试。1872年4月20日，上海《申报》刊登美国作家欧文的短篇小说《一睡七十年》，中国读者接触美国文学已有一百四十多年历史。包括美国文学在内的外国文学与中国现代化进程、与中国现代文学和文化的演进有密切关系。林纾1901年出版《黑奴吁天录》，在跋文中指出："今当变政之始，而吾书适成。人人既蠲弃故纸，勤求新学；则吾书虽俚浅，亦足为振作志气，爱国保种之一助。"①鲁迅读完该小说后，在给友人信中说中国人要以黑奴为前车之鉴："曼思故国，来日方长，载悲黑奴，前车如是，弥益感喟。"②1934年大型文学杂志《现代》推出"现代美国文学专号"，编者在《导言》中指出："现在的美国是在供给着到20世纪还可能发展出一个独立的民族文学来的例子"，正在"独立创造中的中国新文学"不但能从中获得"新鼓励"，而且应该学习美国现代文学的"创造"和"自由"的精神。③中国对美国文学的接受一直没有停止，即使在1960年，著名作家老舍还曾撰文纪念马克·吐温逝世50周年。

南京与美国文学有不解之缘。1921年，赛珍珠随丈夫来到南京，在多所大学任教。她在南京大学的小楼里创作了诺贝尔文学奖获奖小说《大地》。今年5月，南京大学赛珍珠纪念馆落成，正式向外开放。我和我的同事专门举办了"赛珍珠与民国时期的南京"国际学术研讨会。在此之前，我们组织翻译"赛珍珠作品选集"共七卷，我翻译了《群芳亭》部分章节。

南京大学是国内为数不多的较早进行美国文学教学与研究的高校。南京大学目前是全国美国文学研究会驻所单位，拥有江苏高校哲学社会科学重点研究基地当代外国文学与文化研究中心，编辑出版 CSSCI 来源期刊《当代外国文学》。我们有一批研究美国文学的专家学者，在美国小说、诗歌、戏剧、文学批评理论等领域开展工作。2002年问世的四卷本《新编美国文学史》研究不同时期主要的流派、作家和作品，总结美国文学走向世界、成为独立的民族文学的成功经验，并凸显中国学者的主体意识，对美国的一些重要作家与中国文学、中国文化的互动关系进行较为深入的考察，是国内迄今为止规模最大的美国文学通史。近年来，我的同事出版了美国文学与文化研究专著《美国当代文学与美利坚民族认同》(2008)、《美国文艺复兴经典作家的政治文化阐释》(2009)、《现代性的焦虑——菲茨杰拉德与1920年代》(2009)、《20世纪美国华裔小说研究》(2010)和译著《西方正典》(2005)。我本人关注诺贝尔文学奖得主、美国黑人女作家托妮·莫里森,撰写了我国第一部莫里森小说研究专著《性别·种族·文化——托妮·莫里森的小说创作》,该书通过解读莫里森的八部长篇小说,对莫里森的文学创作思想和艺术特色进行了全方位的探讨和细致的阐释,展示出莫里森对美国文学发展作出的贡献。

从20世纪80年代起,美国文学开始走进中国大学课堂。美国文学是绝大多数高校英语系本科生的必修课。从2009年起,我和我的同事设计了为全校本科生开设的通识课程"英美文学与文化",该课程理念是将文学视为一种观念文化,从中选取和提炼出若干与当下时代相关的主题,课程目的是让学生通过文学作品了解英美文化及其核心价值,在深层次上认识中西观念文化的异同,树立全球化语境中的国际视野。我们指导学生阅读富兰克林、爱默生、梭罗、麦尔维尔、惠特曼、德莱塞、克莱恩、菲茨杰拉德、罗斯、桑塔格、任璧莲、莫里森等人的作品,搭建一个跨文化交流的平台。

在研究生教育方面,美国作家成为许多研究生学位论文的研究对象。我历年来指导的博士论文研究德莱塞、霍桑、斯坦贝克、当代华裔美国文学研究、冯尼格特、斯泰因、杰克·伦敦、欧茨、罗斯、弗洛斯特、纳博科夫、贝娄、斯奈德。我的博士生研究领域涵盖了美国文学经典作家,这些年轻的学者在研究中广泛阅读相关论著,对美国文学和文化有较为深刻的认识,并力图从中国视角阐释文本。他们毕业后已成为所在单位学术骨干,不少人担任了院长系主任,为提升教学研究水平、促进中美文化交流发挥作用。

南京大学的美国文学教学与研究得益于一支非常优秀的教师队伍,同时,国际学术交流特别是中美大学之间的交流,使我们的老师了解国外研究最新进展。目前,南京大学与美国布朗大学实施校合作项目,设立"性别与人文研究中心",与美国埃默里大学、宾州州立大学的英文系建立了定期学术交流机制。

中国改革开放以来,经济快速增长,文化教育事业也迎来大发展时代。位于南京的译林出版社是一家专业翻译出版社,自1988年成立以来，出版了一大批包括美国国家图书奖获奖作品在内的经典和当代外国文学作品。目前，美国文学几乎所有重要作家的作品都有中译本。中国读者了解美国文学要超过美国读者了解中国文学。

在中国大学从事美国文学教学与研究，我们自然会对美国文学中的中国因素感兴趣。实际上，有不少美国作家，如爱默生、梭罗等人的思想曾受到中国文化影响。金斯伯格以其长诗《嚎叫》著称于世，是美国"垮掉的一代"文学文化思潮的主要代言人。他曾于1984年访问中国，写了"中国组诗"，其中《读白居易抒怀》怀念白居易，跨越了时空，视唐代诗人为知己，能产生共鸣：

> 头痛，头依着枕躺下
> 仍然在读着有关唐代古道的诗篇
> 白居易叙述的这些事使我把手指
> 捂住双眼哭泣——也许这是他对
> 一个诗人老朋友的情意，而我的
> 脸颊上和秃顶上的毛发也已花白。

金斯伯格对中国传统文化和中国古诗情有独钟，他的《读白居易抒怀》第五首显然是受到张继《枫桥夜泊》的启迪：

> 在苏州石桥下
> 的一条小巷，张继在这儿度过了
> 一个不眠之夜，被寒山寺的钟声唤醒，
> 千年前河水拍打着他的小船

金斯伯格十分赞赏白居易，中美诗人的思绪和情感能够有交汇，融为一体：

> 我的脸颊靠在枕头上午睡
> 思绪起伏逆流而上
> 流向三峡以西的忠县

> 白居易曾在那里为官
> ……
> 我的思绪正在漂流,像河水、像风。
> "两种思绪已在梦中同时迸发,
> 如果我醒来拿起笔,
> 两个世界将成为一体。"

"中国组诗"独具魅力,为美国读者了解中国提供了一条途径。研究中美文化在文学中的交流,是我们中国学者担当的任务。

英国著名作家福斯特在《小说面面观》中讨论人物时将历史学家和小说家做比较:历史学家记录的是人物实际的言行,他也对人物的性格感兴趣,但他对人物性格的总结是从其外部言行推断出来的。小说家的职责是挖掘、揭示人物的内在心理和情感。在现实生活中,人与人之间无法完全地互相了解,只能通过对彼此的外部行为的观察来做一个大致的勾勒,而在小说中,小说家向我们展示小说人物的内心世界,"读者可以完完全全地了解小说人物",其生命的一切,从内心世界到外在言行,都可以把握。在这个意义上,小说比历史更真实。文学是人学,是描写人性。这正是美国文学吸引力之处:它帮助我们认识作为普通人的美国人,认识美国民族,洞悉超越了国别、政治、意识形态、肤色限制的普遍人性,而这是连接中美两国人民最根本的纽带,正如金斯伯格在"中国组诗"中所说,"两个世界将成为一体"。

---

① 斯土活:《黑奴吁天录》,林纾、魏易译,北京:商务印书馆,1981年,第206页。
② 《鲁迅全集》第11卷,北京:人民文学出版社,1981年,第321页。
③ 《现代美国文学专号导言》,《现代》第五卷第六期(1934年10月)。

Teaching and Study of American Literature in Nanjing

Wang Shouren

Professor of the Foreign Language College of Nanjing University, Head of the Center for the Studies of Contemporary Foreign Literature and Culture

---

Abstract: Foreign literature, including American literature, is closely related to the development of China's modernization and evolution of contemporary Chinese literature and culture. Nanjing has run close together with American literature. In 1921, Pearl Buck came to Nanjing with his husband and taught in several universities. She composed the Good Earth that won the Nobel Prize of Literature in a house in Nanjing University. Nanjing University is one among the few colleges that teaches and studies on American literature at an early time. Novelists are responsible to excavate and unveil characters' psychology and emotions. In the real life, people cannot completely understand each other, but can only briefly outline others characters by observing their behaviors. However, in novels, novelists can unveil the inside world of the characters in the novel. "Readers can completely comprehend the characters" and get to know both the heart and acts of the character. From this aspect, novels are more real than the history. Literature is essentially the studies on men and aims to describe the human nature. This is the attractive point of American literature. It helps Chinese understand ordinary American people, American nation and the common human nature beyond the nationality, politics, ideology and race, which is the most fundamental link between American and Chinese people and the value of our teaching and studies on American literature.

Nanjing as a coastal city in East China has been a transport and communication hub in the country, active in establishing connections with the outside world. It was the base from which China's earliest intercontinental maritime expeditions, led by the great navigator Zheng He, set out six centuries ago. It was one of the earliest cities in China's history that opened up to the world. After the Revolution of 1911 led by Dr. Sun Yat-sen which overthrew the Qing Dynasty rule, Nanjing became capital of China. This is a city with many stories, boasting of the riches of the Chinese culture, and absorbing the quintessence of foreign cultures. Nanjing is both traditional and modern.

Foreign literature constitutes an important part of foreign culture. The translation, transmission and reception of foreign literature are closely related to China's modernization drive, and to the development of Chinese modern literature and culture. Foreign literature has participated in China's social transformation by serving as an anti-traditional discourse, an instrument of political revolution, and a window to the outside world. There are many ways for Chinese and American people to get to know each other, and American literature is one of the important channels to facilitate Sino-American cultural exchanges.

American poet Longfellow's "A Psalm of Life" was translated by Thomas Francis Wade, a British diplomat and Sinologist, and Dong Xun, Minister of Finance of the Qing Dynasty in 1864. This was the first attempt to translate American literature into Chinese. On April 22, 1872, the famous Shanghai-based newspaper Shun Pao, also known as Shanghai Daily, published a Chinese version of Washington Irving's "Rip Van Winkle," titled "A Sleep of Seventy Years." The Chinese reader's encounter with American literature has a history of over 140 years. Foreign literature, of which American literature constitutes an important part, is closely related to China's modernization drive, and to the development of Chinese modern literature and culture. In 1901 Lin Shu (1852-1924) translated Uncle Tom's Cabin by Harriet Beecher Stowe into Chinese, and in the "Afterword" to his translation he said:

My book has just been completed when the political reform is beginning at the moment. Everyone is now throwing away old Chinese books and seeking new ideas and thoughts. Although it is common and shallow, this book is powerful enough to boost our fighting spirit, and helpful in the cause of saving the nation. [1]

Lu Xun (1881-1936), having read the novel, wrote in a letter to his friend that the Chinese should learn a lesson from the black slaves: "Our ancient nation has a long way to go. The black slaves set a predecessor for us, and it is really sad to think about their fate." [2] In 1934 the Modern magazine published a special issue on Modern American Literature. The editor wrote in the "Introduction": "Now the United States is providing a fine example of developing an independent national literature in the 20th century", and "Chinese new literature which is in the on-going process of independent creation" can not only find "inspirations" from American literature, but also learn its "creative" and "free" spirit. [3] China's reception of American literature has never been stopped since then, and even in 1960 when the country was virtually isolated from the outside world, Lao She (1899-1966) the well-known Chinese novelist delivered a speech to mark the 50th anniversary of Mark Twain's death.

Nanjing has a special connection with American literature. In 1921, pearl S. Buck and her husband moved to Nanjing after a 5-year stay in North China. In the following years she taught English in universities in the city. It was on the campus of Nanjing University where she wrote the Nobel prize-winning novel The Good Earth (1931). In May this year, Pearl S. Buck Memorial House was open to public, and on the occasion, my colleagues and I organized an "International Conference on Pearl S. Buck and Her Nanking Years". In the 1990s, we launched a translation project of Selected Works of Pearl S. Buck in seven volumes, and I translated parts of her novel Pavilion of Women into Chinese.

Nanjing University is among the few pioneering Chinese institutions of higher learning which started teaching and study of American literature in the latter part of the 20th century, and now hosts China Association for the Study of American Literature. With its Center for the Study of Contemporary Foreign Literature and Culture, the university publishes the peer-reviewed journal Contemporary Foreign Literature, and attracts a team of scholars working in the fields of American fiction, poetry, drama and literary criticism. One of our academic achievements is the four-volume New Literary History of the United States, the most comprehensive history book on American literature ever written by Chinese scholars. The project, which was supported by the Chinese National Fund for the Humanities and Social Sciences, examines major American writers and their works from the Chinese perspective, and looks into how American literature has grown into an independent national literature. The literary and cultural relationships between China and the United States are discussed whenever possible. My colleagues' recent publications include Contemporary American Literature and American National Identity (2008), American Renaissance Authors: A Political and Cultural Reading (2009), Anxiety of Modernism: F. Scott Fitzgerald in the 1920s (2009), Studies in 20th Century Chinese-American Literature (2010) and the Chinese translation of The Western Canon by Harold Bloom (2005). I wrote Gender, Race and Class: A Study of Toni Morrison's Novels, the first book in China on the Nobel-Prize winning African American woman novelist. In this monograph, I conduct a comprehensive analysis of her eight novels, and evaluate her contribution to the development of American literature.

It was not until the 1980s when American literature began to be taught in Chinese universities. American literature is now a required course for English majors. Starting from 2009, my colleagues and I have been developing a general education course in Anglo-American Literature and Culture. The aim of the course is to develop students' critical understanding of the core values of Anglo-American culture, analyze the similarities and differences between Chinese and Western cultures, and broaden their vision in a global context. We introduce undergraduate students across disciplines to the major texts by American authors such as Benjamin Franklin, Ralph Waldo Emerson, Henry David Thoreau, Herman Melville, Walt Whitman, Theodore Dreiser, Stephen Crane, F. Scott Fitzgerald, Philip Roth, Susan Sontag, and Gish Jen. By identifying certain key issues relevant to the community and individuals in contemporary China, the course connects our Chinese students to the American texts, setting up a platform for intercultural communication.

The postgraduate program in American literature is well developed in many Chinese universities, and attracts students all over the country. In the past decades, I have supervised over 20 PhD students' dissertation writing, and half of them chose American literature as their field of study, working on the following authors: Theodore Dreiser, Nathaniel Hawthorne, John Steinbeck, Contemporary Chinese American Literature, Kurt Vonnegut, Gertrude Stein, Jack London, Joyce Carol Oates, Philip Roth, Robert Frost, Vladimir Nabokov, Saul Bellow, and Gary Snyder. My students' research has covered major writers in American literature. These young scholars read extensively, focus in-depth on meaningful topics, and engage effectively with individual authors. The rigorous training provides them with solid foundations for future development. After graduation, some of them have become heads of departments or schools, and played an important role in improving the quality of teaching and research, and promoting the cultural exchange between Chinese and American cultures.

Nanjing University's teaching and study of American literature are supported by a strong faculty. The active international exchanges, the academic exchanges between Chinese and American universities in particular, keep our faculty members well informed of the recent developments in the field of study. As part of its initiative to strengthen the international programs, the university and Brown University launched Nanjing-Brown Joint Program, and set up the Centre for Gender Studies and the Humanities in Nanjing this year. The English Department here maintains exchange relationships on a regular basis with their counterparts in Emory University and the Pennsylvania State University.

Since China adopted its "Opening-up" policy in the 1980s, the country has undergone rapid and sustained economic growth, presented great opportunities for development in education and culture. Yilin Press, which was founded in 1988 and now based in Nanjing, is the leading press of translation in China. Known for its dedication to the translation and publishing of world culture and literature, Yilin Press publishes over 800 titles every year, among which are works of Nobel Prize winners, American National Book Award winners, and National Book Critics Circle Award winners. Thanks to the publishers like Yilin, the Chinese translations of the books by almost all the major American authors are available in China. The Chinese reader knows more about American literature than the American reader knows about Chinese literature.

Teaching and studying American literature in the Chinese context, we are very much interested in Chinese elements in American literature. In fact, many American authors, notably Emerson and Thoreau were influenced by Chinese culture and Chinese way of thinking. Allen Ginsberg, known for his long poem "Howl", was the spokesman for the "Beat Generation". In 1984 he visited China, and wrote "China poems" which include "Reading Bai Juyi". Transcending the limits of time and space, Ginsberg regarded the Chinese poet of the Tang Dynasty Bai Juyi as his old friend, and was able to respond to his poems:

> Lying head on pillow aching
> still reading poems of Tang roads
> Something Bai said made me press my finger
> to my eyes and weep—maybe his love
> for an old poet friend, for I also
> have gray on my cheek and bald head

Ginsberg was fond of Chinese culture and classic Chinese poetry. The fourth poem in "Reading Bai Juyi" was inspired by Zhang Ji's poem "A Night-Mooring Near Maple Bridge"
> From the stone bridge at Suzhou where Jiang Ji spent
> A sleepless night wakened by the bell of Cold Mountain Temple,
> Water lapping against his boat a thousand years ago,

Ginsberg appreciated Bai Juyi very much, and the two poets' thoughts are merged together:

> I lay my cheek on the pillow to nap
> and my thoughts floated against the stream
> up to Zhong Xian west of the Three Gorges
> where Bai Juyi was Governor.
> ......
> So flowed my mind like the river, like the wind.
> "Two thoughts have risen together in dream therefore
> Two worlds will be one if I wake and write."

Ginsberg's "China poems" have their unique charms, helping American readers to understand China and Chinese culture. It is the mission of the Chinese scholars to study the cultural exchanges and interactions between Chinese and American culture in the field of literature.

British novelist E. M. Forster discusses people in his Aspects of the Novel (1927). In his opinion, "the historian deals with actions, and with the characters of men only so far as he can deduce them from their actions"; the novelist, however, is able to enter the mind of people: "it is the function of the novelist to reveal the hidden life at its source." Forster asserts: "In daily life we never understand each other, neither complete clairvoyance nor complete confessional exists. We know each other approximately, by external signs."

But people in a novel can be understood completely by the reader, if the novelist wishes; their inner as well as their outer life can be exposed. And this is why they often seem more definite than characters in history or even our own friends; we have been told all about them that can be told; even if they are imperfect or unreal they do not contain any secrets, whereas our friends do and must, mutual secrecy being one of the conditions of life upon this globe.

Literature is about people and about humanity. This is what American literature fascinates us. American literature enables us to understand Americans as ordinary people completely by having access to "their inner as well as their outer life" and insight into the national character. It helps us to transcend the national, political, ideological, and racial barriers and reach humanity which is the bond that unites two peoples and constitutes the basis of our mutual understanding. It is in literature where "Two worlds will be one," as the American poet Ginsberg tells us in his "China poems".

---

① Lin Shu, Uncle Tom's Cabin by Harriet Beecher Stowe (Beijing: The Commercial Press, 1981), 206.
② Lu Xun, The Complete Works of Lu Xun, vol. 11 (Beijing: The People's Literature Publishing House, 1981), 321.
③ "Introduction" to the Special Issue on Modern American Literature, Modern, vol 5, no. 6 (October 1934).

江苏及南京地域文化简述

徐耀新

江苏省文化厅厅长

内容提要： 地域环境的差异，影响人类的生活方式，进而影响文化精神。本文以江苏和南京为例，对地域和文化的关系作简要论述。第一部分：论述地域文化的概念、基本属性、主要内涵及形成原因。第二部分：论述江苏地域文化的内涵和外延。江苏地域文化大致可以分为"四主区"和"四亚区"。"四主区"主要包括楚汉文化、吴文化、金陵文化、淮扬文化。"四亚区"主要是指镇江文化、淮安文化、南通文化、盐城文化。第三部分：论述金陵文化的内涵和外延。金陵文化以南京为核心，包括六朝文化、明文化和民国文化。在建设历史文化名城的进程中，要着重保护南京古都的自然遗产和历史遗产，从根本上确保古都神韵永驻。要着重打造"六朝文化"、"明文化"、"民国文化"和"革命文化"，提升城市文化品格。

大自然是多彩斑斓的，人类的文化是丰富多样的。各民族各地区文化精神、文化特征之差异，究其根源就在于地域环境有差异、地域历史积淀有差异、生产生活方式有差异，甚至是政治制度的沿革有差异等。可以说是不同的地域孕育了各自的文化。今天论坛的主题是文化与地域，下面我就以论坛闭幕式所在地——江苏和南京为例，对地域和文化的关系作一简要论述，同时也期待向各位来宾介绍江苏及其首府南京文化的概貌。

一、地域与文化的关系

什么是地域文化？我们的理解一般是指特定区域源远流长、独具特色，传承至今仍发挥作用的文化传统，是特定区域的生态、民俗、传统、习惯等文明表现。

地域文化的基本属性：一是独特性。任何文化都是地域性的知识体系，只是不同的文化涵盖的范围不同。二是传统性。文化是历史性的产物，文化的形成源于人类长久的发展和积累。三是多元性。地域文化的内涵、表现形式等都不是完全同质的。四是界限的模糊性。地域文化的界限是模糊的，要想精确地标出具体的地域文化边界是枉然的。五是行政区划的限定性。从特定意义上讲，有的时候一种政治实体就是一个文化体系。

地域文化的主要内涵：主要是指地域范围内的人们在长期历史过程中创造出来的物质和精神财富的总和。通常以方言、饮食（特别是民间的日常饮食）、民间信仰、民间建筑等形式直观表现出来。

地域文化的形成原因：一是自然地理环境。不同的自然环境，在文化上所产生的差异就很难消逝，会长期保存。二是移民。如江南的文化直接受益于西晋末年开始的一个世纪的移民。三是政治权力与行政区划。旗袍与所谓的唐装都是满人入关后强制推广的，现在反而成了中国文化的一种体现。四是民族分布。各民族的文化不尽相同，对地域文化的形成具有一定的影响。五是外来文化。外来文化的影响不同形成了区域文化的差异，如海派文化明显受到西方文化的影响。六是宗教。有些地方的文化明显带有宗教色彩。

二、江苏地域文化的内涵和外延

1667年，江苏因清代江苏省东西分置而建省，省名取自江宁府、苏州府两府首字。江苏位于我国大陆东部沿海中心、长江下游，东濒黄海，介于东经116°18′—121°57′，北纬30°45′—35°20′之间，属于亚热带向暖温带的过渡区。江苏国土面积10.26万平方公里，占全国的1.06%，现设13个省辖市，常住人口7898万。作为华夏长江文化的发祥地之一，江苏山明水秀、风物清嘉、人文荟萃，始终保持着地域文化的稳定因素，深藏着异于其他地域文化的基本特点和个性。江苏的地域文化大致可以分为"四主区"和"四亚区"。

"四主区"主要包括楚汉文化、吴文化、金陵文化、淮扬文化。

（一）楚汉文化。楚汉文化是以国家历史文化名城徐州为中心的区域性文化，它以六千年前的青莲岗文化、大墩子文化乃至更早的下草湾新人文化为渊源。楚汉文化融合先秦黄河、长江两大文化体系，是两汉文化的先声，它凝聚着中华民族奋发向上、自强不息的斗争精神，是中华文化的重要组成部分。它的显性特征是刚强雄浑。汉代"三绝"之汉墓、汉兵马俑和汉画像石刻是其代表。楚汉文化中的非物质文化遗产主要有：江苏梆子、柳琴戏、淮海花鼓、徐州琴书、淮海戏、邳州年画、沛县武术、徐州香包等。

（二）吴文化。吴文化的地域通常指靠近太湖的苏、锡、常地区。吴文化是中华民族史的重要部分，在史学研究中占有重要地位。吴文化具有清新气息、柔美风格、鲜活灵性，形成了聪颖灵慧、细腻柔和而又视野开阔、乐于创新等显性特征。淹城遗址、苏州古城、苏州文庙、太平天国忠王府、三星村遗址、惠山寺等是吴文化中的珍贵历史文化资源。吴地工艺门类齐全，据不完全统计有12大类近100种，主要有苏绣、宋锦、缂丝、紫砂陶器、惠山泥人、檀香扇、常州梳篦、桃花坞木版年画等。形成于苏锡常地区的戏曲主要有昆曲、苏州评弹、锡剧、苏剧等。

（三）金陵文化。金陵文化以国家历史文化名城南京为中心。东晋——南朝的300年不仅使得长江流域历史性地成为中国经济的重心，也在中原主流文化与南方文化融合的基础上形成了金陵文化，其显性特征是南北交汇、兼容并蓄、开放包容，可谓独树一帜。金陵文化主要包括六朝文化、明文化和民国文化，而这三大块历史文化又可统属于"都城文化"。但是主流的都城文化并不排斥其他文化，如盛极一时的秦淮文化，不仅反映了红粉文化、市井风情，而且还包含了民族气节和爱国精神。在秦淮河上，朱自清、俞平伯曾同时泛舟又同时写下了内容不同的《桨声灯影里的秦淮河》历史名篇。金陵文化我将在第三部分重点论述，在此不赘述。

（四）淮扬文化。淮扬文化的中心城市是国家历史文化名城扬州。淮扬地区河多水多，船多桥多，呈现出古、文、水、绿、秀的地域风貌，在南北文化交流中形成了清新优雅与豪迈超俊相结合的显性特征。淮扬文化中的历史文化遗产主要有：龙虬庄遗址、九里——千墩汉墓群、瓜洲古渡、文昌阁、御码头、隋炀帝陵、大明寺等；扬剧、木偶戏、扬州弦词、扬州清曲、扬州漆器、扬州玉器等为世人所熟知。

除了上述的四个主区，江苏的地域文化还包括四个亚区：

一是地处金陵文化、吴文化和淮扬文化结合部的镇江文化（京口文化）。镇江文化融汇了吴文化和中原文化，可以概括为"多元积淀型"，具有兼容并包、多元多样的特点。

二是地处楚汉文化、淮扬文化结合部和我国南北文化结合部的淮安文化。明清时期，淮安因中枢漕运、集散淮盐、河道治理地位显赫而成为"运河之都"，京杭大运河贯穿淮安，兼有南北文化特点的运河文化也随之而生。

三是地处海派文化、吴文化和淮扬文化结合部的南通文化（江海文化）。地处"淮南江北海西头"的江苏南通，是一座有着数千年文化遗存的苏中古城，襟江负海，南风北韵。历史与现实、古老与时尚、外地文化与本土文化在这里交汇互存，形成了极具特色的绚丽多彩的江海文化。

四是远离各文化主区、特色显著的盐城文化（海盐文化）。盐城位于江苏沿海中部，在南有吴越文化、北有楚汉文化的历史条件下，海盐文化位于南北文化过渡带，虽兼容并蓄却又不倚不靠。[1]

三、金陵文化的内涵和外延

南京是中国著名的四大古都及历史文化名城之一，有35万年的人类活动史，近2500年的建城史和450年的建都史，留下了光辉灿烂的历史文明。

（一）独具特色的自然和人文

南京具有雄视长江、领袖东南、近海控淮的地缘优势，是最适合作为都城的城市之一。历史上除汉、唐之间作为"六朝都城"之外，从元末到1949年的581年时间内，南京与北京这两个古都的互动主导着整个中国的政治格局和民族命运，充分体现了南京的独特地位和非凡的区位优势。

1. 独特的地理条件和环境风貌特征。古都南京襟江带河，依山傍水，是龙蟠虎踞、山环水抱、滨江近海、四季分明的"帝王洲、佳丽地"。"春牛首、秋栖霞、夏钟山、冬石城"体现了南京与自然融为一体、四季分明的独特景色和气候。"山水城林，融为一体"，"山在城中、水在林中、人在景中"，是自然风貌与人文景观相结合的最佳典范。

2. 丰厚的历史文化积淀。南京的魅力，不仅在于自然赋予的山水城林之美，更在于文化传承的历史之美。作为六朝古都、十朝都会，南京拥有世界文化遗产1处、国家级文物保护单位27处81个点，省级文物保护单位100处107个点。数十万件珍贵文物，3条主要历史轴线、10片历史文化保护区和12片环境风貌保护区等都是南京历史文化积淀的见证。

3. 雄厚的当代科教实力。南京拥有各类高校七十余所，在校大学生八十多万人，科技人员近40万人，在宁"两院院士"79人。研究领域十分广泛，其中天文、古生物等领域的研究处于世界领先水平。

(二) 总体保护古都的风貌和格局

建设文化南京，打造历史文化名城，要着重保护南京古都的自然遗产和历史遗产，从根本上确保古都神韵永驻。

1. 还原和保护南京城的古都风貌。根据"显山、露水、见城、滨江"的城市建设方针，保老城，建新城，在老城区腾出更多的空间彰显自然环境，营造人文环境。严格控制普通民居和高层建筑，逐步拆除违章建筑和现代低水平建筑，还原和美化老城的古都风貌。

2. 重点保护以"三条历史轴线、明代四重城郭"的古都格局。南京的三条历史轴线：一是六朝及南唐时期的都城中轴线，即今天的中华路，它既是南京城南地区的中轴线，又是传统的商市区。二是明代的都城中轴线，即今天的御道街，它既是南京城东地区的中轴线，又是城市目前的主要出入口之一。三是民国时期形成的城市轴线。这是一条由中山北路、中山路、中山东路组成的"Z"字轴线，它是现今南京道路系统的主要骨架。明代南京都城由宫城、皇城、京城和外郭四圈城垣组成。闻名于世的南京城墙(明城墙)，至今仍保存有21.35公里，是全国重点文保单位。明代四重城郭构成了古都南京城的轮廓，都要坚持适当保护。上述"三条轴线、四重城郭"是南京历史上"繁华竞逐"的地方，一定要保护好这些历史的记忆、历史的符号。

3. 保护一批历史文化街区和环境风貌区。如果说保护南京的三条历史轴线和明代四重城郭，是从线状上总体保护南京古都风貌和格局，而保护一批历史文化街区和环境风貌区，则是从片状上深化这种总体保护。

(三) 纵向打造四大历史文化品牌

在南京历史文化的长河中，地位重要、独具特色并有可能规模化的是"六朝文化"、"明文化"、"民国文化"和"革命文化"，应当把它们打造成南京的城市品牌。

1. 打造"六朝文化"品牌。六朝时期，北方战乱，大量居民包括许多政治家、艺术家、科学家纷纷"衣冠南下"（约90万之众），实现了中华文化的一次大融合。以南京为中心，以汉族为主体的"六朝文化"，上承汉晋，下启隋唐，为后来盛唐文化的兴起奠定了坚实基础，在中华文明史上具有救亡图存、继往开来的重要地位。中西方史学家把六朝文明与西方古罗马文明相媲美，打好"六朝文化"牌，具有全国和世界意义。

2. 打造"明文化"品牌。在南京古代文化中，明代文化历史规模博大、底蕴深厚、气度恢宏。要积极建设明故宫遗址公园，使其产生重大的旅游观光价值。修复并凸显明城墙，使之再展雄姿。充分利用世界文化遗产——明孝陵，打造出具有国际意义的文化和旅游品牌。围绕"龙江宝船厂遗址公园"，深入挖掘郑和这一世界历史名人资源。同时积极开发明文化旅游纪念品。

3. 打造"民国文化"品牌。1927—1949年，中华民国国民政府以南京为首都，这一为期不长的特殊历史时代，在南京也留有许多珍贵的文化遗产，在中华文明史上有着独有的地位。要以孙中山先生的"民主共和"、"天下为公"等先进思想为主线，以海内外炎黄子孙爱我中华的共同理想为纽带，以总统府等民国建筑为依托，辅之以对其他民国文化资源的有效开发和利用，把南京"民国文化"品牌做得更亮、更大。

4. 打造"革命文化"品牌。南京是一座革命之城，历经太平天国定都南京、孙中山建立中华民国、抗日战争、解放战争等重大历史事件，留下了天王府、瞻园、总统府、中山陵、大屠杀纪念馆、雨花台革命烈士陵园等珍贵文化遗存，既是人们接受爱国主义教育、弘扬民族精神的宝贵精神财富，也是南京历史文化和城市旅游的重要品牌。要进一步挖掘和利用这些文化资源，将南京的"革命文化"品牌打造的更有成效，进一步凸显革命历史名城特色。

在纵向打造"四大历史文化品牌"过程中，还要充分挖掘历史文化名人资源，进一步发挥名人效应。南京自六朝以来文化名人辈出，李白、刘禹锡、杜牧、韦庄等诗家名士留下了与金陵有关的许多不朽诗篇。在文化领域，有留下大量传世佳作的南唐二主李煜、李璟，《文心雕龙》的作者刘勰，《儒林外史》的作者吴敬梓，《随园诗话》的作者袁枚，《红楼梦》的作者曹雪芹等。在戏剧领域，有《桃花扇》的作者孔尚任。在书画领域，有著名的画家顾恺之，大书法家王羲之、王献之，有"金陵八大家"之首的龚贤,有美术教育家徐悲鸿,著名山水画家傅抱石,当代草圣林散之等。②

优秀地域文化是传统文化的承载者和历史文化节点,它所肩负的文化基因深深地影响着现代人的精神世界。新的时代赋予了我们新的责任和新的使命,我们当积极研究地域文化现象并深入挖掘地域文化资源,致力于打造特色地域文化品牌,为区域经济社会发展提供精神动力、智力支持和文化条件,以更好地推动经济社会全面协调可持续发展。

---

① 该章节主要参考周欣著《江苏地域文化源流探析》一书。
② 该章节主要观点见本人发表于2002年9月7日《中国文化报》《建设"文化南京"与打造历史文化名城》一文。

On Regional Culture of Jiangsu Province and Nanjing

Xu Yaoxin
Director of Jiangsu Provincial Department of Culture

Abstract: Differences in the geographical environment will affect people's lifestyle and further influences on the culture and spirit. This article will briefly discuss on the relation between the geography and culture, with Jiangsu and Nanjing as an example. Section I: Discuss on the concept, basic property, main connotation and causes of the regional culture. Section II: Discuss on the denotation and connotation of the regional culture of Jiangsu. The regional culture of Jiangsu can be basically divided into four major areas, Chu Han culture, Wu culture, Jinling culture and Huaiyang culture and four secondary areas, Zhenjiang culture, Huai'an culture, Nantong culture and Yancheng culture. Section III: Discuss on the denotation and connotation of Jinling culture. With Nanjing as the center, Jinling culture includes the six-dynasty culture, Ming culture and the culture of the Republic of China. The protection of the natural and historical heritages in Nanjing shall be put emphasis on in the construction of historical and cultural city, in order to fundamentally maintain the charm of the old city. Importance shall be attached to the construction of six-dynasty culture, Ming culture, culture of the Republic of China and Revolutionary culture, to raise the cultural level of the city.

forms. The difference on the cultural spirit and cultural characteristics among different regions and nationalities is essentially related to the difference among the regional environment, regional historical accumulation, production and life style, and even the evolution of political systems, etc. We can say that different regions have fostered their unique cultures respectively. Since the theme of today's forum is culture and region, I will take Jiangsu and Nanjing—where our closing ceremony takes place--as the example, to give a short presentation on the relationship between region and culture. I also hope this can let you have an overview on the culture of Jiangsu Province and its capital Nanjing as well.

I.Relationship between region and culture

What is regional culture? Our general understanding is that, it is the cultural tradition in a certain area which is of long standing and unique characteristics, and which has been passed down till today and still plays an important role in nowadays.

Basic attributes of regional culture: firstly, the uniqueness. Every culture is a regional knowledge system, only the scopes covered by different cultures are not the same. Secondly, the traditionality. Culture is the product of history, the forming of a culture is related to the long-term development and accumulation of human being. Thirdly, the pluralism. The connotation, expressing form, and so on of the regional culture are not completely homogenous. Fourthly, the ambiguity of boundary. The boundary of the regional culture is not clear, any effort to precisely mark out a specific regional cultural boundary will end up in vain. Fifthly, the limitation of administrative division. In this particular sense, sometimes, one political entity means one cultural system.

Major connotation of regional culture: it mainly refers to the sum total of material wealth and spiritual wealth created by human being in a specific regional area, over the long course of history. It is normally expressed in the direct forms as the local dialect, diet (especially the daily folk diet), folk beliefs, and folk architecture etc.

Formation causes of regional culture: firstly, the natural geographical environment. The difference in cultures that generated in different natural environments can hardly fade away and will retain for a long time. Secondly, the immigration. For instance, the Jiangnan Culture was directly benefited from the immigration over a hundred years, starting from the last years of Western Jin Dynasty. Thirdly, the political power and the administrative division. Cheongsam and the so called "Tang Suit" were forcefully introduced after the invasion of Manchurian, while today they are reviewed as one of the expressions of Chinese culture. Fourthly, the distribution of ethnic groups. The culture of each ethnic group differs from each other, which has certain impact on the forming of regional culture. Fifthly, the foreign culture. Different impacts of the foreign culture lead to the difference among regional cultures, for example, Shanghai regional culture was apparently influenced by the western culture. Sixthly, the religion. The cultures of some regions are with distinctive religious features.

II.Connotation and denotation of Jiangsu regional culture

In A.D. 1667, Jiangsu was first established as a province, when Jiangnan Province was split into the eastern part and the western part by the government of Qing Dynasty. Its name comes from the first two characters of Jiangning Prefecture and Suzhou Prefecture respectively. Jiangsu is located at the center of eastern coastal area of mainland China, along the lower reaches of Yangtze River, and bordering the Yellow Sea to the east. It is between 116°18—121°57,east longitude and 30°45—35°20,north altitude, and belongs to the transition zone from sub-tropical to warm temperate. Jiangsu covers a land area of 102.6 thousand km2, accounting for 1.06% of that of China; it currently has 13 provincial cities, with a resident population of 78.98 million. As one of the birthplaces of Chinese and Yangtze River culture, Jiangsu has picturesque scenery, excellent natural products, and a galaxy of notable talents, which always maintains the stable factors of the regional culture and embodies the basic characteristics that distinguish itself from other regional cultures. The regional culture of Jiangsu can be roughly divided into "Four Main Regions" and "Four Sub-regions"

The "Four Main Regions" mainly include Chu-han culture, Wu culture, Jinling Culture, and Huai-yang culture.

(I) Chu-han culture. Chu-han culture, centered at Xuzhou--a national famous historical and cultural city, can be traced back to Qingliangang culture, Dadunzi culture over 6000 years ago, and Xiacaowan culture of even earlier time. Chu-han culture is the integration of the two major cultural systems as the pre-Qin Yellow River culture and Yangtze River culture. As the herald of Han Dynasty Culture, it demonstrates the national spirit of constant striving for self-improvement, and becomes an important part of Chinese culture. The dominant feature of this culture is the strength and robustness. It is represented by the "Three Wonders" of Han Dynasty, as the Han Tombs, Han Terra-Cotta Warriors and Horses, and Han Stone Reliefs. The Intangible Cultural Heritages of Chu-han culture mainly contains: Jiangsu-bangzi opera, Liuqin drama, Hua-hai flower-drum, Xuzhou story-telling opera, Huai-hai opera, Peizhou new year paintings, Pei county martial arts, and Xuzhou sachet, etc.

(II) Wu culture. The region of Wu culture mainly refers to the areas of Suzhou, Wuxi and Changzhou, which are nearby the Tai Lake. Wu culture is an important part of Chinese national history; it occupies a critical position in historiography research. Wu culture has fresh flavor, soft style, and vivid spirituality, which jointly form its dominant features as intelligent, subtle and tender, while with broad view and interest in innovation. The Yancheng ruins, Ancient City of Suzhou, Suzhou Confucius Temple, King Zhongwang's Residence of Taiping Heavenly Kindom, Sanxingcun Ancient Ruins, and Huishan Temple are the precious historical and cultural resources of Wu culture. Wu region has a full range of traditional arts and crafts, according to the incomplete statistics, there are about 12 categories and 100 kinds, mainly including Suzhou embroidery, Song brocade, silk tapestry with cutting designs, purple-clay earthenware, Huishan clay figurine, sandalwood fan, Changzhou comb, and Taohuawu Woodblock Prints etc. The operas formed in Suzhou, Wuxi and Changzhou areas mainly include Kun opera, Suzhou Pingtan, Xi opera, and Su opera etc.

(III) Jinling Culture. Jinling culture is centered at the national famous historical and cultural city—Nanjing. The history of 300 years from Eastern Jin Dynasty to the Southern Dynasties had not only historically turned Yangtze River Basin into the focus of Chinese economy, but also formed the Jinling culture on the basis of fusion between the central China mainstream culture and the southern culture. It has the unique dominant features as the integration between the south and north, inclusiveness, and open and tolerance. Jinling culture mainly consists of the Six-Dynasty Culture, Ming-Dynasty Culture, and Minguo Culture, while all these three historical cultures can be incorporated in the "Capital Culture". However, the mainstream capital culture does not expel other cultures, for example, the Qinhuai culture flourished in the early years was not only the reflection of courtesan culture and local customs, but also contained national integrity and patriotic spirit. On the Qinhuai River, Zhu Ziqing and Yu Pingbo once was boating at the same time, and composed the master works under the same topic "Qinghuai River in Oaring Sound and Light Shadow" of different contents. Since Jinling culture is the focus in the third section of my presentation, I will not go into further details here.

(IV) Huai-yang culture. The central city of Huai-yang culture is the national famous historical and culture city—Yangzhou. Huai-yang region is of rivers with abundant water, and excessive bridges and boats, which maintains the ancient, green, cultural, water and delicate regional style, and forms a dominant feature combining elegance with heroism, in the course of cultural exchange between the north and south. The historical and cultural heritages of Huai-yang culture mainly contains: Longqiuzhuang Ruins, Jiuli—Qiandun Han Tombs, Guazhou Ancient Ferry, Wenchang Pavilion, Royal Pier, Mausoleum of Emperor Suiyang, and Daming Temple etc; Yangzhou opera, puppet opera, Yangzhou Tanci, Yangzhou Ditty, Yangzhou lacquer ware, and Yangzhou jade articles are also well-known to the public.

Besides the above-mentioned four main regions, Jiangsu regional culture also consists of four sub-regions:

The first one is Zhenjiang culture (Jingkou culture), which is located in the junction area of Jinling culture, Wu culture and Huai-yang culture. As the fusion of Wu culture and the Central China culture, Zhenjiang culture can be summarized as "diversified and accumulative type" which has the characteristics of all-embracing and diversity.

The second one is Huai-an culture, which is located in the junction area between Chu-han culture and Huai-yang culture, and the junction area between the northern culture and southern culture of China. In the period of Ming and Qing dynasties, Huai-an had become the "Canal City" due to its position as the center of canal transportation, the distributing center of Huai salt, and the critical location for canal regulation. The Grand Canal passes through Huai'an, and the canal culture with both characteristics of the southern culture and the northern culture ensues.

The third one is Nantong culture (water culture), which is located in the junction area of Shanghai regional culture, Wu culture, and Huai-yang culture. Situated in the area to the "south of Huai River, north of Yangtze River, and west of the sea", Nantong is an ancient city with cultural heritages over thousands of years. Facing the river and against the sea, it combines the style of southern area and the charm of northern area. The history and the reality, the ancient and the modern, and the outside culture and the local culture interact with each and co-exist in this city, where a unique and colorful water culture came into being.

The fourth one is Yancheng culture of unique characteristics (Sea Salt Culture), which is far away from every main cultural region. Yancheng is located in the middle of costal area in Jiangsu Province. Under the historical condition with Wu-yue culture to its south and Chu-han culture to its north, the Sea Salt culture is exactly on the transition zone between the northern and southern cultures, which takes an independent position while embracing the features of both sides. [1]

III. Connotation and denotation of Jinling Culture

Nanjing is one of the famous four ancient capitals of China and the national famous historical and cultural cities; it has a history of human activities for 350 thousand years, a history city for approx. 2500 years, and a history of capital for 450 years, which left us with splendid history and civilization.

(I) Distinctive humanity and nature

With the geographic advantages that facing the Yangtze River, leading the southeast China, closing to sea and controlling the Huai River, Nanjing is one of the most suitable cities to be chosen as a capital. On the history, a part from the period of "Capital of Six Dynasties" between Han Dynasty and Tang Dynasty, over 581 years from the end of Yuan Dynasty till 1949, Nanjing and Beijing dominated the political situation and the fate of nation alternatively and interactively, which well displayed the unique status and extraordinary location advantages of Nanjing.

1. The unique geographical conditions and environmental landscape characteristics. The ancient capital Nanjing is adjacent to the rivers and surrounded by the hills, it is the "blessed land of Kings, and place of the best sceneries" of strategic importance and four distinct seasons. The expression as "Niushou Mountain for spring outing, Qixia Mountain for autumn hiking, Purple Mountain for summer cooling, and Stone city for winter enjoyment" reflects Nanjing's unique scenery that integrates into the nature, and the climate of four distinctive seasons. With "mountains, rivers, city and woods perfectly blended with each other", "hills in the city, streams in the woods, and people in the scenery", Nanjing becomes the best example of combining the natural scenery with human landscape.

2. Profound cultural and historical accumulation. The charm of Nanjing does not only lie in the beauty of hills, rivers, city and woods that given by the nature, but also lies in the historical beauty of cultural inheritance. As the ancient capital of six dynasties, and the metropolitan of ten dynasties, Nanjing has one site of world cultural heritage, 27 national cultural relic protection units of totally 81 spots, 100 provincial relic protection units of totally 107 spots. All the hundreds of thousands of priceless relics, the three 3 historic axes, the 10 history and culture preservation districts, and the 12 environmental landscape protection districts are the evidences of historical and cultural accumulation of Nanjing city.

3. Powerful strength of contemporary science and education. In Nanjing, there are more than 70 university and colleges of various kinds, over 800 thousand undergraduate students, nearly 400 thousand scientific and technological personnel, and 79 academicians of the Chinese Academy of Sciences and Chinese Academy of Engineering. They are researching in very broad fields, among which the reaches in astronomy, paleontology etc. are in the leading place of the world.

(II) Overall protection of ancient capital appearance and patterns

In order to construct a cultural Nanjing, and build a famous historical and cultural city, we shall emphasize on the protection of natural heritages and historical heritages of Nanjing as an ancient capital, thus to fundamentally ensure the maintaining the ancient charm for long time.

1. To restore and protect the ancient capital appearance of Nanjing city. Following the urban construction principle of "showing the mountains, exposing the rivers, viewing the city walls, and along the riverside", we will protect the old city and construct a new city, in order to have more space for the exposure of natural environment and creation of human environment. The construction of common residences and high-level buildings will be strictly controlled, and the unauthorized constructions and modern low-standard buildings will be removed step by step, so as to restore and improve the ancient capital appearance of the old city.

2. To emphasize on the protection of the ancient capital pattern of "three historical axes, quadruple city walls of Ming Dynasty". The three historical axes of Nanjing refer to: 1) The central axis line of the ancient capital in the period of the Six Dynasties and the Southern Tang Dynasty, i.e. today's Zhonghua Road, which is not only the axis line of the southern district of Nanjing city, but also the traditional commercial and market district. 2) The central axis line of the ancient capital in Ming Dynasty, i.e. today's Yudao Street, which is not only the axis line of the eastern district of Nanjing city, but also one of the major accesses to the city. 3) The axis of the city formed during the period of the Republic of China. This a Z-shaped axis formed by the North Zhongshan Road, Zhongshan Road, and the East Zhongshan Road, which is the main frame of today's road system of Nanjing. The ancient capital of Nanjing in Ming Dynasty was formed by four circles of city walls, including the inner palace wall, imperial palace wall, capital wall and the outer city wall.Up till today, there still exists 21.35 km of the famous Nanjing city wall (Ming city wall), which has been listed as one of the national key units of cultural relics protection. The quadruple city walls of Ming Dynasty constitute the contour of the ancient capital of Nanjing, which shall be protected properly and persistently. All the above-mentioned "three historical axes and quadruple city walls" are the "busy and prosperous" places in the history of Nanjing, and these memories and symbols of history must be well preserved.

3. To protect a batch of historical and cultural blocks and environmental landscape districts. If we consider the protection of the three historic axes and the quadruple city walls of Ming Dynasty as the overall protection of ancient capital appearance and patterns from the view of lines, then the protection of a batch of historical and cultural blocks and environmental landscape district is the deepening of this overall protection from the view of planes.

(III)Building the four major historical and cultural brands along the longitudinal historical sequence

In the long history and culture of Nanjing, the "Six-Dynasty Culture", "Ming-Dynasty Culture", "Minguo Culture" and "Revolutionary Culture" are of important positions, unique characteristics, and potentiality of scaled development, which should be built as the city brands of Nanjing.

1. To create the brand of "Six-Dynasty Culture". In the period of the Six

Dynasties, the northern part of China was in chaos caused by war, a large population of inhabitants, including many politicians, artists, and scientists, had been "migrating towards south" (at a population of approx. 900 thousand), thus realized the a big fusion of Chinese cultures. Taking Nanjing as the center, the Han nationality as the main group, the "Six-Dynasty Culture" was preceded by Han Dynasty and Jin Dynasty and followed by the Sui Dynasty and Tang Dynasty, which had established a solid foundation for the flourishing Tang Dynasty Culture, and played a significant role for national salvation and heritance in the history of Chinese civilization. The Chinese and western historians viewed the Six-Dynasty Culture as comparable to the ancient Roman civilization, therefore the success establishment of the "Six-Dynasty Culture" brand has the significance in the nation and the world.

2. To create the brand of "Ming Dynasty Culture". Among all the ancient cultures of Nanjing, the Ming Dynasty Culture is the one of large historical scale, profound foundation, and magnificent bearing. We will actively construct the Ming Palace Ruins Park, so as to attach great tourism values to it. We will restore and expose the ancient city wall of Ming Dynasty, so as to re-exhibit its majestic appearance. We will make full utilization of the World Cultural Heritage—Xiaoling Mausoleum of Ming Dynasty, so as to create a cultural and tourism brand of international significance. Around the "Longjiang Treasure Fleet Shipyard Ruins Park", we will also explore the resource of the world historical famous name – Zheng He in depth. In the mean time, we will also actively develop the tourism souvenirs of Ming Dynasty Culture.

3. To create the brand of "Minguo Culture". From 1927 to 1949, the Nanjing was established as the capital of the Republic of China by its national government. In this short period of a special historical time, there were still a lot of precious cultural heritages being left in Nanjing, and this period also has its unique position in the history of Chinese civilization. We will focus on the advanced thoughts of Dr. Sun Yat-Sen, such as "Democratic Republic", "the World is for All" etc., combine the descendants of the Chinese nation at home and abroad with the common ideal of shared love to our country, and rely on such buildings of the Republic of China as the former Presidential Palace etc., supplementing with the effective exploration and utilization of other Minguo cultural resources, so as to further brighten and enlarge the brand of "Minguo Culture" of Nanjing.

4. To create the brand of "Revolutionary Culture". Nanjing is a city of revolution, which had experienced a serious of significant historical events such as that the Taiping Heavenly Kingdom made Nanjing as its capital, the establishment of the Republic of China by Dr. Sun Yat-Sen, the Anti-Japanese War, and the Liberation War etc. There are precious cultural heritages including the Mansion of King Tianwang of Taiping Heavenly Kingdom, Zhan Garden, the former Presidential Palace, Dr. Sun Yat-Sen's Mausoleum, the Memorial Hall of Nanjing Massacre, and Yuhuatai Martyrs Memorial Park etc., which is not only a valuable spiritual wealth for receiving patriotism education, and cultivating the national spirit, but also an important brand of Nanjing historical culture and urban tourism. We will further explore and utilize these cultural resources, in order to establish the brand of "Revolutionary Culture" of Nanjing effectively,

and further stress on the characteristics of Nanjing as a famous revolutionary historical city.

In the process of "building the four major cultural and historical brands", we will also explore the resources of those famous historical and cultural names to the full extent, and make full play of the celebrity effects. Since the beginning of the Six Dynasties, the cultural celebrities had come forth one after another, and many poets and scholars, including Libai, Liu Yuxi, Du Mu, Wei Zhuang etc., had written immortal pomes related to Jinling. In the field of literature, there were the two Kings of Southern Tang Dynasty—Li Yu, Li Jing, who had left us with a large amount of great works, the author of "Wen Xin Diao Long"—Liu Xie, the author of "The Scholar"—Wu Jingzi, the author of "Essays of Suiyuan on Poetry"—Yuan Mei, and the author of "A Dream of Red Mansion"—Cao Xueqi etc. In the field of dramas, there were the dramatist of "Peach Blossom Fan"—Kong Shangren. In the field of painting and calligraphy, there were the famous painter—Ku Kaizhi, the great calligraphers—Wang Xizhi and Wang Xianzhi, the leader of the "Eight Masters in Jinling"—Gong Xian, the art educationist--Xu Beihong, the famous painter of landscape paintings--Fu Baoshi, and the contemporary script-sage--Lin Sanzhi etc.②

An excellent regional culture can be the carrier of traditional culture and the joint between history and culture, the culture gene bearing on which will deeply affect the spiritual world of modern people. The new era gives us new responsibility and mission, we should research on the regional cultural phenomenon actively and explore the regional cultural resources in depth, we should make efforts to build regional cultural brands of special characteristics, so as to provide spiritual drive, intellectual support and cultural conditions for regional economic and social development, and better promote the all-round, balanced, sustainable development of the economy and society.

---

① This chapter mainly refers to the book "Study on the Origin of Jiangsu Regional Culture" written by Zhou Xin.
② For the main opinions of this Chapter, please refer to my essay "Construction "Cultural Nanjing" and Building the Famous Historic and Cultural City" published on the "Chinese Culture Daily", dated on Sept. 7, 2002.

美国/墨西哥边境地区的文化与空间

拉蒙·萨尔迪瓦

美国斯坦福大学英语与比较文学系教授,"人文与科学学院"霍格兰德家庭教授

内容提要: 导致形成现今美/墨边境地区多元文化形式的各种因素可追溯至16世纪。西班牙探险家及其土著随从和梅索蒂斯混血儿随从自美国西南部向北部转移,并开始了对现在的墨西哥北部、德克萨斯州以及美国西南部其他地区的殖民。这些定居者带来了他们的文化传统、宗教、民俗、文学和语言。自1749年琼斯·德·埃斯坎东建立了新桑坦德省以来,现今的德州与墨西哥边境就成为了一个独特的地方,在这里新旧世界的文化传统相互碰撞,并由此产生新的社会现实。

要正确地理解美洲的殖民和后殖民历史,我们必须明白种族和种族划分的问题,特别是种族通婚和混血的问题。至17世纪以来,拉丁(西班牙裔、葡萄牙裔和法国裔)美洲人的血统就远比英裔美洲人的血统要复杂。

在非裔加勒比地区和西班牙加勒比地区,以及北美新西班牙大陆——也就是当时的主要殖民社会中,种族混合的后代黑白混血儿(非洲裔与欧洲裔的混血儿)以及许多其他混血民族梅索蒂斯混血儿(指欧洲人与美洲印第安人的混血儿),代表了历史上一个既非黑人又非白人但又具有鲜明特征的种族身份,且这些混血儿在非裔加勒比和西班牙加勒比社会一直问题重重。我们可以通过研究那些造成这种边境地区相互冲突的身份区别、种族融合、阶级和政治上的力量,进而了解跨国主义如何深刻地改变了这些边境居民的生活,以及跨国主义如何建立了这样一个至今仍然影响当今世界的历史框架。

塑造当前美国/墨西哥边境地区的文化与历史力量可以追溯至16世纪。西班牙探险家及其土著随从和梅索蒂斯混血儿随从自墨西哥腹地北上,开始了对今天的墨西哥北部、得克萨斯州、新墨西哥州、亚利桑那、加利福尼亚以及美国西南部其他地区的殖民进程。这些定居者带来了他们的文化传统(西班牙)、宗教(罗马天主教)、民俗、文学和语言(西班牙语)。

1620年，清教始祖们在新英格兰建立普利茅斯殖民地。这是英国人在北美建立的最早的殖民地。10年后，清教徒在波士顿普利茅斯殖民地以北定居，由此建立了马萨诸塞湾殖民地。要想正确理解美洲殖民和后殖民时期的历史，就必须了解种族和族裔问题，特别是种族通婚和混血问题。截至17世纪英国殖民地建立时，拉丁美洲的种族谱系（西班牙裔、葡萄牙裔和法国裔）已经存在了一个多世纪，其种族关系远比英属美洲的种族关系复杂得多。

通过理解造成这些身份冲突以及种族融合的力量，以及边境地区的文化地理学，我们就能初步了解跨国主义的真正意义，正是它深刻塑造了生活在西班牙和英属美洲边界地带的那些人的生活，并铸就了迄今仍影响当代世界的历史结构。

在这份报告中，我想谈一下美国西部和西南部边境地带的文化史，然后，从跨国主义的角度指出美国研究领域不断重组的某些特点[①]。最近，美国研究的最新成果开始转向一种跨国主义的历史解释框架，鼓励学者超越多数美国边境史采用的以北部—南部为轴心的典型视角。更为重要的是，它展现了超越国家的文化与空间的经验主义现实，补充甚至取代了墨西哥和美国两国国家大事的重要性。

16世纪的全球化

16世纪初期，西班牙帝国的版图遍及全球。那个时期的一张地图上写着："太阳不会在西班牙的领土上落下。"在同时期的北美，阿兹特克帝国被击溃后，殖民状况逐渐形成并一直延续到19世纪中期。新西班牙殖民地发展的头等大事是延长阿兹特克人修建的完善的"道路"系统——时至今日，该系统仍在继续深刻影响着墨西哥与美国两国之间的移民模式。由于当时的阿兹特克人既没有车轮也没有畜力可供用于运输人员或商品，一切只能靠走路，脚力的速度、范围和耐力决定了道路只能延伸到徒步可及的地方。所以，可以说他们的道路系统实际上是走出来的。

西班牙征服者们发现，阿兹特克的道路完全不适合马车和牲畜拉的车行使。因此，他们不得不花重金对道路进行大规模的路线重置、路面平整、加宽和升级。1550年，他们开始修建皇家公路第一段，这段路经过位于墨西哥湾沿岸的韦拉克鲁斯港连通了墨西哥城与西班牙。随着这条新路的开通,人们可以更方便地与西班牙进行沟通交流,将阿兹特克的黄金运回西班牙和将西班牙的商品运到墨西哥腹地。皇家公路后来又延伸到其他重要城市和矿区。截至1600年,它径直北上,延伸至奇瓦瓦,后又延伸至圣菲(位于今天的新墨西哥州)。

随着道路系统的扩建,1565年,西班牙人认为,穿越太平洋向东经过墨西哥,将从菲律宾殖民地攫取的亚洲商品运送回西班牙,要比绕过南亚和非洲西行更安全。250年来,西班牙大帆船将墨西哥的白银运到马尼拉,然后将香料、丝绸、瓷器、漆器以及其他来自东方的异国特色商品带回西班牙。在这个过程中,墨西哥城成为重要的中转站,它连通了西班牙、亚洲和美洲,缔造了新的世界经济。

祖国的缔造

今天的美/墨边境地区充斥着各种文化形式,造成这一局面的各种因素可追溯至16世纪,它们是早期殖民时期的直接产物。

在该地区,新型建国模式正在逐步形成。西班牙美洲殖民地的开创者们首先学会了对遥远的欧洲君主保持忠诚,然后于1821年墨西哥独立后,又作为西班牙臣民转而效忠新建立的墨西哥君主。

用历史学者曼纽尔·贾米奥的名言来说:墨西哥现在正全力投入到"缔造祖国"的工程之中[②]。西班牙裔美洲居民设想并确立了将其从君主制臣民转变为共和国公民所需的政治制度。而今天位于边境地区的西班牙裔美国居民实际上正努力实践公民身份的文化典故和实际含义。

作为西班牙君主制下的殖民地臣民,他们受君主统治,受其法律管辖。作为共和国的公民,他们现在共享君主的权力,并且有权制定自己的法律。他们新建立的政治体制能否使其在保留作为西班牙(并非墨西哥)臣民的血统观念的同时,将它与作为墨西哥(和梅索蒂斯)国家公民所遵从的新的、由其自由选择的政治忠诚结合在一起?谁是受共和国管辖的公民,而谁又不是呢[③]?

卡斯塔绘画

在16—17世纪的殖民时代,有一个在文化与空间之间建立纽带的特征具有极其重要的意义。要想正确理解美洲的殖民和后殖民历史，我们必须解决种族和族裔的问题，特别是种族通婚和混血的问题。

"被称为'卡斯塔绘画'的绘画流派是墨西哥殖民地时期最引人注目的艺术表现形式。这些绘画描绘了新西班牙普遍存在的种族混血。"（卡祖，5）这些由一系列连续的形象构成的作品描绘了在殖民地定居的三大主要群体：印第安人、西班牙人和非洲人（卡祖，5）。这种画一般画在单独的画布或铜板上，最典型的内容是"不同种族的男人和女人与他们的一两个孩子在一起。每幅画都配以题字，说明所描绘的种族混血"。（卡祖，5）

按照18世纪的排序和分类标准，在墨西哥殖民地时期，该地区的作家、哲学家、画家和历史学家记录了超过六十个不同的种族等级。在非洲人定居的加勒比海地区、西班牙人定居的加勒比海地区以及北美的新西班牙大陆地区——也就是当时的主要殖民社会中——遍布着种族混合的后代黑白混血儿（非洲裔与欧洲裔的混血儿）以及许多其他不同级别的混血民族梅索蒂斯混血儿（指美洲印第安人与欧洲人的混血儿），尽管在非洲人定居的加勒比海地区和西班牙人定居的加勒比海地区仍问题重重，但它们代表了历史上一个既非黑人又非白人而是具有鲜明特征的种族身份。这种种族身份最终由其种族血统确定。

卡斯塔绘画代表着"画家创造形象的方式，以及观察者如何依靠其对先前视觉经历的回忆"赋予意义（卡祖，9）。他们"对种族与社会异质性的强调并非是要暗示不同种族和谐共处，而是要提醒人们……墨西哥是一个有序的等级制社会。在其中，每个群体都占据着一个特定的社会——经济地位，这一地位主要取决于种族。"（卡祖，39）

美国/墨西哥边境地区

尽管不同种族、阶级和政治立场之间确实存在差异，然而，在19世纪初墨西哥独立战争之后，西属美洲巩固国家权力的紧迫性远远超过了创造种族认同的迫切性。人们在法律和社交问题上也保持了高度的一致性。④

墨西哥的北部省份——这个新国家边疆地带的最外缘——远离"正在该国中部进行的民族整合和国家建设新兴计划"。该地区的居民"成为了墨西哥"的国民和公民⑤。然而，由于远离墨西哥城这个权力中心，墨西哥北部的人与世隔绝,形成一种强烈的地方自治独立意识。因此,他们不认同墨西哥中部精英统治者宏大的国家建设策略,及其想象中的墨西哥一体化民族国家。相反,他们形成了一种不同的认同形式。

通过这些缔造国家的事件,今天美/墨边境地区的特点得以根深蒂固地确立起来。这一地区同样拥有抱负与理想、热情与暴力、憧憬与无信,不同文化在这里交汇、冲突,使其成为一片错综复杂而难以驾驭的地带。

尤其是在1846—1848年美/墨战争之后,随着墨西哥北部地区被兼并,以及为结束战争签订的《瓜达卢佩—伊达尔戈条约》,居住在墨西哥湾沿岸到太平洋之间墨西哥被征服地区的前西班牙殖民地居民以及墨西哥共和国居民成为首批墨西哥裔美国人[6]。他们不再是墨西哥公民,但其公民身份又受到了许多美国人的质疑和否定,他们得不到美国或墨西哥任何一国的法律保护。(格里斯沃尔德·卡斯蒂略,68)他们是第一代名义上而非实际上的墨西哥裔美国公民。(详见地图)

对于这些边境居民中的许多人来说,19世纪中期的事件"标志着拥有殖民地、国家、地区与全球公民身份的人之间长达数年的谈判的开始——尽管美国已经兼并了有关土地和人民,但实地状况远没有确定。"(特鲁特和杨,6)这些遥远边陲地区的居民自身构成了一个独立的群体,居住在"第三空间,他们首先认为自己是天主教徒或基督徒;其次,他们承认自己是当地复杂的家庭或亲属关系网中的一员;第三,他们承认自己属于其所在的地方或地区"。(戴维·古铁雷兹:"第三空间",485)

因此,单纯从墨西哥或美国的角度看待现今美国/墨西哥边境地区的居民的国家忠诚问题,完全属于误入歧途。在整个19世纪,尤其是在19世纪中期以后,居民们所感知的边境地区是一个相对完整的中间地区——一个在许多方面独立于墨西哥和美国的第三空间[7]。"自从1854年勘定边界以来,美/墨边界地区一直孕育着一个复杂的历史关系网——尽管这个网络是伴随美国和墨西哥而出现的,但是它却超越了这两个国家。"(特鲁特和杨,2)有鉴于此,我们可以说,边境地区是研究文化与空间的独特而重要的场所。它们代表着产生分歧的政治和思想边界,这种分歧随后又被用来缔造独特的国民身份。

纵观历史,美/墨边境地区发生了许多独特的文化与空间互动活动。在这里,文化与族群—种族社区得以形成。它们否定了民族与公民身份之间的差别，形成了跨越国境的统一。简而言之，尽管边界分割了地区，但是边境地区仍是一个统一的地区。（艾略特·杨，7）通过理解造成这些边境地区身份冲突以及种族、阶级和政治融合的力量，我们能够初步了解跨国主义如何深刻塑造了这些边境居民的生活，及其如何建立了这样一个至今仍然影响着当今世界的历史框架。

---

① 关于新的从"后民族主义"视角进行的美国研究，参见葆拉·莫亚和拉蒙·萨尔迪瓦编：《泛美想象小说》，载《当代小说研究》，第49卷，第1期（2003年春季号）；埃米·卡普兰：《美国文化形成中的帝国混乱》，坎布里奇：哈佛大学出版社，2002年版；利尔·布兰农、布伦达·格林和全国英语教师理事会：《美国文学反思》，厄班纳：全国英语教师理事会，1997年版；保罗·贾斯：《虚拟美洲：跨国小说与跨大西洋想象》，达勒姆：杜克大学出版社，2002年版；比里：雷诺兹与戈登·赫特纳《国家想象，美国身份认同：美国肖像学的文化成果》，普林斯顿：普林斯顿大学出版社，2000年版；唐纳德·皮斯：《国家认同与后美国主义叙事》，达勒姆：杜克大学出版社，1994年版；约翰·罗《后国家主义美国研究》，伯克利：加利福尼亚大学出版社，2000年版；与古斯塔沃·弗迈特《美洲是否存在共同文学》，达勒姆：杜克大学出版社，1990年版。考虑到"拉丁著述的跨美洲起源"美国文学史学优秀新模式，参见柯尔斯坦·格鲁兹：《文化大使：拉丁著述的跨美洲起源》，普林斯顿：普林斯顿大学出版社，2002年版。以及，历史学者德弗拉·韦伯表明，有关美国社会的"跨国"性质的讨论并非最近出现的。参见德弗拉·韦伯：《墨西哥跨国主义的历史视角》，载《社会正义：犯罪、冲突与世界秩序杂志》，第26卷第3期（1999年）。韦伯引用了兰道夫·伯恩的一篇文章，伯恩认为"历史的先见之明"认识到：双重公民身份"是我们……期盼的'国际公民身份'的基本形式"。参见兰道夫·伯恩：《跨国主义的美国》，载《大西洋月刊》，第118期（1916年）。有关当今世界的"后国家主义"性质，参见M. J. 迪尔、古斯塔沃·莱克莱克、乔安妮·贝雷洛维茨：《后边界城市：加利福尼亚州巴巴拉的文化空间》，纽约：拉ülfèmiè莱奇，2003年版。
② 曼纽尔·贾米奥：《缔造祖国》，墨西哥 Porrúa Hermanos 出版社，1916年版。贾米奥在其整个研究中，使用了冶金学中的铜铁"铸造"来描绘国家建设的艺术与劳动。
③ 墨西哥早期宪法通过废除种族与等级制标标准扩大了公民基础，但与此同时，它又将担任公职和进入公共领域的权力仅限于独立的、有文化的男性财产所有者。一次关于墨西哥"公民身份"演变的优秀讨论可参见克劳迪奥·洛姆尼茨：《墨西哥公民身份的模式》，载迪利普·戈恩卡编：《另一种现代性》，达勒姆：杜克大学出版社，2001年版，第306-307页。另参见，迈克尔·穆恩与凯茜·戴维森：《臣民与公民：从Oroonoko到Anita Hill的国家、种族与性别》，达勒姆：杜克大学出版社，1995年版。
④ Fernando Escalante Gonzalbo, Ciudadanos imaginarios: memorial de los afanes y desventuras de la virtud y apología del vicio triunfante en la República Mexicana: tratado de moral pública, 1. ed. (México, D.F.: Centro de Estudios Sociológicos El Colegio de México, 1992) 372. 另参见洛姆尼茨：《墨西哥公民身份的模式》，第315-317页。
⑤ 戴维·古铁雷兹：《迁移、新兴族群与"第三空间"：大墨西哥地区民族主义政治的变迁，载《美国历史杂志》，第86卷第2期（1999），第484-485页。有关大众民族主义与性别认同之间的关系的分析，参见安娜·阿朗索：《血统的威胁：墨西哥北部边疆的殖民主义、革命与性别、霸权与经验》，图森：亚利

桑那大学出版社，1995年版。
⑥ 有关1848年之后美墨边境地区"美国－墨西哥"文学公民—臣民范式的形成，参见小罗尔·科罗纳多：《与美国殖民地时期现代性的竞争：政治、出版与美国—墨西哥文学文化的形成，1836-1939年》，斯坦福大学博士论文，2004年，第1-47页。 科罗纳多重点强调了该地区文化精英阶层的"殖民地"地位，有时就低估了前墨西哥人群中那些被剥夺了财产和选举权的群体的"抵抗"与"反对"的重要性。但是他提出的有关以殖民主义做伪装兴起的"竞争的现代性"极具启发意义。
⑦ 艾略特·杨：《卡塔里诺·加尔萨在得克萨斯-墨西哥边境的革命》，达勒姆：杜克大学出版社，2004年版，第5-11页。杨指出，加尔萨在19世纪末期的反叛是边境地区的人民在面对两个强大的民族国家的蚕食时长达一个世纪的旷日持久的斗争的一部分。

Ramón Saldívar

Professor of English and Comparative Literature and the Hoagland Family Professor of Humanities and Sciences at Stanford University

Culture and Place on the US/Mexico Border

Abstract: The forces that gave rise to the pluralistic cultural forms of the present U.S./Mexico border region date from the sixteenth century. Spanish explorers and their indigenous and mestizo retinues moved north from the interior of Mexico and began the colonization of what is now northern Mexico, Texas, and the rest of the southwestern United States. These settlers brought with them their cultural traditions, religion, folklore, literature, and language. With the establishment of the province of Nuevo Santander by José de Escandón in 1749, the present Texas–Mexico border region became a place where the cultural traditions of the old and the new worlds collided and created new social realities.

In order to understand the colonial and postcolonial history of the Americas properly, we must understand the issues of race and ethnicity, and especially of racial mixing and hybridity. From the seventeenth century on, the racial chromograph in Latin (Spanish, Portuguese and French) America had been a much more complex thing than in Anglo America.

In both the Afro- and Hispano- Carribbean and the mainland of North American New Spain – the dominant colonial societies of the period – the category of the racially mixed mulatto (African and European) and the many other gradations of mixed race mestizaje (American Indian and European), problematic as it remains for both Afro- and Hispano-Caribbean colonial society, represented historically a class of racialized identity that was neither black nor white but distinct, even if determined in the last instance by its racial pedigree. By understanding the forces that impelled these contradictory divisions of identity and unities of race, class, and political in the borderlands, we can begin to have a sense of how transnationalism profoundly shaped the lives of those who lived on the border and forged the historical structures that continue to affect the contemporary world.

The cultural and historical forces that gave rise to the present U.S./Mexico border region date from the sixteenth century. Spanish explorers and their indigenous and mestizo retinues moved north from the interior of Mexico and began the colonization of what is now northern Mexico, Texas, New Mexico, Arizona, California and the rest of the southwestern United States. These settlers brought with them their cultural traditions

(Hispanic), religion (Roman Catholic), folklore, literature, and language (Spanish).

The earliest English settlements in North America, when Pilgrims settled in New England in 1620 to form Plymouth Colony and ten years later, when Puritans settled north of Plymouth Colony in Boston thus forming the Massachusetts Bay Colony. In order to understand the colonial and postcolonial history of the Americas properly, we must understand the issues of race and ethnicity, and especially of racial mixing and hybridity. By the time of the founding of the English colonies in the seventeenth century, the racial chromograph in Latin (Spanish, Portuguese and French) America had already been in existence for over a hundred years, creating a much more complex racial relationship than existed in Anglo America.

By understanding the forces that impelled these contradictory divisions of identity and unities of race, and identity in the cultural geography of the border region, we can begin to have a sense of how transnationalism profoundly shaped the lives of those who lived on the border between Spanish and English America and forged the historical structures that continue to affect the contemporary world.

In this presentation, I wish to comment on the cultural history of the American western and southwestern borderlands and, more broadly, to suggest some features of the ongoing remapping of the field of American studies from a transnational perspective.[1] Recent new work in American studies has turned to a transnational frame of historical reference, urging a vantage point beyond the typical north-south axis of most US border histories. More significantly, it has illustrated the experiential realities of culture and place beyond the nation, supplementing and sometimes even superceding the importance of both Mexican and American national imperatives.

Sixteenth century Globalization

By the start of the 16th century, the Spanish Empire extended world-wide. As the legend of a map from the period says: "The sun does not set on Spanish dominions." At the same time in North America, the colonial conditions in the wake of the defeat of the Aztec Empire had begun to develop into a pattern that was to hold until the mid-nineteenth century. Of primary importance in the development of Colonial New Spain was the extension of the well-developed system of "roads" constructed by the Aztecs, which continue to be of major importance to current patterns of migration between Mexico and the U.S. Because the Aztecs had neither wheels nor beasts of burden to transport themselves or their goods, the speed, range and endurance of foot power was limited to travel by foot. Their system of roads was essentially a system of foot trails.

The Spanish conquerors found the Aztec roads completely unsuitable for horse traffic and animal-drawn carts and were forced to undertake expensive re-routing, flattening, widening, and upgrading. In 1550, they started construction of the first section of El Camino Real (the royal highway) linking Mexico City with Spain through the port of Veracruz on the Gulf Coast. With the opening of this new road, communication with Spain and the transfer of Aztec gold back to Spain, and Spanish goods into Mexico's interior was greatly facilitated. El Camino Real was later extended to other important cities and mining districts. By 1600 it reached as far north as Chihuahua and was later extended to Santa Fe (in what is now New Mexico).

With the extension of this system of roads, in 1565 the Spanish decided it was safer to ship Asian goods from their colony in the Philippines back to Spain by crossing the Pacific eastward to Mexico rather than westward around South Asia and Africa. For 250 years, Spanish galleons carried Mexican silver to Manila, and returned with spices, silk, porcelain, lacquer ware, and other exotic oriental goods destined for Spain. This process located 16th century Mexico City at the major crossroads, connecting Spain, Asia, and the Americas in a new world economy.

Forging a Fatherland

The forces that gave rise to the pluralistic cultural forms of the present U.S./Mexico border region date from the sixteenth century and are the direct result of these early colonial conditions.

In this region, new forms of nation building were being enacted, as the founding Spanish American colonials learned first how to retain loyalty to a far-off European sovereign, and then later to shift allegiance as subjects of the Spanish monarchy to the newly proclaimed constitutional Mexican monarchy after independence in 1821.

In historian Manuel Gamio's celebrated phrase, Mexico was now deeply engaged in the project of forjando patria, or, "forging a fatherland." [2] First imagining then enacting the political institutions required to transform themselves from subjects of a monarchy to citizens of a republic, the Spanish American inhabitants of the present-day borderlands in effect were also working out the cultural idioms and practical implications of citizenship.

As colonial subjects of the Spanish monarchy, they were under the authority of the monarch and were governed by his laws. As republican citizens, they now had a share in the power of the sovereign and the authority to formulate their own laws. Would their newly constructed political forms allow them to retain a notion of blood heritage as Spanish (not Mexican) subjects while simultaneously combining it with a new, freely chosen political allegiance as citizens of a Mexican (and mestizo) nation? Who was and who was not a subject citizen? [3]

Casta Paintings

One feature from the colonial era of the sixteenth and seventeenth centuries linking culture and place is of tremendous importance. In order to understand the colonial and postcolonial history of the Americas properly, we must address the issues of race and ethnicity, and especially of racial mixing and hybridity.

"The pictorial genre known as 'casta painting' is one of the most compelling forms of artistic expression from Colonial Mexico. These paintings portray the extensive mixing of races in New Spain" (Katzew 5). Created as sets of consecutive images, the works depict racial mixing among the three major groups that inhabited the colony: Indians, Spaniards, and Africans(Katzew 5). On separate canvases or copper plates the paintings typically "portray a man and a woman of different races with one or two of their children and each is accompanied by an inscription that identifies the racial mix depicted" (Katzew 5).

Following the 18th century trend to order, classify, and categorize, in colonial Mexico over sixty different castes were chronicled by writers, philosophers, painters, and historians of the region (Carrera). In both the Afro- and Hispano-Carribbean and the mainland of North American New Spain – the dominant colonial societies of the period – the category of the racially mixed mulatto (African and European) and the many other gradations of mixed race mestizaje (American Indian and European), problematic as it remains for both Afro- and Hispano-Caribbean colonial society, represented historically a class of racialized identity that was neither black nor white but distinct, even if determined in the last instance by its racial pedigree.

Casta paintings represent the ways that "an artist creates images and how the viewer draws upon his or her recollection of prior visual experience" to produce meaning (Katzew 9). Their "emphasis on racial and social heterogeneity was not meant to imply a harmonious coexistence of the diverse races, but instead to remind . . . that Mexico was . . . an ordered, hierarchical society in which each group occupied a specific socioeconomic niche defined largely by race" (Katzew 39).

U.S./Mexico Borderlands

Despite real differences between races, classes, and political affiliations, the imperative to consolidate state power in Spanish America after the early nineteenth-century wars of independence was far more urgent than the need to create racial identity and led to a high degree of accord on matters of law and sociability. [4]

In the northern tier of Mexican provinces, the frontier periphery of the new nation, isolated from "the nascent projects of national integration and state building unfolding in central Mexico," the residents of the region "became Mexican" nationals and citizens. [5] However, because of the huge distances from the central seat of power in Mexico City, the people of northern Mexico remained isolated and acquired a fiercely independent sense of local autonomy. Thus, rather than identifying with the grand nation-building strategies of the ruling elites in central Mexico and their notion of an imagined integrated nation-state of Mexico proper, they acquired alternative forms of identity.

In the aftermath of these nation-forging affairs, the present characteristic feature of the United States-Mexican borderlands was firmly established. With equal measures of ambition and idealism, enthusiasm and violence, hope and faithlessness, the region became an intricately refractory zone where different cultures met and clashed.

Particularly after the United States - Mexico War of 1846-1848, with the annexation of the northern territories of Mexico by the United States, and the signing of the Treaty of Guadalupe Hidalgo ending hostilities, former Spanish colonials and republican Mexicans residing in the conquered Mexican territories from the Gulf Coast to the Pacific Ocean now became the first U.S.-Mexicans. [6] No longer citizens of Mexico and with their citizenship contested and denied by many Americans, they were left without the juridical protection of either nation (Griswold del Castillo 68). They were the first of many generations of Mexicans to become United States citizens in name but not in fact. (See Map).

For many of these border people, events of the mid-nineteenth century "marked the beginning of years of negotiation between colonial, national, regional, and global coordinates that were – despite the U.S. annexation of land and people – anything but fixed" (Truett and Young 6). The inhabitants of these remote borderlands districts constituted themselves as a separate people, residing in a "third space [and] identified themselves first as Catholics or Christians, second as members of intricate local networks of familial or kinship association [and only] third with their patrias chicas (their localities or regions)" (Gutiérrez "Third Space" 485).

To see the national allegiances of the inhabitants of the present U.S./Mexico borderlands in exclusively Mexican, or American, terms is therefore very misleading. Throughout the nineteenth century, but especially after mid-century, the inhabitants experienced the borderlands as a relatively coherent, in-between region, a third space separate in many ways from Mexico and the United States.[7] "Ever since the border was mapped in 1854, the [U.S./Mexico] borderlands have supported a complex web of historical relationships that transcended – even as they emerged in tandem with – the U.S. and Mexican nations" (Truett and Young 2). For all these reasons, we can say that borders are uniquely important sites for the study of culture and place; they represent political and ideological boundaries that produce differences that are then used to forge unique national identities.

In the U.S. - Mexico borderlands, a unique interaction between culture and place ocurred historically. Cultural and ethnoracial communities came into being that gainsaid the differences between nationality and citizenship and remained unified even across national boundary lines. In short, while borders have divided the region, the borderlands have remained a united region (E. Young 7). By understanding the forces that impelled these divisions of identity and unities of race, class, and political in the borderlands, we can begin to have a sense of how transnationalism profoundly shaped the lives of those who lived on the border and forged the historical structures that continue to affect the contemporary world.

---

[1] For examples of the new "post-nationalist" American studies, see Paula Moya and Ramón Sald í var, eds., Fictions of the Trans-American Imaginary. Modern Fiction Studies, vol. 49, no. 1 (Spring) (2003); Amy Kaplan, The Anarchy of Empire in the Making of U.S. Culture (Cambridge: Harvard University Press, 2002); Lil Brannon, Brenda M. Greene and National Council of Teachers of English., Rethinking American Literature (Urbana: National Council of Teachers of English, 1997); Paul Giles, Virtual Americas: Transnational Fictions and the Transatlantic Imaginary (Durham: Duke University Press, 2002); Larry J. Reynolds and Gordon Hutner, National Imaginaries, American Identities: The Cultural Work of American

Iconography (Princeton: Princeton University Press, 2000); Donald E. Pease, National Identities and Post-Americanist Narratives (Durham: Duke University Press, 1994); John Carlos Rowe, Post-Nationalist American Studies (Berkeley: University of California Press, 2000); and Gustavo Pérez Firmat, Do the Americas Have a Common Literature? (Durham: Duke University Press, 1990). An excellent new model for American literary historiography that takes into account the "transamerican origins of Latino writing" is Kirsten Silva Gruesz, Ambassadors of Culture: The Transamerican Origins of Latino Writing (Princeton: Princeton University Press, 2002). Further, historian Devra Weber demonstrates that the discussion of the "transnational" nature of American society is not a recent development. See Devra Weber, "Historical Perspectives on Mexican Transnationalism: With Notes from Angumcutiro," Social Justice: A Journal of Crime, Conflict & World Order 26.3 (1999). Weber cites an essay by Randolph Bourne where Bourne urges the "historically prescient" recognition that dual citizenship is "the rudimentary form of that 'international citizenship' to which we . . . aspire" Randolph Bourne, "Trans-National America," Atlantic Monthly 118 (1916). Discussions of the "post-national" character of the contemporary world are the focus of the essays in M. J. Dear, Gustavo Leclerc and Jo-Anne Berelowitz, Postborder City: Cultural Spaces of Bajalta California (New York: Routledge, 2003).

② Manuel Gamio, Forjando patria (Pro Nacionalismo) (México: Porrúa Hermanos, 1916). Throughout his study, Gamio uses the metaphor of the metallurgic "forging" of bronze and iron to describe the art and labor of nation-building.

③ Early Mexican constitutions moved to broaden the base of citizenship by abolishing race and caste as criteria of inclusion while simultaneously restricting access to public office and the public sphere to independent and literate male property owners. An excellent discussion of the evolution of "citizenship" in Mexico is Claudio Lomnitz, "Modes of Citizenship in Mexico," Alternative Modernities, ed. Dilip Parameshwar Goankar (Durham: Duke University Press, 2001) 306-7. See also, Michael Moon and Cathy N. Davidson, Subjects and Citizens: Nation, Race, and Gender from Oroonoko to Anita Hill (Durham: Duke University Press, 1995).

④ Fernando Escalante Gonzalbo, Ciudadanos imaginarios: memorial de los afanes y desventuras de la virtud y apología del vicio triunfante en la República Mexicana: tratado de moral pública, 1. ed. (México, D.F.: Centro de Estudios Sociológicos El Colegio de México, 1992) 372. See also Lomnitz, "Citizenship in Mexico," 315-17.

⑤ David G. Gutiérrez, "Migration, Emergent Ethnicity, and the "Third Space": The Shifting Politics of Nationalism in Greater Mexico," The Journal of American History 86.2 (1999): 484-85. For a discussion of the relationship between popular nationalism and gender identity, see also Ana María Alonso, Thread of Blood: Colonialism, Revolution, and Gender on Mexico's Northern Frontier, Hegemony and Experience (Tucson: University of Arizona Press, 1995).

⑥ On the making of a "U.S.-Mexican" literary citizen-subject in the post-1848 borderlands, see Raúl Coronado Jr., "Competing American Colonial Modernities: Politics, Publishing, and the Making of a U.S.-Mexican Literary Culture, 1836-1939," Ph. D. Dissertation, Stanford University, 2004, 1-47. Coronado's emphasis on the "colonized" status of the lettered elite of the region makes him at times undervalue the importance of "resistance" and "opposition" among the dispossessed and disenfranchised sectors of the former Mexican population but his argument about the emergence of "competing modernities" in the guise of colonialism is powerfully illuminating.

⑦ Elliott Young, Catarino Garza's Revolution on the Texas-Mexico Border (Durham: Duke University Press, 2004) 5-11. Young argues that Garza's rebellion at the end of the nineteenth century was part of a century long struggle of borderlands peoples to maintain their autonomy in the face of two powerful and encroaching nation-states.

全球化冲击下的文化融合与
文化差异

蔡佳禾

南京大学－约翰斯·霍普金斯大学中美文化研究中心副主任

内容提要： 本文要讨论的是全球化在推进世界文化产生趋同运动的同时，也在推动文化的融合。本文虽然也会提到文化的多样性，对此持乐观的态度，但更多地要讨论全球化时代文化差异的问题。研究经济文化学的波士顿大学教授彼得·伯格指出，全球化并没有产生一种单一、完整、统一的世界或全球文化或信仰体系，相反全球化经常加强现存的文化差异，并在许多地区与情况中导致了冲突。本文试图在这一基础上讨论文化融合与文化差异的关系，并以此为背景讨论中美文化关系。

　　本次论坛的一个议题是文化与地域问题。文化领域的学者近年来一直在讨论在全球化的冲击下，地域性或者民族性的文化是否能生存下去。中国学者扈海鹂认为，发展中国家在接受全球化观念时面对着两方面的问题：一是为推进民族的社会进步必须参与到世界的现代化和全球化过程中去；二是作为民族国家在参与世界现代化、全球化过程中，面临着如何保持自身文化的民族性的困难。[①] 虽然中国学者坚持参加全球化的必要性，但他们还是对地域文化的未来前景存在担忧。

　　美国学术界也存在着类似的争论。很多人认为，市场会摧毁文化与多样性。保罗·雷格就认为，同质化的全球消费文化具有巨大的扩散能力，各种文化因此面临着"覆灭的威胁"。只有美国在政治文化方面具有普世性价值（因强调自然权利不可剥夺），同时也引领着通俗与消费文化，所以美国文化已经"在世界文化的生存斗争中占有上风"。[②]

本文要讨论的是全球化在推进世界文化产生趋同运动的同时，也在推动文化的融合。本文虽然也会提到文化的多样性，对此持乐观的态度，但本文更多地要讨论全球化时代文化差异的问题。研究经济文化学的波士顿大学教授彼得·伯格指出，全球化并没有产生一种单一、完整、统一的世界或全球文化或信仰体系，相反全球化经常加强现存的文化差异，并在许多地区与情况中导致了冲突。③本文试图在这一基础上讨论文化融合与文化差异的关系，并以此为背景讨论中美文化关系。

全球化造成了文化差异的扩大

中美关系证实因全球化带来文化差异的扩大与冲突的增加。在最近20年里，全球化已经深刻改变了中国的经济发展方向，中国与包括美国在内的世界经济的相互依赖变得更为紧密。"中国甚至现在越来越走向基于消费型的经济，尤其是中国的中产阶级正在崛起"。2007年中国只占世界消费的5.4%，和意大利的水平差不多，"2012年，中国占世界总消费的14.1%，超过日本，成为世界第二大消费国，仅次于美国。"④在此基础之上，中国经济其实不再是单纯的出口依赖型经济，它正在成为更大的商品进口国与消费驱动型经济。这意味着中国的市场需求将为包括美国在内的发达国家经济提供更多的机会。

尽管中美两国存在着高度的经济相互依赖，中美关系同时也充满不确定性，两国贸易与金融领域的摩擦经常出现在各种媒体上，两国意识形态的差异的对立更是人尽皆知。双方都怀疑对方的深层意图。美国一些国际关系学者认为，中国人的所谓"韬光养晦"意味着要推翻美国主导下的现存国际秩序。中国当然也怀疑美国在对中国进行"和平演变"，要推翻中国现有的政治制度。这种怀疑也存在于两国公众之中。最近的民意调查表明，尽管中美民众至今有着较高比率的相互喜欢，但同时他们之间也存在着明显的互不信任。双方表现出"印象良好，互信不足"的特点。⑤尽管信息技术在中美两国都有很高的覆盖率，"美国民意对中国持重力、不确定态度。"他们对当代中国的文化与中国民众的价值观很不了解。⑥另一方面，中国公众也完全不理解美国为何如此热衷于在世界上推进民主。这种互不信任主要是同两国有些媒体在公众中的民主主义宣传有关，但也与全球化导致的文化差异扩大有关。对另一方文化的深层内容缺乏了解，加深了中美双方的怀疑甚至敌意。

中国由于同全球体系的联系而获得了经济繁荣和社会进步，这一成就不仅揭示了计划经济理论的错误，也揭示了依附理论和政治现代化理论的局限性。东亚各国深受全球化和美国文化的影响，但是东亚国家并没有被吸入"同质性"和"现代性世界文化"。[⑦]不同文化对于现代化和全球化的适应性是不同的。许多东亚与南亚国家，包括日本、中国及印度文化都有很强的适应创造能力。起源于西方的全球化"已经在它到达的一切地方成功地实现了本地化"。而且"在文化全球化过程中还存在不同文化间的紧张与趋同"。[⑧]情况的确如此，在20世纪70—80年代，当中国经济与世界还没有什么联系的时候，中美之间的互不信任并不严重，中国经济20年的高速发展结果之一是中国与美国之间文化方面的互不信任不断加强。

与其他东亚国家一样，中国在全球化进程中保持了自己的文化特性。伯格注意，当前已经出现了一些并非起源于西方的全球扩展性的文化运动，并对西方文化产生了很大的冲击。这种替代性的文化全球化"不仅纠正了非西方和非美国的文化只能对文化全球化作出简单反应，而且意味着有可能存在不止一条通往现代性的道路"。[⑨]中国文化对世界的影响力有限，但它巨大的经济总量，以及强调维护自身制度与文化的坚定性在客观上可能鼓动了当前各国多种文化差异相互撞击。中国即使还处于发展中阶段，社会问题严重，但却被看作是美国霸权和美国价值观的挑战者。

文化融合的必需性

全球化在文化列与是多种文化或意识形态的互动、冲突与妥协，同时它也是这些观念相互吸收与融合的过程。它是各种意识形态与文化的"相互构成（Mutually Constitutive）的过程"。经济全球化推动了文化领域某种程度的趋同运动，这一运动推动世界走向消费社会、法治社会和民主政治。乔治·梅森大学的Tyler Cowen教授指出，从历史角度看，"西方文化的基础正是多样性文化的产品，它们来自国际间商品、服务和思想的交换，在不同程度上，西方文化从希腊人得到了哲学遗产，从中东得到了宗教思想，从中国和阿拉伯得到了科学的基础，而他们的核心人口和语言来自欧洲。"[⑩]任何先进文化本质上都是文化融合的结果。全球化时代的美国文化是否还需要吸收其他国家的先进文化和价值呢?

根据 Cowen 的视角,中国文化同样是多样性文化的产品,它从早期北方草原文化吸收了青铜技术与冶铁技术,从印度次大陆吸收了佛教文化,从西亚和东亚吸收了音乐、舞蹈与雕塑等艺术,自己创造了儒家、道家和兵家等文化思想。当前,中国文化正在学习包括西方文化在内的一切先进文化。中国社会科学院的党国英教授认为:"人类的普世价值别不是抽象的浪漫主义幻想,而是关乎人类福祉的具体的行动准则。自由、公正、民主与和谐这样一些制度范畴不仅是人类获取自尊、独立和富裕的手段,同时也是人类精神福利的组成部分。"[11]当代中国的文化进程正经历着主动地同世界其他先进文化融合的过程,并且正在这一过程中艰难地接纳自由民主公正等普世价值。尽管存在着争论,但中国不可能再走"自我封闭"的老路。全球化时代文化的融合是世界文化发展的主流,那些衰落甚至消失的文化一定程度上就是拒绝或没有机会融合的文化。

说到全球化条件下的文化融合,那些将美国化当作是全球化的观点正在阻碍美国文化的融合过程。今天的美国文化同样也忽略了很多重要的普世价值,譬如,就世界范围看,平等是得到普遍认同的价值。起源于欧洲的社会福利制度体现的是一种社会平等的价值,如今福利制度不仅在欧洲、日本成为不可或缺的社会制度,而且已经在美国扎下根基。即使在发展中国家,福利制度也是各国民众为努力追求和推动的目标。在北美殖民地时代,平等观念曾经有过重要的地位。在美国独立宣言中"平等"曾是最为鼓舞人心的价值。但是今天平等这一价值尤其是其社会意义在美国已经成为有争议的观念,它不是美国"意识形态"的一部分。作为价值的和平也一样,认为全球化就是美国化的学者几乎不会提及这一价值。人类及国际社会不可能放弃如此美好和如此重要的价值观,联合国等众多的国际制度正反映了世界各国对和平价值的追求。但在当代美国对外政策中,和平的意义远没有人权与民主重要,为了后者,它甚至可以被轻易放弃。

文化差异的两面性

全球化推动着文化的融合,但这并非是一种简单的单向的同质化进程,因为在文化融合的过程中文化差异仍然会出新,更不用说文化冲突导致更严重文化的差异产生。全球化不仅推动各国文化的趋同,而且也通过创新制造各种文化的差异。文化的差异的不断出现表明,全球化也是一种带来异质化的进程。"跨文化的交流,当它改变和撕裂每一个它所接触的社会,也会支持创新与创造性的人类能量",Cowen 指出:"文化的同质化与异质化并不是二者选一或互为替代,相反,它们倾向于同时到来。"⑫

北美殖民地时代的思想家和神学家约计约翰·温斯洛普曾经说过,他希望"第一个人都将需要其他人。由此他们都将被紧密地编入到兄弟情感的纽带中去"。他清楚地意识到人们之间差异的存在,但是他解释道:造物主之所以循序这种差异与变化的存在是因为他并不要建立单一化的世界,这种差异让人们进行互补,因此对人类社会是有好处的。⑬透过温斯洛普的思想的宗教语言,可以看到这种思想与中国传统文化中的"和而不同"的思想有着相似性,中国古人认识到"和实生物,同则不继"(《国语·郑语》),也是强调了差异的积极意义。

全球化仍为参与这一运动的各国各地区保留着选择先进速度与具体形式的可能性。"将人类文明的普世价值和民族特色结合起来的要义,是根据自己的历史条件选择迈向人类文明的具体道路。"⑭所有的文化自身都会发现变化,例如美国殖民地时期的主流文化的新教思想,一百多年后却让位于以洛克主义为代表的自然权利原则。⑮社会的发展和文化的互动是推动新的文化观念不断产生的动力,每一代人,每一地区的人都会创造出他们的文化。而文化差异就是因此产生,创新而不是模仿是人类作为高等动物的本能。正是文化差异的存在,文化融合才会有取之不尽的资源。从这一观点看,文化的差异是值得欢迎的,因为它可以是一种正能量。

但文化差异带来的消极性也是不容否认的。第一次世界大战以前,全球化已经在快速比较,但欧洲国家密切的经济往来带来了严重的利益冲突,以及与此相对应的化敌对,这些对立逐渐超过他们的合作,并最终酿成了史无前例的大规模战争和巨大的破坏。现存的国际制度及国际秩序以及支撑它们的规范其实是一个世纪以来人类经历了惨烈战争教训后形成的。这一秩序与制度试图限制国家之间的对立与冲突,以共享的价值规范来应对损害他人的利益冲动,组织文化差异的恶性发展。当前世界上所有大国,包括美国和中国,都是这一秩序与制度的受益者。中国并不谋求颠覆国际秩序,相反中国是这一秩序维护者。同时也正在经历着对相关国际规范内化的过程,虽然这种内化因为文化的差异而有困难。

但是也要看到,文化差异会引起各级紧张的理论也经常被歪曲性的解释。当代世界诸多地区存在着根深蒂固的流血政治冲突。因此,有政治家以文明和文化差异来解释这种冲突的原因。根据英国"卫报"7月30日的报道,美国共和党总统候选人罗姆尼最近在以色列访问时说,相比巴勒斯坦人,以色列的经济成功是由于"文化上差异和上帝的意愿"而形成的。[16]落姆尼实际上要强调以色列在巴勒斯坦持久的流血冲突的道义优势,但他夸大文化与宗教差异在国际冲突中的影响,忽略了以色列—巴勒斯坦问题的政治因素,以及巴勒斯坦公众当年来所受到非人道的待遇。当代世界没有一种文化是鼓励压迫和屠杀的,除非它被某些意识形态当做工具所利用。而将中东地区的流血冲突与文化或文明冲突相联系是常见的现象。所以要允许差异的存在,也要限制差异的恶性发展。

全球化时代文化差异不是一种可以绕开的障碍。不管存在多少问题,"全球化的好处超过了它的代价",当前的面临的问题是要"找到强化其好处并减轻其代价的道路"。并且要承认将存在着关于什么是好处和什么是代价的差异。[17]过去的半个世纪里经济学理论对于世界的和平与发展作出了重大的贡献。未来,文化学必须扮演更为重要的角色。中国的儒家思想有着丰富的有关社会和谐的思想,美国在一百年前也出现过强大的和平运动,在其背后,同样是追求世界和平与和谐的基督教文化理念。这些理念其实出现在所有的文明之中。在当前国际秩序面对新的挑战之时,中美两国的思想家必须扩大共同的文化理念,防止以趋同压制差异,同时也找到限制差异的途径。

国际关系的构建主义理论告诉我们,不同文化之间的认同与敌视其实并非是永久的。一个多世纪前,西方社会中曾经存在严重的排斥犹太人的思潮,反犹主义即使不能算是欧洲与北美主流文化,也是主流文化所能容忍的文化与社会现象。美国在第二次世界大战以后的最初十年里也并没有亲以色列的对外政策。但今天的美国社会已经具有强烈的亲以色列特点,以至于没有哪位美国政治家敢于认真批评以色列的对外政策。即使在学术界,对美以关系的学术批评也很容易被套上一顶反犹主义的帽子。⑱因此,国家和个人都可以有多个认同,虽然认同并不能随意建立,但是在一定条件下,它是可以因利益因文化等转换的。

---

① 扈海鹏:《全球化与文化整合》,《哲学研究》2000年第1期。
② [美]保罗·雷格:《美国:美国是一个全球性国家吗》,第97-98页。
③ [美]霍华德·威亚尔达:《结论:全球化:单一和多元》,《全球化:普遍的趋势,区域的影响》,第266页,波士顿:东北大学出版社。
④ 龙永图:《民意基础很不错 中国人对美国人很友好》,http://money.163.com./12/0608/14/83G1H606000254RD6.html。
⑤ 《希望与疑虑:百人会民意调查报告》,http://survey.commitee100.org/2007/TC/P1-12-TC.php。
⑥ 《中国首次赴美民意调查幕后》,《国际先驱导报》2011年03月02日。
⑦ [美]彼得·穆迪:《东亚的全球化》,《全球化:普遍的趋势,区域的影响》,第151页。
⑧ [美]彼得·伯格:《多元全球化:全球化文化及其影响》,霍华德·威亚尔达编《全球化:普遍的趋势,区域的影响》,第29-30页。
⑨ [美]彼得·伯格:《多元全球化:全球化文化及其影响》,霍华德·威亚尔达编《全球化:普遍的趋势,区域的影响》,第30页。
⑩ 泰勒·科文:《创造性毁灭:全球化如何改造世界文化》,第6页,普林斯顿和伦敦:普林斯顿大学出版社,2002年。
⑪ 党国英:《立足民族特色,拥抱普世价值》,《南方周末》,2007年10月25日。
⑫ [美]泰勒·科文:《创造性毁灭:全球化如何改造世界文化》,第16-17页。
⑬ [美]保罗·雷格:《美国:美国是一个全球性国家吗》,第84-85页。
⑭ [美]保罗·雷格:《美国:美国是一个全球性国家吗》,第84-85页。
⑮ [美]保罗·雷格:《美国:美国是一个全球性国家吗》,第86-91页。
⑯ http://www.guardian.co.uk/world/2012/jul/30/mitt-romney-israel-economic-success。
⑰ 穆迪教授认为全球化并没有带来文化领域的一致性的道义支撑,因此对于这些好处与代价要小心分辨与对待。彼得·穆迪:《东亚的全球化》,《全球化:普遍的趋势,区域的影响》,第165页。
⑱ [美]约翰·米尔斯海默、斯蒂芬·沃尔特:《以色列游说集团与美国外交政策》,法劳·斯特劳斯·吉罗出版社,2007年版。

Cultural Integration and Cultural Differences under the Impact of Globalization

Cai Jiahe

Deputy Director of
The Johns Hopkins
University - Nanjing
University Center
for Chinese and
American Studies

Abstract: This paper focuses on globalization that promotes the integration of cultures in the world while making them converge. Though the paper touches on cultural diversity and is optimistic about it, more attention is paid to the issue of cultural differences in an era of globalization. Peter L. Berger, Professor of Economic Culture at Boston University, noted that globalization didn't bring about a single, complete and unified world or global cultural or religious system and, instead, reinforced existing cultural differences more often than not and led to conflicts in many regions and circumstances. This paper is an attempt made on the basis of this to deal with the relationship between cultural integration and differences and talk about the relationship between Chinese and American cultures in this context.

One topic for this forum is about cultures and regions. Scholars in cultural studies have in recent years been debating whether a regional or national culture can survive under the impact of globalization. Chinese scholar Hu Haili holds that a developing country faces two problems in accepting the idea of globalization: on the one hand, it must take part in the world's process of modernization and globalization to advance its social progress; on the other, in participating in the world's modernization and globalization, it, as a nation, faces the difficulty of how to maintain its national culture[1]. Though insistent on the necessity of participating in globalization, Chinese scholars are still concerned with the prospect of regional cultures.

Similar debate also exists in the American academia, with many arguing that markets will destroy culture and diversity. Paul Rego holds that, as a homogenized global consumption culture has a huge ability to diffuse, cultures are facing "a threat of destruction". Because only the United States has politically and culturally universal values (for its emphasis on inalienable rights), which also takes the lead in popular and consumption cultures, the American culture already "has an edge in the fight for survival among worldwide cultures". [2]

This paper focuses on globalization that promotes the integration of cultures in the world while making them converge. Though the paper touches on cultural diversity and is optimistic about it, more attention is paid to the issue of cultural differences in an era of globalization. Peter L. Berger, Professor of Economic Culture at Boston University, noted that globalization didn't bring about a single, complete and unified world or global cultural or religious system and, instead, reinforced existing cultural differences more often than not and led to conflicts in many regions and circumstances.③ This paper is an attempt made on the basis of this to deal with the relationship between cultural integration and differences and talk about the relationship between Chinese and American cultures in this context.

Globalization Widening Cultural Differences

The Sino-U.S. relationship demonstrates that globalization has widened cultural differences and provoked more conflicts. Over the past 20 years, globalization has profoundly changed the economic development direction of China, and interdependence between China and the rest of the world, including the United States, has become closer still. "China is even making more efforts to move towards a consumption-based economy, and in particular China's middle class is rising." In 2007 China accounted for only 5.4% of the world's total consumption, about the same as Italian level; this figure rose to 14.1% in 2012, making China overtake Japan to become the world's second largest consumer market, only after the United States. ④ The Chinese economy, in fact, is no longer merely an export-dependent economy, and is becoming a bigger importer of goods with a consumption-driven economy. It means that China's market demand will provide more economic opportunities for developed countries including the United States.

Though China and the United States are highly interdependent economically, the Sino-U.S. relationship is full of uncertainties, bilateral frictions in trade and finance are often reported by various media, and ideological confrontation between them are widely known. They both speculate about each other's deep-seated intentions. Some U.S. scholars in international relations hold that the so-called Chinese phrase "Tao Guang Yang Hui", translated as "hide one's capacities and bide one's time", is meant to overthrow the present U.S.-dominated international order. China, of course, also suspects that the United States would likely stage peaceful evolution meant to topple China's present political system. Such suspicion also exists among the public of the two countries. A recent opinion poll suggested that, though people of the two countries to date have a fairly high opinion of one another, there is conspicuous distrust between them. ⑤ Though there is high IT coverage in both countries, "the American public holds an attitude of neutrality and uncertainty towards China", and they have little understanding of the Chinese contemporary culture and values. ⑥ On the other hand, the Chinese public finds it totally incomprehensible why the United States is so keen on promoting democracy in the world. Such mutual distrust is related to democracy publicity by some media in both countries, and also to widening cultural differences as a result of globalization. It is the lack of deeper understanding of each other's culture that has deepened both sides' suspicion and even hostility towards each other.

It is because of its connection with the global system that China has achieved economic prosperity and social progress, an achievement which revealed not only mistakes in planned economy theory but also the limitations of the attachment theory and political modernization theory. Though deeply influenced by globalization and the American culture, East Asian countries were not absorbed into a "homogenized and modern world culture". ⑦Different cultures differ from each other in their adaptability to modernization and globalization. Cultures of many East Asian and South Asian countries, including Japan, China and India, have strong adaptability and creativity. Globalization which originated in the West "has been successfully localized everywhere it reached", and "there also were tension and convergence between different cultures in the process of cultural globalization".⑧ It is indeed true. When the Chinese economy was not connected much with the rest of the world during the 1970s and 1980s, distrust between China and the United States was not unacceptable, but the ensuing 20 years of rapid economic development of China resulted in, among other things, growing distrust between the two countries.

Like other East Asian countries, China has retained its own cultural traits in the process of globalization. Berger noted that there have already been some cultural movements with a global outreach, originating outside the Western world and indeed impacting on Western cultures. Such alternative cultural globalization "not only corrects the notion that non-Western and non-American cultures could only have simple reaction to the forces of cultural globalization, but implies that there may be more than one path to modernity". ⑨The Chinese culture has a limited influence on the world, but China's enormous economic aggregate and its determination to maintain its own system and culture might, objectively, have encouraged the collision of different cultures. Though China is still a developing country with severe social problems, it is regarded as a challenger to the U.S. hegemony and values.

Necessity of Cultural Integration

Culturally, globalization is a process of the interaction, collision and compromise of diverse cultures or ideologies, and also a process of mutual assimilation and integration of these notions. It is a "mutually constitutive process" of various ideologies and cultures. Economic globalization promotes the cultural convergence to a certain degree, which in return drives the world towards consumer society, society ruled by law, and democracy. Prof. Tyler Cowen at George Mason University points that from the historical perspective, "the very foundation of the West is multicultural products, resulting from the international exchanges of goods, services, and ideas. To varying degrees, Western cultures draw their philosophical heritage from the Greeks, their religions from the Middle East, their scientific base from China and Arab countries, and their core population and languages from Europe". ⑩Any advanced culture is in essence a result of cultural integration. Does the American culture in an age of globalization still need to absorb advanced cultures and values of other countries?

From Cowen's point of view, the Chinese culture is a multicultural product alike, which drew its bronze technology and iron smelting technology from the early northern grassland culture, its Buddhist culture from the Indian subcontinent and its music, dance, sculpture and other forms of art from West Asia and East Asia, and established Confucian, Taoist and military thoughts itself. At present, the Chinese culture now is learning from all advanced cultures including those of the West. Prof. Dang Guoying at the Chinese Academy of Social Sciences opines that "universal values of man are not an abstract romantic vision, but a concrete code of conduct concerned with human happiness and benefit. Some institutional concepts like freedom, fairness, democracy and harmony are not only instruments through which man seeks dignity, independence and wealth, but also part of their cultural wealth." ①The contemporary culture of China is experiencing a process in which it voluntarily integrates with other advanced cultures in the world, and in this process it is making efforts to accept such universal values as democracy and fairness. Though there is controversy, it is impossible for China to continue its "self-closed" old path. Cultural integration in the era of globalization is the mainstream of cultural development in the world; those cultures on the decline and even disappearing have, to a certain degree, refused or enjoyed no chance to integrate with other cultures.

As for cultural integration in the context of globalization, those views merely regarding Americanization as globalization are hindering the American culture from integration. The American culture today ignores many important universal values, too, for example, equality – a generally accepted value worldwide. The social welfare system originating from Europe, a value highlighting social equality, is not only an indispensable social system in Europe and Japan, but has taken root in the United States too. Even in developing countries, social welfare is also a goal that people are striving to pursue and promote. In the colonial age of North America, the notion of equality was once held in high esteem; "equality" included in the Declaration of Independence of the United States was once the most inspiring value. But today, equality as a value, especially its social significance, is controversial in the United States, and it is not part of the American "ideology". Peace as a value, too, is almost not mentioned by scholars who regard globalization merely as Americanization. It is impossible that human beings and the international community discard such great and important values, and the international institutions of the United Nations just reflect the countries' pursuit of the value of peace throughout the world. In contemporary foreign policies of the United States, the meaning of peace is far less important than human rights and democracy, and for the latter, peace could even be discarded easily.

Cultural Differences as a Double-edged Sword

Globalization drives the integration of cultures, but it is not a simple process of one-way homogenization, for in the process of cultural integration new cultural differences still emerge, to say nothing of more serious cultural differences arising from cultural collision. Globalization not only drives the cultural convergence from different countries, but also breeds all sorts of cultural differences through innovation. The fact that cultural differences emerge continuously suggests that globalization is also a process that brings about heterogenization. "Cross-cultural exchange, while it will alter and disrupt each society it touches, will support innovation and creative human energies," Cowen noted, "Cultural homogenization and heterogenization are not alternatives or substitutes; rather, they tend to come together." ⑫

John Winthrop, a thinker and theologian of the colonial age in North America, once said he wished that "we must be knit together in this work as one man, we must entertain each other in brotherly affection". He was clearly aware of the differences between human beings, but he explained that God allowed the existence of such differences and changes because God didn't want a monotonous world, and that such differences were meant to make human beings complementary to each other and thus were good for human society. ⑬ Winthrop's thought is similar to what traditional Chinese culture says, "He Er Bu Tong", translated as "harmony but not uniformity"; the ancient Chinese phrase "He Shi Sheng Wu, Tong Ze Bu Ji", literally meaning "harmony generates and sameness stops vitality", also stresses the positive aspect of differences (Discourses of Zheng in Discourses of the States).

Globalization still reserves possibilities for countries and regions involved in the movement to choose what pace and specific form they take towards it. "The essence of combining universal values of human civilization with characteristics of a nation is to choose a specific path to human civilization in light of its own historical conditions." ⑭ All cultures change in themselves; for example, the Protestant thought as the mainstream culture of the colonial age of the United States gave way more than one hundred years later to principles of natural rights, most notably John Locke's classical liberalism . ⑮Social development and cultural interaction continuously drive the creation of new cultural ideas, and people of every generation and every region create their own cultures. Cultural differences are thus created, and it is the instinct of man to innovate, rather than imitating, as a higher species of animals. It is just the existence of cultural differences that provides an inexhaustible source of cultural integration. From this point of view, cultural differences deserve to be acclaimed, for they can be a sort of positive energies.

But cultural differences have their negative side that is undeniable. Globalization had already been developing fast before World War I, but close economic contacts between European countries brought about severe conflicts of interest, as well as corresponding antagonisms – which gradually overtook cooperation between those countries and eventually led to the unprecedentedly large war and enormous destruction. The existent international regimes, international order, and norms that underpin them, were in fact formed after human beings experienced the brutality of wars over the past century. And they are intended to restrict confrontation and conflict between countries, cope with the impulse of hurting others' interests through shared values and norms, and curb the vicious development of cultural differences. All big countries in the world now, including the United States and China, benefit from these regimes and order. China has no intention to overthrow the international order;

instead it tries to safeguard the order. Meanwhile, China is now in a process of internalizing relevant international rules, despite some difficulties arising from cultural differences.

It should be noted, however, that the notion that cultural differences create tensions is frequently distorted. As there are deep-rooted bloody political conflicts in many regions throughout today's world, some politicians attribute them to differences between civilizations and cultures. According to a July 30 report by The Guardian, during his visit to Israel, the US Republican presidential candidate Mitt Romney said that the Jewish state's economic success compared with its Palestinian neighbors was due to "cultural" differences and the "hand of providence" . ⑯By saying that, Romney actually meant to stress the moral superiority Israel had in the long-standing bloody conflict with Palestine, but he exaggerated effects that cultural and religious differences have in international conflicts, and ignored the political factors concerning the Israeli-Palestinian issue, as well as the inhuman treatment that the Palestinians suffered in those years. Not a single culture in the contemporary world encourages oppression and slaughter, unless it is employed as an instrument by some ideologies. But linking bloody clashes in Middle East with cultural or civilization conflict is commonplace. Therefore, we ought to allow the existence of differences and to curb the vicious development of them.

Cultural differences in the era of globalization are not a barrier that can be evaded. No matter how many problems there are, "the benefit of globalization exceeds the cost for it", and the problem now ahead is to "find a path that increases its benefit and reduces its cost". And it is necessary to accept differences in what the benefit is and what the cost is. ⑰ Over the past half century, economic theories contributed much to the world's peace and development. In the future, cultural sciences must play a more important part. China's Confucianism contains rich thoughts on social harmony; the United States also experienced a mighty peace movement a century ago, behind which were Christian cultural ideas for world peace and harmony. These ideas actually exist in all civilizations. At present, the international order is facing new challenges, thinkers in both China and the United States must broaden cultural ideas that are shared by both sides, prevent cultural convergence from suppressing cultural differences, and find out ways whereby differences are restricted.

Constructive theories on international relations tell us that one culture's identification with and hostility to another is not permanent. Over a century ago, there was once widespread anti-Semitism in Western societies, which, even if not mainstream in Europe and North America, was a cultural and social phenomenon tolerated by mainstream cultures. The United States had no foreign policy in favor of Israel in the first ten years after World War II, but the American society today has showed so strong pro-Israel features that no American politicians dare to seriously criticize Israel's foreign policies. Even in the academia, academic critiques of U.S.-Israel ties are also very easily labeled as anti-Semitism. ⑱ Therefore, a country or an individual may have multiple identifications, which, though not established at discretion, may change with interest and culture under certain conditions.

① Hu Haili. Globalization and Cultural Integration. Philosophical Researches, Issue 1, 2000.
② Paul M.Rego, The United States, is America the Universal Nation.Pp.97-98.
③ Howard J.Wiarda,Conclusion,Globalization in Its ONE and Many Forms,in Globalization,Universal Trends,Regional Implications.ed.by Howiarda,Northeastern University Press,Boston,2007,p266.
④ Long Yongtu: Popular opinion is fairly good and the Chinese is friendly to the American people. http://money.163.com./12/0608/14/83G1H606000254RD6.html.
⑤ Hope and Doubt: An Opinion Poll Report by Committee of 100, http://survey.commitee100.org/2007/TC/P1-12-TC.php.
⑥ Behind China's First Opinion Poll in the United States, International Herald Leader, March 2, 2011.
⑦ Peter R.Moody Jr.,Globalization in East Asia,in Globalization,Unversal Trends,Regional Implication,p.151.
⑧ Peter L.Berger,Many Globalization:The cultural and its Implications of Globalization,in Globalization,Universal Trends,Regional Implications.ed.by Howard J.Wiarda,pp.29-30.
⑨ Peter L.Berger,Many Globalization:The cultural and its Implications of Globalization,in Globalization,Universal Trends,Regional Implications.ed.by Howard J.Wiarda,p.30.
⑩ Tylor Cowen,Crdattive Destruction,How Globalization is Changing the World's a Cultures,Princeton University Press,Princeton and London,2002,P.6.
⑪ Dang Guoying. Uphold National Characteristics, Embrace Universal Values. South Weekend, October 25, 2007.
⑫ Tyler Cowen, creative Destrucion,pp.16-17.
⑬ Pau M.Rego,The United States,is America the Universal Nation,pp.84-85.
⑭ Pau M.Rego,The United States,is America the Universal Nation,pp.84-85.
⑮ Pau M.Rego,The United States,is America the Universal Nation,pp.86-91.
⑯ http://www.guardian.co.uk/world/2012/jul/30/mitt-romney-israel-economic-success.
⑰ Prof. Moody holds that, as globalization didn't bring about uniform moral support to the culture field, such benefit and cost should be carefully distinguished and treated. Peter R.Moody Jr.,Globalization in East Asia,in Gobalization,Universal Trends,Regionao Impication,pp.165.
⑱ John J.Mearsheimer&Stephen M.Walt,The Israel Lobby and U.S Foreign Policy,New York;Farrar,Straus and Giroux,2007.

ADDRESS AT THE CLOSING CEREMONY

闭幕致辞

美国国家人文基金会主席詹姆斯·利奇闭幕致辞
Address at the Closing Ceremony by James Leach,
Chairman of US National Endowment for the Humanities

中华人民共和国文化部对外文化联络局副局长李鸿闭幕致辞
Address at the Closing Ceremony by Li Hong, Vice Director-General of the Bureau for External Cultural Relations, Ministry of Culture, People's Republic of China

詹姆斯·利奇

★

美国国家人文基金会主席

我谨代表来访的美国代表团,向中国文化部和江苏省文化厅的盛情款待致以诚挚的谢意。中国东道主是最慷慨大方的。

1979 年我曾作为美国官方代表团的一员来到中国,与邓小平一起参加关系正常化仪式,现在我继续惊讶于中国变化的步伐,两国关系纽带的稳步加深给我留下了深刻的印象。

对于本次第三届中美文化论坛,我相信所有参会者都会同意,本次对话非常令人振奋,并开拓我们的视野。我们相互学习并深受善于思考的学生与会者的激发。

正式和非正式的会议中都提到了孔子和杰斐逊。因此,让我来总结我对中国的孔子文化传统和美国的杰斐逊传统对比的一点观察。

作为哲学家和伦理学家的孔子认为,"己所不欲,勿施于人"。这和犹太教和基督教的肯定"推己及人"的黄金法则似乎没有区别。然而,以否定而非以肯定表达一个意见反映了两个社会之间一定的文化差异。

例如,谈到人权问题时,孔子和杰斐逊可能在公民尊严被滥用的个别情况下看法一致。毕竟,两者都落笔反对当前政府的过度行为。但仍有几个重要的区别。杰斐逊的民主根植于信仰赋予的权力,不仅涉及一个时代的殖民者,也推定为适用于任何地方、任何时候的个人。美国的独立宣言不仅是一个国家建设的信条,它还是一个普遍的生活原则。因此,在国外和国内都践行这些价值是杰斐逊子孙后代的自然本能。在美国的环境下,它经过了内战以及随后的普选和民权运动，这才给我们在独立宣言中所作的宣誓带来了完整的意义。

孔子的教导可能与杰斐逊关于在其他社会提倡社会事业可能带来不适的思想有所出入。道德箴言"勿施于人……"本质上对于个人和整个社会比基于神学的呼吁"……及人"具有较少的侵入性。从20世纪的意识形态来看，这种哲学区别可能很复杂，但是，重要的是我们彼此都认识到，对于一方而言似乎是傲慢和侵入性的内容，对于另一方或许是善意的公民倡议。

我们在北京的发言人之一，著名美国印第安土著部落权威斯科特·斯蒂文斯博士描述了莫霍克族神圣带——有两条平行线的简单设计的带子，表示在同一个地方友好生存的、相互尊重对方领地的两个不同传统的民族。在某些方面，莫霍克带所代表的理想可能和儒家及任何美国政治思想一致。然而，由于现代通信、旅行和贸易使得我们成为近邻，似乎我们今天努力要系上的带子是有着许多交织线头的带子，而非两条非接触的条纹。

另一位与会者，南京大学-约翰斯·霍普金斯大学中美文化研究中心副主任的詹森·帕滕特博士引用社会学家的理论，认为人类进化的物种生存需要有一种对于他人的自然的不信任。根据该理论，人们可能在遗传上就倾向于对非同类的人保持警惕，因为那些人可能很危险，正如老虎对其祖先一样。另一方面，人们可以很容易推测到，人的思维足够强大，想要与类似人群结成联盟，保护自己免受其他非类似群体的侵犯。事实上，文明的起源可能是人类联合起来保护自己及其后代免受狼和其他食肉动物的侵犯。而且，如果我们进一步回过头来看进化，文明的命运取决于地球上的各民族在心理上是否倾向于认为他们都是互相保护的亲人，而非其是否接受所有生命形式都是从海洋进化过来——或许是最简单的有机体海绵——的科学假设，或正如各种信仰教义中所称的，来自亚当和夏娃。唯一清晰的是，对于人性主题，科学无法给出明确答案，宗教的解释亦五花八门，尽管大部分信条都承认人类的缺点，甚至罪行。

人类的经历告诉我们，不同背景的民族之间，以及有着更多类似历史的民族之间爆发了冲突。第一类可能是各民族国家之间或地域上更广阔的民族群落之间的战争；第二类是内战，如19世纪中国和美国的内战、非洲几个世纪以来各部落之间的冲突，以及相对近期的希特勒和波尔波特的种族灭绝。引发冲突并不难，但控制暴力却很难。那就是为什么法治以及实施法律的方法如此重要。

从态度的角度来看，解决冲突的最有效方法就是对于其他民族和文化有更多的了解，对许多人来说造成心理冲击的是：要接受这一理念，即如果人们尊重并与各种背景的民族而不是单单与类似教养的民族相联系，则生活会更加有趣和充实。

对于他人更多的理解和欣赏只有在严格关注人文和人类生存条件时才会达到。套用今天上午一位发言人的话语，历史照亮过去，教训指引未来；哲学阐明人类的思维；文学揭示动机和愿望；诗人说出我们心中所思；艺术丰富人类的经历。结合起来，历史、文学、哲学和艺术美化了文明生活，并给之带来了意义。

拓宽相互理解并不能保证可以避免冲突，但是减少了不可避免的、可能导致战争的紧张局势。那就是为何欣赏人文科学和世界各地无数文化差异如此关键的原因，特别是，对是否为世界带来相对和平和繁荣的世纪起着决定性作用的两个国家而言。

谢谢。

James Leach

★

Chairman of US National Endowment for the Humanities

On behalf of the visiting American delegation, I would like to emphasize how appreciative we are of the generous hospitality of the Chinese Ministry of Culture and the Department of Culture of Jiangsu Province. Our Chinese hosts have been most gracious.

Having first come to China in 1979 as a member of the official delegation representing the United States at the normalization of relations ceremony with Deng Xiaoping, I continue to be startled with the pace of change in China and impressed with the steady increase in ties between our two countries.

In regard to this 3rd China-U.S. Cultural Forum, I am sure I speak for all participants in noting how uplifting and informative the dialogue has been. We have learned from each other and been stimulated by the thoughtful student participants.

Throughout our meetings, formal and informal, there have been references to Confucius and Jefferson. So let me conclude with an observation about one contrast between the Confucian tradition in China and the Jeffersonian legacy in America.

Confucius argued as a philosopher and ethicist that individuals should not do unto others what one would not want done unto oneself. This may seem to be no different than the Golden Rule in the Judeo-Christian tradition which affirms that an individual should do unto others what one would want done unto oneself. Nonetheless, the difference between stating a proposition in the negative as opposed to the affirmative is reflective of certain cultural tensions between our two societies.

When it comes to the subject of human rights, for instance, Confucius and Jefferson would likely be in full agreement on a case by case basis when citizen dignities are abused. Both, after all, put pen to paper in opposition to excesses of existing authorities. But several important distinctions exist. Jeffersonian democracy is rooted in faith-endowed rights that pertain not only to the colonists in one era but are presumed to apply to individuals everywhere in any time frame. The American Declaration of Independence is not simply a nation-building creed; it is a living set of universal principles. Accordingly, it is the natural instinct of the sons and daughters of Jefferson to reflect these values abroad as well as at home. In an American setting, it took a Civil War, and follow-on suffrage and civil rights movements to bring full meaning to the pledges we made to ourselves in the Declaration of Independence.

Where Confucius's teaching might depart somewhat from Jeffersonian thought relates to possible discomfort in advocating social causes in other societies. The ethical "do not do unto others..." prescription is inherently less intrusive on individuals and societies at large than the theologically based call "to do unto others..." This philosophical distinction may be complicated by 20th Century ideologies but it is important that we mutually recognize that what may seem arrogant and intrusive to one side may be well-meaning citizen advocacy by the other.

One of our speakers in Beijing, Dr. Scott Stevens, a noted authority on America's indigenous Indian tribes, described the sacred belt of the Mohawks – a simply designed strap with two parallel lines, symbolizing two peoples of different traditions living amicably in one space, respecting each other's place. In some ways the ideal represented in the Mohawk belt may be as Confucian as any American political thought. Nevertheless, as modern communications, travel and trade make each of us closer neighbors, it would seem that the belt we should strive to wear today would have one line with many interwoven threads rather than two non-touching stripes.

Another conferee, Dr. Jason Patent of the Nanjing branch of Johns Hopkins University, referenced social anthropologists who have theorized that in human evolution survival of the species required a natural distrust of the other. According to this theory, man may be genetically predisposed to be wary of categories of people different than his own because they might be dangerous, just as tigers were to his ancestors. On the other hand, one could just as easily hypothesize that man is thoughtful enough to want to align with similar beings to protect against predators that are more unlike. Indeed, the origins of civilization may be humans banding together to protect themselves and their offspring against wolves and other predators. And, if we look further back in evolution, it may be that the fate of civilization hinges on whether all peoples of the earth become psychologically predisposed to consider themselves mutually protective cousins, regardless of whether they accept the scientific assumption that all life forms evolved from the sea, perhaps the simplest organism, a sponge, or from Adam and Eve as various faith systems affirm. The only clarity is that science is not definitive on the subject of human nature, and religious explanations are varied, though most creeds acknowledge human flaws, indeed sins.

What human experience tells us is that conflict breaks out between peoples of different background as well as between those with more similar histories. The first category might define wars between nation-states or perhaps more geographically expansive groupings of people; the second includes civil wars such as occurred in China and America in the 19th Century, various tribal conflicts over the centuries in Africa, and the relatively recent genocides of Hitler and Pol Pot. It doesn't take much to spark conflict. It takes a lot to hold violence in check. That is why the rule of law and the means to enforce it are so important.

From an attitudinal perspective, the most effective antidote to conflict is greater understanding of other peoples and cultures and what for many is a psychological jolt: an embrace of the notion that life is more interesting and fulfilling if one comes to respect and interrelate with peoples of diverse background rather than simply those with a similar upbringing.

Greater understanding and appreciation of the other can only come from a disciplined attention to the humanities and the human condition. To paraphrase a speaker this morning, history illumines the past with lessons for the future; philosophy clarifies human reasoning; literature reveals motives and aspirations; poets tell us about the heart; and art uplifts the human experience. In combination, history, literature, philosophy and art are what embellish and give meaning to civilized life.

Broadening mutual understanding is no guarantee that conflict can be avoided, but it reduces the prospect that inevitable tensions lead to war. This is why appreciation of the humanities and the myriad of cultural distinctions across the world are so critical, particularly for the two countries that will hold the key to whether this century will be relatively peaceful and prosperous.

Thank you.

李 鸿

★

中华人民共和国文化部对外文化联络局 副局长

尊敬的詹姆斯·利奇先生，各位学者、嘉宾，女士们先生们：

大家好！

经过北京、南京两地的交流和讨论，第三届中美文化论坛即将在南京落下帷幕。在过去三天，中美两国学者围绕文化与人类、文化与历史、文化与地域的关系，展开了热烈而深入的对话，话题涉及哲学、文学、艺术、电影、社会学、本土文化保护、非物质文化遗产保护、文化融合、跨文化交流、当今社会文化发展现状等，我庆幸和美国朋友们共同设计了一个包容性比较强的议题，尽管如此，双方学者思维的活跃和发散性，所涉及领域的广博，还是一次又一次给我们带来惊喜和启示。中国有句古话，"听君一席话，胜读十年书"，我很想从组织者和听众的角度谈两点对论坛的感受：

第一，此次双方学者来自不同的国家，不同的历史文化背景，不同的学术领域，探讨问题的角度也有所不同，但有一点是共同的，那就是双方都抱有极其诚恳的交流善意，极高的交流热情，也表现出极强烈的交流需求和意愿。在北京，学者们总是有说不完的话，我们总是被迫限制他们的发言时间，在南京，嘉宾和学生们的对话成为此次论坛最精彩、最令人激动的亮点，很好地诠释了真正的交流和互动。

第二，大家知道，中美双方现在互为最大的贸易伙伴，中美关系是最重要的双边关系。中美建交以来，双方开展了很多人文交流，但我们仍感觉双方的相互了解还是不够，尤其是对各自思维方式的文化基础了解不够，双方互相了解的程度也不对称。举个例子，在美国，有大量的中国学生在学习，在座的许多中国学者都去过美国。在中国的大学里，所有英文专业的学生都开设美国文学这样一门课程。在中国的外文书店里，有大量关于美国社会与文化的书籍。相比之下，美国对中国的了解实在是不多，比如这次代表团绝大部分成员是第一次访华。我事先没有征求美国朋友的意见，但是这次论坛我觉得双方已经达成了一个共识，那就是中美两国应该多来往、多交流。中美文化论坛就是这样一个平台，它对双方增进对对方国家历史文化、思维方式、当代社会和文化发展现状的了解，恰恰能起到帮助作用。正如文化部部长蔡武所说，中国文化部为能和美国国家人文基金会合作，为搭建这样一个交流平台而感到骄傲，我们愿意把这个论坛做下去，并且不断增加参与交流的学者和嘉宾，让更多的学者和参加者受益。同时我们也鼓励两国文化界、学术界把中美文化论坛不仅当成一个思想交流平台，也当成一个尽力联系、推动下一步文化合作的契机。

今天上午有两件事让我很受触动，一个是毕飞宇先生通过参加爱荷华大学国际写作计划和克里斯托弗结下友谊，并在南京重逢。还有丽莎女士坚持30年的文化实践。我在大学的时候读了一本书，是中国作家王蒙写的，叫作《在那片绿草地上》，那本书打开了我了解美国的窗口，那本书就是王蒙参加爱荷华计划以后回国写成的，可能连当时的举办者也没有想到，这本书在中国有多么受欢迎，对当时渴望了解世界的中国人有多么大的帮助。丽莎女士从事的事情也是非常有意义的，其意义之长远，对学生一生的影响之大，可能要过几十年才能看得更加清楚。不管是国际写作计划的推行者，还是进行文化实践的丽莎女士，他们都是中美文化交流的先行者和实践者，我们希望看到更多的文化机构和个人加入他们的行列中，中国文化部愿意推动更多的中美文化交流，并且提供相应的支持。

我想美国朋友会与我有同感，这次论坛是一次成功的论坛！作为中方组织者，我愿代表中国文化部向美国国家人文基金会，向出席论坛的所有中美专家、学者，表示热烈的祝贺。

明天，美国代表团的朋友们将有机会参观南京这个历史悠久、人文荟萃的城市，亲自感受其历史积淀和当代文化发展状况。我相信，他们会非常喜欢这个城市。南京之所以能成为分论坛，我们首先要感谢江苏省人民政府，我们是应他们的强烈要求，把南京作为论坛的分论坛会场。其次，南京的同事们为论坛做了大量精心的准备，并提供了热情周到的招待。我谨代表文化部对为本次论坛成功举办付出大量心血的江苏省文化厅、江苏新华报业传媒集团，表示衷心的感谢！也想再次向中国艺术研究院表示感谢！

我宣布，第三届中美文化论坛圆满闭幕！谢谢大家的参与！

Li Hong

--- ★ ---

Vice Director-General, Bureau for External Cultural Relations
Ministry of Culture, People's Republic of China

Respected Mr. James A. Leach, distinguished scholars & guests, ladies and gentlemen:

Good morning afternoon!

The Third China-US Cultural Forum will soon come to a close in Nanjing. In the past three days, Chinese and US scholars have been engaged in heated and in-depth discussions in Beijing and Nanjing to explore the relationship between culture and mankind, culture and history, and culture and locality. The discussions cover subjects as diverse as philosophy, literature, art, movie, sociology, protection of local culture, protection of intangible cultural heritage, cultural integration, cross-cultural communication and present status of social and cultural development. I am very glad that I had, together with our US friends, designed an inclusive theme for the forum, however, we were still surprised and inspired, again and again, by the creative and original thinking of the scholars of both sides and the wide range of fields they explored. As an old Chinese saying goes "talking with a wise man is better than reading books for ten years", I would like to share my feelings about the forum as both an organizer and a member of the audience.

First, though coming from different countries and varying in their historical and cultural background, field of expertise and perspective, scholars share one thing in common: good will and passion for communication. In Beijing, scholars had so much to say that we had to limit the length of their remarks; and in Nanjing, dialogues between guest speakers and students, the highlight and the most exciting part of the forum, were fine examples of earnest communication and interaction.

Secondly, as we know, China and the US are the biggest trade partner to each other, and China-US relationship is the most important bilateral relationship. Since the establishment of their diplomatic relationship, cultural exchanges have been greatly promoted between the two countries; however, we still feel an inadequacy of mutual understanding, especially about the culture that underlies the way of thinking in the other country. Moreover, there also exists an asymmetry in the understanding about each other. For example, there are many Chinese students in American colleges and many Chinese scholars present today have been to the US. American literature is taught to English majors in Chinese colleges, and in foreign language bookstores in China, a large number of books about the American society and culture are sold. By comparison, Americans have a far more limited knowledge of China. For example, it is the first time for most US delegates to visit China. I have not asked our US friends beforehand, but I think the forum delivers a clear message of consensus that there needs to be more communications and exchanges between the two countries. The China-US Cultural Forum is a platform to help us understand each other's history and culture, way of thinking and contemporary social and cultural development. As Minister of Culture Cai Wu noted, the Chinese Ministry of Culture is proud to work with US National Endowment for the Humanities to establish such an exchange platform and is willing to move forward to include more scholars and guests in the forum and benefit more scholars and participants. Meanwhile, we also encourage the cultural and academic communities of both countries to make the most of the opportunities offered by the forum in liaison and cultural cooperation, rather than merely take it as a platform for the exchange of ideas.

I was deeply impressed this morning by two things. One is the meeting of Mr. Bi Feiyu and Christopher in Nanjing who have become friends after attending the International Writing Program at the University of Iowa. The other is the three-decade-long cultural pursuit of Lisa. When I was in college, I read a book written by the Chinese writer Wang Meng after his return from the Iowa Program. Titled On that Green Meadow, the book opened a window for me to better understand the US. The organizer of the Program may have never expected how popular this book would be in China and how helpful it would be for Chinese desiring to know the outside world. What Lisa has done is also very meaningful and has such far-reaching influence on the life of students that we may only see it fully decades later. Both the initiator of the International Writing Program and Lisa who has been engaged in cultural pursuit are pioneers and practitioners of the China-US cultural exchange. We hope more cultural institutions and individuals could join them. The Chinese Ministry of Culture is ready to provide more support to promote the cultural exchanges between China and the US.

This forum has made great success and I believe our US friends would have felt the same. As the organizer of the Chinese side and on behalf of the Ministry of Culture of China, I would like to congratulate the US National Endowment for the Humanities and all Chinese and American scholars and experts present at the forum.

The US delegates will have a chance to tour around Nanjing tomorrow, a city with long history and brilliant culture, and feel personally its historical appeal and contemporary cultural development. I believe they will love this city. Now, I want to thank Jiangsu People's Government who had earnestly requested to make Nanjing a sub-venue for the forum. Then I would like to express my appreciation to our colleagues in Nanjing for their painstaking preparations and warm hospitality. On behalf of the Ministry of Culture, I would like to express my gratitude to Jiangsu Provincial Department of Culture and Jiangsu Xinhua Press Group for their painstaking efforts for the forum, and again to Chinese

National Academy of Arts for their great support.

Now I declare the close of the Third China-US Cultural Forum. Thanks for your participation!

COLLECTION OF SCHOLARS' VIEWPOINTS

与会学者论点撷英

从中美文艺的互动之旅看文化交流 —— 以《便条》和《英雄》为案例

王一川
北京大学艺术学院院长,教授

中美两国文化交流的推进,需要考虑文化语境、地域等因素的差异。有两则案例可帮助阐明。一则是美国诗人威廉斯(William Carlos Williams, 1883—1963)的诗《便条》(This Is Just to Say, 1934)。它曾在近三十年前被引进中国,但起初为中国读者所不解。这种不解虽与诗歌文本的语词内涵等文内语境有关,但更与它所呈现的社会语境及个人生活状况有关。其时的中国读者对美国人的日常生活缺少了解或了解不足,本身又缺乏相同的日常生活境遇,因而难以形成同情式共鸣。但随着中国国门的开放程度加大以及中国人日常生活的变化,对该诗的阅读与理解障碍就越来越小,理解趋于顺畅。另一则是中国导演张艺谋执导的古装武侠大片《英雄》,它于2004年在美国上映,取得高票房业绩。之所以如此,与中美两国同处于"冷战"后剧烈动荡的"文明的冲突"境遇中,战争与和平成为两国公众共同关怀的焦点性问题。了解中美两国文化语境、生活境遇等的异同,有助于推进文化交流。

传统内外的当代中国:政治领导、对外政策及其中国特性

时殷弘
中国人民大学国际关系学院教授

当代中国政治领导已经体现了几个深刻特征,这些特征都有其在中国百年传统或现代/当代创造性实践中的根源,他们或对中国的外交政策具有决定性的影响,或通过其对外行为显著反映出来。它们分别是:改革的本质区别、"保持"的中心思想、"统治宇宙的生物圈"的概念、平等问题的悖论、强调道德、外交政策对国内的压倒性功能、对追求中国特色及其压倒性重要性的坚定

保护与发展：中国电影的文化发展难题

周星

北京师范大学艺术与传媒学院院长，教授

信念、"富强中国"长期背景下的政治审慎。特别是中国实行国内和外交政策的改革开放以来，无论是对中国人自己还是其他人来说，最后一项都是一个非常重要的长期的基本主题。

真正理想化的电影业应该是健全的市场化加上对本土电影的保护。良好的市场化是市场准则，但是中国电影的市场成熟度跟国外还有差距，中国好的本土电影的文化影响力又不足，有了一定的保护，好的本土电影才不会被好莱坞强势的文化所遮蔽。现实是好电影缺乏，一些不该被保护的电影也被保护了，导致观影群体产生对于国产电影的逆反心理。电影毕竟是文化产品，而产品的市场需要和文化上的心理应和的确有值得研究的问题。由此，中国电影的难题再一次呈现在面前：电影到底在文化层面存在还是在市场层面存在？我们越来越受到市场生存的威胁，因此为了生存而理直气壮的追求导致电影文化品性的淡漠，实际上反过来威胁到电影的生存。我们也许难以避免内地电影市场予夺与文化追求之思，但偏离电影文化的市场生存的短视恶果，却迟早要影响到国产电影的生命存留。

我们的电影不乏喧闹却缺少思想和人文观照，这是一个需要反思的问题。

我们不能不思考中国电影的文化现实和未来图景，本土电影文化品性之丧失的忧虑已经无法回避，现实主义精神如何在市场予夺中保持的难题无可回避。电影最触动人心的，还是人们内源性、心理上的情感体会，这是技术无法取代的。所以，我们自身对于电影的内在精神的把握才是重要的前提。中国电影长远发展需要纠偏市场唯一的认识。而无论是本土市场还是世界电影节的中国电影身影，需要的是我们自己精神文化的张扬，否则无论多少国内票房都难以避免给他人分羹，而不被电影世界所看重。

文化多样性与国际文化贸易

李小牧
北京第二外国语大学副校长，国家文化发展战略研究院院长

当今世界进入了一个全球资源共享、文化边界日渐模糊的新时代，任何国家都不可避免地参与到日益复杂多元的竞争中，各国文化在走出国门的同时，也会受到外来文化的吸引与冲击。发展文化贸易可以最大限度地减轻外来文化对中国国内文化市场的冲击，同时也最大限度地弱化国家间的意识形态冲突。

文化如水，具有独特的渗透力，文化产品和服务承载着价值观念和生活方式，社会价值超过其商业价值，与其他贸易相比，在意识形态等方面会对输入国消费者潜移默化地产生影响。因此，设计制作更多的符合受众偏好内容和创意的文化产品与服务，培育国内国际文化市场，在世界文化经济生态圈中找到中国文化应有的位置，培育起更多民众对中国文化的认同感，使得中国文化和谐地融入世界多样性文化中，从而达到稳固中国核心价值、增强民族自豪感、强化文化凝聚力的目的。

国际金融危机的文化反思和发展模式竞争

齐勇锋
中国传媒大学文化发展研究院学术委员会主任，教授

由美国次贷危机引发的金融海啸重创了美、欧等西方发达经济体，导致全球性的经济衰退。金融危机的成因，从现象看是以美国为首的西方金融制度存在缺陷，而深层原因在

中美电影的文化张力：冲突与融合

陈旭光

北京大学艺术学院北京大学影视戏剧研究中心主任，教授

于西方文明的缺失。这场继20世纪30年代世界经济危机以来的全球性金融危机和经济危机，不仅改变了世界经济的走向，而且对未来世界地缘政治和文明发展格局产生重大影响。随着"美国式的资本主义从神坛上跌落下来"，而中国、印度、巴西、俄罗斯等新兴市场经济国家的崛起，事实上世界文明格局和发展模式已经不可逆转地从以西方文明主导的美国模式而进入"多元文明共存和多种发展模式竞争"的新时代。在国际形势已经发生了深刻变化的条件下，面对"欧债危机"和不断动荡的世界局势，如何通过文化对话、文化价值的重构而凝聚共识，求同存异，形成广泛的文化认同，推动国际经济、政治新秩序的构建，从而避免已经发生和可能再次发生的"金融危机"和"文明冲突"，使人类社会在多元文明共存与和谐发展的基础上保持持久的发展繁荣，已经成为摆在我们面前的一个不容回避的重大课题。中美两国作为世界上最大的经济体，在这方面负有重大的历史性责任。

电影是国家文化形象建构与文化软实力的重要载体。美国是电影大国和电影强国，百余年来一直强力输出电影也输出美国文化。中国是巨大的电影市场。近年来美国电影在题材、主题等方面不断调整策略以更适应中国市场。

中国电影近年来不断崛起，电影产业迅速发展。但"2·28"以来，美国电影对中国电影市场的压力剧增。一方面，中国电影要向美国学习成熟的电影工业管理机制，走类型化生产的道路；另一方面，中国电影也有自己的文化坚守，有自己的文化形象建构与传播的使命。中国电影在坚守的前提下又应

有对美国电影文化的大胆吸取、借用。

中国近期魔幻大片《画皮2》的成功引人思考。它把中国文化中居于边缘、民间、非主流地位的关于狐妖鬼魅的"鬼文化"或"妖仙文化",用电影的方式"大众文化化",且融合了美国魔幻电影的诸多类型要素。以《画皮2》的成功为个案,我们可以深入地思考中国电影如何向美国学习(如以制片人为中心的制片管理机制),中美文化如何在电影中既冲突又互相融合,中国电影既坚守又开放宽容的辩证文化态度和电影生产策略等。

新型、和谐、富有生机与活力的世界文化只有在冲突与融合的必要的张力中才能健康和谐地发展。

教育、出版与社会转型

肖东发

北京大学新闻与传播学院
现代出版研究所所长,教授

一、历史的回顾——教育、出版的转型与社会转型

1.春秋战国的私人著述、私人藏书、有教无类与社会转型。

2.晚清出版教育的近代化变革与社会转型。

3.印刷术在东西方不同的命运及社会作用之比较。

4.出版与社会的互动关系。

二、经验的总结——几点启示及规律探讨

1.关于社会转型、文化转型和出版转型。

2.生产力与生产关系——技术先行。

3.社会转型规律的探讨。

三、教训的反思——如何建设文化强国

1.20世纪初的教育与出版——张元济与蔡元培。

2.新中国60年两次着重点转移(去虚务实,不迷信数字,不再一味变更生产关系,不急功近利,

重视新媒体在跨文化传播中的作用

唐润华

新华社新闻研究所中外媒体发展战略研究中心主任

既重硬件建设,更重软实力。)

3. 欲使国家振兴舍教育而无他。

4. 重视出版,提高全民阅读率提高公民素质。

过去,跨文化传播面临的困难除了意识形态之外,还有地域上的、语言文字上的以及技术上的障碍——由于这些因素的影响,跨文化传播平台和渠道比较少,传播的广度和深度受到极大限制,效果也大打折扣。如今,迅猛发展的新媒体,尤其是社会化媒体,正在日益消减这些障碍,为不同文化间建立起顺畅而和谐的交流提供了空前的机会。

各种技术先进的新媒体终端正在成为越来越重要的跨文化传播平台。除传统的PC机之外,智能手机、平板电脑的用户在全世界以几何级数增长,这些新的终端不但便于使用和携带,而且具有非常完备的功能,可以为跨文化传播提供极其便利的条件。正是由于这些新媒体终端的迅速普及,使得跨文化传播不但有了多样化的渠道,而且有了广泛的受众和影响。

蓬勃发展的社会化媒体则为跨文化传播提供了互动交流的绝佳平台。例如,中国的新浪微博3亿多用户里,也有外国使馆、外国媒体、国际组织,以及诸如澳大利亚前总理陆克文这样的外国政要及知名人士,他们在微博里可以与普通的中国百姓进行广泛而深入的交流。同时,也有很多中国人和媒体机构等在Twitter、Facebook开设了账号,与外国网民交流信息。

随着智能翻译技术的不断发展,新媒体正在攻克跨文化传播最为困扰的语言障碍,有望在世界各国不同语言文字使用者之间架起可以顺畅进行交流的桥梁。

西方文明与中国融合文化观的建构：从辛亥革命到"中国走向全球化"

刘琛

北京外国语大学英语学院跨文化研究中心主任，副教授

对中国文化价值观的要义尤其是其现代性的两种论争由来已久。一种研究范式认为自唐代以来，中国不再有文化意义上的发展（H.G. Wells 著《世界史纲》）；另一种范式则指出中国文化建设从未停滞，且在与西方文明的交流会通中逐渐形成了现代性的融合文化价值观。以此为背景，系统梳理了从近代到21世纪全球化背景下中国文化价值观的建构历程及其一贯保持的基本思想，得出结论认为：中国文化转型，特别是自1978年改革开放以来的突出特点是融合吸收式。这说明中国文化理念的现代化进程是内发的，是积极主动地探索与思辨的结果。在此基础上，本研究总结了当下中国文化观与西方文明接轨的主要元素。

电影历史与现代化

丁亚平

中国艺术研究院电影电视研究所所长，研究员

走向当代的电影历史评价体系，包括电影复兴，经济发展、社会发展和电影历史本身的发展，电影史学者素质、电影史创新、电影史料、影像史学、电影史影响等多个方面。这些年来，电影史学开始获得一个更广阔的全球视野，一个新的不断发展的电影历史和文化观念。其中，史料作用、口述史以及其他一些超现状、超战略的史学问题，成为电影历史关心与探究的事情。电影历史资料搜集、电影历史写作、影像史学与在大火之中宝器名画同样有着刻不容缓的性质。在不

冲击抑或机遇——论好莱坞"加强型"影片的引进对中国电影的影响

赵卫防

中国艺术研究院电影电视研究所副所长、研究员

同的环境中进行历史研究,所表现出的一种社会义务、使命和颠覆的姿势值得肯定。在新社会和新语境之中,普遍主义终将取代种种现实主义,而成为电影历史现代化的必然趋势。

自2012年开始,中国每年将增加14部美国进口大片,以IMAX和3D类的"加强型"电影为主。今年上半年,中国国产电影的市场占有率似乎应声而落。其实这其中更多的是机遇而非冲击。

首先,在具有稳固的民族电影基础的地区,尽管外来的商业电影有时十分强悍,但一般不会对民族电影造成质的冲击,韩国电影便是如此。经过数年的产业化发展,中国电影已经形成了稳固的基础,国产电影不会受到太大的冲击。

其次,2012年上半年中国国产电影遭遇一定的低迷,主要是近年来特别是2011年其美学同质化达到极致后的市场冷淡回应。

最后,好莱坞"加强型"影片的增加,能够为中国电影市场有效扩容,这对国产电影来说,更主要的是机遇而非冲击。同时,亦使中国电影市场趋于高端,这为中国电影的创作营造出了高端的创作氛围,特别是为3D国产电影营造出了较佳的创作语境。

中外舞蹈交流中亟待解决的四个问题

欧建平

中国艺术研究院舞蹈研究所所长、研究员

古往今来,中国舞蹈的兴旺发达从来都是对外交流的硕果。作为26年来游学亚、澳、欧、美二十余国共四十余次的学者,以及17年来二十多个国

家一百多个舞团访华演出的顾问,我认为,随着中国经济的稳步发展,我们在全国范围内实施"文化大发展大繁荣"和"走出去"国策的进程中,应尽快制定方案,拿出措施,解决以下四个中国舞蹈乃至整个中国文化发展的大问题:1.中外舞蹈的进出口至今依然存在着严重的逆差;2.中国政府、企业、个人等多级资助体制与相关政策至今尚未颁布;3.尽管外来的当代舞已使包括民间、古典、芭蕾、现当代、国标和音乐剧在内的整个中国舞蹈受益匪浅,但至今依然没有长期引进"洋教头"的计划;4.把中国建设成"芭蕾强国"的宏伟蓝图至今依然只是我们的梦想。

从郭明达到沈伟 —— 中美舞蹈交流的逆向输出

江东

中国艺术研究院舞蹈研究所副所长、研究员

虽然中国是一个有着几千年舞蹈史的国度,但在如今已经风靡世界的现代舞运动中,中国却是个后来者。中国现代舞的发生与发展,与中美之间的舞蹈交流直接相关。

早在上世纪40年代,如今已逾九旬高龄的郭明达先生,曾在纽约等地跟随阿尔文·尼克莱等美国现代舞名家学习现代舞艺术,他成为中国赴美学习现代舞的第一人。上世纪50年代中期他返回中国,但这位在当时有理想、有抱负的舞者,却始终没有找到可以发挥自己所学专业的地方。

改革开放后,情况发生巨变。80年代末期,中国广东率先与美国舞蹈节(ADF)合作,先后邀请了六位美国现代舞蹈家前来广州培训中国第一批职业的现代舞人。在这批学员之中,就有如今在纽约现代舞领域中大红大紫的沈伟。在2008年北京奥运会开幕式上的开场舞蹈中,沈伟让更多的人见识到了他富有中华意味的现代舞艺术以及他不羁的才气。

近半个世纪的历史跨度，见证了中国现代舞艺术的历史性转折和跨越：从开始的汲取到后来的输出，中国舞者在这个领域中的后发优势和天才能力，得到了国际观众的尊重。而这个跨越，除了有中国舞者的不懈努力之外，自然离不开频繁而有效的中美间的舞蹈交流。

走向跨文化的中国当代艺术

王端廷
中国艺术研究院美术研究所外国美术研究室主任，研究员

1989年东西德的统一、苏联的解体和东西方冷战的结束，开启了世界政治历史新篇章。紧随着意识形态对立的解除，全球贸易协定出台，世界进入经济全球化的崭新时代。2001年12月10日，中国正式成为世贸组织成员，中国经济自此成为世界经济有机体的组成部分。

经济全球化是人类史无前例的生活方式，对于中国人来说更是一种崭新的生存经验。经济全球化给中国社会的发展带来了机遇，也给我们的生存能力提出了挑战。由经济全球化引发的世界文明的发展问题对全人类而言都是一个全新的课题，这使中国人第一次获得了与世界各国人民平等参与、共同探索人类生存发展道路的机会和权利。

在全球化时代，中国艺术家与世界各国艺术家站在了同一起跑线上，那些以超凡的智慧和独特的创造表达了人类共同心声和普遍关切的中国艺术家迅速走上了当代国际艺术的舞台。全球化不仅给中国当代艺术家带来了全新的艺术观念，也给他们提供了丰富的艺术语言，在20世纪90年代的"政治波普"和"玩世现实主义"之后，一种既表达了中国人的生命意志又符合全人类共同审美趣味的跨文化的中国当代艺术在21世纪悄然兴起并不断走向成熟。

跨文化艺术意味着在艺术家个人与世界之间再

也没有屏障，意味着个人的独立和相互之间的平等，它尊重个体生命的价值，鼓励个人创造力的充分发挥，同时标榜人类文化价值的一体性。我认为，跨文化是人类文明的未来。

差异与共融——中美绘画艺术的合作与交流

刘万鸣
中国艺术研究院美术创作院副院长

一、中美艺术之渊源

中国是东方文明发源地之一，地处亚欧大陆最东侧，由于自给自足的社会发展，文化艺术曾长期形成守静状态，平静含蓄。而美国的艺术由于理念源于西方文明，社会的开放、民族的豪放外露性格，使其求真的艺术风格快速彰显，进而形成本民族的东西。

二、审美体系的差异

中国艺术的审美观念是同伦理道德相联系的，美近于善，在从事艺术创作过程中注重修炼人格，提高精神境界。而美国艺术则是以自然科学的现实去理解美、认识美。美近于真，追求艺术对生活的再现，追求符合科学的形式美。具体在绘画上，中国绘画近于音乐和诗歌，具有象征性；美国绘画近于小说，具有写实性。所以，中国绘画是依据精神的升华而至善，美国绘画则通过对生活的认知而教人为善。

三、中美艺术的交融

人类艺术的终极关注点都是人，关注的是天、地、人之间的关系。世界文化的开放与交流使艺术更趋于多元化的自由形态。中国近现代绘画艺术之父徐悲鸿先生在20世纪40年代就已提出：美术应该忠于现实，离开现实则言之无物。科学之天才在精确，艺术之天才亦然，艺术中之韵趣，一若科学中之推论。宣真理之微妙，但不精确则感情浮泛，彼此无从沟通。能精于形象,自不难求得神韵。20世纪的呼声并未过时,具体到当代中国画亦势在必行。当今科学迅猛发展的美国,其绘画艺术的科学求真性正是我们借鉴、融合的一大契机。科学与绘画并不矛盾,二者是和谐统一的。相反美国绘画艺术虽然始终向欧洲的潮流靠拢,随着世界艺术的大同,期间不少人接触东方艺术思想,意识到绘画内涵的重要性,他们突破现实,强调艺术的纯粹,关注自然,通过人性的视点无限地挖掘大自然的情趣。更多是受中国老庄和禅学的渗透,而今已成为美国当代艺术的一大主流。值得欣慰的是,中国人看到了具有中国意味的美国艺术,美国人看到了具有美国情致的中国艺术,中美艺术的共融将会使人类艺术达到至真、至善、至美。

也谈中美文化交流的出发点和努力的目标

陈飞龙

中国艺术研究院马克思主义文艺理论研究所所长,研究员

中美文化交流实在是一个敏感而困难的论题。这是因为在历史的记忆里,中美关系极其复杂,特别是20世纪里有过一波三折的历史纠结,至今令人困扰,而在现实世界里,又有许多经济的和政治的纠纷和难堪,确实又令人难解。于是有人试图从观念形态的对比分析中找出文化上的差异来破解中美文化交流这个难题,有人想避开社会制度和意识形态的差异寻求中美文化交流的发展,还有人企图以实用超脱的思想,只从现实的需要出发强调中美文化交流的重要性。然而,不同的国家和不同的民族在其历史发展的过程中,由于生产力的高低不可避免地导致经济、技术乃至政治制度、法律、文化等领域的参差不齐。所谓的经济全球化,穷富各国之间以及南北之间的差距不是被缩小而是在拉大。由于文化的差异、意识形态的

不同和战略利益的冲突，我们可以清楚地看到中美关系包括中美文化关系不可避免地变得十分敏感和微妙。在我看来，中美文化交流中最需要的是大学者和大思想家。美国是一个重商主义的国家，利益高于一切，文化也是按照资本逻辑运作。中国改革开放三十多年来以经济为中心，利益的趋势遮蔽了文化逻辑。今天我们最需要具有跨过历史、超越现实，能站在人类历史和文化的制高点上的大学者、大思想家，他们需要拿出睿智和良知去探寻更加公平合理的经济制度、更加完备健全的政治制度、更加开明公正的制度文化，这样的新文化将催生出人们对理想的不断追求和对未来的无限向往，最终造福于两国人民，造福于全人类。这是中美文化交流的出发点和努力的目标。

中美文化对话的背景和问题

祝东力
中国艺术研究院马克思主义文艺理论研究所副所长，研究员

冷战后历史可分为三个阶段：一、从1991年年底苏联解体开始，主题是全球化；二、从2001年"9·11"开始，除全球化主题，又加入反恐主题；三、从2008年美国金融危机开始，又加入世界经济衰退主题。第三阶段的危机和衰退可能正是前两个阶段的经济扩张和反恐开支的结果。这是中美文化对话的第一层时代背景。美国霸权由三个支柱构成，即高科技-军事霸权、美元——金融霸权、意识形态——话语霸权。在这三方面，美国都遇到了挑战或挫折。同时，尽管中国自身面临诸多难题和瓶颈，但综合国力上升，应当是一个长时段的历史性趋势。中美国力相对接近。这是第二层时代背景。中国是最大生产国，美国是最大消费国，因此 Niall Ferguson 提出"Chimerica"（中美国）概念。中美合作对于世界经济、政治具有重大意义。

傩与21世纪中国民间祭祀文化

刘祯
中国艺术研究院戏曲研究所所长，研究员

这是第三层时代背景。这些时代背景导致这一结论：中美文化对话、交流、合作具有前所未有的重要性。就中美文化关系而言，当前最大问题是彼此缺乏了解。美国方面不必说了。中国方面，尽管几十年来对美国表现出浓厚兴趣，但以主观投射居多，客观了解为少。例如，对美国的个人主义价值观，中国人往往从权利角度，而不是从责任角度理解，所谓责任，即为自己和社会负责。

傩，起源于中国远古驱逐法术和巫术，是原始宗教信仰的产物；是驱邪除疫、禳凶纳吉的一种历史悠久的祭祀仪式；是中国最古老、传统文化意蕴最深厚，也最具生命力的活态非物质文化遗产。它包括傩仪、傩戏、傩舞、傩俗等领域。傩、傩文化，不仅有其历史价值、文化价值和艺术价值，而且傩、傩仪、傩文化所体现出的千百年来民间百姓、族群一种精神的联系和凝聚力，对走向21世纪民间文化的构建和发展具有启示意义。也因此，对傩文化的重视、保护和研究，对全面、完整和深刻地认识中国传统文化、思想，尤其是民间草根思想文化的一脉相承具有积极的意义。剥离其裹在身上神秘、表层的"面具"，它所呈现的内容不仅丰富多彩，而且鲜活、生动，魅力无限，这是这种民间祭祀文化的生命力所在。

比如临武傩戏，俗称"神狮子"，历史悠久，传统有自，心口相传，形成一套完整的祭祀程序，由"许愿"和"还愿"两部分组成，其表现形式有傩仪、傩舞和傩戏，而很多时候这三者又是混融一体的，临武傩戏涵育多种民间艺术和音乐元素，弥漫着神秘的巫楚文化气息，在当地及周边广大地区有广泛的影响。同时，临武傩戏也是傩文化家族里一座待开垦的富矿。

20世纪80年代以来，我国对傩文化的发掘、抢救、保护和研究取得了丰硕的成果，进入21世纪，随着国家对非物质文化遗产保护工作的开展和重视，各地许多傩文化项目进入国家和省市"非遗"名录。于上世纪成立的中国傩戏学研究会专事傩戏、傩文化研究，聚集了国内外一大批专家学者，重视理论联系实际，重视田野考察与学术研讨结合，二十多年来与各地有关单位在十余个省、区举办了十多次大型国际学术研讨会，为中国傩戏研究作出了重要贡献。

中美文化交流中的传统表演艺术

王馗
中国艺术研究院戏曲研究所研究员

昆曲、粤剧、京剧、藏戏、皮影戏是列入"人类非物质文化遗产代表作名录"中的五项中国戏剧表演艺术形态，代表了中国传统戏剧在不同演进历程中各具特色的演剧体系。作为中华民族创造的文化艺术，它们亦因不同的方式走出中国，为人类所共同享有。在中美文化交流中，中国戏剧样式最初主要因族群移民历史和商业市场开发而为外域了知。建立在政府协作机制中的戏剧交流，进一步促使多元的中国传统戏剧艺术，以其特有的文化品格得以传播，并因此而保持更加稳定的传承系统。不过，随着文化艺术交流的渐趋深入，理性而客观的学术推广在政府和民间协作中的作用显得尤为重要。

随着经济全球化和社会现代化的不断加快，"地球村"已然不再只是一个文学和修辞意义上的比喻性概念，而是一个切切实实的当下现实。比如互联

用文化的意识调适发展的姿态

吴文科
中国艺术研究院曲艺研究所所长,研究员

网络的沟通方式与喷气飞机的交通便利,使得人类从未像今天这样相互亲近又相互依存;不同地域、种族、信仰与文化背景下的各类人群,愈来愈因时空距离的日益拉近而站在同一的历史场域中,并且因此而面临着更为一致的利益诉求与更加迫切的发展挑战。借用政治家们的话语,"和平与发展"确是我们时代的追求主题!

然而,环顾当今的世界,"地球村"的景象很不让人舒心:不同的意识形态、不同的国家利益、不同的宗教信仰和不同的生活方式之间,还存在着诸多的偏见、争论、对抗乃至战争……由此而引起的许多人道主义悲剧,包括不当发展带来的环境污染恶果,严重地影响着整个地球和人类的健康生存与持续发展。

造成这些悲剧与恶果的根源,主要是人类基于某种偏见、狭隘与贪婪秉性的野蛮表现。这就使对文明的追求和对文化的尊重,成为矫正野蛮并救赎人类的最好方式与途径。也从一个侧面印证了美国学者塞缪尔·亨廷顿(Samuel Huntington)于20世纪90年代初期提出的"文明冲突"理论(Clash of Civilization)的某种现实客观性。

由此,我们有理由为本次论坛所设定的话题框架即"文化的语境:地域·人类·历史"的学理价值及积极意义进行喝彩!因为,它给我们提供了通过文化视角思考人类发展的交流可能,同时也向我们昭示出这样一些通过文化的交流方式,增进人类文明而又智慧地生活的诸多思想方法与有益理念:

——在"全球化"和"现代化"的背景下,人类更应将"对话"和"共享"作为发展的主要追求,而非将"对抗"与"瓜分"作为生存的经营之道。在地球的"开发"史或者说人类的"进化"史上,某些对抗性手段可能推动了历史的发展与社会的进步;但在"全球化"和"现代化"的今天,不当的过度"开发"与愚蠢的盲目"进化",则有可能毁灭整个地球与人类。这就更加需要理性思想、文化姿态与美好情怀的引领,学会用文化的方式而非其他的手段解决人类面临的重大问题。

——生活在"地球村"里的人们,不应再将某些"人群"的眼前诉求,借助强权凌驾于整个"人类"的利益之上;而要站在历史的高度——为子孙后代着想,立足地球的实际——为全体人类着想,着眼持续的发展——为地球环境着想。

——解决人类发展的重大问题,需要全体人类的团结合作;实现人类的健康发展,有赖文明的创造进步,而非资源掠夺、技术封锁、经济制裁与军事要挟。人类作为"万物之灵",应当学会文化地生活,将文化的追求作为幸福的目标,而非将自身异化为可悲的经济动物、可笑的政治傀儡和可怕的军事机器。

地球因人类而拥有灿烂的文明,人类因文化而享有美好的生活。只有当我们明确了自身发展的真正目的,明白了自己所处的时代语境,我们才有可能走出各自的狭隘圈子,摒弃一己的思想偏见,实现人类的共同发展。

文化语境中的中国曲艺

田莉
中国艺术研究院曲艺研究所副所长,副研究员

作为中国传统的艺术,曲艺是颇具民间性质的表演艺术。它源自民间,发展于民间,一直活跃在民间,讲述老百姓自己的故事,显示出鲜明的民间文化性质和民间艺术精神。同时又和中国传统艺术一样,曲艺蕴含着中国文化精

神和中国艺术的基本精神。因此，相对于官方正统文化而言，中国曲艺属于民间文化范畴；相对于中国艺术主流的文人艺术而言，中国曲艺属于中国文化中非主流的艺术；与官方和文人的高雅艺术相比较，曲艺无疑是一种通俗艺术。尽管在某些人眼中曲艺不能登大雅之堂，但它却能把中国文化传统和民间生活融为一体，把民众的精神诉求和娱乐需要相结合。

与其他中国艺术一样，曲艺注重兴象与意趣的中国艺术精神，通俗易懂，娱情悦心，是中国民众主要的娱乐方式之一。千百年来，中国曲艺培育了中国人基本的艺术趣味和审美习惯。甚至在文化教育并不普及的时代，它更是民众最初的学习方式。

曲艺是中国民众延续了千百年的精神生活方式与文化娱乐方式。中国各阶层民众喜爱曲艺艺术，把听书听曲当作日常生活的一部分。在许多中国人的心目中，与曲艺联系在一起的，是乡音乡情的亲切感，是对家乡抹不去的印象。可以说，曲艺不仅有着独特的艺术魅力，还是一种独特文化的记忆。

城市发展与戏剧发展

刘彦君
中国艺术研究院话剧研究所所长，研究员

在当代中国，文化的建设发展和日益加速的城市化进程之间的关系正变得日益紧密。戏剧艺术由于其自身的社会性和公众性质，与城市的关系也变得愈发密切。我们可以很容易地论证出戏剧对于城市发展的重要性来，也可以很容易地找到戏剧演出对一个城市的物质进步和精神成长的见证。剧场作为城市中一个具有交流和沟通作用的公众场所，能够汇聚一个城市的文化风情、人文图景、精彩瞬间，能够汇聚这块土地上的人们共同的情感、意志、想象力和创造力。历史精神和时代愿望，自强不息、开放宽容的情怀和信念，都能从这个城市的剧场中找到，并最终为来自不同城市的人们所接受和认同。实践正在日益决定着戏剧与城市发展之间的关系与走向。在当代中国，随着近年来城市化进程的加速，随着戏剧在社会生活中重要性的逐步提高，全国各类演出场所的建设也越来越多。一些大城市，如上海、北京两地，率先仿照着纽约百老汇、伦敦西区、日本涩谷等模式，开始了建立中国城市戏剧园区的探索。本文分别从剧场、非剧场、网络与资金这几个近年来出现的新现象等方面论述了戏剧与城市之间的关系。指出随着城市建设的进一步发展，戏剧文化与城市发展之间的关系必将越来越紧密，其前景也一定会越来越光明。

阿瑟·米勒与当代中国话剧

宋宝珍
中国艺术研究院话剧研究所副所长，研究员

回溯中美戏剧文化交流，我们无法忘怀一位对于中国当代戏剧颇具影响的美国剧作家阿瑟·米勒（Arthur Miller, 1915—2005）。这不仅是因为他曾两度踏上过中国的土地，与北京人民艺术剧院有过良好的合作，还因为中国人喜欢他真诚的个性、顽强的生命力、敏锐的社会洞察力，及其剧作所蕴含的深刻哲理。

1978年9月18日至10月12日，阿瑟·米勒偕妻自费来华访问，游历了京、沪、广和桂林等地。这是中国结束"文革"后，首次迎接美国戏剧界的朋友。当时，米勒对当代中国一无所知，而中国人对美国戏剧也相当隔膜。米勒在北京观摩了《丹心谱》、《蔡文姬》、《彼岸》等戏剧演出，与曹禺、英若诚等就戏剧问题展开讨论。在上海，他见到了著名导演黄佐临。回国后，米勒在1979年

3月于《大西洋月刊》上发表长文《在中国》,大谈他的访华观感。他说:"中国人在剧场里的喜怒哀乐,同我们是一样的。东西方文化固然很不相同,但是产生这种文化的心却完全是一样的。"

1981年,经由黄佐临导演,上海人民艺术剧院在上海演出了《炼狱》,演出时更名《萨勒姆的女巫》,首轮连演五十多场。1983年春,米勒携妻再度来华,为北京人艺亲自导演《推销员之死》。5月7日,此剧在首都剧场首演轰动,演到七十多场还欲罢不能。

而今,阿瑟·米勒及其剧作对中国人来讲不再陌生。2002年5月19日,王晓鹰导演的《萨勒姆的女巫》由中国国家话剧院在京首演。2006年5月,此剧在京复演。2006年12月,上海话剧艺术中心演出此剧。2005年2月北京人艺复排《推销员之死》,2012年3月再度复排此剧。

摄影中的"看法"、"关系"与一种比较研究的方式

李树峰
中国艺术研究院摄影艺术研究所所长,研究员

摄影作为记录和表达手段,位于技术与艺术的交融处,核心内容即"看法"——看世界的方法。看世界的方法,以摄影者介入生活的身份和机位为前提,以叙事中的语态、时态选择为表现方式,以作品编辑方式为归纳手段,进入传播过程。"看法"的本质是对可能进入镜头的现实事物之间关系的认识。摄影的文化价值来源于"关系","关系"即意义。"关系"有两种,一种是摄影活动过程中人的关系,包括拍摄者、被拍摄者和观众三者之间的关系;另一种是在将三维现场空间转化为二维平面空间过程中必须处理的信息点之间的关系。前一种关系决定着机位高低、距离远近和作品感染力强弱;后一种关系决定着一幅作品的认识价值高低和艺术效果的好坏。

针对前一种关系,我们提倡的是拍摄者、被拍摄者和观众三者之间的平等与尊重,摒弃傲慢与偏见,摄影者秉持真诚之心关注和凝视他人,把目击到的事物转化为具有客观性的图像。针对后一种关系,我们特别需要考虑的是选取信息点并处理其中关系的问题。即照片中信息点之间的关系与现实世界中相应事物之间关系的比对,发现这两处关系的相同点与不同点,传给社会,在读者那里发挥启智和通情的作用。要使拍摄更有文化价值,我们不得不在发现信息点和处理信息点之间关系上下工夫,要有意识地用取景器的四条边框勒住有效信息(常常分出主要信息和次要信息,这是一个矛盾的两个方面),并在现场中逼迫信息点之间发生关系,利用构图和景深控制,焦点、瞬间选取等手段,把信息点之间的关系展开,并且能够用言语表述其主要内容。做到这一点,生存在真实性和艺术性之间、文字和图像之间的照片,就能进入文化传播,也就是说,其文化价值生成了。

中华礼乐文明、礼仪之邦的历史与现代意义

项阳
中国艺术研究院音乐研究所研究员

中华民族的文化传统渗透着礼乐文化的基因,如此被称之为礼乐文明、礼仪之邦。本文对周公制礼作乐以来的礼乐文明之内涵进行辨析,探讨当下学界对礼乐认知的误区,把握礼乐与礼制、礼俗仪式中相须为用,礼乐文化是中国传统文化中乐之国家意义的代表。从乐的本体视角与礼的类分对应,探求中华礼乐文明、礼仪之邦传统延续,重建礼乐体系之可能与可行性意义,使传统礼乐观念以其实在的表现融入中华现代文明之中。

文化多样性认同与文化交流融合

郑长铃
中国艺术研究院文化发展战略研究中心副主任，研究员

当今世界，文化（狭义的文化概念）发展被经济、政治的发展裹挟着，相伴而显现的是其独立品质的丧失。

文化本来就如空气自在存续着，并在人们生活的时空中，自然地显示着其行为及价值取向诸等（广义的文化概念）。随着社会的发展，文化逐渐被对象化、分化，甚至被作为商品、产业化……于是强权政治和经济寡头就很自然地将自己的文化及其价值观兜售给别国他人，世界文化趋同在所难免。

基于这样的现实，联合国教科文组织通过的《世界文化多样性宣言》（2001），已经充分认识到并明确肯定了文化多样性对于人类的今天和未来发展的意义；随后颁布的《保护和促进文化表现形式多样性公约》（2005），指出："维护文化多样性将保持乃至创造一个更为多姿多彩的世界。文化多样性使人类有了更多的选择，施展和提高自身的能力，并形成价值观，进而成为各社区、各民族和各国可持续发展的一股主要推动力。在民主、宽容、社会公正以及各民族和文化间相互尊重的环境中，繁荣和发展文化多样性对于维护地方、国家和国际层面的和平与安全是不可或缺的。要在承认文化多样性，认识到人类是一个统一的整体和发展文化间交流的基础上，开展广泛的团结互助。"

公约是共同遵守的约定，认同是基础。本文拟通过以下几点的梳理——文化多样性认同与维护世界文化多样性，中国在维护世界文化多样性方面的努力，中国在促进世界各国各民族文化交流方面的作为来说明问题，并提出：文化多样性认同基础上的交流融合才是人类文化健康发展之途径。

Looking into Culture Exchange from the Interactive Tour on Sino-US Arts-with This is Just to Say and Heroes as the cases

Wang Yichuan

Professor and Dean of School of Arts, Peking University

Differences among cultural context, region and so forth shall be taken into account when advancing Sino-US cultural exchange, which can be clarified by two cases, that are This is Just to Say (This Is Just to Say, 1934), a poem of American poet-William Carlos Williams (William Carlos Williams, 1883-1963) and Heroes-the Ancient-Costume & Martial-Arts directed by Zhang Yimou (a Chinese director). Of these two cases, the first one was introduced into China thirty years ago, but could not be understood by Chinese people at the beginning. Although, such non-understanding was caused by language environment in the context like connotations of words and expressions of poem, it was also related to social context appearing and personal life situation. At that time, Chinese readers lacked of understanding on American daily life or only knew little, and they also lacked of the same daily life situation themselves, therefore, it was difficult to form sympathy resonance; however, the obstacles for reading and understanding the poem became smaller and smaller with deeper open degree of China and change of Chinese people's daily life, so the understanding trended to smoothness. The latter one was on in America in 2004, which obtained high box-office. The reason for this is that America and China were both in the situation of violent and unrest "Clash of Civilizations" after "cold war", so war and peace became focus concerned both by the public of China and America. Therefore understanding differences among cultural context, life situation, etc. were helpful for boosting culture exchange.

The Contemporary China In and Out of Tradition: Political Leadership, Foreign Policy, and Their Chineseness

Shi Yinhong

Professor of School of International Studies, Renmin University of China

There have been several profound features embedded in the contemporary Chinese political leadership, all having their roots in the Chinese centuries-long traditions or the modern/contemporary creative practice, together with their shaping impacts upon China's foreign policy or remarkable reflections in her external behavior. They are: reforms inherently differentiated; central idea of "maintenance", notion of "biological circle governing universe", paradox in the question of equality, the emphasis on morality, overwhelmingly domestic function of foreign policy, firm belief in the Chineseness per sue and its

Dean and professor of the School of Art and Communication, Beijing Normal University

Zhou Xing

Protection and Development: Difficulties in the Cultural Development of Chinese Films

overwhelming importance, and political prudence in the perennial context of "Strong China, Weak China." In particular, the last one is a very significant perennial basic theme since reform and opening up for China's domestic and foreign policy, a theme for both the Chinese ourselves and others.

A truly idealized film industry shall be established based on a perfect market system and the protection of local films. The favorable market system is the standard of a market, but Chinese films are still falling behind foreign countries. Moreover, the cultural influence of good Chinese local films is insufficient, so a certain protection is necessary to protect the good local films from being shielded by Hollywood. However, it turns out to be that the good films are in short while some films that should not be protected are protected, giving rise to the antagonistic psychology on domestic films of the audience. Films are essentially cultural products, and the problems in the market demand and cultural psychological reaction of the products shall be profoundly considered. Therefore, a difficulty lies in front of Chinese films that whether the films shall exist in the cultural level or the market level. Chinese films are increasingly threatened by the market, so pursuit in market is leading to the indifference on the cultural character of films, which conversely also threatens the existence of films. It is inevitable to prevent the conflict between the market and cultural pursuit, but the film market that deviates from the culture will necessarily affect the existence of domestic films, sooner or later. Chinese films are lively but lacking introspections on thoughts and humanity. A reflect on these problems is necessary.

We have to think about the cultural reality and future prospects of Chinese films. It is inevitable that local movies may lack the cultural character and the realism spirit may dominate the market. However, films are precious because they touch people's endogenous and psychological sensibility and heart, which cannot be replaced by technologies. Therefore, only the inherent spirit of the films is the important premise. The idea of market-only shall be corrected for the long-term development of Chinese films. Both the local market and Chinese films in the world film festival need to promote Chinese own spirit and culture, otherwise Chinese market has to share the benefits with

Cultural Diversity and International Cultural Trade

Li Xiaomu

Vice President of Beijing International Studies University, and President of National Institute of Cultural Development

other countries and Chinese films will not be recognized by the film world, regardless of the domestic tickets.

As the world is entering a new era in which resources are shared globally and boundaries between cultures become increasingly blurry, any country is unavoidably involved in increasingly complex and plural competition, and the cultures of countries, while going abroad, are also attracted and impacted by foreign cultures. Developing cultural trade may minimize the impact of foreign cultures on the domestic cultural market of China, and maximally weaken ideological conflicts between China and other countries.

Like water, culture has a peculiar penetrative force. Cultural products and services carry values and lifestyles, have more social value than commercial value, and compared with other types of trade, have a subtle influence on the consumers of importing countries in such aspects as ideology. It is therefore important to design and produce more cultural products and services which are creative and meet consumer preferences, to foster domestic and international cultural markets, to find a position that the Chinese culture is due to have in the global cultural and economic ecosphere, and to develop more people's identification with the Chinese culture, so that the Chinese culture blends harmoniously with diverse cultures of the world and the goal of stabilizing China's core values, enhancing the national pride and strengthening cultural cohesion is attainable.

Cultural Reflection on International Financial Crisis and Competition of Development Mode

Qi Yongfeng

Director of Academic Committee of the Institute of Cultural Development of Communication University of China, Professor

The financial tsunami triggered by the U.S. subprime mortgage crisis hit the United States, Europe and other developed economies in the West, leading to a global recession. The cause of financial crisis is that the western financial system led by the United States is defective viewing from the phenomenon, but the deeper reason lies on the lack of western civilization. This global financial and economic crisis following the world economic crisis in the 1930s, not only has changed the direction of the world economy, but also has impacted the future of the world geopolitical and civilization development pattern significantly. As "American-style capitalism falls down from the altar", and the rise of China, India, Brazil, Russia and other emerging market economies, the pattern and development model of world civilization have been irreversibly shifted from the United States-led western civilization mode into a new era of "the coexistence of diverse civilizations and competition of multiple development models" actually. Under the conditions that the international situation has undergone profound changes and in face of "European Debt Crisis" and the ever-turbulent world, it has become a major issue which cannot be evaded on how to seek common ground while reserving differences, form a wide range of cultural identity and promote the construction of a new international economic, political order by forging consensus through cultural dialog and reconstruction of cultural values, so as to avoid the "financial crisis" and the "clash of civilizations" which have occurred and may occur again, and maintain human society in sustainable development and prosperity based on coexistence and harmonious development of multiple civilizations. As the two largest economies in the world, China and the United States bear a heavy historical responsibility in this regard.

The Cultural Tension of American and Chinese Films: Conflicts and Integration

Chen Xuguang

Head and professor of the Institute of Film, Television and Theater Peking University of the School of Arts Peking University

The film is an important carrier for the construction of the national cultural image and cultural soft power. As a giant and power in films, America has vigorously exported its films and culture to the outside world for more than a century. In recent years, American films are constantly adjusting their subjects and themes to adapt to Chinese market, a huge film market.

China has experienced a constant rise of films and rapid development of the film industry. However, since the "Feb. 28", American films have unceasingly put on increasingly greater pressure on Chinese film market. On one hand, Chinese films shall learn from the mature management system of American film industry and lead the way of production of categorized production; and on the other hand, Chinese films shall adhere to Chinese culture and build and spread the cultural image of their own. Based on the adherence, Chinese films shall be bold to learn and borrow from the culture of American films.

The success of the Painted Skin Resurrection, a recent magic film of China, is a thought-provoking phenomenon. It presents folk and non-mainstream edge culture, the "ghost culture" or the "evil spirit and immortal culture" on fox ghosts and goblins, in movies and makes it a "mass culture"; and meanwhile, it combines many elements of American magic films. With the success of the Painted Skin Resurrection as a case, we can profoundly think about how Chinese films should learn from America (the film producer-oriented film production management system), how Chinese and American culture conflict and integrate with each other in films, how Chinese films should adhere to Chinese culture and be open to the outside culture and the strategies for the film production.

The new-style, harmonious and vigorous world culture can only healthily develop in the conflicts and integration of cultures.

Transformation of Education, Publishing and Society
Abstract:

Xiao Dongfa

The head and professor of Modern Publishing Research Institute of News and Communications College of Peking University

I. History Review-Transformation of Education, Publishing and Society

1. Private writings, private collection, no social distinctions in teaching and social transformation in the Spring and Autumn.

2. Modern transformation of publishing and education, and social transformation in late Qing Dynasty.

3. Comparison on different destiny and social function of art of printing between east and west.

4. Interactive relationship between publishing and society.

II. Afterthoughts on Experience-Several Inspirations and Discussion on Law.

1. About transformation on society, culture and publishing.

2. Technology going ahead of productivity and production relations

3. Discussion on laws of social transformation.

III. Self-examination on Lessons-How to Construct Culture Power

1. Education and publishing at the beginning of last century Zhang Yuanji and Cai Yuanpei.

2. Two-time transfer on focus within 60 years of new China (seeking facts instead of false, not superstitious about numbers, no longer blindly changing production relationship, not eager for a quick access, not only focusing on hardware construction, but also on soft power.)

3. Intending to develop the country, giving education but without others.

4. Focusing on publishing, improving the national reading rate and citizen quality.

Attaching Importance to the Role of New Media in the Trans-Cultural Transmission

Tang Runhua

Head of the Sino-Foreign Media Development Strategy Research Center, Journalism Institute of Xinhua News Agency

In addition to the problem of ideology, the trans-cultural transmission was also encountered with obstacles in geography, language and technologies. Due to these causes, the trans-cultural transmission had only a few platforms and channels, which seriously restricted the extent, depth and effect of the transmission. Currently, the new media under rapid development, particularly the social media, is eliminating these obstacles and provides an unprecedented opportunity for the smooth and harmonious exchange among different cultures.

Technically advanced new media terminals are becoming a more and more important platform for trans-cultural transmission. In addition to the traditional PC, smart phones and tablets are increasing in a geometric ratio in the world. They are convenient and portable of complete function, which significantly benefit the trans-cultural transmission. The rapid popularity of these new media terminals enables the diversified channels for the trans-cultural transmission and exerts wide influence on the crowd.

The social media of vigorous development provides a great exchange platform for the trans-cultural transmission. For example, the 300 million users of Sina Weibo in China also include the foreign embassy, foreign media, international organizations and important foreign political figures and men of distinction such as Mr. Rudd, the former premier of Australia, who can conduct wide and in-depth communication with ordinary Chinese people. At the same time, many Chinese people and media register accounts in Twitter and Facebook to communicate with foreign netizens.

Along with the constant development of intelligent translation, the new media is trying to overcome the obstacle of language, the major obstacle in the trans-cultural transmission, to erect a bridge of communication among users of different characters and languages around the world.

The theories and debates on the transformation of China's cultural values have been part of the history of cultural studies. Some critics argued that the development of Chinese cultural values has remained to a remarkable degree stationary even since Tang Dynasty, her glory time (For instance, H. G. Wells Outline of History). Other studies, however, addressed that the construction of modern Chinese cultural values which is crystalized into "integrity" is in large

The Civilization of the West and Construction of Chinese Cultural Integrity Values: from 1911 Revolution to "China Goes Global"

Liu Chen

Director and Associate professor of the Cross-culture Research Center of English School of Beijing Foreign Studies University

part a result of the communication with the world, above all, the Western civilization.

Focusing on writings of leading Chinese scholars and important official documents of China, the study probes is tropically into the construction of Chinese cultural integrity values from Modern China to China under the context of globalization and discusses the core spirits interpreted as national identity by Chinese people from generations to generations to date. The study finds that the transformation of Chinese cultural ideas, in particular, that from Reform and Opening-up launched in 1978 on going primarily is the outcome by the touch of the active communication and exchange with the outside world. Also, the paper concludes the key elements that are essentially the same between Chinese cultural values and that of the Western culture.

Four Major Problems Demanding Prompt Solution in Dance Exchanges between China and Foreign Countries.

The History of Films and Modernization

Ding Yaping

Research Fellow and Head of the Film and Television Institute, Chinese National Academy of Arts

The assessment system for the history of modern films consists of renaissance of films, economic development, social development and the development of the history of films itself, as well as the quality of scholars on the history of films, innovation of the history of films, materials on the history of films, history of images and influence of the history of films. In recent years, the study on the history of films has seen a broader global vision, while the history of films and the cultural concept are constantly developing. The role of historical materials, oral history and some other historiography problems beyond the current situation and strategies have drawn great attention of the history of films. It is as emergent as saving precious jewels and drawings from the fire to collect historical materials of films write the history of films and study on the history of images. The historical studies in different environments show the social responsibilities and tasks as well as innovations. The universalism will finally replace various kinds of realism in the new society and context and become the inevitable trend of the modernization of the history of films.

Challenge or Opportunity: the Influence of the Import of Hollywood Enhanced Movies on Chinese Films

Zhao Weifang
Research Fellow and Deputy Head of the Film and Television Research Institute, Chinese National Academy of Arts

Starting from 2012, China will allow the entry of additional 14 3-D or large-screen IMAX movies per year from the US. Speciously because of this, the market share of domestic movies declined in the first half of the year. However, as a matter of fact, importing Hollywood blockbusters will bring more opportunities than challenges to the Chinese film industry.

First, in regions where the national film industry has a solid base, the entry of foreign commercial films, despite their sometimes menacing manner, generally would not bring qualitative impact to national movies, as is the case with the Korea. After years of development, the Chinese film industry has gained a strong foothold, and thus importing more US movies will not generate much impact on domestic movies.

Second, in the first half of 2012, China's domestic film industry suffered a downturn, mainly because of the lukewarm market response to aesthetic homogenization in recent years especially in 2011.

Third, the increase in Hollywood enhanced movies will help expand the Chinese film market, which is an opportunity rather than impact for domestic movies. It will also help steer the domestic film market on a high-end path, stimulating a high-end atmosphere for the creation of Chinese movies, especially for 3D movies.

Four Major Problems Demanding Prompt Solution in Dance Exchanges between China and Foreign Countries

Ou Jianping
Research Fellow and Director of Dance Research Institute, Chinese National Academy of Arts

Throughout the ages, the prosperity of Chinese dance has always been the rich fruits of exchanges between China and foreign countries. As a visiting scholar to 21 foreign countries for over 40 times in the past 26 years, and as a consultant to the China tours of over 100 dance companies from over 20 foreign countries for the past 17 years, I strongly believe that in conducting the dance exchanges between China and foreign countries while carrying out our national strategies of "Promoting and Prospering the Chinese Culture on a Larger Scale" and "Chinese Culture Going Abroad," four major problems are shouting for prompt solution through a systematic plan and relevant measures, and should take advantage of the steady growth of Chinese economy:1.There has always been a severe unfavorable balance between the Chinese and foreign dance imports and exports; 2. The multi-level funding system for our Chinese government, enterprises and individuals has not been issued; 3.There has been no long-term scheme of inviting contemporary dance teachers from foreign countries, although this western style has greatly benefited all the Chinese styles of folk, classical, ballet, modern-contemporary, ballroom and musical theater dances; 4. To develop China into a "Powerful Ballet Country" has merely been a beautiful blue print in our dream.

From Guo Mingda to Shen Wei – the Reverse Export in the Sino-US Exchange on Dance

JIang Dong

Vice director and Research Fellow of Dance Research Institute, Chinese National Academy of Arts

Despite with a dance history of several thousand years, China is only a new arrival in the worldwide popular modern dance. The emergence and development of the modern dance in China is directly related to the Sino-US exchange on dance.

In 1940s, Mr. Guo Mingda, who is now in his 90s, had learned the modern dance from many American masters of modern dance such as Alwin Nicholai in New York and some other places, as the first Chinese people learning modern dance in America. He returned to China in mid-1950s. However, at that time, he could not give play to his specialty though he was a dancer of aspirations and ambitions.

After reform and opening up, China has experienced a great change. In late 1980s, Guangdong Province of China cooperated with American Dance Festival (ADF) and invited six famous American dancers of modern dance to Guangzhou to train the first batch of Chinese professional modern dancers, including Shen Wei, who is now very popular in the modern dance of New York. In the opening dance for 2008 Beijing Olympic, Shen Wei presented the modern dance of Chinese characteristics and his own superb talents to the world.

Chinese modern dance has seen a historical turn in the half a century, from the absorption to export. Chinese dancers have won respect from international audience based their innate talents and acquired advantages. In addition to unremitting efforts of Chinese dancers, the frequent and effective Sino-US exchange on dance also significantly contributes to the development.

The unification of West Germany and East Germany in 1989, the dissolution of the former Soviet and the end of the Cold War between the East and the West opened

The Modern Arts of China toward Cross-culture

Wang Duanting

Research Fellow and Head of the Research Room for Foreign Fine Arts of the Art Research Institute, Chinese National Academy of Arts

the new era of the world politic history. Following the release of the ideological opposition and the issue of the International Trade Treaty, the world entered a brand-new era of economic globalization. On December 10, 2001, China became a former member of the WTO (World Trade Organization), as a result, the economy of China becomes the organic integral part of the world economy.

Economic globalization is the unprecedented living style in the human history and a kind of brand-new survival experience to Chinese. Economic globalization has brought us not only opportunities for the social development of China but also challenges to our survival capabilities. The issue of the development of the world civilization resulting from economic globalization is a brand-new topic to all human beings and grants Chinese the opportunity and right for the first time to equally participate in and joint explore the survival and development route of human together with all the nations in the world.

In the times of globalization, the Chinese artists and the artists of the other countries in the world stand at the start line; those Chinese artists that express the common aspiration and universal concern of human with extraordinary wisdom and unique creativity have quickly stood on the present international art stage. Globalization not only brings the present Chinese artists with brand-new art values but also provides them with rich art languages. After the "Political Pop" and "Cynical Realism" in the 1990s, the present art of China that either expresses the life significance of the Chinese or conforms to the common aesthetic interest of all human beings springs up sorrowfully and goes toward maturity.

Cross-culture means there will never be barriers between individual artists and the world, indicates the independence of and mutual equality among individuals. It respects the life value of individuals, encourages individual creativity and advertises the unity of human cultural values. The author thinks that cross-culture is the future of human civilization.

I. Origins of Chinese and US Arts

Located on the easternmost side of Eurasia, China is one of the cradles of Oriental civilization. Due to its self-sufficiency in social development, the Chinese culture and arts were long in a stage of tranquility. By contrast, U.S. arts originated in Western civilization, and social openness and

Difference and Integration: China-US Cooperation and Exchange in the Art of Painting

Liu Wanming
Vice President of Fine Arts Creation Institute, Chinese National Academy of Arts

the extrovert character of the nation made the art style of realism soon to the fore and proceed to become part of the nation.

II. Difference in Aesthetics

Aesthetic ideas in Chinese arts is connected with ethics, likening beauty to good, and the process of art creation emphasizes the cultivation of moral integrity and the improvement of spirituality. US arts, by contrast, understand and appreciate beauty from the reality of natural science, likening beauty to truth and pursuing the artistic reproduction of life and the formalist beauty in line with science. In painting, specifically, Chinese painting is close to music and poetry, which is symbolic; US painting approximates novel, which is realistic. Therefore, Chinese painting approaches good by virtue of spiritual sublimation, while US painting instructs people to behave morally through cognition of life.

III. Integration of Chinese and US Arts

The ultimate focus of human art is man and the relationship between nature, earth and man. The openness of and exchange between worldwide cultures has made art tend to be diversely free in form. Mr. Xu Beihong, the father of Chinese modern art of painting, pointed out in the 1940s that fine arts should be loyal to reality and divorce from reality leads to empty verbiage. Scientific genius lies in precision, so does artistic genius; the lasting appeal is like deduction in science, which, if not precise, is superficial and makes it impossible to connect one to another part of it. Proficiency in image makes it not that hard to acquire romantic charm. The call from the past century is not outdated and still applies to modern Chinese painting. The truthfulness of painting in the US, where science is developing rapidly, offers us a great chance for us to learn and blend. Science and art are not in contradiction to each other; they are of harmonious unity. Though US painting had always drawn close to European art, with worldwide art integrating, many Americans came into contact with Oriental art thoughts and became aware of the importance of the meaning of painting. They broke reality, underscored the purity of art and shift their focus on nature, tapping into the greatness of nature from the human perspective; some of them, much more influenced by China's Laozi and Zhuangzi and their Taoism, have become a mainstream of modern art in the US. It is pleasing notice that the Chinese have seen US art of Chinese flavor and the Americans have seen Chinese art of American style. The integration of Chinese and US arts will lead human art to consummate truth, good and beauty.

Discussion about the Starting Point and the Target to Achieve of the Cultural Exchange between China and US

Chen Feilong
Director and Research Fellow of Marxist Literature and Art Theory Research Institute of China Academy of Arts

The cultural exchange between China and US actually is a sensitive and difficult topic. This is because, in the memory of history, the relationship between China and US is very complicated; in particular, in the 20th Century, the two countries had a series of historical entanglements, which have been puzzling people until now; however, in the present world, the two countries have many disputes and troubles in economy and politics, which are hard to be solved. As a result, some people attempt to find out cultural differences through ideological comparison to solve the hard issue of the cultural exchange between China and US, some want to avoid the differences in social system and ideology so as to seek for the development of the cultural exchange between China and US and some attempt to stress the importance of the cultural exchange between China and US only from the actual demand with the practical and unconventional thought. Nevertheless, different countries and nations are inevitably uneven in economy, technology and even in politic system, law, culture, etc. due to different productivities; in terms of the so-called economic globalization, the gap between the poor countries and the rich countries and between the South and the North does not narrow but expand. Because of cultural differences, ideological differences and strategic interest conflict, it can be seen clearly that the relationship between China and US, including cultural exchange, inevitably becomes very sensitive and delicate. To the author, great scholars and great ideologists are the most needed for the cultural exchange between China and US. As a country of mercantilism, US regards its interest above everything else and its culture operates on basis of capital logic. For more than 30 years since its Reform and Opening-up, China has been focusing on economy with the trend to interest hiding cultural logic. Today, what we need the most is the great scholars and great ideologists who can stride over history, overstep the reality and stand at the commanding height of the history and culture of human. They need to spend their wit and wisdom and intuitive knowledge to seek for more fair and reason economic system, more perfect and sounder politic system, more enlightened and impartial institutional culture. Such new culture, without doubt, will result in the continuous pursuit of people to ideals and their unlimited wishes to the future and will finally bring benefit to the two nations and all the human beings. This is the starting point and target for the cultural exchange between China and US.

Background and Problems of the Cultural Dialogue between China and US

Zhu Dongli

Vice director and Research Fellow of Marxist Literature and Art Theory Research Institute of China Academy of Arts

The history after the Cold War is classified into three stages: the first stage started from 1991 where the former Soviet was dissolved and had the topic of globalization; the second stage started from the September 11 Event in 2011 and had the topic of anti-terrorism in addition globalization; the third stage started from the Financial Crisis of US in 2008 and had one more topic of world economic recession. Possibly, the crisis and depression at the third stage originated from the economic expansion and anti-terrorism expenditure at the first two stages. This is the first times background for the cultural dialogue between China and US. The hegemony of US consists of three backbones, i.e. hi-tech-military hegemony, the US Dollars-financial hegemony and the ideology-speech hegemony. In these three aspects, US has encountered challenges or setbacks. Meanwhile, although without many difficulties and bottleneck problems, the rise of the national comprehensive strength of China should be a historic trend of long term. The national power of China is approaching to that of US, which is the second times background. China is the largest production country while US is the largest consumption country; therefore, Niall Ferguson brings forward the concept of "Chimerica". The cooperation between China and US is very significant to the economy and politics of the world, which is the third times background. These times backgrounds result in one conclusion that the dialogue, exchange and cooperation between China and US have unprecedented importance. At present, in terms of the cultural relationship between China and US, the largest problem is that both parties are short of understanding. Let alone US, in China, although people have been interested in US for decades, they are more subjective other objective. For example, regarding the value of individualism, the Chinese often understand it from right rather than responsibility. The responsibility aforesaid refers to being responsible for oneself and society.

Originating from China's ancient ejection spell and witchcraft, nuo is a product of primitive religion beliefs; a time-honored traditional rituals for driving out evil spirits, plague and fierce and bringing luck in; and also a China's most ancient and most vital living intangible cultural heritage with most profound traditional culture implication. It covers areas like nuo ceremony, nuo opera, nuo dance, nuo customs, etc. Nuo and nuo culture not only have historical

Nuo and China's Folk Sacrifice Culture in 21st Century

Liu Zhen

The head and Research Fellow of Opera Research Institute of Chinese National Academy of Arts

value, culture value and art value, but also the emotional association and cohesion of people in the folk and ethnic group in a period in history embodied by nuo, nuo ceremony and nuo culture would be an embarrassment to construction and development of folk culture moving forwards to 21st century, therefore, attaching great attention to and protection of nuo culture has an positive significance for overall, complete and profound recognition on Chinese traditional culture and thought, especially for remaining connected with grass-roots' ideology and culture in the folk. Peeling off mystery wrapped on the body and the "mask" on the surface layer, it displays not only rich, but also alive and vivid contents with infinite charm, which is just the source of vitality of sacrificial culture in the folk.

For instance, Linwu Nuo Opera, commonly known as "Lion of God", has a long history and tradition and has been passed on from generation to generation, with a complete sacrifice procedure formed which is constituted by "wishing" and "redeeming a wish". Linwu Nuo Opera is manifested in nuo ceremony, nuo dance and nuo opera, however, those three forms are mixed into one sometimes. Containing many elements of folk art and music while diffusing with mysterious ambience of Witch Culture of the State of Chu, Linwu Nuo Opera impacts the local and wide area around extensively. Meanwhile, it is also a rich ore to be ploughed in the nuo culture family.

Since 1980s, our country has made great achievement on exploring, rescuing, protecting and researching on nuo culture; entering the 21st century, many nuo culture projects in various regions have been listed in the national, provincial and municipal intangible cultural heritage directories with unfolding and attaching great attentions to protection of intangible cultural heritage by the state. The Research Society of China's Nuo Opera Theory established in the last century engages in research on nuo opera and nuo culture, and has gathered a large number of experts and scholars at home and abroad. The Research Society focuses on linking theory with practice, and field study combing with academic discussion, having made an important contribution to research on China's nuo opera.

Kunqu Opera, Cantonese Opera, Beijing Opera, Tibetan Opera and the shadow play are listed as the five performing arts of Chinese opera in the "Human Beings Intangible

Traditional Performing Arts in the Sino-US Cultural Exchange

Wang Kui

Research Fellow of the Opera Research Institute, Chinese National Academy of Arts

Cultural Heritage Representative Work", which represent the opera system of their own unique features in the different evolution stages of Chinese traditional opera. These cultural arts created by Chinese nations have stepped to the world stage in different ways and been jointly enjoyed by all the people around the world. In the Sino-US cultural exchange, Chinese opera of different styles become known by the foreign world due to the history of group immigrants and development of the commercial market. The exchange on opera under the governmental coordination has further facilitated the promotion of Chinese traditional operatic arts based on their unique cultural characters and therefore maintained a stable imparting system. However, along with the deepening exchange on culture and arts, the rational and objective academic promotion is playing an extremely important role in the governmental and non-governmental coordination.

Adjusting the Posture of Development with Cultural Awareness

Wu Wenke

Director of Research Institute, Chinese National Academy of Arts

With the accelerating economic globalization and social modernization, the "Global Village" is no longer just a figurative concept in literary and rhetorical sense, but a definite reality. The Internet and jet aircraft, for instance, have allowed people to be closer to and more independent on each other than ever before; groups of people in different geographical, ethnic, faith and cultural context are now standing in the same historical domain because of the shortened temporal and spatial distance, thereby having more consistent interest demands and facing more urgent development challenges. To put it in political words, "peace and development" is the theme of our times!

However, looking around the world today, we may find the Global Village far from palatable: widespread prejudices, controversies, confrontations, or even wars, still exist between different ideologies, different national interests, different religious beliefs and different lifestyles, giving rise to many humanitarian tragedies such as the environmental pollution caused by irrational development that poses great threat to the planet and the health, survival and sustainable development of human.

The root cause of these tragedies and consequences is the human's barbaric behavior based on some kind of prejudice, narrow-mindedness and the greedy nature. Therefore, the pursuit for civilization and the respect for culture become the best approach to the rectification of savage and the redemption of mankind. Such tragedies and consequences have also, in one way, reflected the objectivity of the theory of "clash of civilizations" proposed by American scholar Samuel Huntington in early 1990s.

As a result, we have every reason to applaud for the theoretical value and the positive significance of the forum themed Cultural Context: Geography • Human • History. The forum allows us to reflect on the development of human from a cultural perspective, and reveals to us some useful thoughts and concepts to promote human civilization and live a life of wisdom through cultural exchanges:

— In the context of globalization and modernization, we human beings should take "dialogue" and "sharing" as the main pursuit for development, rather than take "confrontation" and "carving up" as the approach to survival. In the "development" history of the Earth or in other words, the "evolutionary" history of human, some confrontational means might have promoted historical development and social progress. However, in the present era featuring globalization and modernization, excessive "development" and blind "evolution" may destroy the entire Earth and humankind. Thus, it is necessary to learn to address the major issues faced by the mankind in a civilized approach and with rational thinking, a cultural posture and sympathetic feelings.

— People living in the Global Village should no longer allow the supremacy of the immediate demands of some particular group over the overall interests of the human. Instead, they should take a historical stance for the benefits of future generations, base their behaviors on the actual situation of the Earth for the sake of all mankind, and concentrate on sustainable development for the sake of the environment.

— To resolve major issues of human development requires the solidarity and cooperation of all human beings, and the sound development of human depends on the creation and progress of civilization, rather than resource exploitation, technology blockade, economic sanctions and military threat. The human, as the wisest of all creatures, should learn to live a civilized way of life and consider cultural pursuit as the goal of happiness, rather than alienate ourselves into a deplorable economic animal, ridiculous political puppet or terrible military machine.

The world has witnessed a splendid civilization created by human, and the human live an enjoyable life thanks to the culture. Only when we are clear about the real purpose

Chinese Folk Art Forms in Cultural Context

Tian Li

Associate Research Fellow and Deputy Head of Folklore Research Institute, Chinese National Academy of Arts

of development and the context of the era can we get out of our own narrow circle, abandon ideological biases and accomplish the common development of mankind.

As the traditional China's art, Chinese Folk Art Forms is a performing art having folk nature. Originating from the folk, developing in the folk as well as being active in the folk, Chinese Folk Art Forms narrates common people's stories and displays bright folk cultural attributes and art spirits. Meanwhile, as the same as Chinese traditional art, Chinese Folk Art Forms contains Chinese cultural spirit and the basic spirit of Chinese art. Therefore, Chinese Folk Art Forms belongs to folk cultural category relative to official orthodox culture, and a non-mainstream art in Chinese culture relative to mainstream literati art of Chinese art; while comparing with official and literati classic arts, Chinese Folk Art Forms is undoubtedly a pop art. Although some people think that China play is unpresentable, it still can mix Chinese culture tradition with folk life, and combine people's spiritual pursue with entertainment.

As the same with the other Chinese arts, Chinese Folk Art Forms focuses on the spirit of Chinese art with Xing (a technique of expression from Book of Songs) image and interest, which is popular and easy to understand; and it can cultivate one's entertainment and relax people's mind, so it is considered as one of main entertainments for Chinese people. In a period in history, Chinese Folk Art Forms has fostered Chinese people's basic artistic taste and aesthetic habits. Even in the age that cultural education was not popular, Chinese Folk Art Forms was the initial learning style for people.

Chinese Folk Art Forms is Chinese people's spiritual life way and cultural entertainment way lasting for thousands of years. Chinese people at various levels are fond of Chinese Folk Art Forms, and regard listening to books and Chinese Folk Art Forms as a part of daily life. In many Chinese people's mind, it is cordial feeling of sounds and call of home, and also an inerasable impression to the hometown when connecting with Chinese Folk Art Forms. It can be said that Chinese Folk Art Forms not only has unique artistic charm, but also is a unique culture memory.

Urban and Drama Development

Liu Yanjun

The head and Research Fellow of Drama Research Institute, Chinese National Academy of Arts

In contemporary China, relationship between construction and development of culture and the rapid urbanization process is becoming tight day by day. Due to its social and public property, drama has tighter and tighter relationship with the urban. It is easy for us to prove the importance of drama to the urban developments, and also easy to find out witness by drama shows to material progress and spirit growth of a city. As a public place with functions of exchange and communication in the city, theater is able to converge cultural programme, humanistic prospect and wonderful moment of a city, as well as common feelings, will, imagination and creativeness of people living in the land. Historical spirit, desire of the age, motivated, open and tolerant feelings and beliefs can all be founded in dramas in the city, and also be accepted and recognized by people from different cities. Practice is increasingly determinant factor for relationship between drama and urban development and their trend. In contemporary China, various performance places are constructed nationwide more and more with acceleration of urbanization process and importance of drama to the social life being increasingly improved currently. Some cities, such as Shanghai, Beijing, imitated models like New York Broadway, West End of London, Shibuya of Japan to begin its exploration on construction of urban drama zone in China. The Article discusses the relationship between drama and the urban from new phenomenon such as theater, non-theater, website and fund emerging in recent years. It points out that relationship between drama culture and urban development will be tighter and tighter, and its prospect will also be brighter and brighter with the further development of urban construction.

Arthur Miller and Contemporary Chinese Drama

Song Baozhen

The deputy head and Research Fellow of Drama Research Institute, Chinese National Academy of Arts

we cannot forget an American dramatist-Arthur Miller (Arthur Miller, 1915-2005) who brought a considerable influence on contemporary Chinese drama when looking back to Sino-US drama culture exchange, that is not just because he had ever set his foot on China's land and had good cooperation with Beijing People's Art Theatre, but also due to that Chinese people are attracted by his sincere personality, indomitable vitality, sharp social insight and profound philosophy contained in his drama.

From September 18 to October 12, 1978, Arthur Miller visited China with his wife at his own expense, and travelled Beijing, Shanghai, Guangzhou, Guilin, etc, this is considered as the first time for welcoming friends from American Theatre-land after the end of culture revolution in China. At that time, Arthur Miller knew nothing about contemporary China, so did Chinese people to American drama. After watching drama shows, such as Song of Loyalty, Cai Wenji, the Opposite Bank, he unfolded discussion with Cao Yu, Ying Ruocheng, et al with regards to drama issues, and he met famous director Huang Zuolin in Shanghai. When he came back to his country, Arthur Miller published in China in the Atlantic Monthly in March 1979 for talking about impressions on visiting China. "Chinese people's happiness and sorrows in the drama are the same as us. It is no doubt that oriental culture is very different from western one; however, ambition for the culture is completely same." He said.

In 1981, Shanghai People's Art Theater showed Purgatory which was renamed as "the Crucible" when being played, with more than 50 continuous play at first run through being directed by Huang Zuolin. In spring in 1983, Arthur Miller visited China again with his wife to personally direct Death of a Salesman. On May 7, the play was resoundingly showed at Beijing Theater for its first run, which could not be stopped even it had been played for more than 70 times.

Currently, Chinese people are no longer stranger to Arthur Miller and its drama. In May 19, 2002, the Crucible directed by Wang Xiaoying was played in Beijing by National Theatre Company of China for the premiere, and was re-played in Beijing in May 2006. In December 2006, such drama was played in Shanghai Dramatic Arts Centre. In February 2005, performers from Beijing rehearsed Death of a Salesman which was rehearsed again in March 2012.

"View", "Relation" and a Kind of Comparative Study in Photography

Li Shufeng

Head and Research Fellow of Photographic Art Research Institute, Chinese National Academy of Arts

As the method of record and expression, photography combines the technology and art, with the "view", the way to view the world, as the core content. The way to view the world is delivered to others based the photographer's status in the life by selecting the voice and tense of the presentation and editing the work. The essence of the "view" is the understanding of the relation among the objects taken into the camera. The cultural value of photography derives from the "relation", i.e. the meaning. Two kinds of "relations" are included. The first is the relation among people engaged in photo-taking, including the photographer, people in the camera and the viewer. The second is the relation among the information points in the transition from the 3D venue to the 2D picture. The first relation determines the height of the position of the camera, the distance and the affection of the work, while the latter relation decides the value and artistic effect of the work.

Regarding the previous relation, it is advocated that the equality and respect shall be ensured and the pride and prejudice shall be avoided among the photographer, people in the camera and the viewer, and the photographer shall sincerely focus on others and transfer the things in his eyes to objective pictures. For the latter relation, the selection of information points and the treatment of the relations shall be taken into serious consideration, which means to figure out the relations among the information points in the photo and the relations among these corresponding objects in the real world, find out the similarities and differences between the two kinds of relations, deliver to the society and inspire viewers' sensitivity and intelligence. For the sake of more cultural value, it is necessary to work hard on figuring out and dealing with the relations among the information points, consciously take effective information (often including primary and secondary information, two sides of a conflict) into the viewfinder, stimulate the relations among the information points, unfold the these relations based on the composition, control of the depth of field and selection of the focus point and moment, and present the main content with the language. If the above process is completed, the photos combining the truth and art and characters and images can be incorporated in the cultural communication. In other words, the cultural value is generated.

Historic and modern significance of rituals □ music and state of ceremonies of China

Xiang Yang

Research Fellow of Music Research Institute, Chinese National Academy of Arts

Cultural tradition of China is on basis of rituals music culture, thus named as rituals music civilization and stage of ceremonies. The author discriminated to connotation of rituals music civilization made by Zhou Gong, discussed the misunderstanding to rituals music in current academic, mastered and had a knowledge of mutual relations between rituals music and ritual system, customs and ceremonies, rituals music culture is representative in Chinese traditional music culture. Explore traditional continue of rituals music

Cultural Diversity Recognition and Cultural Exchange and Merging

Zheng Changling

Researcher Fellow and Deputy director of Cultural Development Strategy Research Center, Chinese National Academy of Arts

civilization and stage of ceremonies from view of music and classification of etiquette, the possibility and feasibility of reestablishing rituals music system have made traditional rituals music idea integrate in modern civilization of China on its real representation.

In the world today, the development of culture (in narrow sense) is swept forward by the development of economy and politics; meanwhile, its independent quality disappears remarkably.

Culture exists freely like air and fills in the time and space of human life, naturally presenting its action, value orientation, etc. (in wide sense) As society develops, culture has gradually become one object, or has been split up and even been used as goods and has been industrialized, etc., therefore, the power politics and economic oligarch may naturally impose their own culture and values onto others and the convergence of the cultures in the world is inevitable.

With such reality, Universal Declaration on Cultural Diversity (2001) passed by UNESCO has fully recognized and clearly affirmed the significance of cultural diversity to the development of human at present and in the future. Convention on the Protection and Promotion of the Diversity of Cultural Expressions (2005) later issued by UNESCO points out: "Being aware that cultural diversity creates a rich and varied world, which increases the range of choices and nurtures human capacities and values, and therefore is a mainspring for sustainable development for communities, peoples and nations. Recalling that cultural diversity, flourishing within a framework of democracy, tolerance, social justice and mutual respect between peoples and cultures, is indispensable for peace and security at the local, national and international levels. It is required to widely develop unity and mutual aid on basis of acknowledging cultural diversity and recognizing human as a unified entirety and developing cultural exchange."

The conventions are the agreements that all countries and nations shall abide by while recognition is the basis. By means of discussing the following points:

Cultural diversity recognition and maintaining world cultural diversity;

Efforts of China to maintain world cultural diversity; and

Conducts of China to promote the cultural exchanges among all countries and nations in the world;

This Thesis is to stress the subject and bring forward that only the exchange and merging on basis of cultural diversity recognition is the approach to develop human culture healthily.

NEWS ROUNDUP

新闻综述

任慧
中国艺术研究院文化发展战略研究中心副研究员

沟通·融合·将无同
"跨文化双边对话：第三届中美文化论坛"隆重举行

为了进一步深化中美两国的文化交流，开辟中美文化合作的新路径，由中华人民共和国文化部和美国国家人文基金会共同主办、中国艺术研究院和江苏省文化厅共同承办的"跨文化双边对话：第三届中美文化论坛"于2012年9月6日在北京隆重举行。

"中美文化论坛"是根据2008年中华人民共和国文化部同美国国家人文基金会签署的《关于鼓励人文学科学术性研究和文化遗产保护合作事宜的谅解备忘录》而举办，其宗旨是为中美两国在文化领域建立一个公共性、学术性、互动性的定期对话机制，通过此机制探讨文化艺术的发展方式和文化遗产保护等问题，加深中美两国在文化艺术和人文科学领域的相互了解，促进双方在文化艺术和人文科学领域的友好合作，推进两国文化交流的深入发展。2009年，中国国家主席胡锦涛与美国总统奥巴马发表的《中美联合声明》，明确提出要在美国举行第二届中美文化论坛。2010年，国务委员刘延东和美国国务卿希拉里·克林顿在北京联合主持了"中美人文交流高层磋商机制成立仪式暨第一次会议"，将"中美文化论坛"列为中美文化交流的重要项目。在前两届论坛成功举行的基础上，今年第三届中美文化论坛如期在北京举行，表明中美两国高层文化交流已经步入了制度化的发展轨道。

出席开幕式的有中华人民共和国文化部副部长赵少华，美国国家人文基金会主席詹姆斯·利奇，美国驻华使馆公使王晓珉，中华人民共和国文化部外联局局长侯湘华，中华人民共和国文化部外联局副局长李鸿，中国艺术研究院党委书记、副院长高显莉，中国艺术研究院副院长王能宪、吕品田，中国艺术研究院中国非物质文化遗产保护中心常务副主任李新风，中国艺术研究院院长助理、文化发展战略研究中心主任贾磊磊等。中国艺术研究院终身研究员、中国文化研究所所长刘梦溪，著名文化学者余秋雨，中国美术馆馆长范迪安，中国社会科学院荣誉学部委员、民族文学研究所刘魁立，中国社会科学院美国研究所所长黄平，中国艺术研究院艺术创作研究中心及陶艺艺术中心主任朱乐耕，中国艺术研究院中国文化研究所研究员摩罗等国内文化艺术界知名的专家在开幕式上做主题发言。美方出席论坛的有来自美国国家图书馆、斯坦福大学、波莫纳大学、罗格斯大学、爱荷华大学以及美国总统人文艺术委员会的专家、学者和艺术家。此外，还有来自中国艺术研究院、北京大学、中国人民大学、北京师范大学、北京第二外国语大学等高校和科研机构的代表以及来自《人民日报》、《光明日报》、《中国文化报》和中央电视台、中央人民广播电台、新华社等数十家新闻媒体的记者。

赵少华在开幕式上说：中美两国都是幅员辽阔的大国。两国广博壮丽的土地、山川、河流孕育着杰出的人民和灿烂的文化，并赋予他们人民特有的民族性格和精神气质。本届论坛"文化的语境：文化与人类、文化与历史"的议题将使两国学者从地域、历史与人类发展的角度，对比中美文化，从而以更为宏大、高远的视角来看待两国文化与两国关系。她说，不可否认，中美两国在文化传统、社会制度和发展阶段等方面存在着差异和不同。但问题的关键是如何看待差异和不同。中国尊崇"和而不同"的文化理念，相信文化交流有助于缓解冲突、消弭误解和矛盾。赵少华说，作为全球最大的发展中国家和最大的发达国家，中美双方加强交流、增进互信、促进合作，共建"相互尊重、互利共赢的合作伙伴关系"，对两国乃至全世界都是最大的福音。她呼吁中美两国有识之士能更多思考如何减少由于两国存在差异和不同所造成的误读、误解、误判，在增进文化间互相了解方面下工夫。

詹姆斯·利奇在致辞中回顾了中美两国在历史上对人类文明作出的杰出贡献，提出中国和美国的文化虽有差异，但这并不意味着不能尊重彼此的创造和成就以及更重要的人类环境，因为文化的内涵比政府的概念更深远、更持久。如果说文化是海洋，那么国家就是航行在文化滔滔巨浪中的船只。如果人们尊重彼此的文化，认识到不同背景下人们面临的共同挑战，就可以大大降低因差异导致矛盾的可能性。而要想增进对彼此的尊重,就必须重视人文交流。

来自中美两国的五十余名专家、学者和艺术家将从中美两国由于历史、地域、民族等原因所形成的文化差异为切入点,以"文化的语境:地域,人类,历史"为主要议题展开深入地交流与探讨。中美两国的文化各自具有独立鲜明的特征,通过两国学者积极的人文交流,必将加强并增进理解、共鸣和信任,从而推动中美两国文化的深入交流,并促进两国人民之间的友谊。

一

钱锺书先生说过:"东海西海,心理攸同;南学北学,道术未裂。"东方和西方,各个国家民族的不同人群,彼此的心理结构和心理指向,常常是相同的。人类历史上的许多惊心动魄或者惊天动地的争执和论争,到后来都因趋同而化解,或由于折中而和合。文化与人类,最终是和谐发展的。

中国艺术研究院终身研究员、中国文化研究所所长刘梦溪提出,人类历史上的许多惊心动魄或者惊天动地的争执和论争,到后来都因趋同而化解或由于折中而和合。正像中国历史上学术思想最活跃的魏晋时期所出现的"将无同"这三个字,其所代表的就是世界上不同的文化、不同的"文明体国家",不必然发展为冲突,而是需要通过交流与对话达成文化的互补与融合。人类的未来,世界历史的大趋势,是走向文明的融合而不是相反。著名文化学者余秋雨先生指出早在16世纪,意大利传教士利玛窦根据在中国生活三十多年的考察调研,就已经得出了"中国文化四千年的历史证明了它不扩张、不侵略的农耕文化本性"的结论,推翻了他本来欧洲海洋文化的逻辑。因此我们应该认识到,不同的文化虽然有着明显的差异,但文明的敌人不是别的文明,而是野蛮,所以文化和文化之间不应该冲突,而应该互相包容、互相理解,甚至互相欣赏,总之一句话"文化差异不应该导致人类冲突"。由此亨廷顿教授将文化差异解释为冲突的根源,无视"中华文明几千年来内部斗争激烈,却从来没有与周边的其他文明发生长时间的冲突"的现实,也就抹杀了文明间可以和谐共生的特性。中国社科院美国研究所所长黄平也认为在各个国家尤其是非西方国家走向现代的过程中,必然面对现代性问题的二元对立思维:未来与过去,现代与传统,西方与非西方,民主与专制,善与恶等。但中国古代的哲学,尤其是《易经》所包含的阴阳思想,就是一种超越此种二元对立的思维,足以提供解决这类问题的无限可能性。

中国艺术研究院中国非物质文化遗产保护中心常务副主任李新风从努力建设符合中国实际的、富有实效的非物质文化遗产保护制度,注重整体性的保护,大力推进文化生态保护区的建设,高度重视非文化遗产保护的法律建设,积极探索、实践其他各种保护方式以及重视非物质文化遗产基础理论研究与学科建设五个方面介绍了中国在非物质文化遗产保护方面所进行的一系列宝贵的、富有创造性的探索和实践,希望共同保护这些全人类的共同精神财富。美国国会图书馆"美国国家民俗中心"名誉主任佩姬·巴尔杰认为,"美国文化"的独特性正是源于世界文化的融合和(或)共存,这种多样性对于维护21世纪可持续发展的文化社群至关重要。因此致力于在全世界范围内保护和支持全球所有非物质文化遗产,同时必须认识并尊重由于人口流动和不可避免的文化元素共享所形成的整体文化表述。因此,在保护传统文化表述的同时,应当对这个流动化、全球化、依赖于新技术并维护知识产权的现代世界中可能出现的文化变化持支持态度。美国纽伯瑞图书馆"美洲印第安人和原住民研究"达西麦克尼克尔中心主任斯科特·曼宁·史蒂文斯发表了题为《建立档案与美国印第安研究间的桥梁》的讲话,指出图书馆及其他致力于收藏美洲印第安人资料的文化机构所长期面临的问题,最主要的是如何建立研究机构(如纽伯瑞图书馆)和它所代表的美国印第安人社区之间的最佳联系,更好地促进美国原住民和学术界的联系与关系。图书馆有义务使馆藏的文化材料尽量不脱离美国印第安人的生活,而这个人群正是能从馆藏资料受益最多的人群。对于美国境内的美洲原住社群而言,记载着本土历史、文化传统及本土居民母语的资料都是极其重要的资源。而对于蕴藏在广大民众中间的最普遍、最常用、最基础的非物质文化的重要性却认识不足。

中国美术馆馆长范迪安发表了题为《中国当代艺术:在全球与本土之间》的演讲,指出伴随着中国社会的历史性变革,中国艺术呈现出多元的发展态势,"当代艺术"成为新的社会文化现象。与20世纪以来西方现代艺术发展的文化逻辑不同,中国当代艺术在经济与资本的作用下、在全球化的文化条件下,呈现出新的生态结构,艺术博物馆、艺术市场、艺术空间、艺术传播几个方面的蓬勃发展，构成了艺术从创造到消费的文化格局。在中美艺术交流中，如何克服以"符号化"的视角观察和评价中国当代艺术，如何在信息时代与全球文化语境中认识中国艺术的当代特征与文化价值，是一个急迫的问题。美中学术交流委员会北京办事处主任阿瑟·泰用大量具体的数字统计结果，对中美两国在人文艺术领域三十年以来的学术交流情况进行了回顾与展望。

二

具有五千年文明史的中华文化以儒家思想为代表，"修身、齐家、治国、平天下"，具有深厚的人文修养和历史情怀。美国虽然只有两百多年历史，但凝聚多民族文化形成独特的美国精神和价值观。尊重历史，正视现实，放眼未来，通过文化这座桥梁，一定会为未来全人类的繁荣发展起到积极的推动作用。

中国艺术研究院院长助理、文化发展战略研究中心主任贾磊磊以中国电影这个具有世界性的艺术表现形式为例，指出中国电影最突出的价值表达是体现在对于中国传统文化精神的信守方面，而在对传统文化精神的表达方面最关键的又在于对传统文化核心价值取向的认同方面，它集中体现在对于"仁爱"精神的阐释中。作为一种凝聚着中国古代这种千年文化价值观，"仁爱"思想贯穿在政治、哲学、伦理、艺术等不同的精神领域，它是整个中华民族核心价值体系的有机组成部分。中国艺术研究院艺术创作研究中心主任、陶瓷艺术研究中心主任朱乐耕结合自身创作谈道，作为中国工艺美术史中唯一延续最久又没有中断过的艺术形态的陶瓷艺术，在现代中国社会背景下的蓬勃发展情况，希望可以通过艺术搭起一座座友谊的桥梁，让不同的文明得到相互的理解和尊重。

中国社会科学院荣誉学部委员刘魁立指出，在文化保护方面对于非物质文化遗产的偏见，容易造成文化的民族性、广泛性及其深厚历史底蕴的丧失，使文化日益趋同化，缺乏应有的生命力和创造力。我们应该尊重联合国教科文组织关于非物质文化遗产保护的理念，为人类社会寻求一个超越物质独占、消弭以及由此造成的人与人、社会与社会之间的纷争，从而推进人类文化的持续的繁荣发展。中国艺术研究院中国文化研究所研究员摩罗就《文化权利是国家主权和国家利益的组成部分》发表了主题演讲，他认为文化是构成民族国家实体的因素之一，理所当然也是国家主权的组成部分。现代国际社会处处以尊重他国主权相标榜，这种尊重也应该相应地坐实为尊重其利益诉求，尊重其文化传统、文化精神及文化权利。

"美国历史文物保护顾问委员会"副主席、美国罗格斯大学董事会杰出服务教授、罗格斯大学"种族、文化与现代经验"学院院长克莱门特·普莱斯从非洲裔美国历史领域的研究视角指出，美国南北战争所造成的恐怖影响已经是举世公认的事实。在此基础上，他认为美国南北战争的150周年纪念和所谓的黑奴大解放对美国历史文化意识的一次重大调整相重合，而这次重大调整的发展是美国南北战争和黑奴大解放的重要遗产之一，也是对世界范围内历史文化叙事的一次贡献。美国现代语言学会学术传播部主任、美国波莫纳学院媒介研究教授凯萨琳·菲茨帕特里克以《我们怎样阅读与写作：社会网络与文学社群》为题，谈到很多美国作家都认为互联网影响并干扰了现代人的感知能力，在媒体高度饱和的现代文化中，阅读的重要性不断下降，而阅读正是一种可能改变了美国历史进程的主要严肃认知形式。但同时，因为现在的图书销售量比以往任何时候都高，所以可以推论阅读和写作在当代美国生活中继续占据着重要地位。

三

一方水土养一方人，一方文化具有特有的民族性格和精神气质。以文化交流消除地域差异，增进理解和信任，有利于全人类的和谐共生。

第三届中美文化论坛还在南京设立了分会场，继续讨论"文化与地域"的相关议题。江苏省人民政府副省长曹卫星、江苏省委宣传部常务副部长章剑华、江苏省委宣传部副部长司锦泉等领导莅临大会。

江苏省文化厅厅长徐耀新以江苏和南京为例对地域和文化的关系作了简要论述，提出地域环境的差异影响人类的生活方式，进而影响文化精神。对于南京而言，在建设历史文化名城的进程中，要着重保护南京古都的自然遗产和历史遗产，从根本上确保古都神韵永驻，提升城市文化品格。江苏省人民政府参事室主任宋林飞从"城市多元化及其融合"的角度入手，谈到中国正在从农业社会转变为城市社会，由此带来了城乡文化的多元交融，以及城市化过程中的很多难题，为了解决中国城市社会面临的挑战，应该立足中国实际，适当向西方学习成功经验，采取科学的发展思路，确保中国的城市化进程能够提高质量，能够使中国更多的国民享受城市优良的生活方式。美国斯坦福大学英语系主任，比较文学系教授、"人文与科学学院"霍格兰德家庭教授拉蒙·萨尔迪瓦通过以美国/墨西哥边境地区为研究对象，通过研究那些造成这种边境地区相互冲突的身份区别、种族融合、阶级和政治上的力量，进而了解跨国主义如何深刻地改变了这些边境居民的生活，以及跨国主义如何建立了这样一个至今仍然影响当今世界的历史框架，进而凝练这段历史与记忆的社会美学价值。

南京大学—约翰斯·霍普金斯大学中美文化研究中心副主任蔡佳禾认为中国的儒家思想有着丰富的有关社会和谐的思想，基督教文化也有追求世界和平与和谐的理念。在当前国际秩序面对新的挑战之时，中美两国的思想家必须秉持和寻求共同的文化理念，找到克服文化差异的途径。在全球化的过程中，文化的差异不是一种可以轻易绕开的障碍，但也绝对不是永恒的，未来文化学在维护世界和平方面必须扮演更为重要的角色。南京大学—约翰斯·霍普金斯大学中美文化研究中心美方合作主任詹森·帕滕特以《思维定势与世界观：对空间如何决定思想的反思》为题，谈道几个世纪以来许多学科的学者一直在探讨和争论文化共性和文化相对主义的议题，通过介绍近几十年来的主要研究成果，表明确空间作为一种关键决定因素在人类体验中的重要地位。

江苏作家协会副主席毕飞宇从个体与环境以及身体与观念的角度，谈道地域文化虽然具有稳固性，但通过不同文化的交流、渗透以及彼此之间的化学反应，也会发生改变。而任何一种地域文化，只要有益于人类的发展与交流，就是有价值的，有生命力的，才能成为人类文化的有机成分。通过越来越多的丰富的多元的文化交流，我们可以发现国人变得更好、更自信、更个人，也更属于这个世界。同时，从文化交流当中获得好处的绝对不仅仅是中国人，从文化交流当中获得好处的应该是世界上的每一个人。南京大学外国语学院当代外国文学与文化研究中心主任王守仁重点介绍了南京地区关于美国文学教学与研究情况，指出包括美国文学在内的外国文学与中国现代化进程、与中国现代文学和文化的演进有着密切的关系，而南京大学是国内为数不多的较早进行美国文学教学与研究的高校。1921年，知名作家赛珍珠在南京大学的小楼里创作了诺贝尔文学奖获奖小说《大地》。文学是人学，具有超越国别、政治、意识形态、肤色限制的普遍人性意义，是连接中美两国人民的纽带，也是我们讲授和研究美国文学的价值所在。美国爱荷华大学国际写作计划主任克里斯托弗·梅瑞尔从地域和文学的关系出发，探讨了地理环境在沃尔特·惠特曼、亨利·戴维·梭罗和马克·吐温的作品中的主导地位，分析《草叶集》、《梭罗日记》和《密西西比河上》三部具有奠基意义的作品。

作为一个文明古国，中国文化拥有"海纳百川"的博大胸襟，崇尚尊重文化的多样性选择。在全球化时代共同应对未来挑战的背景下，包括中美两国在内的全世界人民加强文化交流与合作，必将具有更加广阔的前景与更加辉煌的未来。

Ren Hui

Associate Research Fellow of Cultural Development Strategy Research Center, Chinese National Academy of Arts

Communication, Integration and Jiang Wu Tong
—"The Third China-U.S. Cultural Forum: A Binational Conversation on Bridging Cultures" was grandly Held

To deepen China-U.S. cultural exchanges and blaze trails for bilateral cultural cooperation, the Third China-U.S. Cultural Forum: A Binational Conversation on Bridging Cultures, co-sponsored by the Ministry of Culture of China and U.S. National Endowment for the Humanities (NEH) and jointly organized by Chinese National Academy of Arts and Jiangsu Provincial Department of Culture, was held in Beijing on September 6.

Held according to the memorandum of understanding on encouraging academic studies on humanity science and stepping up cooperation in the protection of cultural heritage signed by the Ministry of Culture of China and the NEH in 2008, the China-U.S. Cultural Forum aims to build a regular dialogue mechanism in a public, academic and interactive way in the cultural field of the two countries. The mechanism is intended to provoke discussions on development pattern of culture and art and the protection of cultural heritage so as to deepen the two countries' mutual understanding and friendly cooperation in culture, art and the humanities, and promote the cultural exchanges between them. Chinese President Hu Jintao and U.S. President Barack Obama issued the U.S.-China Joint Statement in 2009, according to which the Second China-U.S. Cultural Forum would be held in the U.S. In 2010, Chinese State Councilor Liu Yandong and U.S. Secretary of State Hillary Clinton co-chaired in Beijing the Inauguration Ceremony and First Meeting of the China-U.S. High-Level Consultation on People-to-people Exchange, at which the China-U.S. Cultural Forum was recognized as an important part of China-U.S. cultural exchanges. On the success of the previous two forums, the Third China-U.S. Cultural Forum was held in Beijing as scheduled, marking the institutionalization of high-level cultural exchanges between the two countries.

The opening ceremony was attended by China's Vice Minister of Culture Zhao Shaohua, NEH Chairman James Leach, Robert S. Wang, Deputy Chief of Mission at U.S. Embassy Beijing, Hou Xianghua and Li Hong, respectively Director-General and Deputy Director-General for External Cultural Relations, Ministry of Culture, Gao Xianli, Party

Secretary and Vice President of Chinese National Academy of Arts, Wang Nengxian and Lv Pintian, Vice Presidents of Chinese National Academy of Arts, Li Xinfeng, Executive Deputy Director of China Intangible Cultural Heritage Protection Center, Chinese National Academy of Arts, and Jia Leilei, President Assistant of Chinese National Academy of Arts and Director of Cultural Development Strategy Research Center. Liu Mengxi, lifelong research fellow and Director of Chinese Studies Institute of Chinese National Academy of Arts, famous cultural scholar Yu Qiuyu, Fan Di'an, Director of National Art Museum of China, Liu Kuili, honorary academician of the Chinese Academy of Social Sciences and research fellow of the Institute of Ethnic Literature, Huang Ping, Director of the Institute of American Studies, Chinese Academy of Social Sciences, Zhu Legeng, Director of the Artistic Creation Research Center and the Ceramic Art Research Center, Chinese National Academy of Arts, Mo Luo, research fellow of the Institute of Chinese Culture, Chinese National Academy of Arts, and many other famous scholars from China's arts and cultural sector made keynote speeches at the opening ceremony. Attendees from the U.S. side included experts, scholars and artists from Library of Congress, Stanford University, Pomona College, Rutgers University, University of Iowa and President's Committee on the Arts and the Humanities. Also present at the ceremony were representatives from institutions of higher learning and research institutes such as Chinese National Academy of Arts, Peking University, Renmin University of China, Beijing Normal University, and Beijing International Studies University as well as journalists from dozens of media agencies including People's Daily, Guangming Daily, Chinese Culture Reported, CCTV, China National Radio and Xinhua News Agency.

As Zhao Shaohua said at the ceremony, China and the U.S. are both great powers with a vast territory. Their magnificent land, mountains and rivers have nurtured outstanding peoples and splendid cultures and give their peoples the unique national character and ethos. The theme of this forum "The Context: Place, People, History" will provide Chinese and U.S. scholars with an opportunity to make comparison between Chinese and American cultures in terms of region, history and human development so that they will view their the cultures of and relations between the two countries from a more lofty and macroscopic perspective. She said, "undoubtedly, there are differences between China and the U.S. in terms of cultural tradition, social system, and the stage of development, but the crux of the problem is how to look at such differences. China enshrines the philosophy of 'seeking harmony rather than uniformity', and believes that cultural exchanges contribute to the alleviation of conflicts and elimination of misunderstanding and tension." It will best serve the interests of the two countries and even if the world's largest developing country and largest developed country could improve communication, enhance mutual trust, promote cooperation, and work together to build a "partnership featuring mutual respect and mutual benefit". She called on insightful people of both countries to think more about how to reduce misinterpretation, misunderstanding and misjudgment between China and the U.S. that arise from their differences and work hard at enhancing mutual understanding between them.

James Leach reviewed in his speech the outstanding contributions made by Chinese and American people to the human civilization. As he said, China and the U.S. have different cultures, but that doesn't mean we cannot respect each other's creativity and social achievements, and more importantly human condition. Culture is vastly larger and more sustaining than government. Culture is the ocean and nations are like ships attempting to navigate culture's tumultuous waves. If people have respect for each other's culture and for the mutual challenges individuals of all backgrounds face in the sea of life, the chances that differences will cause conflict vastly diminish. To enhance mutual respect, we should attach importance to people-to-people exchanges.

Over 50 experts, scholars and artists from China and the U.S. had in-depth discussions on the cultural differences caused by historical, geological and ethnic factors under the theme "The Context: Place, People, History". Given the distinctive features of Chinese and American cultures, the exchanges between scholars of the two countries are bound to boost mutual understanding, sympathy and trust, deepen cultural communication, and cement the friendship between the two countries.

I

Mr. Qian Zhongshu once said: "From the east or west, people think in the same way; in the south and north, the Tao is nothing dissimilar". It means that people's psychological structure and preference tend to be the same in various countries of the East and the West. Many fierce or earthshaking debates and arguments in history were eventually resolved by a tendency toward common ground or reconciled through compromise. Culture and humanity develop in harmony after all.

Mr. Liu Mengxi pointed out that many fierce or earthshaking debates and arguments in history were eventually resolved by a tendency toward common ground or reconciled through compromise. It is just like the meaning of the three-word epigram "just the same" (jiang wu tong) which dates back to the Wei and Jin Dynasties (c. 220-420 AD), a period seeing the liveliest academic thoughts in Chinese history. Conflict is not inevitable between different cultures and civilizations in the world. Instead, it is necessary to achieve cultural fusion and mutual complementation through exchange and dialogue. The future of the humanity and the general trend of the world is the cultural integration rather than the opposite. Mr. Yu Qiuyu, a famous cultural scholar, pointed out that, the 30-year-long investigation and research by Italian missionary Mattew Ricci early in the 16th century led to the conclusion that the 4,000-year-long history had proved that the Chinese culture is by nature a farming culture which seeks no invasion or expansion. That is quite different from the European marine culture. Therefore, we should realize that despite obvious differences, what runs counter to civilization is barbarism rather than other civilizations. There should not be any conflict between different cultures, but mutual tolerance, understanding and even appreciation. In one word, cultural differences should not cause human conflicts. Professor Huntington attributes conflicts to cultural differences, ignoring the fact that "despite the intense internal struggles over the thousands of years, the Chinese civilization has never been involved in longstanding conflicts with other civilizations" and thus denying the distinctive feature of harmonious co-existence of different civilizations. Huang Ping holds the similar idea that all countries, especially non-Western countries, will inevitably face the dual way of thinking in the process of modernization: future and past, modern and traditional, Western and non-Western, democracy and dictatorship, good and evil, etc. However, ancient Chinese philosophy, especially the concepts of Yin and Yang in the Book of Changes, breaks the confrontation in the dual way of thinking and provides infinite possibilities of solving such problems.

In hope of protecting the spiritual treasure shared by the whole mankind, Li Xinfeng introduced China's valuable and innovative efforts in protecting intangible cultural heritage in five aspects including establishing an effective protection mechanism in line with China's realities, focusing more on overall protection, building cultural and ecological reserves, attaching importance to establishment of the legal framework for the protection of intangible cultural heritage, experimenting with other protection approaches, and paying attention to the basic theoretical research and discipline building concerning intangible cultural heritage. Peggy Bulger, Director Emerita of the American Folklife Center at the Library of Congress, holds that the uniqueness of the American culture is rooted in the fusion and/or coexistence of world cultures, and such diversity is essential to maintaining the sustainable development of cultural communities in the 21st century. Therefore, to protect intangible cultural heritage across the world, we must realize and respect the integrated cultural expression caused by population mobility and inevitable sharing of cultural elements. Therefore, while protecting the expression of traditional culture, we should be supportive to possible cultural exchanges in a modern world featuring dynamism, globalization, dependence on new technologies and intellectual property right protection. Scott Manning Stevens, Director of the D'Arcy McNickle Center for American Indian and Indigenous Studies at the Newberry Library, delivered a speech entitled "Build a Bridge between Archives and American Indian Studies", pointing out that the major problem confronting libraries and other cultural institutions committed to collecting materials about American Indians for long was to best connect research institutes (like the Newberry Library) and American Indian communities they represented and better promote the relationship between American Indians with the academic community. Libraries are obliged to prevent cultural materials they have collected from being divorced from the life of American Indians who are supposed to benefit most from such materials. All materials recording indigenous history, culture and tradition and mother tongue are very important resources for aborigines in the U.S. However, insufficient importance is attached to intangible culture which is most often seen and used and most fundamental in people's daily life.

Fan Di'an made a speech entitled "Contemporary Chinese Art: Between Globalism and Localism", in which he said that along with the historic changes in the Chinese society, the Chinese art had become increasingly diverse, and the contemporary art had become a new social and cultural phenomenon. Different from the cultural logic underlining the development of Western modern art, the contemporary Chinese art presents a new ecological structure under the influence of economy and capital and against the backdrop of cultural globalization. Art museums, market, space and communication have prospered to form a cultural pattern featuring the shift from artistic creation to consumption. In China-U.S. artistic exchanges, it is imperative to change the mindset in viewing and evaluating contemporary Chinese art with a "symbolized" perspective and to understand the contemporary characteristics and cultural value of Chinese art in the information age and the global cultural context. Arthur D. Tai, Director of the Beijing Office of the U.S. Committee on Scholarly Communication with China, reviewed the academic exchanges between China and the U.S. in the past three decades with huge amounts of data and took a glance of future communication.

II

Confucianism, the most representative of the 5,000-year-long Chinese culture, values cultivating one's personal character, keeping a family in order, governing a state well and bringing peace to the world, and shows profound cultural accomplishment and historic vision. Despite a history of just more than 200 years, the cultures of multiple ethnic groups have shaped the unique American spirit and values. With respect for the past, courage to face the present and expectation for the future, we will undoubtedly promote the prosperity of the whole mankind through the bridge of culture.

Jia Leilei took Chinese movies, a global form of artistic expression, as an example, and pointed out the most outstanding value of Chinese movies was its observation of traditional Chinese culture, while the key to depicting the traditional culture was to identify its core values, which is mainly reflected in the interpretation of "benevolence". As the crystallization of the thousands of years of Chinese culture, the thought of benevolence is felt in many fields like politics, philosophy, ethics and art, and is an integral part of the core values of the Chinese nation. Zhu Legeng shared his personal experience of artistic creation and said that ceramics, as an artistic form with longest and continuous development in China's history of arts and crafts, was expected to build a bridge of friendship to facilitate mutual respect and understanding between different cultures against the background of modern prosperity in China.

Liu Kuili pointed out the bias against the protection of intangible cultural heritage possibly resulted in the loss of the nationality, universality and historical foundation of culture, and thus led to increasing homogeneity of culture which lacks due vitality and creativity. We should respect UNESCO's idea of protecting intangible cultural heritage, so that the transcendence of material exclusiveness can be sought for human society and the caused disputes between peoples or between societies can be eliminated. Moreover, the continued prosperity of human culture can be promoted. Mo Luo made a keynote speech entitled "Cultural Rights are an Integral Part of National Sovereignty and National Interests". As he said, as a constituent of nation state entity, culture is naturally an integral part of the national sovereignty. The respect for the sovereignty of other countries in modern international community should correspondingly be crystallized into the respect for their interest demands, cultural traditions, cultural spirit, and cultural rights.

Clement Price, Vice Chair of the Advisory Council on Historic Preservation and Board of Governors Distinguished Service Professor of History and Director of the Institute on Ethnicity, Culture and the Modern Experience at Rutgers University, pointed out based on his research on the history of American Africans that the horrible impact of the American Civil War was recognized across the world. He argued that the 150th anniversary of the Civil War and the so-called slave emancipation coincided with a major adjustment to Americans' historic and cultural awareness, whose development was among the important legacies of the Civil War and the slave emancipation as well as an important contribution to the historical and cultural narration worldwide. Kathleen Fitzpatrick, Director of Scholarly Communication, Modern Language Association and Professor of Media Studies (on leave), Pomona College, delivered a speech entitled "How We Read and Write: Social Networking and Literary Community", in which she said that many American writers blamed the Internet for affecting and messing with people's perception. The importance of reading is increasingly ignored in the modern culture with high media saturation, while reading is a major serious form of cognition which may change the American historical process. However, we can conclude that reading and writing is still important in American people's life as book sales are higher than ever before.

III

A particular place nurtures a particular group of people. A particular culture gives its people unique national character and ethos. Eliminating geological differences and enhancing understanding and trust via cultural exchanges is conducive to the harmonious coexistence of all mankind.

Nanjing is a sub-venue to further discuss topics related to culture and place. The conference was attended by Cao Weixing, Vice Governor of Jiangsu Provincial People's Government as well as Executive Deputy Director Zhang Jianhua and Deputy Director Si Jinquan of the Publicity Department of the CPC Jiangsu Provincial Committee.

Xu Yaoxin, Director General of Jiangsu Provincial Department of Culture, talked briefly about the relationship between place and culture by taking Jiangsu and Nanjing as an example, and argued that the differences in geological environment affect people's way of life and thus influence the culture. Nanjing should focus on the protection of its natural and historical heritage in the process of building itself into a historical and cultural city, so as to preserve its ancient charm and enhance its cultural image. Song Linfei, Director of Counselors' Office of Jiangsu Provincial People's Government, made a speech on urban diversification and integration. He pointed out in the speech that China's transformation from an agricultural to an urban society has caused diversity and integration of urban and rural cultures and also brought about many problems in the process of urbanization. To meet the challenges confronting China's urban society, we should take China's actual conditions into consideration, learn from the successful experience of Western countries and follow the scientific outlook on development so as to ensure the better quality of China's urbanization and offer more people the opportunity to enjoy a healthy way of life in cities. Ramon Saldivar, Chair of Stanford University Department of English, Chair of Comparative Literature Department, and the Hoagland Family Professor in Humanities and Sciences, studied the identity differences, racial integration, class and political forces causing conflicts in border areas between the U.S. and Mexico, to understand how transnationalism has deeply changed the life of residents in the border areas and how it has established the historical framework stilling affecting the whole world, and conclude the social and aesthetic value of this special period of history.

Cai Jiahe, Deputy Director of Jones Hopkins University-Nanjing University Center for Chinese and American Studies, argued that the Confucianism of China abounds in ideas of social harmony, and the Christianity also pursues world peace and harmony. When the current international order is confronted with new challenges, both Chinese and American thinkers should seek common cultural concepts and find the way to overcome cultural differences. In the process of globalization, cultural differences can hardly be dodged but are by no means eternal. In the future, culturology will play a more important role in maintaining world peace. In his speech entitled "Stereotype and World View: Reflection on How Space Determines Thoughts", Jason Patent, Co-Director of John-Hopkins University-Nanjing University Center for Chinese and American Studies, talked about the cultural commonality and cultural relativism that had been discussed and debated by scholars of many disciplines, and argued for the importance of space as a decisive factor in people's experience by introducing his major research findings over the past decades.

Bi Feiyu, Vice President of the Writers' Association of Jiangsu Province, based his speech on the relationship between individuals and the environment as well as between body and mind. As he said, regional culture is stable, but may change because of the exchanges, integration and chemical reactions with other cultures. All regional cultures are valuable and vital, and can become an integral part of the human culture, as long as they are conducive to human development and communication. People will be better, more confident, more personal and more attached to this world through more and diverse cultural exchanges. Moreover, it is not only the Chinese people but also everyone in the world that can benefit from cultural exchanges. Wang Shouren, Director of the Center for the Study of Contemporary Foreign Literature and Culture, School of Foreign Studies Nanjing University, introduced the teaching and research on American literature in Nanjing. He pointed out that foreign literature including American literature is closely related to China's modernization and the evolution of China's contemporary literature and culture, and that Nanjing University is among the few universities in China that took the lead to teach and research American literature. Famous writer Pearl S. Buck wrote her Nobel-winning novel The Good Earth in her studio in Nanjing University. Literature is a science of people and has universal significance that transcends the limits of nationality, politics, ideology and race, and it is the bond between Chinese and American people, which explains why it is worth teaching and researching American literature. Christopher Merrill, Director of the University of Iowa International Writing Program, analyzed groundbreaking works including Leaves of Grass, The Journal: 1837-1861 and Life on the Mississippi respectively by Walt Whitman, Henry David Thoreau and Mark Twain, and talked about the leading role of geological environment in them, from the perspective of the relationship between place and literature.

As an ancient civilization, the Chinese nation is broad-minded and respects the diversity of cultures. Facing the same challenges in the context of globalization, peoples in the world, including Chinese and Americans, should reinforce cultural exchanges and cooperation for a better future.

肖庆
中国艺术研究院文化发展战略研究中心助理研究员

构筑文化交流与认知的世纪平台

——"第三届中美文化论坛：跨文化双边对话"

在全球化趋势不可逆转的多元文明共存的世界，跨文化双边对话不仅成为人们相互理解的新模式，同时也为各国认识自身、实现自我超越提供了一条可行之路。正是在这样的时代语境下，"跨文化双边对话：第三届中美文化论坛"如期举行。

中美文化论坛是中美人文交流高层磋商机制框架下文化领域的重要项目，其宗旨是为中美两国在文化领域建立一个公共性、学术性、互动性的定期对话机制。中美文化论坛于2008年、2010年先后在中国和美国成功举办了两届，汇集了两国众多的专家学者和有识之士参与，双方从不同视角进行了广泛交流探讨。2012年9月6—8日，在北京和南京，来自中美两国的五十余名专家、学者和艺术家围绕"文化的语境：文化与地域、文化与人类、文化与历史"的议题，探讨中美两国由于不同的地理环境、民族渊源、历史发展等原因形成的文化特质，从而寻求相互认知、理解与认同的基础，并着意为中美两国人民的心灵沟通，增进相互之间的理解和信任搭建起一座世纪桥梁。

全球与本土之间的文化抉择

随着经济全球化和社会现代化的不断加快，"地球村"已然不再只是一个文学修辞意义上的比喻，而是一个真真切切的当下现实。不同地域、种族、信仰与文化背景下的各类人群，愈来愈因时空距离的日益拉近而站在同一的历史场域中，并且因此而面临着更为一致的利益诉求与更加迫切的发展挑战。正如美国国家人文基金会主席詹姆斯·利奇所说："当今世界瞬息万变,平衡困境不断增加,后果愈发严重。"利奇主席列举了三种特别敏感的困境:"1. 贸易中的竞争与合作之间的平衡。若要维持建设性的关系,国家和公司之间必须实现互利。2. 地方化和全球化之间的平衡。所有的地方政治都受到全球性事件的影响。当政治(包括由贸易问题引发的关注)变得愈发全球化,外交政策愈本地化,而不再是统治精英的专属特权。政府在决策时必须以某种方式兼顾城市和农村民众的利益。3. 国家自由与内、外部秩序的平衡。在世界许多地方,这种平衡变得越来越不稳定。没有任何一个国家能够规避决策及其衍生的其他后果。"

在这种时代背景下,中美双边关系对经济繁荣和世界和平的影响越发重要。夹杂在这种既合作又博弈的错综复杂的关系体系中,如何对待他国他族文化,如何与文化传统相异的他国他族相处,成为国际交往中一个非常重要的问题。与会的中国学者普遍认为,现代国际社会中对于他国主权的尊重,应该相应地坐实为尊重其利益诉求,尊重其文化传统、文化精神及文化权利。自由、公正、民主、和平的社会制度,不仅是人类获取自尊、独立和富裕的手段,同时也是人类精神的组成部分。南京大学教授蔡佳禾认为目前在美国的对外政策中,平等、和平的价值观变得愈发有争议。他说:"尽管人类通过两次世界大战,建立了联合国这样的一系列国际化制度,来维护和确保世界和平。但是,在美国的对外政策当中,和平的意义并没有人权和民主重要,甚至为了人权和民主,和平就可能被削弱。"面对各种冲突的现实,中国艺术研究院著名学者刘梦溪呼吁将"对话"和"共享"作为发展的主要追求,而非将"对抗"与"瓜分"作为生存的经营之道。他说:"冲突是人类文明的'反动',是礼仪文化的'弃物'。所以,孔子说:'礼之用,和为贵。''和'才能成礼,冲突是愚蠢的失礼行为,为人类文明所不取。人类如果因文化的差异与'不同'而出现偶然的对立,彼此当事方应该采取'和而解'的态度,而不是走向'仇而亡'的道路。这是中国古老文化的智慧,也是人类本性和人类理性所应该指向的目标。"

面对这一世界性的问题,与会的西方学者认为,虽然民族国家之间的差异有时难免会不断深化。但是,如果人们认识到不同背景下人类面临的共同挑战,就可以大大降低因差异导致矛盾冲突的可能性。正如美国国会图书馆民俗中心荣誉主任玛格利特·博格尔所说:"文化并不是一种单纯的竞争关系,美国性不是最好的,中国性也不是最好的。我们应该合在一起,把自己当作一个'人类'来看待,这样才能避免一种害怕失去的恐慌。"

此岸与彼岸之间的价值博弈

世界各种来自不同文化的群体既有人类所共有的思维规律,也有在自己文化氛围中形成的具有各自特色的考虑问题、认识事物的习惯方式和方法。在跨文化交际中,很多人都倾向于认为对方也用与自己同样的方式思维,从而导致文化接受的变形。中华人民共和国文化部副部长赵少华在致辞中说,不可否认,中美两国在文化传统、社会制度和发展阶段等方面存在着差异和不同,但问题的关键是如何看待差异和不同。中国尊崇"和而不同"的文化理念,相信文化交流有助于缓解冲突、消弭误解和矛盾。赵少华希望中美两国有识之士能更多思考如何减少由于两国之间的差异和不同所造成的误读、误解、误判,在增进文化间互相了解方面下工夫。

文化接受的变形普遍存在于文化交流的各个领域,"中国当代艺术在西方出现的面貌,常常被弱化甚至简约化为一种政治符号的图像。"中国美术馆馆长范迪安认为,在中美艺术交流中,美国评论界如何克服以"符号化"的视角观察和评价中国当代艺术的思维定势,如何在信息时代与全球文化语境中认识中国艺术的当代特征与文化价值,成为急迫问题。他认为,了解不充分、认识有盲点,以及由文化中心主义导致的文化偏见,让中国当代艺术在西方视野里,成为一种被遮蔽的存在。中国艺术研究院中国文化研究所研究员摩罗认为,中国人和美国人文化心态的调适,需要双方的相互支持和频繁互动。

美国民意对中国持着一种不确定的态度。而且他们对中国当代的文化、中国公众的价值观念是很不了解的,南京大学"中国与美国研究中心"美方合作主任詹森·帕滕特根据自己在中国工作20年的感受得出了同样的认识:"美国是一个高度差异化的社会,中国也是一个高度差异化的社会,所以,要做一概而论的结论,是非常危险的。"据美国国际教育学会发布的年度报告,2010—2011年中国留学美国的人数超过15万,同期，美国赴中国留学人数不足2万。在第三届中美文化论坛中，出席的中国学者几乎人人都可以用英语演讲，绝大多数都有留美经历，而美国学者却很少有人能用汉语交流。"如果美国公众也像中国公众一样，更加积极地了解中国人的生活状况、文化语境和文化传统，那么中美两国的文化交流可能会更加顺利地开展，误读和误解也会相应大大减少。"北京大学艺术学院院长王一川说。文化交流的魅力就在于彼此渗透，彼此谦让，彼此影响，并最终保持独立。江苏省作家协会副主席著名作家毕飞宇谈道，在文化上做出妥协和退让，在内心一定是极其痛苦的。然而，这个世界从来就不存在不妥协、不退让的文化交流。任何一种地域文化，只有有益于人类，有益于人类的发展与交流，这种文化才是有价值的，才是有生命力的，才能成为人类文化的有机成分。中国艺术研究院艺术创作研究中心主任、陶瓷艺术研究中心主任朱乐耕结合中国陶瓷艺术的发展情况，希望可以通过艺术推动彼此的理解和尊重。

历史与现实之间的认同空缺

哈佛大学教授亨廷顿于20世纪90年代提出"文明冲突论"，其中"世界冲突的根源在于文明的差异"一直饱受争议。在论坛上，著名学者余秋雨引述了意大利传教士利玛窦的结论反驳了这一对西方思想界影响甚广的理论。400年前的意大利传教士利玛窦，在研究了中国"4000年的历史"和长达30年的调研后，在其晚年完成的《中国札记》里得出了一个重要的结论：中国人真的没有要扩张国界、企图侵略远方的野心。余秋雨对比了以农耕文明为主体的中华文明与海洋文明、游牧文明的不同，分析说："海洋文明和游牧文明大多具有生存空间上的拓展性、进犯性、无边界性。它们的出发点和终点，此岸和彼岸，是无羁的，不确定的。相反，中国农耕文明的基本意识是固土自守、热土难离。它建立精良军队的目的，全都在于集权的安慰和边境的防守。"

中国艺术研究院院长助理、文化发展战略研究中心主任贾磊磊分析说："欧洲人初识中国的马可·波罗时代，正是中国人走向强盛之时；而美国人初识中国，恰恰是中国走向衰败的晚清时代，这种历史上的落差造成中美两国在许多领域理解的差异。"贾磊磊以电影为例分析了中美文化在价值观方面的异同。他说："文化的价值观是一个民族、一个国家中体现的关于个人、家庭、国家乃至人类社会的终极理想，它决定着人们在政治、社会、伦理、艺术领域对于是非、善恶、正邪、美丑的基本判断。文化价值观决定我们文化生存方式的思想根基，也主导着我们的基本文化认同倾向。"

在对未来的展望中，中国社会科学院美国研究所所长黄平认为中美之间应该告别"非黑即白"的思维定式，正视差异，摒弃误解，他说："中国古代哲学，尤其是《易经》所包含的阴阳思想，是一种超越二元对立的思维，足以提供解决这类问题的无限可能性。不管你的历史多么悠久，也不管你的文化多么优越，我们放下架子，以最平常的心来探讨，一同跨越我们现有的文化的屏障、束缚、边界。"美国爱荷华大学国际写作计划主任克里斯托弗·梅瑞尔在演讲中深情地提起法国诗人圣－琼·佩斯，这位1960年诺贝尔文学奖获得者，20世纪初历时一个月时间探寻了成吉思汗的故乡，并在北京西山的道观中完成了他的长篇杰作《远征》。这位法国诗人的东方足迹激励着梅瑞尔的文学创作，让他在文化的传承中感受着东西方文明的互融互通。

借鉴与创新之间的发展维度

文化如水，具有独特的渗透力，文化产品和服务承载着价值观念和生活方式，社会价值超过其商业价值。中国社会科学院荣誉学部委员刘魁立认为："长期以来，对文化的认识存在一定程度的偏差：人们常常特别关注文化的物质层面，而轻视了物质中蕴含的思想和精神以及整个非物质文化的重要意义和价值。这种对于文化的偏见，容易造成文化的民族性、广泛性及其深厚历史底蕴的丧失，使文化日益趋同化，缺乏应有的生命力和创造力。"

保护自己的优秀文化传统不仅仅是单纯地涉及一个国家、一个民族文化建设的重要问题，也是人类文化多样性发展的基础和保证。中国艺术研究院文化发展战略研究中心副主任郑长铃说，文化交流是人类文化的存续、发展的需要，而真正认同文化多样性，并以此为基础，才能有效地实现文化的交流，促进文化的包容、涵化、融合、发展。

文化的差异，是可能带来创造性的，只有差异的存在，才能带来创新性和新的事物的发生，为文化的融合提供源源不断的充分的资源。

美国学者关注了当前高科技背景之下文化发展所呈现的新特点。美国国会图书馆美国国家民俗中心名誉主任佩姬·巴尔杰认为，在保护传统文化的同时，应当对现代世界中可能出现的文化变化持支持态度。美国现代语言学会学术传播部主任凯思琳·菲茨帕特里克谈到，很多美国作家都认为互联网影响并干扰了现代人的感知能力，使阅读的重要性不断下降。实际上，当前美国的图书销售量比以往任何时候都高，阅读和写作在当代美国生活中继续占据着重要地位。

对于非物质文化遗产的保护也是论坛讨论的热点，中国艺术研究院中国非物质文化遗产保护中心常务副主任李新风表示，近年来中国在非物质文化遗产保护方面进行了一系列探索和实践，如努力建设符合中国实际的、富有实效的非物质文化遗产保护制度，注重整体性的保护，大力推进文化生态保护区的建设等。在美国，非物质文化遗产的保护也受到了广泛的重视，美国国会图书馆美国国家民俗中心名誉主任佩姬·巴尔杰介绍了美国学界在传承其传统文化方面所作出的积极努力。她认为美国文化的独特性正是源于世界文化的融合和共存，在全世界范围内保护和支持全球所有非物质文化遗产、认识并尊重因人口流动和文化元素共享所形成的整体文化表述至关重要。美中学术交流委员会北京办事处主任阿瑟·泰博士对中美之间的学术交流进行了全面地考察，他说，中美交流已经从以前单一领域的学习和研究，过渡到多边、多领域、多学科，融合多个利益相关方情况的多层级交流活动，包括个人对个人、个人对机构以及机构对机构之间的关系。美国纽伯瑞图书馆"美洲印第安人和原住民研究"达西麦克尼克尔中心主任斯科特·曼宁·史蒂文斯认为，图书馆及其他致力于收藏美洲印第安人资料的文化机构所长期面临的问题，主要是如何建立研究机构和它所代表的美国印第安人社区之间的最佳联系，以及更好地促进美国原住民和学术界的关系。

在对中美文化发展未来的展望中，刘梦溪引述了中国历史上学术思想最活跃的魏晋时期所提出的"将无同"，这三个字所代表的即是不同文化、不同"文明体国家"，通过交流与对话达成文化的互补与融合。中美文化论坛在东西方文化之间架起了一座沟通与交流的桥梁，希望这座友谊的桥梁能够不断延伸，在中美两国之间构建起一条通衢大道，向着人类理想的文化生存方式不断前进。

Xiao Qing

Assistant Research
Fellow of Cultural
Development
Strategy Research
Center, Chinese
National Academy of
Arts

Build a Century Platform for Cross-cultural Communication and Understanding
—The Third China-U.S. Cultural Forum: A Binational Conversation on Bridging Cultures

In a world where diverse cultures coexist and globalization rushes onward irreversibly, cross-cultural bilateral dialogue has become a new way for people to understand each other, and has provided a feasible approach for all the countries to understand themselves and to realize self-transcendence. In such a context, "The Third China-U.S. Cultural Forum: A Binational Conversation on Bridging Cultures" has been held as scheduled.

As an important cultural project under the framework of China-U.S. High-Level Consultation on People-to-People Exchange, China-U.S. Cultural Forum aims to build a regular dialogue mechanism in a public, academic and interactive way in the cultural field of the two countries. The forum was successfully held in China and the United States respectively in 2008 and 2009, during which a great number of experts, scholars and other learned people from both countries were brought together and had an extensive exchange of views from different perspectives. From September 6 to 8, 2012, over 50 experts, scholars and artists from both China and the U.S. gathered in Beijing and Nanjing. Centering around the theme "The Context: Place, People, History", they discussed the cultural traits of China and the U.S. shaped by their different geographical environments, ethnic origins, and historical development, with a view to seeking the foundation for mutual understanding and acceptance, and to building a bridge for deepening heart-to-heart communication, mutual understanding and confidence between the peoples of China and the U.S.

I. Cultural Choices between Globalism and Localism

With the acceleration of economic globalization and social modernization, "global village" is no longer just a figurative concept in literary and rhetorical sense, but a definite reality. Different human groups in different places, of different races, with different beliefs and cultural backgrounds increasingly stand in the same historical domain with the narrowing of space and distance, and thereby face more identical interest demands and more pressing challenges from development. As James Leach, Chairman of the U.S. National Endowment for the Humanities (NEH) pointed out, "in a world of escalating change, balancing quandaries grow rapidly in number and consequence." Mr. Leach listed three particularly sensitive quandaries of our times: 1) the balance between competition and cooperation in trade. For constructive relations to be sustainable, mutual advantage must accrue to countries as well as companies; 2) the balance between localism and globalism. All local politics is affected by global events. When politics, including trade-driven concerns, becomes globalized, foreign policy comes to be a localized consideration, rather than the near exclusive province of governing elites. In one way or another, public sentiment in cities and rural hamlets must be factored into policy considerations; and 3) the balance between freedom and order externally as well as internally in the affairs of the state. In many parts of the world this balance is increasingly precarious. No country escapes the necessity of choice-making and the ramifications of the judgment calls of others.

Against such a backdrop, China-U.S. relations exert greater impacts on the economic prosperity and peace of the world. In such a complicated system of relationships featuring both cooperation and competition, how to treat the cultures of other nations and how to get along with other countries with different cultural traditions have become very important issues in developing international relations. Chinese scholars at the conference agree that the respect for the sovereignty of other countries in modern international community should correspondingly be crystallized into the respect for their interest demands, cultural traditions, cultural spirit, and cultural rights. A free, equitable, democratic and peaceful social system is not only the means for human beings to acquire dignity, independence, and wealth, but also a constituent part of human spirit. Professor Cai Jiahe of Nanjing University thinks that in the current U.S. foreign policy, the values of equality and peace have become increasingly controversial. "Although humankind has established a series of international institutions like the UN following the two world wars to maintain and guarantee world peace, in the U.S. foreign policy, peace is less significant than human rights and democracy, and it even may be undermined for the sake of human rights and democracy." Recognizing the reality of recurrent conflicts, Liu Mengxi, a distinguished scholar at the Chinese National Academy of Arts, advocated "dialogue" and "sharing" as the major pursuits in development, instead of taking "antagonism" and "partitioning" as the way of life. As he pointed out, "conflict is 'reactionary' to human civilization and something 'eschewed' by ritual culture. That's why Confucius said, 'in the application of the rites, harmony is to be prized.' Only harmony can lead to propriety, whereas conflict is a foolish breach of propriety to be avoided in human civilization. In the case of occasional confrontation arising from cultural differences, the parties involved should try to become reconciled instead of hating and trying to beat the other. Such is the wisdom in the ancient Chinese culture and also an objective that human nature and reason inclines one to."

As to such a world problem, Western scholars think that although the differences between nation states may unavoidably deepen sometimes, if the common challenges facing people with different backgrounds are recognized, the possibility of causing conflicts due to cultural differences may be reduced dramatically. As Margaret Bulger, Director Emerita of the American Folklife Center at the Library of Congress, said, "the relationship between cultures is not simply a competitive one. The American culture is not the best, neither the Chinese culture. They should be integrated. We should regard ourselves as one group, i.e., humankind, so as to avoid the panic caused by the fear of losing. "

II. Different Values Held by China and the U.S.

People from different cultures have something in common in terms of the way of thinking, but they do have their particular approaches to problems and ways of understanding things due to their distinctive cultural atmospheres. In cross-cultural communication, many people tend to think that the other side thinks in the same way as they do, which causes the distortion of cultural acceptance. As China's Vice Minister of Culture Zhao Shaohua said in her address, undoubtedly, there are differences between China and the U.S. in terms of cultural tradition, social system, and the stage of development, but the crux of the problem is how to look at such differences. China enshrines the philosophy of "seeking harmony rather than uniformity", and believes that cultural exchanges contribute to the alleviation of conflicts and elimination of misunderstanding and tension. Ms. Zhao expressed her hope that insightful people of both countries would think more about how to reduce misinterpretation, misunderstanding and misjudgment between China and the U.S. that arise from their differences, and work hard at enhancing mutual understanding between them.

The distortion of cultural acceptance is prevalent in all fields of cultural exchanges. "The emergence of contemporary Chinese art in the West is often attenuated or even simplified into an image of political symbol." According to Fan Di'an, Director of National Art Museum of China (NAMOC), in China-U. S. artistic exchanges, it's imperative for American critics to change the mindset in viewing and evaluating contemporary Chinese art with a "symbolized" perspective and to understand the contemporary characteristics and cultural value of Chinese art in the information age and the global cultural context. He holds that insufficient understanding, blind spots, and cultural prejudice resulting from cultural centralism make contemporary Chinese art a hidden existence in the eyes of Westerners. Mo Luo, research fellow of the Institute of Chinese Culture, Chinese National Academy of Arts, thinks that the adjustment of the cultural mentality of Chinese and Americans requires the mutual support and frequent interaction between the two sides.

The American public have an obscure attitude towards China. Moreover, Americans have little understanding of China's contemporary culture and the values of the Chinese public. Jason Patent, American Co-Director of John-Hopkins University-Nanjing University Center for Chinese and American Studies, makes a similar observation based on his experience in China in the past two decades: "Both the U.S. and China are highly differentiated societies, so it's very dangerous to generalize." According to the annual report of the Institute of International Education, between 2010 and 2011, there were over 150,000 Chinese studying in the U.S. but no more than 20,000 Americans studying in

China. Almost all the Chinese scholars attending the Third China-U.S. Cultural Forum can make speeches in English, and most of them have studied abroad. In contrast, few American scholars at the forum can talk to others in Chinese. As suggested by Wang Yichuan, Dean of the School of Arts, Peking University, "if the American public make more efforts to understand the life, culture and tradition of the Chinese people, as the Chinese public do to understand them, there will be more smooth cultural exchanges and much less misinterpretation and misunderstanding between the two countries." The charm of exchange between two cultures is about recognizing and influencing each other without losing independence. Bi Feiyu, a famous writer and Vice President of the Writers' Association of Jiangsu Province, mentioned that making compromises and concessions in cultural exchanges are surely painful at heart. However, there are no cultural exchanges in this world that involve no compromises or concessions. For any regional culture, only when it's beneficial to the development and communication of humankind, can it be valuable or dynamic, and become an integral part of human culture. Zhu Legeng, Director of the Artistic Creation Research Center and the Ceramic Art Research Center, Chinese National Academy of Arts, expressed his hope to promote mutual understanding and respect between China and the U.S. via art in light of the development of the ceramic art in China.

III. Understanding Gap between History and Reality

In the 1990s, Professor Samuel Huntington of Harvard University proposed the theory of the Clash of Civilizations, which has since been highly controversial, particularly the idea that the source of conflict in the world is the differences between civilizations. At the forum, the famous Chinese scholar Yu Qiuyu cited the conclusion of Italian missionary Matteo Ricci to refute the theory which has exerted extensive impacts on Western intellectuals. Four hundred years ago, after studying China's 4,000-year history and the Chinese society for three decades, Matteo Ricci came to an important conclusion in The Journals of Matthew Ricci written he wrote in his later years: China has never had the ambition to expand its national border, or attempted to invade remote countries. Mr. Yu compared the differences between the Chinese civilization featuring farming culture, the marine civilization, and the nomadic civilization, and concluded that "most marine and nomadic civilizations are characteristically expansive, aggressive, and borderless. Their starting point and destination are indefinite. Contrarily, the fundamental consciousness of the Chinese civilization is to cling to the land. The purpose of establishing a well-equipped army is to protect the centralized power and to defend the border."

Jia Leilei, President Assistant of Chinese National Academy of Arts, and Director of Cultural Development Strategy Research Center, pointed out: "During the times of Marco Polo when Europe came to know about China, China was on its way to prosperity; whereas, when Americans got to know about China in late Qing Dynasty, China was on the decline. This historical fault line has resulted in the understanding differences between China and the U.S. in many areas." Taking movies as an example, Mr. Jia analyzed the differences in values between the two cultures. "A culture's values are its ideas about what is good, right, just and beautiful in the political, social and ethical and artistic domains. They embody the ultimate ideal of a nation and a country about individuals, family, country and even human society. The values serve as the ideological foundation of lifestyle and define the cultural identity."

Looking into the future, Huang Ping, Director of the Institute of American Studies, Chinese Academy of Social Sciences, insisted that both China and the U.S. should say goodbye to the mindset of viewing things as "either black or white", face up to the differences, and abandon misunderstanding. As he pointed out, "ancient Chinese philosophy, especially the thought of Yin and Yang proposed in the Book of Changes, is a way of thinking that transcends the binary dichotomy. It provides infinite possibilities for solving such problems. No matter how long your history is, and no matter how superior your culture is, we should get off our high horses, and talk with a calm mentality about how to break existing cultural barriers, restraints, and borders." Christopher Merrill, Director of the University of Iowa International Writing Program, fondly mentioned French poet Saint-John Perse who was awarded the Nobel Prize for Literature in 1960. He spent a month exploring the hometown of Genghis Khan in early 1900s, and completed his lengthy masterpiece Anabase at a Taoist temple in the Western Hills of Beijing. The footprints of this French poet in the East have inspired Mr. Merrill's literary creations, and lent him a perspective on the integration of Eastern and Western cultures over time.

IV. Development Dimension between Learning and Innovation

Culture is like water, and it possesses unique penetrating force. Cultural products and services embody values and lifestyles, and generate more social than commercial benefits. As Liu Kuili, Honorary Academician of the Chinese Academy of Social Sciences, said, "for a long time, people have some misunderstanding about culture. They usually pay special attention to the material layer of culture, and overlook the thought and spirit contained in the material, as well as the significance and value of intangible culture. Such cultural prejudice may result in the loss of the nationality, universality, and profound historical foundation of culture, and thus leads to increasing homogeneity of culture which lacks due vitality and creativity."

Protecting one's own excellent cultural traditions not only involves the efforts of a country and a nation to promote cultural progress, but also provides the foundation and guarantee for the world's cultural diversity. As pointed out by Zheng Changling, Deputy Director of the Cultural Development Strategy Research Center, Chinese National Academy of Arts, communication is essential for the survival and development of cultures. Only based on the recognition of cultural diversity can we have effective cultural exchanges, and promote the inclusiveness, acculturation, fusion, and development of different cultures.

Cultural differences may bring about creativity. The existence of differences may give incentive to innovation and the birth of new things, and provide endless and sufficient resources for cultural fusion.

American scholars have paid attention to the new features of cultural development in the current high-tech context. Peggy A. Bulger, Director Emerita of the American Folklife Center at the Library of Congress, believes that in protecting the traditional culture, we should support the possible changes in the cultures in contemporary world. As pointed out by Kathleen Fitzpatrick, Director of Scholarly Communication at the Modern Language Association, many American authors have argued that the Internet has affected and messed with modern perception, leading to the declining awareness about the importance of reading. However, the fact is that book sales in the U.S. are higher than ever. Reading and writing still occupy an important place in contemporary American life.

Protecting intangible cultural heritage is a hotspot issue at the forum. According to Li Xinfeng, Executive Deputy Director of China Intangible Cultural Heritage Protection Center, Chinese National Academy of Arts, in recent years, China has done a lot in the protection of intangible cultural heritage, including the efforts to build an effective protection system in line with China's realities, focus more on overall protection, and promote the construction of cultural and ecological reserves. In the U.S., the protection of intangible cultural heritage has attracted great attention. Peggy A. Bulger, Director Emerita of the American Folklife Center at the Library of Congress, introduced the efforts of American academia in passing down their traditional culture. She holds that the uniqueness of the American culture comes from the fusion and/or co-existence of world cultures. It's critical to safeguard and support the world's intangible cultural heritage and to recognize and respect the full spectrum of cultural expression that results from population mobility and the sharing of cultural elements. Arthur D. Tai, Director of the Beijing Office of the U.S. Committee on Scholarly Communication with China, fully examined the scholarly communication between China and the U.S. As Mr. Tai argued, China-U.S. academic exchanges have shifted the focus from single-field study and research to multilateral, multi-field, multi-discipline, and multi-level activities involving multiple stakeholders, covering person-to-person, person-to-institution, institution-to-institution relationships. Scott Manning Stevens, Director of the D'Arcy McNickle Center for American Indian and Indigenous Studies at the Newberry Library, Chicago, Illinois, held that the primary issue facing libraries and other cultural institutions with collections focused on American Indians is how to establish the best contacts between a research facility and the American Indian community it represents, and foster better relations between Native Americans and the academic world.

When talking about the future of China-U.S. cultural development, Mr. Liu Mengxi cited the epigram "just the same" (jiang wu tong) put forward during the Wei and Jin Dynasties, a period which saw the liveliest academic thoughts in Chinese history. The three words mean that different cultures and civilizations can complement and integrate with each other through communication and dialogue. The China-U.S. Cultural Forum has built a bridge of communication and exchanges between Eastern and Western cultures. Hopefully the friendship between China and the U.S. will help to build a broad avenue that leads the two countries to the ideal state of cultural coexistence.

图书在版编目（CIP）数据

跨文化双边对话　文化的语境：地域·人类·历史
——第三届中美文化论坛文集/贾磊磊主编．—北京：
文化艺术出版社，2013.4
ISBN 978-7-5039-5583-9
Ⅰ.①跨… Ⅱ.①贾… Ⅲ.①中美关系－文化交流－
文集 Ⅳ.①G125-53

中国版本图书馆CIP数据核字(2013)第063347号

跨文化双边对话　文化的语境：地域·人类·历史
——第三届中美文化论坛文集

主　　编	贾磊磊
责任编辑	胡　晋　谢　阳
书籍设计	姚雪媛
出版发行	文化艺术出版社
地　　址	北京市东城区东四八条52号　100700
网　　址	www.whyscbs.com
电子邮箱	whysbooks@263.net
电　　话	(010) 84057658　84057666（总编室）
	(010) 84057696　84057697（发行部）
经　　销	新华书店
印　　刷	北京卡乐富印刷有限公司
版　　次	2013年4月第1版
印　　次	2013年4月第1次印刷
印　　张	27.25
开　　本	710×1000　1/16
字　　数	400 千字
书　　号	ISBN 978-7-5039-5583-9
定　　价	68.00 元

版权所有，侵权必究。印装错误，随时调换。